URBAN FOOD SYSTEMS IN LATIN AMERICA

Drawing on a range of case studies from across Latin America, this book highlights the ways that urbanization shapes the food systems that feed this region's cities, approaching the problem of food in cities as a particularly urban problem.

Latin America is the most urbanized area in the world, with nearly 80% of the population living in cities, where rates of food and nutritional insecurity are persistently high, and where the social and spatial organization is characterized by inequality and segregation. The broader questions addressed in this volume are as follows: How do the specific processes and dynamics of Latin American urbanization influence or shape food systems? How can urban food systems develop forms of governance that supports food security and sustainability? After a general introduction, this volume is organized into three main sections: Territories, mobilities, and governance. The chapters consider how specific elements such as urban planning, zoning, migration, gentrification, informal settlements, logistics, retailers, wholesale markets, and street vendors, among others, contribute to shaping how food is distributed, sold, and bought in cities. Drawing on studies and theoretical approaches written by scholars and practitioners from Argentina, Brazil, Chile, Ecuador, and Mexico, this book provides a Latin American perspective on global discussions surrounding the role of cities in ensuring food access to urban populations.

This volume will be of great interest to students, scholars, and policymakers interested in food systems, urban food, urban planning, sustainable urban development, and Latin American studies.

Tiana Bakić Hayden is Anthropologist and Professor of Urban Studies at El Colegio de México, Mexico. Her research focuses on cultures of food commerce and consumption and on the relationship between food and mobilities.

Joaquín Pérez Martín is Professor and Researcher of agrifood systems at Universidad de Buenos Aires, Argentina. His research focuses on urban food supply, food infrastructure, logistics, governance, and policies.

Routledge Studies in Food, Society and the Environment

American Farming Culture and the History of Technology
Joshua T. Brinkman

Transforming Food Systems
Narratives of Power
Molly D. Anderson

The Real Cost of Cheap Food
Michael Carolan

Plant-Forward Cuisine
Basic Concepts and Practical Applications
Ole G. Mouritsen, Klavs Styrbæk and Mariela Johansen

Ethical Omnivores
Better Eating for Everyone
Samantha Noll

Urban Food Systems in Latin America
Territories, Mobilities and Governance
Edited by Tiana Bakić Hayden and Joaquín Pérez Martín

For more information about this series, please visit: www.routledge.com/Routledge-Studies-in-Food-Society-and-the-Environment/book-series/RSFSE

URBAN FOOD SYSTEMS IN LATIN AMERICA

Territories, Mobilities and Governance

Edited by Tiana Bakić Hayden and Joaquín Pérez Martín

Routledge
Taylor & Francis Group
LONDON AND NEW YORK

earthscan
from Routledge

Designed cover image: Getty Images

First published 2025
by Routledge
4 Park Square, Milton Park, Abingdon, Oxon OX14 4RN

and by Routledge
605 Third Avenue, New York, NY 10158

Routledge is an imprint of the Taylor & Francis Group, an informa business

British Library Cataloguing-in-Publication Data
A catalogue record for this book is available from the British Library

Library of Congress Cataloging-in-Publication Data
Names: Hayden, Tiana Bakić, editor. | Martín, Joaquín Pérez (Food supply researcher), editor.
Title: Urban food systems in Latin America : territories, mobilities and governance / edited by Tiana Bakić Hayden, Joaquín Pérez Martín.
Other titles: Routledge studies in food, society and environment
Description: New York, NY : Routledge, 2025. | Series: Routledge studies in food society and the environment | Includes bibliographical references and index.
Identifiers: LCCN 2024050399 (print) | LCCN 2024050400 (ebook) | ISBN 9781032750064 (hardback) | ISBN 9781032750057 (paperback) | ISBN 9781003471929 (ebook)
Subjects: LCSH: Food supply—Latin America. | Nutrition policy—Latin America. | Food security—Latin America.
Classification: LCC HD9014.L32 U73 2025 (print) | LCC HD9014.L32 (ebook) | DDC 381.4/564130098—dc23/eng/20250208
LC record available at https://lccn.loc.gov/2024050399
LC ebook record available at https://lccn.loc.gov/2024050400

ISBN: 978-1-032-75006-4 (hbk)
ISBN: 978-1-032-75005-7 (pbk)
ISBN: 978-1-003-47192-9 (ebk)

DOI: 10.4324/9781003471929

Typeset in Times New Roman
by Apex CoVantage, LLC

CONTENTS

FIGURES, MAPS, AND TABLES

CONTRIBUTORS

Yolanda Alfaro
Sociologist, professor, and researcher. Her research concentrates on analyzing migration trends in the Andean Region and how collective memory and storytelling influence narratives.
Universidad San Francisco de Quito (Ecuador)

Andres Barsky
Professor and Researcher at the Instituto del Conurbano. His research interests focus on public policy frameworks for preserving peri-urban productive areas in Latin American cities.
Universidad Nacional de General Sarmiento, Universidad Nacional de Luján & CONICET (Argentina)

Francisca Basaure
Anthropologist, Master in Cultural Heritage. Based in the Tarapacá region, she researches and publishes on Indigenous communities, religious practices, everyday life, and mobility.
Universidad de Chile (Chile)

Fernando Bercovich
Sociologist specialized in urban studies and economics. His work focuses on the relationship between territory and inequality.
Universidad de Buenos Aires (Argentina)

Adriana Brinck
Archaeologist and urban anthropologist. Her work focuses on ethnographic work on urban issues and archaeological heritage management.
Universidad de Chile (Chile)

Simone Buratti

Urban sustainability professional with extensive experience in civic and academic sectors.

Investigador independiente (México)

Juan Antonio Carrasco

Professor and researcher in transportation engineering and planning. His research focuses on the social context of travel behavior and the interplay between transport planning and modeling.

Universidad de Concepción (Chile)

Adrián Hernández Cordero

Human geographer and professor-researcher. His work focuses on urban dynamics, with a particular emphasis on gentrification, touristification, and foodification in Mexico and Spain.

Metropolitan Autonomous University (México)

María Mercedes Di Virgilio

Full Professor and Senior Researcher. Her research focuses on the residential mobility processes of lower and middle-class families, public policies, spatial mobilities, and urban transformation.

Universidad de Buenos Aires & CONICET (Argentina)

Mercedes Eguiguren

Postdoctoral Fellow. Her research explores the intersections of mobility, socio-spatial inequalities, and the subjective experience of migration, with a focus on the Andean Region.

Balsillie School of International Affairs & Wilfrid Laurier University (Canada)

Irene Farah

Postdoctoral Scholar in Urban and Regional Planning. Her research focuses on urban governance, politics, street vendors, food systems, and spatial methods.

University of Illinois, Urbana-Champaign (United States)

Erick Alejandro Ferrer Sánchez

Sociologist and PhD student in Urban and Environmental Studies. His research highlights the platformization process and the incorporation of food delivery platforms in food environments.

El Colegio de México (México)

Inés Figueroa

Urban anthropologist. Her work focuses broadly on ethnographic work on urban issues.

Universidad de Chile (Chile)

Guadalupe Granero
Urbanist. Her academic and professional activity is focused on territorial justice.
Universidad de Buenos Aires (Argentina)

Tiana Bakić Hayden
Anthropologist and professor of urban studies. Her research focuses on cultures of food commerce and consumption, and on the relationship between food and mobilities.
El Colegio de México (México)

Walter Imilan
Professor and researcher of urban and territorial studies. His work focuses on dwelling practices, everyday life, and planning from ethnographic perspectives.
Universidad Central de Chile (Chile)

Paola Jirón
Professor and researcher of urban and territorial studies. Her work focuses on the relationship between urban planning and dwelling experiences through mobility, care, and mobile methods.
Universidad de Chile (Chile)

Diego Martín
Professor and researcher of International Relations. His research focuses on international cooperation processes, the international action of local governments, and city networks.
Universidad Nacional de Rosario (Argentina)

Julián Monkes
Environmentalist, professor, and PhD student in agricultural sciences. His studies focus on the strategies of small family farmers for agroecological transition.
Universidad de Buenos Aires (Argentina)

Ayari G. Pasquier Merino
Sociologist and researcher at the Centro de Investigaciones Interdisciplinarias en Ciencias y Humanidades. Her research focuses on urban food systems, sustainability, and social inequality
Universidad Nacional Autónoma de México (México)

Joaquín Pérez Martín
Professor and researcher on agrifood systems. His research focuses on urban food supply, food infrastructure, logistics, governance, and policies.
Universidad de Buenos Aires (Argentina)

Cláudio Smalley Soares Pereira

Geographer, professor, and researcher of urban studies. His research focuses on the production of urban space, urban commerce, retail companies, consumption, and medium-sized cities.

Universidade Estadual do Ceará (Brasil)

León Felipe Téllez Contreras

Social geographer and urban studies scholar. His research focuses on urban politics, grassroots organizations, and infrastructure governance.

University of the West of Scotland (Great Britain)

José Antonio Vázquez-Medina

Food Anthropologist and professor of food studies. His current research focuses on urban food systems, tourism, and food heritage.

Center for Food and Development Research (México)

Dhan Zunino Singh

Sociologist and PhD in History. Expert in cities, mobilities, and culture. His current work focuses on infrastructure, material turn, and urban mobility.

CONICET & Universidad Nacional de Quilmes (Argentina)

Introduction

LATIN AMERICAN URBANIZATION AND FOOD SYSTEMS

Integrating perspectives toward a more sustainable food future

Joaquín Pérez Martín and Tiana Bakić Hayden

Urban food systems and global food crises

Recent decades have seen an uptick in interest in urban food systems in a variety of scholarly fields, policy discussions, and grassroots activism. Indeed, after being largely absent from the urban agenda for much of the twentieth century, food is increasingly recognized as an issue that brings together questions of governance, planning, infrastructure, sustainability, health, mobility, and sociality that are integral to life *in* cities and to the life *of* cities. This has been especially the case since 2006, as continuing waves of food price crises have increased food insecurity in many regions (Lang, 2010; von Braun, 2009). Indeed, since 2006, global food prices have increased at rates far outpacing inflation and demonstrated extreme volatility, leading to three distinct global food pricing crisis events in 2007–2008, 2010–2011, and 2021–2022 (FAO, 2024b). At the same time, the global food regime continues to push productive systems toward intensive, input-dependent systems of monocropping which affect biodiversity, deplete soil and water systems, and increase vulnerability to pests and diseases. Food systems are contributing significantly to climate change, at the same time as they are becoming increasingly vulnerable to extreme weather events, droughts, and unpredictable growing conditions.

Faced with economic and ecological crises which affect food systems around the world, national governments and international organizations have overwhelmingly failed to react effectively. Even as global agrifood businesses have thrived, middle-class and working-class consumers in many parts of the world have seen their food expenditures rise, and their food security suffer (Clapp & Moseley, 2020; Cohen & Garrett, 2010; Hawkes et al., 2022). At stake here is not only a failure of political will at the national scale to address global food crises but also a failure of policy imagination in terms of recognizing the changing economic, ecological, and

DOI: 10.4324/9781003471929-2

political contexts in which such crises emerge. Today, after decades of neoliberal policies having weakened state capacity for regulating food systems, and in the context of the climate crisis and continuing urbanization, the need for new scholarly and policy approaches to dealing with food systems crises is key.

Cities, as key sites of consumption, have the potential not only to play a central role in ensuring access to urban populations but also to act as essential nodes for transforming how systems for distribution and commerce are organized and governed (HLPE, 2024). Indeed, the demands of urban consumers for low-priced foods have historically been one of the central concerns of states when it comes to creating food policies. Yet the question of food justice and fair working conditions for farm workers or of sustainability and environmental justice have often been left out of discussions that center primarily on the food security of urban consumers. In recent years, scholars from a variety of disciplines have drawn attention to the need for new theoretical and analytical approaches to understanding food systems, which take planetary urbanization into consideration, given that the majority of the world's population now lives in cities (Pothukuchi & Kaufman, 1999; Sonnino, 2016). While recognizing the continued importance of rural areas for global food security and sustainable food systems, a new wave of scholarship and activism is recognizing cities as new spaces of struggle and negotiation in a neoliberal era.

The notion of *urban food systems* refers to the constellation of places, people, institutions, regulations, and activities that exist within a particular urban context, which connect food production, processing, distribution, consumption, and waste management. It is a deliberately broad definition, but one that aims to draw particular attention to the fact that cities are where the overwhelming majority of consumption occurs, and to the fact that in order to cater to the needs of urban consumers, a wide array of actors, institutions, and infrastructures are involved who are often left out of rural production-centered discussions about food security and sovereignty. This book brings an urban food systems perspective to understanding how Latin American cities today feed themselves. We discuss the challenges which they face in this process, and the potential spaces for building more sustainable and just food systems which emerge in the region.

Feeding Latin America's cities

Nowhere are discussions about urban food systems more relevant than in Latin America, the world's most heavily urbanized region, as well as its most unequal. Since the mid-twentieth century, most Latin American countries have experienced rapid rates of urbanization, coinciding with policies that promoted the expansion of input-heavy, intensive agricultural production. Furthermore, in recent decades, drought and climate-related extreme weather events, political instability, and violence have further created difficult conditions in rural areas and have pushed people out of agricultural livelihoods (Carney, 2024). Between 1980 and 2020 alone, the rural population in Latin America decreased by nearly 50%, while over 82% of the population now lives in cities (UNDESA, 2018). Today, there are 70 cities with over one million inhabitants in the region, and nine metropolitan areas with more than five million residents which account for nearly 18% of the total population (UNDESA, 2018).

In these same cities, meanwhile, rates of food and nutritional insecurity are persistently high, especially among vulnerable populations, and food constitutes a prohibitively high expenditure for many families (FAO et al., 2024). Food expenditures range between 16% of total earnings in the case of Brazil (IBGE, 2020) and 38% in the case of Mexico (INEGI, 2023), with other countries falling between. These average proportions, however, hide the fact that poorer households generally dedicate a far larger percentage of their incomes to food expenses, even as they consume foods that are of poorer quality and higher prices. Thus, across Latin America, an average of 26% of the population suffered from moderate or severe food insecurity between 2021 and 2023, ranging from a low of 16% in Uruguay and Costa Rica to 60% in Guatemala (see Figure I.1). These generally high rates of food insecurity in the region, meanwhile, occur even as many Latin American countries are key global producers and exporters of agricultural and food products, concentrating a great deal of wealth in resources, and with the presence of important international agrifood companies. While, historically, rural food security has been higher than that in urban areas, research increasingly shows that urban food insecurity is a significant issue and one which affects vastly more people than rural food insecurity. Since most cities in the region do not suffer from a lack of food availability overall, the question of urban food insecurity brings to the fore the question of *accessibility* over time, which in turn draws our attention to the mechanisms through which people access food in the urban market. In this context, an urban food systems approach is necessary in order to understand how distribution and commerce are organized, and how profit and

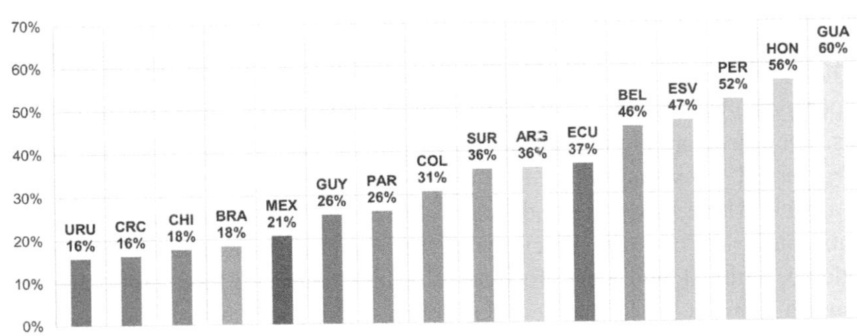

FIGURE I.1 Prevalence of moderate or severe food insecurity (percent) (2021–2023 average)[1]

Source: Own elaboration based on FAO (2024a)

value are accrued in the food systems that feed the region's cities (Bisang & Gutman, 2005; Reardon, 2015).

In Latin American cities, high levels of poverty and marginalization coexist with extreme wealth, territorial segregation is the norm, and high rates of informality characterize labor, housing, and commerce (Silveira, 2011; Schteingart & Pírez, 2015). In the last two decades, for example, despite the fact that per capita income has increased and poverty decreased somewhat, rates of labor informality continue to be high, accounting for nearly 43% of the population, and dependency on monetary assistance programs is widespread (World Bank, 2024b).[2] Indeed, since the COVID-19 pandemic, when poverty rates increased, much of the economic recovery has been located in the informal sector, where precarious working conditions and lack of benefits prevail. Women and marginalized populations, moreover, are particularly vulnerable and likely to suffer from poverty and food insecurity (CEPAL, 2021). In all countries in Latin America, women are disproportionately responsible for unpaid domestic and care work (World Bank, 2024a) and are more likely to experience food insecurity than men (FAO, 2024a).

In recent decades, since the advent of neoliberalism throughout Latin America, cities have become larger and more sprawling, and at the same time more socio-spatially segregated (Janoschka, 2002). Rapid territorial expansion occurs, especially in larger cities, through processes of formal real estate development and speculation, as well as through processes of informal urbanization conducted by poor people. The resulting urban structure is one characterized by high degrees of exclusion, segregation, and informality (Janoschka & Sequera, 2016; Di Virgilio & Perelman, 2014; Reis & Lukas, 2022). Processes of gentrification, urban renewal, and enclosure in gated communities have led to the symbolic and physical expulsion of working classes from central areas (Moctezuma, 2021; Crossa, 2018; Caldeira, 2001). Waves of migration, both from rural areas and from different countries, continue to feed the growth of cities and leave their mark on their demographic and cultural makeup. In addition to all of these political, economic, and social shifts, climate change is affecting cities throughout the region, as they struggle to deal with water shortages, flooding, heat, extreme weather, and other climate-related problems.

These social-spatial dynamics, conditions, and challenges which we find in contemporary Latin American cities have significant implications for urban food systems. They structure the ways in which territories are produced, disputed, defined, and governed. They shape the way in which people and goods circulate. They affect the ways in which foods are produced, distributed, and consumed, and the engagements of a variety of actors. Precisely because Latin American cities are the product of global, regional, and local processes, the neighbourhood food environments go through a complex tension between the globalized food markets and the local actors.

While there has been abundant scholarship on the nature and dynamics of Latin American urbanization, we have little understanding of its implications for the organization and regulation of food production, distribution, trading, and consumption. How do processes and characteristics of urbanization produce distinctive challenges and realities in terms of food systems governance, in the organization of commercial life, and in terms of the kinds of actors and infrastructures that make up the urban food systems upon which people depend? How, for example, do urban planning, zoning and development impact the availability of land and its use for producing, distributing, and selling foods? How does a large informal economy impact the commercial landscape and food availability, and how do recent shifts to supermarket dominance and e-commerce further shift the terrain? How do demographic shifts in cities—through migration, informal and formal urbanization or gentrification—impact the places and networks through which food is sold? How are social movements, such as agroecological and small farmers' associations, creating new opportunities for transforming urban food systems?

This book opens the door to addressing these questions through a series of case studies and theoretical discussions of different Latin American contexts written by scholars, experts, and practitioners from disciplines such as urbanism, geography, sociology, economy, and anthropology, among others. A key premise of the book is that in order to understand the problems and potentials of urban food systems in Latin America, it is necessary to think about the particularities of how cities are planned, governed, and experienced; that is, the book proposes a serious dialogue between urban studies and food studies through a variety of problems, approaches, and cases. While there has been a recent proliferation of publications that explicitly link the question of food to urban studies (Battersby & Watson, 2019; Sonnino, 2016), the vast majority of these works is focused on cities of the Global North, and to a lesser degree Africa. Latin America has been largely absent from these emerging discussions, in spite of the fact that the region's cities have been highly relevant for the development of urban theory in the twentieth century (Gorelik, 2022).

Territories, mobilities, and governance

The volume is organized into three broad thematic sections, each corresponding to key elements of urban life: Territories, mobilities, and governance. This structure seeks to organize the discussion of food systems in relation to existing discussions in urban studies within Latin America. The chapters contained in each section demonstrate how different phases, including production, distribution, and consumption, and different spaces in food systems may be incorporated into the study of traditional arenas of urban studies; that is, the question of territory is not only related to agricultural production, nor mobility solely to the realm of distribution. Rather, as the chapters in each section show, we can see how different dimensions of food systems can and should be considered in relation to all areas of urban life in a transversal manner.

Territories

Following the work of critical geographers and urban scholars, the territory can be understood as a dynamic process of appropriation, dispute, and control over space through different forms of power (Haesbaert & Mason-Deese, 2020; Schwarz & Streule, 2020). In other words, to speak of territory and of processes of territorialization (or deterritorialization) is to speak of the ways in which power, exclusions, and inequalities are constituted through spatial disputes and orders, and how they relate to inequalities. In terms of urban food systems, an emphasis on territories invites us to look critically at questions of how urban land and space are defined, regulated, and appropriated in relation to food production, availability, access, and consumption; that is, to understand that urban food systems exist not in empty or neutral space, but that they entail material and social relations on the ground. In order to understand how urban food systems operate in particular places, then, we need to be attentive to the ways that these intersect with different processes of (de)territorializations.

Following this insight, the chapters in this section reflect on different dimensions of urban territorial processes in Latin American cities, ranging from (formal and informal) urban expansion, contested use of public space for informal commerce, and displacements in contexts of gentrification. The chapter by Hayden and Farah discusses how policies governing the use of public space affect the sale and consumption of street foods through case studies in Mexico City. Cordero and Vázquez-Medina, meanwhile, analyze how different types of gentrification shape food availability and consumption practices in three urban contexts in Mexico. Granero, Bercovich, and Pérez Martín's chapter centers on the question of urban and peri-urban land development, encroachment, and speculation in terms of how they affect urban food production and trading in Argentina, Columbia, and Brazil. Finally, Barksy, similarly, looks at the role of regional planning (or lack thereof) on agricultural peri-urban production in different Latin American countries.

Mobilities

The notion of mobilities in urban studies refers, on the one hand, to an expansion of the ways that transport technologies, planning, and infrastructures shape the urban structure, economies, and circulation of people in cities. In a more expansive way, the mobility studies paradigm, which has emerged in recent decades, has proposed a broader understanding of the role of movement in relation to spaces and temporalities of urban life. The mobilities paradigm, which emerged in the 1990s, critiques traditional, static ways of understanding urban territories and dynamics and posits that understanding the ways that flows and frictions operate in all arenas of urban life is key to understanding 'constellations of power, the creation of identities and the microgeographies of everyday life' (Cresswell, 2011, p. 551). In other words, analyzing the world in terms of mobilities entails looking at what moves (and what doesn't), at how it moves, at the ways that this movement is represented and experienced at different scales.

In the study of foods and food systems, a mobilities framework invites us to look on the one hand at the mobility of foods themselves—in terms of mapping the actors, assemblages, infrastructures, and technologies involved in circulation. We can see, then, the role of packaging, of logistics technologies, of developments such as shipping containers and barcodes, or recipes and the histories, political economies, and socialities of these in shaping food access and inequalities (Deener, 2020; Cronon, 1992; Hayden, 2021). Analyzing mobilities in terms of food can also mean looking at how the mobilities of people—whether for commuting, tourism, leisure, or migration—create different types of demand, consumption patterns, and interactions with food systems.

In this book, we take inspiration from these expansive discussions on mobilities in order to bring together chapters that analyze how urban structures and infrastructures related to the circulation and mobility of goods and persons affect food systems. That is, the chapters look at how foods move through, around, and into cities as well as how the movement of people—from commuters to migrants—is connected to the production of foodways. Thus, Pasquier and Buratti ethnographically analyze the logistical and transportation challenges faced by small-scale producers in Mexico, as they strive to generate local foodways. In Zunino and Ferrer's contribution, we see how the proliferation of food delivery applications is growing throughout the region, as what may be seen as an emerging infrastructure, with implications for how people access food. Meanwhile, the other two chapters reflect on the ways that human mobility intersects with the creation of ways of feeding people. In the case of Santiago, Chile, for example, we see how the public subway system creates opportunities for informal food commerce to meet the needs of urban commuters who need to eat on the go (Jirón et. al.). Urban informality, then, is tied to patterns of everyday mobility, forms of exclusion, and the lack of transport planning, which adequately cares for people and considers their food needs. In the chapter by Hayden, Eguiguren, and Alfonso, meanwhile, we see how historic and contemporary waves of international migration play key roles in shaping the infrastructural and gastronomical dimensions of urban food systems. Through a discussion of Quito, Ecuador, and Buenos Aires, Argentina, the chapter centers the role of human mobility on the production and transformation of urban food systems over time.

Governance

In recent decades, the concept of governance has emerged in urban studies as central to understanding how decisions are made, how power is wielded, and how government is organized. While the state, in its different scales and capacities, is often at the core of discussions of governance, the term has been embraced in large part because it allows for a recognition of the power and centrality of a diversity of state and non-state actors, including citizens, community organizations, corporations, non-governmental organizations, international agencies, criminal groups, bureaucrats, judges, and others, in organizing urban space and structures (Da Cruz et al., 2019; McCann, 2017). In other words, a focus on *governance*, rather than government, policy, or regulation, allows for a recognition of the actual—rather than normative—ways that decisions get made on the ground and in specific urban contexts. In relation to the study of urban food systems, the concept of governance has similarly been used as a way to analyze the heterogeneity of actors, institutions, and interests involved in creating and regulating food systems (Moragues-Faus et al., 2022).

Despite the analytical utility of the governance framework, critics have pointed to the fact that the increasingly broad use of the term can lead to confusion over what governance actually refers to, who is involved, and who are its potential beneficiaries (Whittingham, 2010; Moragues-Faus, 2020). Indeed, while one of the virtues of a governance approach is that it allows for a recognition of the role of different private and public actors, it also risks normalizing the role of non-state actors, avoiding discussions of the political and economic implications of existing governance schemes, and perpetuating neoliberal logics that undermine state governing capabilities (Moragues-Faus, 2020; Mayer, 2006). In relation to food systems, an emphasis on governance, for example, may recognize the roles that large corporations—including agricultural firms, industry, supermarkets, and logistical operators—wield as well as the role played by peasant or informal vendor organizations. Yet, without a critical perspective, governance discourse may contribute to a situation where states, at different scales, bear responsibility for ensuring access to food, even as their ability to deliver is undermined by the interests and powers of other actors (Vivero & Ramírez, 2009).

Nevertheless, while recognizing the critiques of the concept on methodological and political grounds, we find governance to be a useful category for illustrating the role of different types and scales of actors—including social and political organizations, economic actors, and the state— involved in administering and regulating the region's food systems. Here, we see, for example, the strategies that supermarkets, the most important actor in food systems in Latin America and globally, have implemented in order to expand in Argentina, Brazil, Chile, and Mexico (Pérez Martín). Smalley's chapter hones in more closely on supermarket's efforts at a commercial concentration in medium-sized cities in Brazil, demonstrating their hegemonic control over much of the country's urban food system. Tellez, in his chapter on the organizational strategies of vendors and merchants in Mexico City's public markets, shows the centrality of these actors in governing key spaces of food distribution. Monkes' chapter on family farming organizations in Argentina shows the key role of associative and collective organizations in promoting agroecological production and supporting small-scale producers. Finally, Martín's text highlights the role of state actors in relation to international agreements through analysis of how local governments in Brazil, Ecuador, and Argentina have strived to implement urban food policies in dialogue with the Milan Urban Food Policy Pact.

The concluding section of this book, by María Mercedes Di Virgilio, provides a discussion of how the analysis of food, which has historically been absent from urban studies in Latin America, provides insight into broader transformations in cities throughout the region.

Toward a more sustainable urban food future

As various chapters in this book show, Latin American cities face multiple challenges in feeding their populations in ways that are just, equitable, and sustainable. In many ways, the challenges faced in these cities—ranging from periurban expansion and the loss of arable land, to the increased power of corporate food actors, to logistical and organizational challenges among small producers—mirror those found in other parts of the world. Yet there are particularities to the ways in which many global processes take place, including the importance of informal food economies, processes of informal urbanization, modes, and shifting migration patterns. Indeed, as this volume shows, in order to understand the workings of food systems in the region, it is necessary to take seriously the question of urban processes and dynamics. This, too, is important in terms of thinking about how food systems can be transformed to be more sustainable and just. As various chapters in this book show, today a combination of movements, ranging from farmers' associations to local governments, are organizing to promote agroecology, short distribution chains, and forms of certification which can improve the quality of the food and the conditions under which it is produced and distributed.

Notes

1 List of acronyms of Figure 1.1: Uruguay (URU), Costa Rica (CRC), Chile (CHI), Brazil (BRA), Mexico (MEX), Guyana (GUY), Paraguay (PAR), Colombia (COL), Suriname (SUR), Argentina (ARG), Ecuador (ECU), Belize (BEL), El Salvador (ESV), Peru (PER), Honduras (HON), and Guatemala (GUA).
2 Per capita income increased 37% on average (GDP per capita—constant 2015 US$), while poverty decreased 49% on average (Poverty headcount ratio at $6.85 a day 2017 PPP—% of population) and inequality 13% (Gini index).

Bibliography

Battersby, J., & Watson, V. (2019). The planned 'city-region' in the new urban agenda: An appropriate framing for urban food security? *Town Planning Review*, *90*(5), 497–518. https://doi.org/10.3828/tpr.2019.32

Bisang, R., & Gutman, G. E. (2005). Acumulación y tramas agroalimentarias en América Latina. *Revista de la CEPAL*, *2005*(87), 115–129. https://doi.org/10.18356/e8691f11-es

Caldeira, T. P. D. R. (2001). *City of walls: Crime, segregation, and citizenship in São Paulo*. University of California Press.

Carney, M. A. (2024). The climate-food-migration nexus: Critical perspectives. *Global Food Security*, *42*, 100786.

CEPAL. (2021). *Informe Especial COVID-19 No 9. La autonomía económica de las mujeres en la recuperación sostenible y con igualdad*. Comisión Económica para América Latina y el Caribe.

Clapp, J., & Moseley, W. G. (2020). This food crisis is different: COVID-19 and the fragility of the neoliberal food security order. *The Journal of Peasant Studies*, *47*(7), 1393–1417. https://doi.org/10.1080/03066150.2020.1823838

Cohen, M. J., & Garrett, J. L. (2010). The food price crisis and urban food (in)security. *Environment and Urbanization*, *22*(2), 467–482. https://doi.org/10.1177/0956247810380375

Cresswell, T. (2010). Towards a politics of mobility. *Environment and Planning D: Society and Space*, *28*(1), 17–31. https://doi.org/10.1068/d11407

Cresswell, T. (2011). Mobilities I: Catching up. *Progress in Human Geography*, *35*(4), 550–558. https://doi.org/10.1177/0309132510383348

Cronon, W. (1992). *Nature's metropolis: Chicago and the great west* (3rd print). Norton.

Crossa Niell, V. (2018). *Luchando por un espacio en la Ciudad de México: Comerciantes ambulantes y el espacio público urbano* (Primera edición). El Colegio de México, Centro de Estudios Demográficos, Urbanos y Ambientales.

Da Cruz, N. F., Rode, P., & McQuarrie, M. (2019). New urban governance: A review of current themes and future priorities. *Journal of Urban Affairs*, *41*(1), 1–19. https://doi.org/10.1080/07352166.2018.1499416

Deener, A. (2020). *The problem with feeding cities: The social transformation of infrastructure, abundance, and inequality in America*. University of Chicago Press.

Di Virgilio, M. M., & Perelman, M. (Eds.). (2014). *Ciudades latinoamericanas: Desigualdad, segregación y tolerancia* (Primera edición). International Congress of Americanists, Ciudad de Buenos Aires, Argentina. CLACSO.

FAO. (1975). *The state of food and agriculture 1974*. FAO. https://bit.ly/3f2L4LZ

FAO. (2024a). *FAOSTAT – Prevalencia de la inseguridad alimentaria moderada y grave (%) (promedio de 3 años)*. FAO. https://www.fao.org/faostat/en/#country

FAO. (2024b). *Índice de precios de los alimentos de la FAO*. FAO. https://bit.ly/30084XF

FAO, IFAD, UNICEF, WFP, & WHO. (2024). *The State of Food Security and Nutrition in the World 2024 – Financing to end hunger, food insecurity and malnutrition in all its forms*. Roma: FAO. Recuperado de FAO website: https://doi.org/10.4060/cd1254en

Fuglie, K., Gautam, M., Goyal, A., & Maloney, W. F. (2019). *Harvesting prosperity: Technology and productivity growth in agriculture*. World Bank. https://doi.org/10.1596/978-1-4648-1393-1

Gorelik, A. (2022). *La ciudad latinoamericana: Una figura de la imaginación social del siglo XX*. Siglo XXI Editores.

Haesbaert, R., & Mason-Deese, L. (2020). Territory/ies from a Latin American perspective. *Journal of Latin American Geography*, *19*(1), 258–268.

Hawkes, C., Ambikapathi, R., Anastasiou, K., Brock, J., Castronuovo, L., Fallon, N., & Zorbas, C. (2022). From food price crisis to an equitable food system. *The Lancet*, *400*(10350), 413–416. https://doi.org/10.1016/S0140-6736(22)01348-4

Hayden, T. B. (2021). Street food as infrastructure: Consumer mobility, vendor removability and food security in Mexico City. *Food, Culture & Society*, *24*(1), 98–111. https://doi.org/10.1080/15528014.2020.1859920

Hayden, T. B., & Singh, D. Z. (2020). Food and mobility. *The Journal of Transport History*, *41*(2), 278–288. https://doi.org/10.1177/0022526620916889

HLPE. (2024). *Strengthening urban and peri-urban food systems to achieve food security and nutrition, in the context of urbanization and rural transformation*. FAO.

IBGE. (2020). *Pesquisa de Orçamentos Familiares 2017–2018. Perfil das despesas no Brasil. Indicadores selecionados*. Instituto Brasileiro de Geografia e Estatística. https://biblioteca.ibge.gov.br/visualizacao/livros/liv101761.pdf

INEGI. (2023). *Encuesta Nacional de Ingresos y Gastos de los Hogares 2022 (ENIGH)*. Instituto Nacional de Estadística y Geografía. https://www.inegi.org.mx/contenidos/programas/enigh/nc/2022/doc/enigh2022_ns_presentacion_resultados.pdf

Janoschka, M. (2002). El nuevo modelo de la ciudad latinoamericana: Fragmentacióny privatización. *EURE (Santiago)*, *28*(85), 11–20.

Janoschka, M., & Sequera, J. (2016). Gentrification in Latin America: Addressing the politics and geographies of displacement. *Urban Geography*, *37*(8), 1175–1194. https://doi.org/10.1080/02723638.2015.1103995

Kumar, L., Chhogyel, N., Gopalakrishnan, T., Hasan, M. K., Jayasinghe, S. L., Kariyawasam, C. S., Kogo, B. K., & Ratnayake, S. (2022). Climate change and future of agri-food production. In R. Bhat (Ed.), *Future foods* (pp. 49–79). Academic Press. https://doi.org/10.1016/B978-0-323-91001-9.00009-8

Lang, T. (2010). Crisis? What crisis? The normality of the current food crisis. *Journal of Agrarian Change*, *10*(1), 87–97. https://doi.org/10.1111/j.1471-0366.2009.00250.x
Mayer, M. (2006). Contesting the neoliberalization of urban governance. In H. Leitner, J. Peck & E. Sheppard (Eds.), *Contesting neoliberalism: Urban frontiers* (pp. 90–115). New York: Guildford Press.
McCann, E. (2017). Governing urbanism: Urban governance studies 1.0, 2.0 and beyond. *Urban Studies*, *54*(2), 312–326. https://doi.org/10.1177/0042098016670046
Moctezuma, V. M. (2021). *El desvanecimiento de lo popular: Gentrificación en el Centro Histórico de la Ciudad de México*. El Colegio de Mexico AC.
Moragues-Faus, A. (2020). Towards a critical governance framework: Unveiling the political and justice dimensions of urban food partnerships. *The Geographical Journal*, *186*(1), 73–86. https://doi.org/10.1111/geoj.12325
Moragues-Faus, A., Clark, J. K., Battersby, & Davies, A. (Eds.). (2022). *Routledge handbook of urban food governance*. Routledge. https://doi.org/10.4324/9781003055907
OIT. (2022). *Informe Mundial sobre Salarios 2022–2023: El impacto de la inflación y de la COVID-19 en los salarios y el poder adquisitivo*. Oficina Internacional del Trabajo.
OIT. (2023). *Panorama Laboral 2023*. Oficina Internacional del Trabajo – Oficina Regional para América Latina y el Caribe.
Pothukuchi, K., & Kaufman, J. L. (1999). Placing the food system on the urban agenda: The role of municipal institutions in food systems planning. *Agriculture and Human Values*, *16*, 213–224.
Reardon, T. (2015). The hidden middle: The quiet revolution in the midstream of agrifood value chains in developing countries. *Oxford Review of Economic Policy*, *31*(1), 45–63. https://doi.org/10.1093/oxrep/grv011
Reis, N., & Lukas, M. (2022). *Beyond the megacity: New dimensions of peripheral urbanization in Latin America*. University of Toronto Press. https://books.google.com/books?hl=en&lr=&id=STRjEAAAQBAJ&oi=fnd&pg=PT11&dq=nadine+reis+lukas&ots=E0I1y04JWV&sig=Ogo6ttq4M9MptOhRxux49nyqgLo
Schejtman, A. (1988). La seguridad alimentaria: Tendencias e impacto de la crisis. *Revista de la CEPAL*, *36*, 141–162.
Schteingart, M., & Pírez, P. (Eds.). (2015). *Dos grandes metrópolis latinoamericanas: Ciudad de México y Buenos Aires. Una perspectiva comparativa*. El Colegio de Mexico AC.
Schwarz, A., & Streule, M. (2020). Introduction to the special issue "Contested urban territories: Decolonized perspectives." *Geographica Helvetica*, *75*(1), 11–18.
Silveira, M. L. (2011). Urbanización latinoamericana y circuitos de la economía urbana. *Revista Geográfica de América Central*, *2*, 1–17.
Sonnino, R. (2016). The new geography of food security: Exploring the potential of urban food strategies. *The Geographical Journal*, *182*(2), 190–200. https://doi.org/10.1111/geoj.12129
Timmer, C. P. (2010). Reflections on food crises past. *Food Policy*, *35*(1), 1–11. https://doi.org/10.1016/j.foodpol.2009.09.002
UNDESA. (2018). *World urbanization prospects: The 2018 revision*. United Nations Department of Economic and Social Affairs – Population Division. https://bit.ly/3f2VRFZ
Vivero, J. L., & Ramírez, P. (2009). Hambre, derechos humanos y la consolidación del Estado en América Latina. In J. L. Vivero & X. Erazo (Eds.), *Derecho a la alimentación, políticas públicas e instituciones contra el hambre* (p. 336). Ediciones LOM.
von Braun, J. (2009). Addressing the food crisis: Governance, market functioning, and investment in public goods. *Food Security*, *1*(1), 9–15. https://doi.org/10.1007/s12571-008-0001-z
Whittingham Munévar, M. V. (2010). ¿Qué es la gobernanza y para qué sirve? *Revista Análisis Internacional*, *2*(12). http://hdl.handle.net/20.500.12010/891
World Bank. (2024a). *Latin America & Caribbean – Proportion of time spent on unpaid domestic and care work, by sex (% of 24 hour day)*. World Bank – Gender Data Portal. https://genderdata.worldbank.org/en/regions/latin-america-caribbean
World Bank. (2024b). *World Bank, poverty and inequality platform* [Data set]. https://bit.ly/3hENqTe

SECTION I

Territories

1

URBAN GOVERNANCE AND THE REGULATION OF STREET FOOD VENDING IN LATIN AMERICA

Tiana Bakić Hayden and Irene Farah

Introduction

Street vending is a common feature of many Latin American cities which represents an important source of income, goods, and employment for large swaths of the urban population in cities around the region (Alba, 2015; Mattews & Alba, 2015; Cross, 1998; Swanson, 2007; Goldstein, 2016). While street commerce in different cities in Latin America has been documented since precolonial times, it has gained importance since the 1960s, when increased rates of urbanization led to a growth in the 'informal' economy (Rakowski, 1994; Castells & Portes, 1989). Despite its importance to local economies, street vending has historically also been seen as an 'urban problem' by planners, residents, and politicians and has been discursively linked to congestion, dirtiness, criminality, and other problems. Consequently, city governments throughout Latin America have maintained ambivalent relations with street vendor populations over many decades, alternately tolerating and criminalizing them. The different ways in which street commerce has been governed have had effects on working conditions and the organization of street vendors as well as on the way that consumers perceive and interact with their practices.

Street food represents one of the largest sectors of street commerce and an especially important source of employment for women, migrants, and other vulnerable populations (Roever & Skinner, 2016; Skinner & Haysom, 2016). Street foods are also a particularly important source of food for urban residents who increasingly spend large portions of their days outside of the home (Hayden, 2021; Hayden & Villagómez, 2023). In spite of the economic, nutritional, and social importance of street foods, there is surprisingly little literature on the impact of urban governance

DOI: 10.4324/9781003471929-4

policies on street food vendors and consumers in Latin America. In order to address this gap, we draw on ethnographic research conducted with street food vendors in Mexico City, a metropolis where street food is particularly prevalent and important in social and economic terms, and where there is a significant corpus of academic literature on the subject of street commerce more generally (Crossa, 2018; Cross, 1998; Alba & Braig, 2022; Leal Martínez, 2020), and a smaller number of studies of street food in particular (Long-Solís, 2007; Hayden, 2021; Farah et al., 2022; Hayden & Villagómez, 2023; Hayden, 2014). While the case of Mexico City has its particularities, which we will discuss in the methods section, many of the insights may be relevant to other cities in the region.

The chapter's organization proceeds as follows: After briefly introducing the Mexico City context and our research methodology, we go on to review literature on the governance of street vending in Latin America in order to point to key tendencies, challenges, and conflicts that have emerged throughout the twentieth century. We then ask: What are the implications of street vending governance for the sale and consumption of foods? In order to answer this question, we draw on research with street food vendors, in both street markets and stalls in Mexico City, in order to understand the effects of governance strategies on vendors and consumers. In general terms, we suggest that foods have material and symbolic qualities that differentiate them from other types of goods that are sold on the streets.

Context and methodology

Street (food) vending in Mexico City

In 2023, it is estimated that there are 442,482 street vendors operating in Mexico City's public spaces, including sidewalks, transportation hubs, parks, and other areas (using data from National Survey of Occupation and Employment (*Encuesta Nacional de Ocupación y Empleo*) based on Luján Salazar and Vanek (2020)). Street vendors have been incorporated into urban governance structures since the early twentieth century through a patchwork of strategies including political organizing through clientelistic networks (Crossa, 2018; Cross, 1998) and alliances with local authorities, police, and neighbors (Hayden, 2023; Moctezuma, 2021; Barbosa, 2008; Piccato, 2001; Farah, 2024). Since the 1990s, however, changes in local government and the rise of neoliberal urban policies have led to a greater crackdown on vendors in many public spaces, including the subway system, the historic center of the city, and other areas (Serna-Luna, 2020; Giglia, 2013; Moctezuma, 2021; Leal Martínez, 2020; Crossa, 2018; Meneses-Reyes, 2011; Silva-Londoño, 2010). None of these shifts, however, have significantly reduced the overall presence of street vendors in the city, but rather have had implications for their working conditions and forms of organization, as we will discuss in more detail in the literature review, as many of the more recent changes to street vendor governance are common to other Latin American cities.

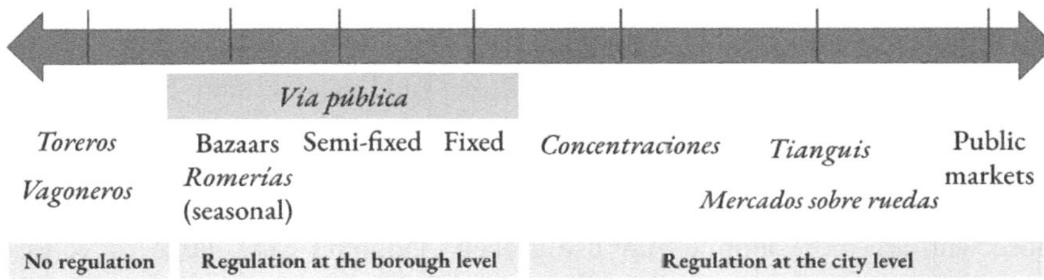

FIGURE 1.1 Street vendors in Mexico City and their range of legal certainty

Source: Own elaboration

In Mexico City, like in other cities, the governance of street vending occurs through an interplay of different government institutions and a diverse array of local stakeholders (such as business associations, neighborhood associations, and political associations). Mexico City's political structure is composed of the head of government (the mayor of the city) and 16 boroughs (intra-city local governments). Boroughs divide street vending under three main subsectors: (1) *vía pública* (public way), (2) *tianguis* (street markets), and (3) public markets. These categories are regulated by different government officials and have varying degrees of social, political, and legal recognition (see Figure 1.1). The legal status of these vending categories is in constant flux, determined by the daily negotiations between vendors, street vending associations, state employees, and politicians at local and city governments. For example, public markets are managed directly by the city government, with boroughs playing a minor role in their supervision. *Toreros* (bullfighters) do not have any regulation, 'dodging' the authorities that persecute them by selling their merchandise on a piece of cloth and running away as they see authorities, as if they were bullfighters. Likewise, *vagoneros* (subway vendors) are not accounted for in the law but have historically been organized to be able to sell within the subway system. Vendors of *vía pública* range from bazaars and *romerías*—having seasonal agreements—to 'fixed' vendors, who have stalls attached to the ground. All vendors of *vía pública* are regulated at the borough level. *Tianguis* and *mercados sobre ruedas* (markets on wheels) are installed daily and are regulated at the city level. *Concentraciones* are agglomerations of vendors which function as precursors of public markets and are regulated at the city level.

These general categories and history of street vending in Mexico City broadly apply to the case of street *food* vending, which represents a large sub-sector of street commerce in the city, with an estimated 118,899 people selling food from public spaces in some capacity in the city in 2019 (Luján Salazar & Vanek, 2020). Indeed, street foods have maintained a presence since precolonial times and through the colonial and modern periods (Long-Solís, 2007; Barbosa, 2008; Bleynat, 2021). Although maligned as 'unhygienic' or unhealthy by some, the sale of street foods has represented an important economic opportunity for women, migrants, and other vulnerable groups, as well as an important source of culturally appropriate and affordable food for consumers 'on the go' (Hayden & Villagómez, 2023; Hayden, 2021; Long-Solís, 2007; Gálvez, 2018). Street food vendors may be divided into those who sell fresh ingredients (produce, meat, and cheese) and those who sell prepared, ready-to-eat goods (juices, cooked stews, tacos, and griddle-fried corn snacks). Food vendors may operate in any of the types of spaces listed earlier, and those who are more mobile may use grocery shopping carts, large tricycles, or pushcarts to move their wares in public spaces.

Methodology

In this study, we focus on *vía pública* and *tianguis* street vending, bringing together material from research conducted by each of the authors independently. Tiana draws on fieldwork conducted in 2012, 2014–2015, and 2018 with *vía pública* vendors selling from fixed and semi-fixed stalls or mobile vendors (selling from bicycles, pushcarts, or grocery carts) in several neighborhoods in Mexico City, including Centro Histórico, Roma, Condesa, and the wholesale market district (la Central de Abasto) in Iztapalapa. Irene draws from research in 2021 and 2023 with vendors and leaders of street vending associations in *tianguis* (street markets) in the following boroughs: Gustavo A. Madero, Álvaro Obregón, and Coyoacán. In both cases, the research in question consisted of ethnographic methods, including in-depth interviews with street vendors and in the case of *tianguis*, with leaders of street vending associations. The research in both cases dealt, at least in part, with how street vendors were regulated, how they managed their relationships with different authorities and stakeholders, and how they articulated their claims to the street.

We focus on *vía pública* vending since it is the most politicized and most conspicuous type of street vending in the city (Crossa, 2018; Leal Martínez, 2016; Meneses-Reyes, 2011). *Vía pública* vendors commonly set up with fixed or semi-fixed stalls on sidewalks, parks, or plazas across the city. Due to their semi-permanent condition, *vía pública* vendors (both fixed and semi-fixed) are subject to clientelism, extortion, and eviction. We also study *tianguis* vending because government permits are given more easily to *tianguis* associations than to other street vendors working in public spaces. Moreover, they have better social acceptance (Gayosso Ramírez, 2009; Gómez, 2012) since they are integral to Mexico City's food system selling mostly healthy foods at accessible prices (Domínguez et al., 2023). Lastly, *tianguis* are critical sites to study since they can cover up to ten kilometers of city streets, revealing the importance of street vending's urban management of public space.

Literature review: Street vending governance in Latin American cities

The governance of street vending in Latin America reflects two conflicting approaches and characterizations of street commerce and informal economies.

On the one hand, street vending is essential for the distribution of goods and services, supplying cities with products from other countries and playing a central role in the economy (Mattews & Alba, 2015; Alba, 2015), as well as a primary activity or alternative source of income for many residents (Cross, 1998; Pradilla, 2005). On the other hand, street vending has historically been understood as chaotic, backward, or unhygienic by governing elites and residents. Street vending is often depicted as the cause of increased neighborhood insecurity due to potential vendor collusion with criminals (Davis & Luna, 2007; Leal Martínez, 2020), obstruction of pedestrian and vehicular movement, and pollution of public spaces (Bromley, 2000). Street vendors are also viewed as unfair competition for established businesses because they typically do not pay property taxes and are often seen as a population that skirts the law and is involved in illicit activities (Bromley, 2000; Crossa, 2018). Street vending thus frequently results in conflicts over public space (Ramírez-Kuri, 2015). Policies governing street commerce for much of the twentieth century and to the present day can thus be understood as contradictory, ambiguous, and ambivalent, as authorities have alternated between tolerating, incorporating, ignoring, scapegoating, and criminalizing street economies, depending on shifting historical or political tides.

There is a significant body of literature on street commerce in Latin American cities, largely dating from the 1960s onward. This boom reflects the fact that in the 1950s and 1960s, a large number of people moved from rural areas to cities in search of better economic opportunities, contributing to the rapid urbanization of Latin American cities. The rapid growth of urban populations in these decades, however, outpaced the ability of cities to provide adequate housing, services, and employment, leading to an increase in housing and labor informality in the region (Meneses-Reyes, 2011; Collier, 1976; Cornelius, 1975). In this context, however, many populations managed to secure housing and work through a combination of collective organization and clientelistic agreements with politicians and political intermediaries that formed membership-based associations (Auyero, 2000; Collier, 1976; Cornelius, 1975; Goldstein, 2004; Meneses-Reyes, 2011). Street vendors, whose very presence on the streets came to represent the excesses and shortcomings of urbanism in the mid-twentieth to late twentieth century, were also emblematic of the ways in which popular economies articulated with political structures of the time (Crossa, 2018; Cross, 1998; Alba & Braig, 2022; Meneses-Reyes, 2011; Donovan, 2002).

Since the 1990s, when neoliberal governments and policies began to proliferate throughout Latin America, urban studies scholars began to take note of the increased move toward forms of spatial regulation and governance that criminalized and displaced street commerce, especially in areas that were targeted for 'renewal' or were undergoing gentrification (Becker & Müller, 2013; Rosemary Bromley, 1998; Bromley & Mackie, 2009; Crossa, 2018; Delgadillo, 2017; Giglia, 2013; Leal Martínez, 2007; Meneses-Reyes, 2013a; Moctezuma, 2021; Nogueira, 2019; Silva-Londoño, 2010; Stamm, 2005; Swanson, 2007). Scholars have argued that the eviction of vendors stems from cities' efforts to modernize urban areas by attracting private capital to improve the urban image (Crossa, 2018; Leal Martínez, 2016; Swanson, 2007) and privatizing city spaces to spur economic growth (Becker & Müller, 2013; Delgadillo, 2017; Leal Martínez, 2020). Physical revitalization practices around Latin America have aimed to 'rescue' the downtown areas from crime and physical deterioration. These 'broken windows' style policies which criminalize the urban poor have promoted changes in land use regulations and fostered real estate development in the name of ensuring security (Davis & Luna, 2007; Meneses-Reyes, 2013a). These policies have associated vendors with poor sanitary conditions, disorder, source of crime, chaos, and underdevelopment (Peña, 1999). As such, street vending in the late twentieth and early twenty-first century has continued to be seen as a symbol of disorder, corruption, and illegality for the ruling class who wish to remain in power, reflecting a 'deteriorating' society that they find undesirable (Crossa, 2018; Leal Martínez, 2016; Swanson, 2007).

In terms of the legal frameworks through which street commerce has been governed in Latin America, the implementation of laws has been the primary formal approach (Meneses-Reyes & Caballero-Juárez, 2014). However, there has been an absence of comprehensive regulatory street vending frameworks. Scholars have argued that a lack of a clear legal framework creates uncertainty and increases criminalization, leading to conflicts and challenges in enforcement (Hayden, 2017; Tucker, 2017; Tucker & Devlin, 2019). The ambiguity of laws leaves room for interpretation and manipulation, allowing for selective enforcement or exploitation by various stakeholders. The ambiguity of regulation creates gray areas in the implementation of norms, opening up space for discretionary practices. Consequently, laws enforced by state authority are temporarily suspended at discretion, depending on the negotiation achieved between the local state and vendors, using these regulatory ambiguities as a tool of the state apparatus to exercise their power (Tucker, 2017). According to Tucker and Devlin (2019), uncertainty works as a mode of planning by which local authorities manage street vending and urban space, exerting their power by creating confusions, ambiguities, and rule-breaking strategies. In this manner, authorities maintain ambiguous spaces between law and everyday practices of enforcement to gain control over public space.

Studies have also noted that existing policies are often used in an exclusionary manner, favoring certain vendors or sectors while marginalizing others (Meneses-Reyes, 2018; Nogueira, 2020). The enforcement of legal frameworks also varies across time, intensifying or dwindling at the convenience of government authorities (Itikawa, 2010; Mackie et al., 2014; Serna-Luna, 2020). This variation is oftentimes attributed to electoral convenience, political willingness, or lack of state capacity. However, Meneses-Reyes (2011) highlights the legal difficulty in enforcing laws that regulate public space, scrutinizing the tensions between protecting the public space of unwanted street vendors while officially recognizing the organizations of vendors and their right to work in public space.

Given the lack of legal certainty and authority abuse, street vendors have historically worked under incessant political and legal uncertainties, being forced to readapt quickly to rapidly changing modes of planning, reinterpreting, and renegotiating their strategies to continue working in public spaces (Azuela & Meneses-Reyes, 2014; Bromley, 2000; Crossa, 2018; Meneses-Reyes, 2013a; Meneses-Reyes & Caballero-Juárez, 2014). Over time, street vendors have learned to contest these logics in multiple ways, by differentiating their work from other type of criminalized work (Crossa, 2016), by using the global market to exchange products (Alba, 2012), or by promoting illicit economic activities that challenge the hegemonic powers of the state (Gago, 2017). In short, vendors have sought to negotiate and struggle over changing power structures in their everyday lives (Cross, 1998; Crossa, 2018). Some vendors have rearticulated their position as vendors by drawing new meanings of themselves by building their identity around artistic performance (Crossa, 2013). Other vendors have gained legal insight to challenge exclusionary policies (Meneses-Reyes & Caballero-Juárez, 2014; Serna-Luna, 2020). In Latin America, countries like Colombia and Mexico have endeavored to protect street vendors by developing the 'right to work' in international documents and constitutional case laws (Meneses-Reyes & Caballero-Juárez, 2014). Within these collective efforts, there is a demand to shift the discourse of street vendors from being an undesirable nuisance for modernizing trends to a discussion of political and legal recognition which would improve their livelihoods and their coexistence with other users of public space.

Contesting exclusionary and ambiguous policies, street vendors have also organized into membership-based associations. These legal changes have been possible due to joint efforts and the integration of international organizations, non-governmental organizations, membership-based organizations, trade unions, and street vendors (Roever, 2010). In fact, some scholars have emphasized how politics and collective action are at the core of street vending governance (Cross, 1998). Even in the presence of regulatory frameworks and vendors willing to comply with the law, there is great difficulty in coordinating the strategies of multiple stakeholders and the heterogeneity of vendors with different political incentives at different levels of government (Crossa, 2016; Roever, 2005).

In particular, research in political science has analyzed how governments promote street vendors to organize to facilitate street vending governance (Hummel, 2022) and tolerate street vendors as a strategy to maximize votes as well as a redistribution strategy among poor constituencies (Holland, 2017). A greater focus on intermediation has shed light on the complexities of street vending governance and the itinerant negotiation that exists to regulate street vending and public space. Across Latin America, these associations have acted as the intermediaries (brokers) between governments and street vendors and are conformed as unions or civil associations which vary in their origin and goals. While some of these associations focus on defending vendors' rights, others have focused on maximizing electoral or economic outcomes. Scholars have focused on the power of street vending associations and how they impact the enforcement of regulations in Peru (Aliaga Linares, 2002; Holland, 2017; Hummel, 2022; Roever, 2005), Colombia (Donovan, 2002, 2008; Holland, 2017; Moncada, 2016), Mexico (Alba, 2015; Cross, 1998; Peña, 1999; Silva-Londoño, 2010; Zaremberg, 2011), Bolivia (Hummel, 2017, 2022), and Brazil (Hummel, 2022). In particular, Aliaga Linares (2002) has scrutinized the alliances these associations build to advocate for their demands with governments, while other scholars have examined the relationship that leaders of the associations maintain with street-level bureaucrats (Cross, 1998; Holland, 2017; Hummel, 2018) and political parties (Holland & Palmer-Rubin, 2015).

In summary, we can see that the majority of existing studies on street commerce in Latin American cities have analyzed the political and economic dimensions of vending and the way that vendors have organized to stake a claim to the street. Here, we wish to draw attention to two key points that have emerged in these studies, which are particularly relevant to our understanding of street *food* vendors. First, the studies cited earlier, which draw attention to the precarity, informality, and sometimes illegality of street commerce, demonstrate that the working conditions of street vendors are difficult and are hampered by the shifting governance structures to which they are subjected. Second, the increasing criminalization of street vendors in the context of neoliberal urbanism has pushed vendors out of many areas, and forced them to change their vending strategies, often becoming more mobile as they sell. Both of these points, while relevant for street vendors more generally, weigh especially heavily on those who sell food on the streets. It is to these vendors in Mexico City that we turn our attention now.

Challenges and opportunities faced by food vendors

Lack of access to urban services

One of the challenges that existing literature on street vending has identified is that the precarious working conditions of street vendors are linked to their lack of stable access to urban services, including water, sanitation, and electricity (Roever, 2014; Skinner & Watson, 2017). While this is a problem for people in popular economies who sell on the streets more broadly, it affects food vendors in particular due to the type of products that they sell.

Lack of clean water, for example, limits the ability of workers to wash their hands and clean their supplies, which contributes to the widespread notion that street food is unsanitary. Indeed, there is a large body of literature related to public health, both in Mexico and globally, that takes as its starting premise the fact that street vendors' lack of access to clean, running water poses a health risk (Pires et al., 2012; Pariza & Cho, 2024). Prepared food vendors are sensitive to the risks that not washing hands represents in their industry, as well as to socially stigmatizing perceptions that they lack hygiene (Hayden, 2014). Vendors take various steps to mitigate the problem of inadequate access to running water. Those who sell from fixed or semi-permanent stands may bring large plastic jugs full of gallons of potable water with them to work to use for washing dishes, their working areas, and for drinking. This is not an option, however, for more mobile vendors who sell from small tables in the street, due to the cost and logistical challenges of storing and transporting water. Due to these challenges and exacerbated by the COVID-19 pandemic, it has become common to see large bottles of hand sanitizer at street food stands, and many vendors use plastic gloves when handling money.

Lack of running water also poses challenges in terms of dealing with dishes and cookware. Since vendors lack running water or sinks, many of them choose not to use reusable plates or cups, even when people consume prepared goods right on the spot rather than for takeaway. In some cases, vendors may place disposable pieces of paper on plastic plates, so that the paper can be thrown away without dirtying the plate. In many cases, however, vendors choose to use disposable plastic or Styrofoam products, since the logistics of washing are complicated. This creates challenges in terms of not only the economic (and ecological) costs of producing disposable waste but also because of the question of waste generation and disposal.

Unlike many cities, Mexico City does not have public dumpsters where people can deposit waste, but rather relies on a network of semi-formalized waste collectors who collect directly from private residences and buildings, but not from the street (Marello & Helwege, 2018; Espinosa-Aquino et al., 2023). In order for waste collectors to take garbage, then, vendors need to coordinate garbage pickups and pay them directly. Food products, meanwhile, generate a large quantity of organic waste, which need to be disposed of quickly in order to avoid unpleasant smells and attracting urban pests. This is especially important because one of the key complaints that neighbors or authorities who are opposed to the presence of street vendors in public spaces may cite is that they create unsanitary conditions on the street, related in large part to food waste and disposal.

In fact, street food vendors themselves are quite aware of the challenges that vending in precarious public spaces entails. As many street food stalls are situated on busy sidewalks, intersections, transport hubs, or other areas with high rates of transit, the vending conditions are characterized by a lack of comfortable space, seating areas, shade or shelter for customers and vendors alike. Yet since setting up seating or shade structures (sun umbrellas or tarps) may be unacceptable to local authorities or neighbors; street vendors are limited in terms of what they can do to attract and retain customers. Some attempt to put down a few plastic stools that cluster around the cooking area, while others invest in larger tarps which allow them to vend even in the rain. Historically, street vendors in Mexico City who sell from semi-fixed or fixed stands have invested in colorful *rótulos*, or hand-painted signs, often of a humorous nature, to give themselves identity, although recently municipal authorities in central Mexico City have prohibited even these forms of aesthetic expression to vendors, forcing them to adopt standardized signage with the city's logo on it (Ibarra, 2022).

Another strategy for appropriating public space to which food vendors turn is related to cleaning and maintenance of the sidewalk. It is common to see vendors scrubbing the sidewalk on which they set up their tables or stalls with soap and water at the beginning and end of the day, much like owners of local brick-and-mortar businesses. Vendors understand this to be part of their duty as small business owners, and as a responsibility which counteracts the commonly held notion that they dirty their surroundings. However, not all vendors clean their working spaces appropriately, often leaving stains of oil or blocking the sewage with trash or food, which create public health hazards and issues with neighbors and authorities.

Lack of reliable access to electricity is another problem street vendors face since those who do not have a permanent stall are unable to secure a legal electrical connection. While a small number of vendors will set up connections, piggybacking off neighboring buildings or through the official state-owned company, the vast majority of street vendors simply lack electricity. Since food vendors sell perishable goods, they need proper storage conditions to maintain the freshness and safety of their food. The lack of refrigeration or cooling systems, which are crucial for storing perishable items such as meat, dairy, fruits, and vegetables, means that food can spoil quickly, leading to significant financial losses for the vendors and posing health risks to consumers. Additionally, vendors may face challenges in accessing fresh ingredients daily. In the case of Mexico City, food street vendors have to invest in either storage to maintain their excess inventory or transportation to access the main supply center that sells food at wholesale prices. Lack of electricity also means that vendors necessarily need to use gas tanks or charcoal grills for cooking, increasing the risk of accidents.

Illegality, criminalization, and mobility

As we discussed previously, one of the fundamental issues faced by street vendors in Latin America is that their claims to public space are often precarious, lacking full legal recognition, and subject to discretional and frequently changing municipal regulations. In recent years, this has led to increased criminalization of vendors and their removal from areas of 'urban renewal' or gentrification (Moctezuma, 2021; Crossa, 2009). In practice, this has meant that many vendors need to become more 'mobile', that is, to be ready to pick and run or hide when authorities come by (Meneses-Reyes, 2013b; Hayden, 2021) or simply cannot set up their stalls. These tendencies and changes affect all street vendors, yet they have particular implications for food vendors for several reasons.

First, as mentioned earlier, the types of products that food vendors sell are generally more delicate and complicated to transport and set up than consumer goods such as cosmetics products, batteries, cell phone cases, t-shirts, or toys. Fresh foods, such as produce, need to be carefully handled in order not to bruise or be damaged. Prepared foods, such as tacos or stews, need to be transported with care in pots, Tupperwares, or other vessels so as not to spill. What this means is that the setup and takedown time for street food businesses is often a much longer affair than for other sorts of goods. In practice, this means that food vendors are not able to simply get up and flee when authorities demand that they do or when they are threatened with fines or confiscations. They are most vulnerable to the heightened mobility that is demanded of vendors in contexts where they may be criminalized and forced to engage in a more cat-and-mouse dynamic with police and other authorities.

Second, and related to the previous discussion about the lack of access to municipal services, increased mobility is particularly challenging to food vendors because of their need for water, energy, and waste disposal. Large water vessels for cleaning and consumption, gas cylinders or coal grills, and bags of organic waste all weigh down food vendors and render them unable to be easily mobile. Whereas vendors who sell non-delicate and non-perishable goods can simply hawk their wares from improvised settings such as a box or blanket on the sidewalk, food vendors generally need tables, grocery carts, or stalls that can be set up and remain stable. Moreover, as mentioned, they frequently require cooking, washing, and cooling equipment such as gas canisters, coal-fired griddles, chopping boards, and tables, which cannot be safely or easily dismantled in rapid fashion. At the end of the workday, it is common to see food vendors on sidewalks scrubbing down large pots, stacking plastic food containers and utensils, washing down the sidewalk with chlorine, and other such tasks. All of this means that food vendors are particularly vulnerable to changing regulatory landscapes which may challenge their right to sell in a particular place.

Finally, in contexts where vendors are displaced by changing regulations or implementation of existing laws, they lose the 'social infrastructure' of relationships with local customers, businesses, waste collectors, police, and others. These social networks are important to all street vendors, since they allow for storage of equipment, access to bathrooms and running water, and protection (Malasan, 2019). Yet, for the reasons mentioned earlier, food vendors tend to have more equipment that cannot be easily transported, and which needs to be stored close to where they sell their goods. Tables, griddles, and sun umbrellas, for example, may be stored in the basements or storage rooms of local businesses or residential buildings for a small fee. Vendors may pay a small amount or have an agreement about cleaning the sidewalk in exchange for access to bathrooms in cafes or businesses nearby. Sometimes, they might even leave their equipment in brick-and-mortar businesses or houses nearby. Local police frequently eat for free with vendors in exchange for keeping an eye out for them and offering some degree of 'protection' from criminals. Customers, of course, represent the economic basis for street food vending, and those networks in particular take time to establish, especially in the context of high-density competition and food cultural heritage such as that which characterizes Mexico City. Urban governance strategies which lead to the criminalization and displacement of vendors, or to their increased spatial precarity and mobility, mean that vendors lose those valuable social connections, which provide them not only with income but also with networks that allow them to access basic services.

Conclusion

In this chapter, we discussed key aspects of the governance of street vending in Latin America and highlighted some of the particular challenges faced by food vendors through the study of street vendors in Mexico City. Existing research shows that governance strategies that regulate public spaces and thoroughfares—including laws, bylaws, clientelistic arrangements with vendor's organizations, and discretionary practices by local police have significant impacts on millions of people throughout Latin America's cities, who work as vendors in the streets. Street vendors in general have thus historically suffered from criminalization, exclusionary policies, and lack of access to urban services. Yet, these challenges are particularly severe for street food vendors, who are more reliant on infrastructures and whose goods are perishable. Indeed, as our analysis earlier mentioned shows, the materiality of food as a good makes the work of food vendors qualitatively different than, for example, that of people who sell batteries or cleaning supplies.

Furthermore, it is not simply the materiality of food which differentiates this type of street commerce from other types but its symbolic and political dimensions as well. Food is an essential good, and the right to food is a human right, which is enshrined in the 1948 Universal Declaration of Human Rights and in Article 4 of the Mexican constitution. Food vendors frequently invoke this notion of food as an indisputable *moral good*, as well as a *human right* when speaking of the legal and political challenges that they face to vending on the street, as well as when responding to popular discourses which attempt to delegitimize their claims. Food vendors claim—and studies back up these claims (see Hayden, 2021; Farah et al., 2022)—that they are contributing an important service for urban populations by feeding people on the go at extremely affordable prices.

To this day, however, urban planning and efforts at governing public space have not recognized the importance of street vendors for urban life and for food security. On the contrary, much recent policy has drawn on negative depictions of street food vendors as unhygienic, disorderly, and problematic. In fact, we can learn from previous state efforts when Mexico City's government in the 1950s—under pressure from its increasing population growth—supported the creation of *tianguis* street markets to supply a newly arrived population with food, when they did not have access to food stores in the steadily growing metropolis (Gómez, 2012). Ever since, *tianguis* have become a vital supply of food in the city (Farah, 2024) and there is still a need to think about ways through which street vendors need better support from governments. Planning and governance of public spaces and places in Latin American cities could therefore benefit from careful attention to the ways that food is bought, sold, and consumed outside of the home and in the streets of the region's cities.

References

Alba, Carlos. 2012. "La Calle Para Quien La Ocupa. Las Condiciones Sociopolíticas de La Globalización No Hegemónica En México DF." *Nueva Sociedad* (blog).

https://nuso.org/articulo/la-calle-para-quien-la-ocupa-las-condiciones-sociopoliticas-de-la-globalizacion-no-hegemonica-en-mexico-df/.

Alba, Carlos. 2015. "Los Líderes de Los Vendedores Ambulantes de Las Calles Del Centro Histórico de La Ciudad de México." In *La Globalización Desde Abajo: La Otra Economía Mundial*, edited by Carlos Alba, Gustavo Lins Ribeiro, Gordon Mattews, and Mario A. Zambudio Vega, 373–406. Ciudad de México: Fondo de Cultura Económica.

Alba, Carlos, and Marianne Braig. 2022. *Las voces del Centro Histórico: la lucha por el espacio en la Ciudad de México*. Mexico City: El Colegio de México.

Aliaga Linares, Lissette. 2002. *Sumas y Restas: El Capital Social Como Recurso En La Informalidad (Las Redes de Los Comerciantes Ambulantes de Independencia)*. Lima, Perú: Alternativa-UNMSM.

Auyero, Javier. 2000. "The Logic of Clientelism in Argentina: An Ethnographic Account." *Latin American Research Review* 35(3): 55–81.

Azuela, Antonio, and Rodrigo Meneses-Reyes. 2014. "The Everyday Formation of the Urban Space: Law and Poverty in Mexico City." In *The Expanding Spaces of Law*, edited by Irus Braverman, Nicholas Blomley, David Delaney, and Alexandre (Sandy) Kedar, 167–89. Stanford, CA: Stanford University Press.

Barbosa, Mario. 2008. *El trabajo en las calles: subsistencia y negociación política en la ciudad de México a comienzos del siglo XX*. México, D.F: El Colegio de México, Centro de Estudios Históricos; Universidad Autónoma Metropolitana, Unidad Cuajimalpa.

Becker, Anne, and Markus-Michael Müller. 2013. "The Securitization of Urban Space and the 'Rescue' of Downtown Mexico City: Vision and Practice." *Latin American Perspectives* 40(2): 77–94.

Bleynat, Ingrid. 2021. *Vendors' Capitalism: A Political Economy of Public Markets in Mexico City* (1st ed.). Stanford, CA: Stanford University Press.

Bromley, Ray. 2000. "Street Vending and Public Policy: A Global Review." *International Journal of Sociology and Social Policy* 20(1/2): 1–28. https://doi.org/10.1108/01443330010789052.

Bromley, Rosemary. 1998. "Informal Commerce: Expansion and Exclusion in the Historic Centre of the Latin American City." *International Journal of Urban and Regional Research* 22(2): 245–63. https://doi.org/10.1111/1468-2427.00138.

Bromley, Rosemary, and Peter K. Mackie. 2009. "Displacement and the New Spaces for Informal Trade in the Latin American City Centre." *Urban Studies* 46(7): 1485–506. https://doi.org/10.1177/0042098009104577.

Castells, Manuel, and Alejandro Portes. 1989. "World Underneath: The Origins, Dynamics, and Effects of the Informal Economy." In *The Informal Economy: Studies in Advanced and Less Developed Countries*, edited by Alejandro Portes, Manuel Castells, and Lauren A Benton, 11–37. Baltimore: Johns Hopkins University Press.

Collier, David. 1976. *Squatters and Oligarchs: Authoritarian Rule and Policy Change in Peru*. Baltimore: The Johns Hopkins University Press.

Cornelius, Wayne. 1975. *Politics and the Migrant Poor in Mexico City*. Stanford, CA: Stanford University Press.

Cross, John C. 1998. *Informal Politics: Street Vendors and the State in Mexico City*. Stanford: Stanford University Press.

Crossa, Veronica. 2009. "Resisting the Entrepreneurial City: Street Vendors' Struggle in Mexico City's Historic Center." *International Journal of Urban and Regional Research* 33(1): 43–63. https://doi.org/10.1111/j.1468-2427.2008.00823.x.

Crossa, Veronica. 2013. "Play for Protest, Protest for Play: Artisan and Vendors' Resistance to Displacement in Mexico City." *Antipode* 45(4): 826–43. https://doi.org/10.1111/j.1467-8330.2012.01043.x.

Crossa, Veronica. 2016. "Reading for Difference on the Street: De-Homogenising Street Vending in Mexico City." *Urban Studies* 53(2): 287–301. https://doi.org/10.1177/0042098014563471.

Crossa, Veronica. 2018. *Luchando Por Un Espacio En La Ciudad de México: Comerciantes Ambulantes y El Espacio Público Urbano*. México: El Colegio de México.

Davis, Diane, and Óscar Luna. 2007. "El factor Giuliani: delincuencia, la cero tolerancia en el trabajo policiaco y la transformación de la esfera pública en el centro de la ciudad de México." *Estudios sociológicos* 25(75): 639–81.

Delgadillo, Víctor. 2017. "Markets of La Merced: New Frontiers of Gentrification in the Historic Centre of Mexico City." In *Contested Markets, Contested Cities*, 1–17. London: Routledge.

Domínguez, Ana Paula, Irene Farah, Nancy López-Olmedo, Carolina Pérez-Ferrer, Yenisei Ramírez-Toscano, Brent A. Langellier, M Arantxa Colchero, Juan A. Rivera, Tonatiuh Barrientos-Gutierrez, and Dalia Stern. 2023. "Changes in the Healthfulness of Food and Beverage Purchases From 2006 to 2020 in Formal, Mixed and Informal Outlets in Mexico." *BMC Public Health*. Under Revision.

Donovan, Michael G. 2002. "Space Wars in Bogotá: The Recovery of Public Space and Its Impact on Street Vendors." *Master in City Planning*. Massachusetts Institute of Technology. https://doi.org/10.1177/0042098007085100.

Donovan, Michael G. 2008. "Informal Cities and the Contestation of Public Space: The Case of Bogotá's Street Vendors, 1988–2003." *Urban Studies* 45(1): 29–51. https://doi.org/10.1177/0042098007085100.

Espinosa-Aquino, Beatriz, Xavier Gabarrell Durany, and Roberto Quirós Vargas. 2023. "The Role of Informal Waste Management in Urban Metabolism: A Review of Eight Latin American Countries." *Sustainability* 15(3): 1826. https://doi.org/10.3390/su15031826.

Farah, Irene. 2024. "The Scramble for the City: Street Vending, Politics, and the Governance of Public Space in Mexico City and San Francisco." PhD in City and Regional Planning. UC Berkeley,

Farah, Irene, Dalia Stern, Yenisei Ramírez, Nancy López-Olmedo, Carolina Pérez-Ferrer, Brent A. Langellier, M. Arantxa Colchero, and Tonatiuh Barrientos-Gutierrez. 2022. "Food and Beverage Purchases at Formal and Informal Outlets in Mexico." *Public Health Nutrition*, October, 1–28. https://doi.org/10.1017/S1368980022002324.

Gago, Verónica. 2017. *Neoliberalism From Below: Popular Pragmatics and Baroque Economies*. Translated by Liz Mason-Deese. Durham: Duke University Press Books.

Gálvez, Alyshia. 2018. *Eating NAFTA: Trade, Food Policies, and the Destruction of Mexico*. 1st ed. Oakland, California: University of California Press.

Gayosso Ramírez, José Luis. 2009. "Los tianguistas de la Ciudad de México: de informales a trabajadores atípicos." *Iztapalapa. Revista de Ciencias Sociales y Humanidades* 30(66/1): 53–67.

Giglia, Angela. 2013. "Between Common Good and the Insular City: Urban Renovation in Mexico City." *Alteridades* 23: 27–38.

Goldstein, Daniel M. 2004. *The Spectacular City: Violence and Performance in Urban Bolivia*. Durham: Duke University Press Books.

Goldstein, Daniel M. 2016. *Owners of the Sidewalk: Security and Survival in the Informal City*. Durham: Duke University Press Books.

Gómez, Norma Angélica. 2012. "Liderazgos y organizaciones en el comercio en vía pública de la Ciudad de México: el caso de la delegación Iztapalapa 1998–2008." Doctoral. Ciudad de México: Colegio de México. https://repositorio.colmex.mx/concern/theses/9593tv37z?locale=es.

Hayden, Tiana Bakić. 2014. "The Taste of Precarity: Language, Legitimacy, and Legality among Mexican Street Food Vendors." In *Street Food: Culture, Economy, Health and Governance*, edited by Ryzia De Cassia Vieira Cardoso, Michèle Companion, and Stefano Roberto Marras, 83–97. Routledge.

Hayden, Tiana Bakić. 2017. "Disambiguating Legalities: Street Vending, Law, and Boundary-Work in Mexico." *Ethnoscripts* 19(2). http://nbn-resolving.de/urn:nbn:de:gbv:18-8-11749.
Hayden, Tiana Bakić. 2021. "Street Food as Infrastructure: Consumer Mobility, Vendor Removability and Food Security in Mexico City." *Food Culture and Society: An International Journal of Multidisciplinary Research* 24(1): 98–111. https://doi.org/10.1080/15528014.2020.1859920.
Hayden, Tiana Bakić. 2023. "Insecure Infrastructures: The Affects and Effects of Violence in Mexico's Food System." *American Anthropologist* 125(1): 89–99. https://doi.org/10.1111/aman.13807.
Hayden, Tiana Bakić, and Paloma Villagómez. 2023. "La Alimentación Como Práctica Socioespacial: Relevancia Para Las Desigualdades Urbanas." In *Desigualdades Territoriales. Miradas Cruzadas*, edited by Martha Schteingart, Clara Salazar, and Jaime Sobrino, 252–71. Mexico City: El Colegio de México.
Holland, Alisha C. 2017. *Forbearance as Redistribution: The Politics of Informal Welfare in Latin America*. New York, NY: Cambridge University Press.
Holland, Alisha C., and Brian Palmer-Rubin. 2015. "Beyond the Machine: Clientelist Brokers and Interest Organizations in Latin America." *Comparative Political Studies* 48(9): 1186–223. https://doi.org/10.1177/0010414015574883.
Hummel, Calla. 2017. "Disobedient Markets: Street Vendors, Enforcement, and State Intervention in Collective Action." *Comparative Political Studies* 50(11): 1524–55. https://doi.org/10.1177/0010414016679177.
Hummel, Calla. 2018. "Bribery Cartels: Collusive Corruption in Bolivian Street Markets." *Latin American Research Review* 53(2): 217–30. https://doi.org/10.25222/larr.342.
Hummel, Calla. 2022. *Why Informal Workers Organize: Contentious Politics, Enforcement, and the State*. New York City: Oxford University Press.
Ibarra, Alejandra. 2022. "Mexico City Trades Colorful Food Stalls for Drab Uniformity." *Washington Post*, June 20, 2022. https://www.washingtonpost.com/world/2022/06/17/mexico-city-rotulo-cuauhtemoc/.
Itikawa, Luciana. 2010. "Clandestine Geometries: Mapping Street Vending in Downtown São Paulo." In *Street Vendors in the Global Urban Economy*, edited by Sharit Bhowmik, 278–96. India: Routledge. https://www.routledge.com/Street-Vendors-in-the-Global-Urban-Economy/Bhowmik/p/book/9780367176471.
Leal Martínez, Alejandra. 2007. "Peligro, proximidad y diferencia: negociar fronteras en el Centro Histórico de la Ciudad de México." *Alteridades* 17(34): 27–38.
Leal Martínez, Alejandra. 2016. "'You Cannot be Here': The Urban Poor and the Specter of the Indian in Neoliberal Mexico City." *The Journal of Latin American and Caribbean Anthropology* 21(3): 539–59. https://doi.org/10.1111/jlca.12196.
Leal Martínez, Alejandra. 2020. "Securing the Street: Urban Renewal and the Fight Against 'Informality' in Mexico City." In *Futureproof: Security Aesthetics and the Management of Life*, edited by D. Asher Ghertner, Hudson McFann, and Daniel M. Goldstein, 245–70. Duke University Press. https://doi.org/10.1515/9781478007517-012.
Long-Solís, Janet. 2007. "A Survey of Street Foods in Mexico City." *Food and Foodways: Explorations in the History and Culture of Human Nourishment* 15(2–4): 213–36.
Luján Salazar, José de Jesús, and Joann Vanek. 2020. "Informal Workers in Mexico: A Statistical Snapshot." Statistical Brief 22. WIEGO. https://www.wiego.org/sites/default/files/publications/file/WIEGO_Statistical_Brief_N22_Mexico_0.pdf.
Mackie, Peter K., Rosemary Bromley, and Alison M. B. Brown. 2014. "Informal Traders and the Battlegrounds of Revanchism in Cusco, Peru." *International Journal of Urban and Regional Research* 38(5): 1884–903. https://doi.org/10.1111/1468-2427.12161.
Malasan, Prananda Luffiansyah. 2019. "The Untold Flavour of Street Food: Social Infrastructure as a Means of Everyday Politics for Street Vendors in Bandung, Indonesia." *Asia Pacific Viewpoint* 60(1): 51–64. https://doi.org/10.1111/apv.12217.

Marello, Marta, and Ann Helwege. 2018. "Solid Waste Management and Social Inclusion of Wastepickers: Opportunities and Challenges." *Latin American Perspectives* 45(1): 108–29. https://doi.org/10.1177/0094582X17726083.

Mattews, Gordon, and Carlos Alba. 2015. "Introducción: ¿Qué Es La Globalización Desde Abajo?" In *La Globalización Desde Abajo: La Otra Economía Mundial*, edited by Carlos Alba, Gustavo Lins Ribeiro, Gordon Mattews, and Mario A. Zambudio Vega, 27–51. Ciudad de México: Fondo de Cultura Económica.

Meneses-Reyes, Rodrigo. 2011. *Legalidades públicas: el derecho, el ambulantaje y las calles en el centro de la Ciudad de México (1930–2010)*. Universidad Nacional Autónoma de México.

Meneses-Reyes, Rodrigo. 2013a. "Crime, Street Vendors and the Historical Downtown in Post-Giuliani Mexico City." *International Journal of Criminology and Sociology* 2(June): 186–98. https://doi.org/10.6000/1929-4409.2013.02.19.

Meneses-Reyes, Rodrigo. 2013b. "Out of Place, Still in Motion Shaping (Im)Mobility Through Urban Regulation." *Social & Legal Studies* 22: 335–56. https://doi.org/10.1177/0964663912469644.

Meneses-Reyes, Rodrigo. 2018. "(Un)Authorized: A Study on the Regulation of Street Vending in Latin America." *Law & Policy* 40(3): 286–315. https://doi.org/10.1111/lapo.12106.

Meneses-Reyes, Rodrigo, and José A. Caballero-Juárez. 2014. "The Right to Work on the Street: Public Space and Constitutional Rights." *Planning Theory* 13(4): 370–86. https://doi.org/10.1177/1473095213503967.

Moctezuma, Vicente. 2021. *El desvanecimiento de lo popular: Gentrificación en el Centro Histórico de la Ciudad de México*. El Colegio de Mexico AC.

Moncada, Eduardo. 2016. "Urban Violence, Political Economy, and Territorial Control: Insights From Medellín." *Latin American Research Review* 51(4): 225–48.

Nogueira, Mara. 2019. "Displacing Informality: Rights and Legitimacy in Belo Horizonte, Brazil." *International Journal of Urban and Regional Research* 43(3): 517–34. https://doi.org/10.1111/1468-2427.12808.

Nogueira, Mara. 2020. "Preserving the (Right Kind of) City: The Urban Politics of the Middle Classes in Belo Horizonte, Brazil." *Urban Studies* 57(10): 2163–80. https://doi.org/10.1177/0042098019872167.

Pariza, Teodora, and Min Jung Cho. 2024. "Food Safety in Latin American Informal Food Establishments." *Frontiers in Sustainability* 4(January). https://doi.org/10.3389/frsus.2023.1325060.

Peña, Sergio. 1999. "Informal Markets: Street Vendors in Mexico City." *Habitat International* 23(September): 363–72. https://doi.org/10.1016/S0197-3975(99)00012-0.

Piccato, Pablo. 2001. *City of Suspects: Crime in Mexico City, 1900–1931*. Duke University Press Books.

Pires, Sara M., Antonio R. Vieira, Enrique Perez, Danilo Lo Fo Wong, and Tine Hald. 2012. "Attributing Human Foodborne Illness to Food Sources and Water in Latin America and the Caribbean Using Data From Outbreak Investigations." *International Journal of Food Microbiology* 152(3): 129–38. https://doi.org/10.1016/j.ijfoodmicro.2011.04.018.

Pradilla, Emilio. 2005. "Estancamiento económico, desindustrialización y terciarización informal en la Ciudad de México 1980-2003 y potencial de cambio." In *Globalização e território: ajustes periféricos*, edited by Ana Clara Torres Ribeiro, Hermes Magallaes, Jorge Natal, and Rosalía Piquet. IPPUR.

Rakowski, Cathy A. 1994. "Convergence and Divergence in the Informal Sector Debate: A Focus on Latin America, 1984–92." *World Development* 22(4): 501–16.

Ramírez-Kuri, Patricia. 2015. "Espacio público, ¿espacio de todos? Reflexiones desde la Ciudad de México." *Revista mexicana de sociología* 77(1): 7–36.

Roever, Sally. 2005. "Negotiating Formality: Informal Sector, Market, and State in Peru." Doctoral. Berkeley, CA: University of California.

Roever, Sally. 2010. "Street Trade in Latin America: Demographic Trends, Legal Issues, and Vending Organizations in Six Cities." In *Street Vendors in the Global Urban Economy*, edited by Sharit Bhowmik, 208–40. India: Routledge. https://www.routledge.com/Street-Vendors-in-the-Global-Urban-Economy/Bhowmik/p/book/9780367176471.
Roever, Sally. 2014. "Informal Economy Monitoring Study Sector Report: Street Vendors." Sector Report. Cambridge, MA: Women in Informal Employment: Globalizing and Organizing (WIEGO).
Roever, Sally, and Caroline Skinner. 2016. "Street Vendors and Cities." *Environment and Urbanization* 28(2): 359–74. https://doi.org/10.1177/0956247816653898.
Serna-Luna, Erick. 2020. "Gobernar bajo la ciudad: etnografía sobre la gobernanza del comercio popular en el metro de la Ciudad de México." Doctoral. Mexico City: Colegio de México.
Silva-Londoño, Diana. 2010. "Comercio ambulante en el Centro Histórico de la ciudad de México (1990–2007)." *Revista Mexicana de Sociología* 72(2): 195–224.
Skinner, Caroline, and Gareth Haysom. 2016. "The Informal Sector's Role in Food Security: A Missing Link in Policy Debates?" Working Paper 44. Cape Town: PLAAS, UWC and Centre of Excellence on Food Security, 1–25.
Skinner, Caroline, and Vanessa Watson. 2017. "The Informal Economy in Cities of the Global South." In *The Routledge Companion to Planning in the Global South*. Routledge. https://doi.org/10.4324/9781315678993.ch11.
Stamm, Caroline. 2005. "Balance de Las Plazas de Comercio Popular Del Centro Histórico de La Ciudad de México." In *El Ambulantaje En La Ciudad de México Investigaciones Recientes*, edited by Jérôme Monnet and Juliette Bonnafé, 1st ed. México, DF: Universidad Nacional Autónoma de México, Coordinación de Humanidades, Programa Universitario de Estudios sobre la Ciudad: Centro Francés de Estudios Mexicanos y Centroamericanos.
Swanson, Kate. 2007. "Revanchist Urbanism Heads South: The Regulation of Indigenous Beggars and Street Vendors in Ecuador." *Antipode* 39(4): 708–28. https://doi.org/10.1111/j.1467-8330.2007.00548.x.
Tucker, Jennifer. 2017. "City-Stories: Narrative as Diagnostic and Strategic Resource in Ciudad Del Este, Paraguay." *Planning Theory* 16(1): 74–98. https://doi.org/10.1177/1473095215598176.
Tucker, Jennifer, and Ryan Thomas Devlin. 2019. "Uncertainty and the Governance of Street Vending: A Critical Comparison Across the North/South Divide." *International Journal of Urban and Regional Research* 43(3): 460–75. https://doi.org/10.1111/1468-2427.12792.
Zaremberg, Gisela. 2011. *¿Corporativismo Informal? Organizaciones de Ambulantes y Partidos Políticos a Partir de La Alternancia Electoral En México, Distrito Federal (2000–2005)*. Buenos Aires: CLACSO.

2

FOOD GENTRIFICATION IN MEXICO

Three urban experiences

José Antonio Vázquez-Medina and Adrián Hernández Cordero

Introduction

Understanding the effects of demographic shifts on urban spaces has long been central to urban planning and studies. In recent years, in Latin America, the category of gentrification—understood as the phenomenon of social and territorial transformation that implies the economic and architectural revaluation of an area of the city, accompanied by the arrival of middle-class sectors and the exodus of working-class inhabitants—has become one of the key analytical lenses through which urban changes in the region's cities have been discussed and debated. Within this broader discussion, however, the role of food systems is only recently emerging as an important site in which the effects of gentrification can be observed. This chapter contributes to this burgeoning line of study on food gentrification through analysis of the transformations of urban food systems and their relationship with the phenomenon of gentrification based on the experiences of three Mexican cities that are experiencing this process at different rates and intensities.

In literature on the phenomenon of gentrification, specifically in the 1980s and 1990s, in what we can call the second wave[1] of studies on gentrification, authors such as Peter Marcuse, Neil Smith, and David Ley focused on studying the issue of residential displacement, posing the question of whether the phenomenon had its origin in the supply or demand for housing. Although it was not the focus of their studies, they observed the changes in the commercial offerings of neighborhoods undergoing gentrification, with the appearance of art galleries, bars, and sophisticated restaurants, a phenomenon that, several years later, became known as commercial gentrification. Given their structuralist vision, these authors tended to leave out certain elements related to micro or everyday life, especially those linked to the emergence and configuration of consumption

DOI: 10.4324/9781003471929-5

patterns of new social actors, that is, middle-income residents and visitors with ample cultural capital.

Subsequent studies that looked at urban transformation through the lens of consumption began to pay attention to issues such as the production and marketing of certain products in changing urban areas (Zukin, 1995). Although the concept of "food gentrification" would only later come into use, studies of the emergence of spaces and products such as specialized coffee (shops) began to draw attention to the ways that the tastes and types of consumption of new inhabitants shaped urban spaces in a process that Zukin called *domestication by cappuccino* (1995). Her argument, which is relevant to various other products or commercial spaces, is that consumption concerning public space implies exclusion since not all people have the capacity and taste to acquire elite forms of coffee (or other goods, such as sushi, or *tapas*). The proliferation of spaces of elite consumption thus contributes to the displacement of certain working-class practices and products, evidencing the tensions that are generated between different sectors in neighborhoods in the process of transformation.

We cannot take for granted, however, that changes in the availability and accessibility of certain types of foods are a simple or predictable consequence of the gentrification process. Each urban environment presents certain particularities that have to do with the particular characterization and interests of the agents involved; the articulation and problems of local food systems; and other exogenous factors that obey broader social processes circumscribed to local realities. In the case of Mexico, the above is evident: We are facing dissimilar moments in the processes of food gentrification in different cities, which cannot be generalized and merit a particular analysis of the contexts in which they are framed. The point is relevant for Latin America in general and beyond: Gentrification is a phenomenon whose specific characteristics vary, depending on territorial, population, economic, and political factors. It stands to reason that the implications for food systems will likewise vary. This chapter accordingly sets out to analyze the effects of gentrification on food systems in three different Mexican cities.

First, we analyze the transformation in the culinary offerings of restaurants and prepared food stands in Santa María la Ribera, a central neighborhood of Mexico City that is undergoing a process of gentrification. The population shift in the neighborhood has led to an increase in restaurants aimed at the new inhabitants of the neighborhood who have a high cultural and purchasing capital. This shift entails deregulation of the food supply in this neighborhood, creating symbolic and material segregation between new and old residents.

The second case we present is Cholula, Puebla. A municipality in the suburbs of the capital of the state of Puebla, that has a diversified population composition due to the presence of several private universities that attract high-income national and foreign students. In general, these students have been the driving force behind the proliferation of more cosmopolitan consumption patterns in the city. At the same time, the presence of a significant tourist economy in the town is based on specialized local or "traditional" fare. In the interplay between these populations, a hybrid food regime of sorts can be identified in Cholula.

Finally, we analyze the case of Mazatlán, Sinaloa, a tourist port located in northwestern Mexico. We study transnational gentrification based on the arrival of older adults from the United States and Canada who settle in the city. The arrival of these inhabitants has encouraged a change in the food supply in several ways, including the strengthening of short distribution chains of agroecologically produced food through the establishment of a local, organic market. This form of consumption, however, is limited to newcomers and is not accessed by the local population.

This chapter condenses the findings of different research studies by the two authors that address the diverse forms of food gentrification in Mexico. It should be clarified that this is not a comparative study, but rather a descriptive multisite analysis that allows us to locate the agents that make the phenomenon dynamic in particular contexts. The findings presented in this work were obtained through an ethnographic approach in the sites studied: With this approach, face-to-face and virtual fieldwork was conducted, as well as semi-structured interviews with key actors who were selected by convenience and snowballing. For the case of Santa María, the fieldwork upon which this text draws occurred in two moments. The first took place between 2018–2019 and 2022–2023. The fieldwork in Cholula took place between 2020 in a face-to-face manner, and later virtual fieldwork was carried out due to the health contingency due to COVID-19. Finally, in Mazatlán ethnographic fieldwork was conducted between 2021 and 2022.

Theoretical approaches to food gentrification

The concept of food gentrification is still in a seminal period of its configuration and is therefore used in a polysemous manner. *Gastrofication, gourmet gentrification, foodification,* and other neologisms have emerged concurrently, both in academia and in the press, to designate and describe this global phenomenon (Lütke & Jäger, 2021; Loda et al., 2020). Although most of the meanings in circulation are based on the notion of identifying the process of transformation of urban centers in relation to changes in the food supply, the concept often glosses over various phenomena of different scopes and magnitudes. Furthermore, the existing literature on food gentrification comes mainly from the Academy of the Global North and may not adequately reflect Latin American context and realities. It is necessary, in other words, to have studies that address the way that urban structures and inequalities in Latin America condition changing food landscapes in contexts of gentrification. In this section, therefore, we engage in a brief discussion of the overlapping concepts and terms that allows us to define and operationalize the concept of food gentrification in order to analyze the three Mexican cases we address.

As a starting point, we take up the notion of *culinary-gastronomic assemblages* proposed by Ayora Díaz (2018) to refer to the dimensions of change and permeability in the culinary and gastronomic spheres of cuisines, as well as their relationship with the food systems and landscapes where they are found. This notion assumes that cuisine, despite having established structures, has a dynamic character that reflects the historical moment in which it is inscribed. Ayora Díaz recognizes the gastronomic assemblage as the structural normative field that regulates and modulates the food phenomenon from a "set of ingredients, recipes, techniques and technologies required for the production and consumption of food, as well as the necessary etiquette for its consumption" (Ayora Díaz, 2018, p. 10); while the culinary assemblage alludes to the dynamic of preparation that allows more easily the mobility and integration of new ingredients and influences according to the context where it is carried out. In this sense, we can infer that food gentrification, at least in the Mexican case, could be located at the intersection of both fields and that it challenges some phenomena that we will discuss later.

The first involves the phenomenon of *gourmetization* of traditional, peasant, working-class, and ethnic cuisines (Matta, 2013; Aguilera Bornand, 2018; Harris & Phillips, 2021; Mariano et al., 2023; Peña, 2023). This process has to do with the "elitization" of traditional cuisines and implies the upward mobility of products, dishes, ways of eating, and cooking that were related to Indigenous, peasant, or marginalized groups and that are reconfigured based on new class distinctions and the values that emanate from them (Peña, 2023). In this sense, products and dishes are decontextualized from their ways of being prepared in their original environments to undergo a technical reinterpretation that adheres to the canons of haute cuisine to be marketed in arenas destined to *fine dining* or to the emerging formats of new food outlets offered in gentrified environments. Gourmetization thus not only legitimizes cultural appropriations and extractivism of traditional forms of culinary knowledge but also appeals to elite diners eager to acquire more cultural capital through new food "experiences." This phenomenon also involves the production of meanings and values that are tied to those of globalization and that involve, among others, respect for local and artisanal production; the cultivation of food with little agrochemical intervention and produced in a sustainable manner; and that also appeal to the rhetoric of ancestry, tradition, and health as an added value within the field of cuisine.

While the rise of *gourmetization,* as a facet of food gentrification is indeed a global phenomenon, its success and form depend on local contexts. For the Mexican case, we can explain the rise of gourmetization as being related at least partially to the recent inscription of "Mexican Traditional Cuisines" in the UNESCO World Heritage List has promoted patrimonial narratives about peasant and ancestral products, which are then in turn marketed to diners with high cultural capital (Vázquez-Medina, 2023; Campos & Favila, 2018). In addition, such cuisines are often marketed through green and sustainable discourses that have underpinned what Johnston and Baumann (2015) call *locavorism,* and that legitimizes the consumption of local products for a rather restricted sector of the population (Espeitx, 1996).

In general, in Mexico and other global sites, we see that the transformation of urban food landscapes in contexts of gentrification entails a shift from more traditional, working-class cuisines to more cosmopolitan and/or specialized or gourmet offerings (Sbicca, 2018, 2020; Zukin, 1993, 1995; Zukin et al., 2017; Vázquez-Medina et al., 2020). Shifts may also occur through new forms or types of consumption, including food delivery applications and the digitization of business promotion through digital social networks. The changes in local foodscapes may entail a change in local offerings, or a restriction in the availability of existing foods as everyday products become prohibitively expensive for sectors of the population.

It is important to mention that not all gentrification entails a replacement of traditional or working-class spaces with new spaces of consumption, at least in the short to medium term. Indeed, certain establishments proudly resist the encroachment of new aesthetics, preserving their traditional character, and turning them into atmospheres that embody the local social memory of neighborhoods as spaces of "authenticity." Yet as Zukin et al. (2017) have argued, it is this very air of authenticity which attracts new settlers to such establishments, and which allows them to be a sort of showcase of authenticity that confers added value to the new consumption and leisure offerings in gentrifying neighborhoods.

Regardless of the form that food gentrification takes—whether it be the emergence of entirely new restaurants, new offerings in grocery stores, or changing prices or menus in existing "traditional" establishments—we can see that food begins to serve as an attraction for new settlers in gentrifying contexts. Food comes to serve as a part of developing a new narrative about a neighborhood's identity. Foodscapes that feature authentic, gourmet, and cosmopolitan offerings thus nurture an imaginary about neighborhoods undergoing gentrification, which in turn draws more elite sectors to the spaces in question. Food, in other words, becomes a *driver* of gentrification and not simply a consequence of shifting urban residential patterns. Yet the way that food acts as a driver, or changes as a result of gentrification, varies in different urban contexts. We now turn to three cases from Mexico to further illustrate this point.

The food gentrification of Santa María la Ribera, Mexico City. Between the cosmopolitan and the popular

Santa María la Ribera is an emblematic neighborhood of Mexico City, located on the edge of the central area of the Mexican capital (see Map 2.1). Its construction in the mid-nineteenth century was part of the first urban expansion of the city, which added new areas for the middle and upper classes. The neighborhood lost its petty bourgeois character around the middle of the twentieth century, when the Mexican capital experienced an important natural population growth, as well as the massive arrival of rural migrants. The social and architectural deterioration of the area was exacerbated by the effects of a massive earthquake in the city in September 1985, which resulted in landslides in Santa María La Ribera, affecting its heritage and causing the departure of many residents, as well as the arrival of inhabitants from working-class sectors in the center of the city, who organized themselves into neighborhood groups (Hernández Cordero, 2021).

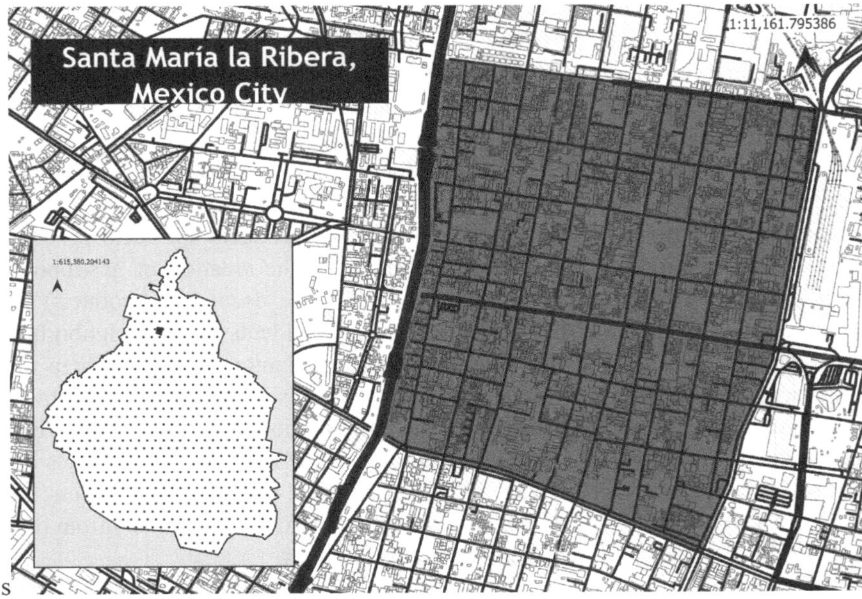

MAP 2.1 Location of Santa María La Ribera

Source: Prepared by Denisse Rosas Fonseca

From that moment on, Santa María La Ribera has been increasingly linked in the popular imaginary with problems of crime and insecurity. In this context and with the implementation of neoliberal urbanism in Mexico City in the early twenty-first century, the city government designed an intervention plan to generate a process of urban renewal because the neighborhood had a high economic potential due to its good location, as well as its important heritage value. The construction of new housing on various derelict lots, the arrival of middle-income residents, and the repurposing of existing public infrastructure were encouraged.

In Santa María la Ribera, gentrification is characterized by the arrival of predominantly young, middle-class Mexican individuals, with a high cultural and economic capital that allows them to demand cosmopolitan food and artistic establishments. With the arrival of new inhabitants with greater cultural and economic capital, Santa María La Ribera has become a *cultural spot* that brings new urbanites to consume what is produced in the neighborhood. As an almost inherent part of the process of population change, restaurants, cafes, and other prepared food outlets immersed in a logic of consumption that appeals to *culinary cosmopolitanism*, have begun to shape the new foodscape. Santa María La Ribera has also become the focus of attention of leisure publications that highlight not only the *cultural movement* but also the gastronomic itineraries that can be carried out in the neighborhood, and that show the presence of new restaurants offering innovative menus, as well as a kind of revitalization of certain *traditional* food outlets that resist and coexist with the new food offerings.

Food gentrification in particular occurs in various ways in Santa María La Ribera. The new inhabitants generally share socio-cultural codes where innovative and gourmet gastronomic offerings are valued, in keeping with global trends which are then adapted to the neighborhood environment. Among them, we can observe the articulation of gastronomic values on menus and in both new and existing establishments (through an emphasis on handmade products and local products, for example). In addition, we can increasingly see the creation of gastronomic *branding* (including the use of certain types of fonts, decor, and products) that is geared toward the tastes of new middle-class residents of the neighborhood (Vázquez-Medina et al., 2020). Indeed, the rise of Santa María La Ribera as a gastronomic cluster in the central area of Mexico City is evidenced in the proliferation of specialized food sales spaces in the neighborhood, including coffee bars, restaurants featuring international cuisines, bakeries, and gourmet specialty stores that sell specific products such as cheeses or pastries. These establishments, furthermore, cater not only to new residents but attract middle-class diners from other parts of the city who seek new, specialized experiences.

This phenomenon coexists with another that celebrates and promotes the "traditional" culinary heritage and identity of the neighborhood. There has been an increase in tourist tours featuring visits to traditional consumption spaces such as *cantinas* (bars) and *pulquerías* aimed at foreign tourists seeking immersive experiences of daily life and who learn about the neighborhood through virtual platforms and digital social networks. New inhabitants, as well, seek out these types of traditional, popular establishments in the neighborhood, which come to constitute a point of confluence between new and old neighbors. In this sense, nostalgia plays a fundamental role in the production of the foodscape, since it acts as a catalyst of the culinary offer that contributes to (re)create imaginaries of a bucolic life of the city, which acquires a new value of consumption, and of which the new inhabitants want to be part of.

Regarding the phases of the local food system that are impacted by food gentrification, we can distinguish that they are mostly concentrated in spaces of consumption. In terms of production and distribution, there is very little in terms of the types of farmer's markets or alternative food networks for elite consumption that have been identified in other global gentrifying contexts. We identified a few efforts to promote alternative food networks in the area, but the efforts are still very incipient. Occasionally, local producers are invited to market some products in artistic events and workshops on urban gardens, and there have been attempts to organize events for the recovery of the culinary memory of edible herbs mostly used in the domestic sphere, sponsored by collectives of professional cooks who have their businesses in the neighborhood. Overall, however, the effects of middle-class, Mexican gentrification in Santa María la Ribera can be observed in the commercial spaces of consumption, whereby the neighborhood has shifted to become a gastronomic cluster with recognition on a metropolitan scale.

Cholula, Puebla, and the food frontier. Gentrification and touristification of a magical town

San Andrés and San Pedro Cholula are two neighboring municipalities of the Metropolitan Zone of Puebla and Tlaxcala, a region located in the central highlands of Mexico (see Map 2.2). Both municipalities share a cultural and historical matrix, and Cholula is generally understood as a social and territorial continuum referred to collectively as simply "Cholula."

Cholula has undergone a process of social and territorial transformation and has become a peri-urban nucleus of the city of Puebla, where middle-class urban sectors that have settled there in recent years converge with the original population. Unlike the case of Santa María la Ribera, Cholula's demographic shift has been more prolonged and complex in nature. In the 1970s Cholula began its transformation thanks to the founding of the campus of the Universidad de Las Américas Puebla (UDLAP) on its territory. Since its inauguration, the rural landscape has been modified, especially in San Andrés, because it was provided with public infrastructure and the inhabitants began to establish lodging businesses, restaurants, and night bars for the university community. A decade later, the Government of Puebla executed an ambitious urban development plan aimed at expanding the city toward the west of the metropolitan area. In this context, Cholula began to turn toward tourist activities, thanks to its patrimonial capital represented by the vestiges of

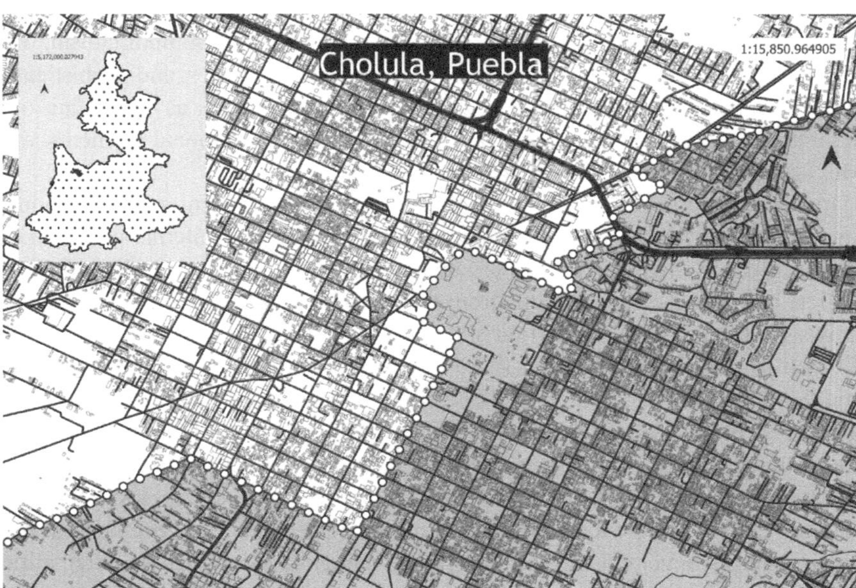

MAP 2.2 Location of Cholula

Source: Prepared by Denisse Rosas Fonseca

a great Pyramid, as well as by the Historic Center of San Pedro. In recent years, the locality has been revalued by government programs, specifically the *Pueblos Mágicos* ("Magic Villages") program that articulates tourism and heritage discourses by promoting towns and villages that have "heritage" characteristics that make them attractive for tourists. The designation of Cholula as a Pueblo Mágico was particular because it encompassed San Andrés and San Pedro, the first time that two municipalities were included in such a designation. Despite the attempt at shared tourism management, the gap between the two became more evident, not only because of the administrative boundaries between them but also because of the border that separates the social and territorial dynamics, especially when viewed from the perspective of the culinary offerings.

In San Pedro, population shifts and food gentrification can be understood in relation to the phenomenon of *touristification*. The historic town center with heritage buildings, its neighboring pyramids, and myriad churches have led to San Pedro drawing national and international tourists. Consequently, many of the restaurants in town cater to tourists' tastes and craft menus and narratives that make references to the "ancient" and "ancestral." The gastronomic offerings that are available in San Pedro demonstrate the intention of promoting "Mexicanness" for tourism purposes through restaurants that specialize in regional varieties of local foods, where authenticity and tradition are promoted as values for tourists.

In San Andrés, on the other hand, gentrification can be understood in relation to the presence of students and creative classes who have settled there over the years. There, restaurants appeal to ideas of modernity and culinary cosmopolitanism, with menus that feature international offerings, ecological discourses, and sophisticated and innovative cuisine. In this sense, San Andrés has served as something of a laboratory for culinary proposals that began to mix international elements with Mexican gastronomy.

In this respect, in San Pedro and San Andrés there is a differentiated gastronomic landscape: The former is more frequented by national and international tourists visiting the city of Puebla and the latter by the new inhabitants of Cholula, as well as by middle-class urbanites from the metropolitan area. However, evidence shows how the processes of touristification and gentrification are increasingly difficult to differentiate, as they share interrelationships such as being driven by middle-income sectors and defined by similar consumption patterns (Judd, 2003). In the case of Cholula, while there is a difference in the type of public that attends one or the other food *spot*, the proximity between San Andrés and San Pedro means that they comprise a complementary foodscape, which is nonetheless shaped by ongoing changes in the local population due to public policies, development programs, and the development of urban spaces which have made the municipalities attractive to students, tourists, and middle-class creative sector workers.

Unlike Santa María la Ribera, in Cholula the impact of urban transformations on the local food system is perceptible in the distribution as well as consumption phases. We can observe, for example, the role of the State about the renovation of the San Pedro municipal food market to promote it as a tourist attraction, and the relocation of the *central tianguis* (open-air itinerant market) that used to be established in the vicinity of the market on Sundays, to an establishment in the peripheral zone of the municipality. Also, given the peri-urban nature of Cholula, which has historically been a place where local agricultural producers have operated, we can see that some of the restaurants have incorporated the use of local products as an added value to their businesses. Thus, restaurants in this area can be seen as agents that favor the shortening of food supply chains in some cases, but due to the middle-class publics which they serve, local products in this context are marketed to certain sectors of the population.

Mazatlán, Sinaloa: Food gentrification and second home tourism

Mazatlán, Sinaloa is a port city located in northwestern Mexico. The *pearl of the Pacific,* as it has been called, has transformed since the beginning of the twentieth century, from being a merchant port to a tourist destination that has emerged as a favorite destination not only for national holidaymakers but also for a very particular sector of foreign tourists.

Although Mazatlán has attracted some tourists from the United States since the first half of the twentieth century, it was not until a couple of decades ago that the port began to position itself as one of the favorite second-home destinations for retirees from the United States and Canada seeking a warm place to go during the winter months (Santamaría, 2009; Lizárraga, 2016; Maldonado, 2017). As a destination that offers a mild, warm climate and affordable prices, Mazatlán gradually became a circular migration site where retirees and older adults from North America have settled for extended periods of time during the winter season, or permanently. Although these "second home tourists" can be found in different parts of the central city, we can identify the formation of a more or less structured enclave within the circuit comprising Mazatlán's Historic Downtown area and the part of the Malecon beachfront area called Olas Altas (see Map 2.3). This is no coincidence: It is due to the renovation of these areas carried out at the beginning of the century and promoted by the municipal and state governments, with the support of local businessmen. The renovation of Mazatlán's Historic Downtown included the remodeling of historic buildings, the repaving of public roads, and the establishment of a circuit of pedestrian streets and gardens.

Various studies have shown that the arrival and settlement of US migrants to Mazatlán has modified the spatial and consumption dynamics in some areas of the city, not only expanding new alternatives aimed at this sector but also modifying the supply of housing, products, and services (Lizárraga, 2008, 2016; Ceballos, 2021; Maldonado, 2017). The arrival of American and Canadian residents has also modified the dynamics of food supply and consumption in Mazatlán. In terms of consumption, the foodscape in the port area has been transformed with the opening of new consumption spaces aimed at the new settlers: Gourmet seafood restaurants, specialty coffee bars, and haute cuisine restaurants that adapt their menus to

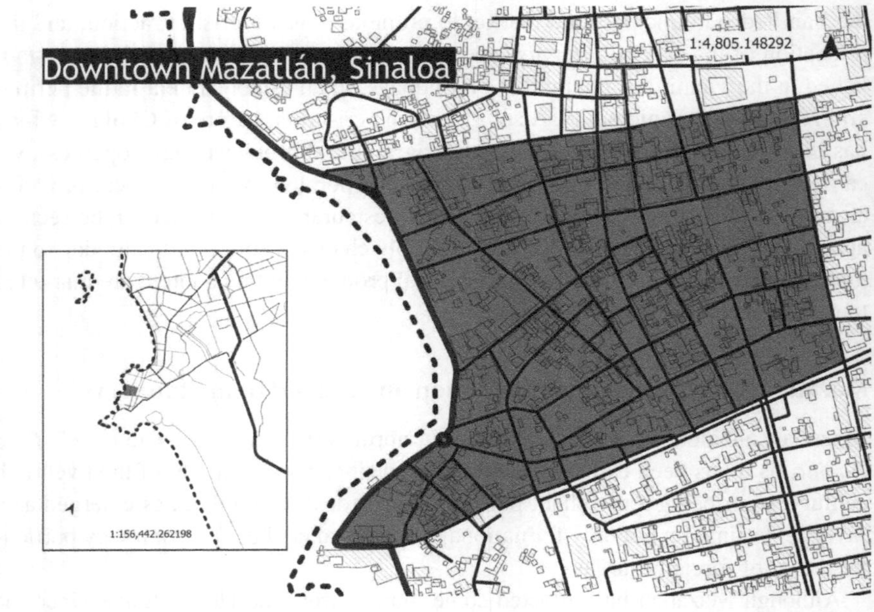

MAP 2.3 Location of Mazatlán's Historic Center

Source: Prepared by Denisse Rosas Fonseca

the tastes, times, and rhythms of the American and Canadian food cultures, now represent a large proportion of the prepared food offerings in the area.

In terms of production and supply, we can see the emergence of new shops that connect to producers that cater to new residents. The Mazatlán Organic Market (MOM), for example, is a street market offering agrochemical-free agricultural products, which operates only during the winter months. The MOM is a self-managed initiative generated by a retired American journalist who settled permanently in the port and who wanted to replicate the *farmer's markets* of California and which has been set up for the past 12 years between November and April. In the Organic Market, one can find farm products harvested around Mazatlán that can be categorized as "specialty" products and that are not marketed elsewhere, as they are aimed at these new inhabitants. Although this type of initiative dynamizes food production and supply chains by shortening the distance between producers and consumers, it is also true that the high cost of the products, and the limited months during which the MOM operates, restrict access to these foods.

Final thoughts

The intersection between urban transformation and food systems has emerged as a phenomenon of global relevance that requires careful attention. Although it is commonly assumed that changes in food supply are merely results of gentrification, this study highlights the complexity and unique dynamics of each environment despite more or less shared patterns, which in some ways, can serve for comparative exercises between cities around the world.

In this chapter we have demonstrated that in Mexico the phenomenon of food gentrification is expressed in very different ways by analyzing diverse case studies: Santa María La Ribera, a central neighborhood of Mexico City undergoing a process of urban transformation; Cholula, a suburban municipality experiencing a tension between the education industry and tourism; Mazatlán, a coastal city specializing in tourism and second homes. The examination of these three cities shows certain similarities across the cases: The stratification of local food systems and inequalities generated in the access to certain types of food due to specialization and increased prices stand out, for example. We can also see that there is a lack of effective State intervention in mitigating some of the more damaging effects of (food) gentrification in the different contexts. Indeed, State policies tend to promote forms of urbanization which cater to middle-classes and tourists rather than more working-class populations.

This study has also shown, however, that we must not assume food gentrification to be a progressive and homogeneous process, in which local offerings play catchup and transform in response to demographic changes. Instead, we can observe how food can play a role in attracting new populations, and in creating new forms of value in urban contexts, acting in this way as an engine for gentrification. The way in which this plays out, however, varies depending on the new populations who arrive in specific territories, the local dynamics of existing residents, and the types of urbanization that exist, in addition to state policies which promote different forms of urban development or renewal. In the case of Mexico, we can see that local middle-class urbanites, international tourists, retirees, and students represent different types of populations who arrive in different types of urban contexts.

Finally, we have drawn attention here to the need to understand food gentrification beyond the sole focus on *commercial* offerings or the consumption side of urban food systems. Instead, we show that (food) gentrification can affect production and supply networks in diverse ways, including through encroaching on periurban productive space, opening up new market spaces, and creating demand for new types of local or international products. These trends may contribute to the fostering of structural inequities that condition and stratify local food systems in the Mexican reality and that open a powerful vein of analysis to study the relationship between territorial dynamics and the way that urban food systems are consolidated.

Note

1 The first wave corresponds to the seminal work of sociologist Ruth Glass in the 1960s.

References

Aguilera Bornand, I. M. (2018). Comida étnica, exotismo y otredad en Chile. El caso del restaurante "Peumayén Ancestral Food". *Chungará (Arica)*, *50*(4), 673–680.

Ayora Díaz, S. (2018). Cocina, gastronomía y modernidad: hacia una definición de lo gastronómico. *Diario de campo*, *4*, 6–14.

Campos, A., & Favila, H. (2018). Culturas alimentarias indígenas y turismo. Una aproximación a su estudio desde el control cultural. *Estudios y Perspectivas en Turismo*, *27*(2), 194–212.

Ceballos, T. (2021). Los desafíos del turismo en Mazatlán. Hacia una nueva estrategia de desarrollo local. In E. Hernández & G. Ibarra (Coords.), *Los Grandes Problemas de Sinaloa* (pp. 45–76). Mexico City: Tirant Lo Blanch.

Espeitx, E. (1996). Los nuevos consumidores o las nuevas relaciones entre campo y ciudad a través de los "productos de la tierra". *Agricultura y Sociedad*, *80–81*, 83–116.

Harris, D., & Phillips, R. (2021). What's better than a biscuit?: Gourmetization and the transformation of a Southern food staple. *Food and Foodways*, *29*(3), 243–263. https://doi.org/10.1080/07409710.2021.1943614

Hernández Cordero, A. (2021). Santa María La Ribera, Santa María La Ratera y Santa Mari La Juarica: Momentos de un barrio en proceso de gentrificación. *Revista De El Colegio De San Luis*, *11*(22), 1–33. https://doi.org/10.21696/rcsl112220211301

Johnston, J., & Baumann, S. (2015). *Foodies: Democracy and distinction in the gourmet foodscape*. New York y London: Routledge Taylor & Francis Group.

Judd, D. (2003). El turismo urbano y la geografía de la ciudad. *Eure*, *29*(87), 51–62. https://scielo.conicyt.cl/pdf/eure/v29n87/art04.pdf

Lizárraga, O. (2008). La inmigración de jubilados estadounidenses en México y sus prácticas transnacionales. Estudio de caso en Mazatlán, Sinaloa y Cabo San Lucas, Baja California Sur. *Migración y Desarrollo*, *11*, 97–117.

Lizárraga, O. (2016). El Turismo Residencial de Retiro en Mazatlán, México. Una propuesta de marca ciudad Revista Anais Brasileiros de Estudios. *Turístico/ABET, Juiz de Fora*, *6*(3), 85–96.

Loda, M., Bonatti, S., & Putilli, M. (2020). History to eat: The *foodification* of the historic centre of Florence. *Cities*, *103*. https://doi.org/10.1016/j.cities.2020.102746

Lütke, P., & Jäger, E. M. (2021). Food consumption in Cologne Ehrenfeld: Gentrification through gastrofication? *Urban Science*, *5*(1), 26.

Maldonado, C. M. (2017). La Competitividad Turistica de los Destinos Costeros en Mexico ante el Mercado de Turismo Residencial: el caso de los norteamericanos en Mazatlán/Sinaloa. *Anais Brasileiros De Estudos Turisticos*, *7*(3), 74–87. https://doi.org/10.34019/2238-2925.2017.v7.3187

Mariano-Juárez, L., Medina, F. X., & Conde-Caballero, D. (2023). Popular cuisines at foodie tables: Social class, distinction, and food transformation and incorporation in contemporary gastronomies. *International Journal of Gastronomy and Food Science*, *33*, 459–479. https://www//journals.sagepub.com/doi/abs/10.1177/1469540515611203

Matta, R. (2013). Valuing native eating: The modern roots of Peruvian food heritage. *Anthropology of Food*. http://journals.openedition.org/aof/7361

Peña, L. (2023). Entre los kosher y lo koolsher: gourmetización de la cocina judía en Buenos Aires (Argentina). *Archives on Food, Culture and Nutrition*, *I*, 43–58.

Santamaría, G. A. (2009). *El Nacimiento del turismo en Mazatlán*. Sinaloa, México: Ed. UAS.

Sbicca, J. (2018). Alimentación, gentrificación y transformaciones urbanas. In J. Sbicca, J. González, G. Ramos, & R. Espelt (Coord.), *Gentrificación, privilegios e injusticia alimentaria* (pp. 5–12). Madrid: FUHEM.

Sbicca, J. (2020). The urban agriculture fix. In *A recipe for gentrification: Food, power, and resistance in the city* (pp. 93–110). New York: NYU Press.

Vázquez-Medina, J. A. (2023). La promoción de la cocina tradicional mexicana en la lógica turístico- patrimonial: entre la autonomía culinaria y la homogenización cultural. In A. Vilchis, E. Coria-Cruz, & A. Martin (coords.), *Turismos del Sur. Claves para reflexionar sobre el turismo desde el pensamiento crítico* (pp. 208–238). Chetumal/Los Mochis:

Universidad Autónoma de Quintana Roo- Ediciones de la Universidad Autónoma de Occidente.
Vázquez-Medina, J. A., Hernández-Cordero, A., Lagos, S., & Rangel-Trujillo, F. (2020). Alimentación y Gentrificación en Santa María La Ribera. *Estudios Sociales, 30*(55).
Zukin, S. (1993). *Landscapes of power: From Detroit to Disney World.* Berkeley; Los Ángeles; London: University of California Press.
Zukin, S. (1995). *The cultures of cities.* Hoboken: Wiley-Blackwell.
Zukin, S., Lindeman, S., & Hurson, L. (2017). The omnivore's neighborhood? Online restaurant reviews, race, and gentrification. *Journal of Consumer Culture, 17*(3).

3

LAND DISPUTES AND THE URBANIZATION PROCESS

Challenges for urban food systems

Guadalupe Granero, Fernando Bercovich and Joaquín Pérez Martín

Introduction

In contemporary disputes over how we as a society use land, the competition between vital needs and the speculative demands of the real estate market is nowhere exemplified so well as in contemporary tensions related to land access in urban food systems. Globally, since the 1970s, market-driven regulatory restructuring has led to forms of territorial organization that are increasingly based on rent-seeking capacities, whereby the state's ability to design and implement public policies related to territorial management is increasingly questioned and weakened (Brenner et al., 2011). While the capitals of the real estate-financial complex exert pressure to develop green spaces in order to maximize the urban rent gap (López-Morales & Klett, 2021), domestic and global demand for foods encourage the use of fertile areas for production and commercialization circuits of different types and scales. In the realm of urban food systems, market-driven, rent-seeking logics of land use have manifested primarily in tensions related to (1) the transfer of productive peri-urban agricultural land to residential or commercial use (Barsky, 2005, 2010), (2) the expulsion of small food merchants due to gentrification processes (Di Nucci & Lan, 2008; Hernández Cordero & Eneva, 2016; Mermet, 2017), (3) the expansion of supermarkets in urban territories (Di Nucci, 2015; Pérez Martín, 2022), and (4) land development for food distribution and commercialization in urban areas (Pérez Martín & Barsky, 2021; Vecslir Peri, 2011). These tensions not only bring to the fore questions of who should have access to land and how—central concerns for urban theory and activism[1] more broadly—but also point to the central role of food as a necessity and right for urban consumers, and the role of food in producing urban space (Steel, 2013).

Latin America is a highly urbanized region with cities that are characterized by high degrees of socio-spatial fragmentation, where the speculative logic of

DOI: 10.4324/9781003471929-6

the market has coexisted and competed since the beginning of the twentieth century with popular forms of urbanization led by citizen groups and organizations (Abramo, 2012; Clichevsky, 2000; Kozak, 2008). In this context, disputes related to land access for food systems, both in productive peri-urban areas and within the urban fabric, are not simply economic or technocratic disputes but rather are related to a series of questions about how the urbanization process should look and what principles should organize the growth of cities. Given the importance of developing sustainable urban food systems in the region and the need for public policies that challenge the current logic of spatial production, critical theory is a must for revising the conceptual framework of land production from and within the context of Latin American urbanization.

This chapter seeks to review which theoretical tools can help to think about territorial food policies and, together with this, which are the contributions that can nurture, expand, or reformulate them from Latin American thought. Based on the analysis of urbanization dynamics oriented to the extraction of residential rents, the objective of this chapter is to reflect on how they impact on food production and access to food. To this end, it is proposed to recover literature that addresses the issue of territorial development with a justice perspective and allows linking it to the problem of food circuits, focusing on understanding the motives and strategies of key actors. Second, the case of the main metropolis of Argentina and its counterpoints with cities in Colombia and Brazil are presented and discussed. In all cases, the issue of access to urban land emerges as an element that hinders or stresses the functioning of urban food systems. Finally, some reflections are articulated with the purpose of guiding territorial planning and development to contribute to the sustainability and sovereignty of urban food systems, within the framework of a just transition.

Theoretical contributions to think about land access conflicts from Latin America

Urbanization as a material process is complex, dynamic, and changing. The urbanizations mutate in its forms, while the different logics coexist in its deployment, and the actors appear and disappear in its materialization. Urbanization as a concept is also complex; its meaning is a field of permanent reformulations. Today, it is difficult not to think of it as a restructuring of the territory that transcends the sphere of cities, as an engine of spatial organization that connects the evolution of urban societies with the natural landscapes that feed their consumption and process their waste, that contain ecological impacts and offer calm to the metropolitan frenzy, that nourish the beginning of the most structural productive chains connecting populations at extreme points of the globe (Harvey, 2012).

In the process of planetary urbanization (Brenner, 2016) the greatest social and territorial inequalities in the world are deepening. This is the general framework for thinking about disputes over rural and peri-urban land, where access to fertile soils with the availability of fresh water and natural goods is coveted for urbanization and energy transition. In short, access to territory is constitutive of social conflict. The same happens in the city, where the configuration and access to infrastructure and services conditions accessibility to the territory in a center-periphery scenario that is also no stranger to conflict. Brenner (2016) proposes a double character in urbanization: *Concentration*, a movement of implosions that explains dense agglomerations—what we can recognize as urban centers—and *extension*, whose explosive forms transform nature into operational landscapes of capitalism in its different geographical scales. Urbanization is, in these terms, a process of planetary scale that shapes buildings, streets, parks, highways and also waterways, forests, fertile plains, carbon sinks, salt flats for lithium extraction, and maritime platforms, among others. What this conception ultimately affirms is the impossibility of conceptually fragmenting the anthropization of the Earth. In doing so, it calls into question the traditional rural–urban territorial dichotomy, which has been put into the discussion (Berardo, 2019; Found, 1971; Von Braun, 2007) and opens questions on how to address issues where spatial categories seem to split those whose boundaries are blurred by social and economic dynamics.

Since the 1970s, urban economics has been the dominant conceptual framework for explaining spatial structuring based on the functioning of urban land markets. In Latin America, Jaramillo González (2009, 2013) is one of the main authors who have placed the theory of urban rent as the axis of conflicts in access to land and the forms acquired by the urbanization process, highlighting the need for planning and the application of different regulatory instruments. In particular, four possible strategies for regulating access to urban land are highlighted: Taxation, zoning, the provision of infrastructure as a tool to stimulate the use and price of land, and, finally, the possibility of acting as a real estate agent. Although the focus of these strategies is precisely on access to urban land, the same logic could be applied to the growth of cities in peri-urban areas. Along the same lines, Pedro Abramo (2012) modeled agencies over space in terms of three logics in tension: That of the State—and its regulatory tools—, that of the market, and that of necessity. The first brings into play the public function of urban planning, not only as the capacity to produce infrastructure for housing, circulation, and logistic and commercial food operations, through state resources but also as the power to dictate norms, plan and organize the territory and guide the actions of third parties in accordance with the common good. Throughout contemporary capitalism, the latter has been the hegemonic mechanism for coordinating decisions on land use in terms of rent extraction. Finally, the logic of necessity contains the actions that produce popular neighborhoods—often defined as *social production of habitat*—in a sequence that Abramo recognizes as occupation/self-construction/self-urbanization/consolidation and that includes spaces for commercialization. This characterization does not intend to propose monolithic and compartmentalized logics, but rather forms of producing the city that overlaps, that coexist even within themselves, and that, inevitably, present contradictions: From the constitution of the "informal" land markets studied by Abramo to the colonization of publicly managed spaces by entrepreneurs linked to the real estate business or phenomena such as small developers engaged in the production of social housing, to mention only a few emerging from these dynamics.

The core of the urban rent theory is that while the market is the dominant form of spatial coordination, it produces morphologically fragmented cities, socially and spatially. Abramo (2012) named this phenomenon as *com-fused* cities: Agglomerates with fabrics more linked to the canon of modern cities of the compact structure together with diffuse fabrics, of extensive land uses and low population density. This model has made it possible to analyze the two central configurations in the dispute for urban land: Gated communities, as enclaves of middle-income and high-income sectors, and lots, villas and informal settlements, and self-produced popular neighborhoods. Based on these socio-spatial characteristics, particular urban food systems are configured, given that, at both extremes and in their intermediate configurations, the conditions of access to urban land both for food production and for its circulation and commercialization determine the characteristics in which each household accesses its food on a daily basis. Thus, while access to urban land for the location of food stores and their supply is hindered or limited in both gated communities and working-class neighborhoods, due to exclusion and lack of urban integration, respectively, the former drive investment—both public and private—in large infrastructures such as highways and supermarkets, while the latter form a network of small stores and retailers (Pérez Martín, 2021).

In this sense, the theory of urban rent consistently explains how Latin American cities grow and who, where, and in what ways they produce that urban space; it is thus a powerful conceptual tool for understanding uprooting, expulsions, and even certain forms of oppression linked to the socio-economic dimension of territorial configurations. It constitutes a fundamental starting point for understanding the scenario of land disputes and has therefore been a privileged tool for urban policies that since the end of the twentieth century have managed the territory under the criterion of the social function of the city and the consequent obligation to redistribute the benefits that are generated collectively.

The question that emerges is how to advance not only on the unjust results of this model but also on the mechanisms that configure it and how, specifically, to deepen the understanding and transformative projections in the framework of access to land for production, circulation, and access to food both in peri-urban areas and in cities. With this approach as a trigger, the analysis in different Latin American territories of the actors involved in contemporary conflicts between the urbanization process and food production will seek to characterize, in terms of responsibilities toward a just transition, who and how they can contribute to the necessary changes.

Urban sprawl, food production, and supply: Cases in Latin America

Taking up the three logics mentioned by Pedro Abramo—that of the State, that of the market and that of necessity—we could broadly group these actors into three spheres: Public management at different levels (programs, plans and projects at local, provincial, and national levels); real estate developers and supermarkets seeking to extract a rent from urban or peri-urban land; social movements and civil society organizations that bring together wills marginalized, to a lesser or greater extent, by the two previous groups of actors. This third group usually aims at a more socio-environmentally sustainable land production. Although these three groupings are useful for the analysis of territorial planning and food production and marketing, or the lack thereof, it is clear that there are communicating vessels between them as they are complex social relations where each of the actors seeks to influence public policy decisions, investments, and other variables that end up shaping a given territorial dynamic and, therefore, the production, marketing, and consumption of food.

The link between urban expansion and the reconfiguration of territories used for food production and marketing is very clear in Argentina, particularly in the Buenos Aires Metropolitan Area (AMBA). According to Cruz-Muñoz (2021), the AMBA has substantially reduced its population density in recent decades: It had a population density of 9,376 inhabitants per square kilometer (hab/km^2) in 1991, while in 2001, this indicator had dropped to 8,877 hab/km^2, and projections for 2020 established an even greater decrease to 5,679 hab/km^2. This 39% reduction between 1991 and 2020 indicates a growth of the low-density urban stain and a transformation of land use—from rural to urban—driven by real estate pressure, to the detriment of the land use planning potential that the State could have. In fact, a study that analyzed the growth of cities between 2006 and 2016 detected an urban expansion of 21,704 hectares of rural land, 84% of which had residential use (Cordara & Duarte, 2018). However, more than half of this new urban land was occupied by the "gated communities" typology, that is to say neighborhoods of middle and high-income families who were physically and socially excluded from the consolidated urban fabric of the rest of the AMBA.

Just as this type of expansion—accelerated, with little state planning and low density—increases the distance, time, and cost of people's commuting to, for example, their places of work, it does the same for foodstuffs that are massively consumed in the consolidated city but which are mostly produced outside it, in the peri-urban areas. Moreover, beyond distance, the cost of supply at the regional level will depend not only on the size of the urban area but also on the form and, above all, the required operating time, where the availability and condition of access roads, streets, and avenues, as well as traffic regulations, are key elements. In turn, the operation time will also be determined by the density and spatial organization of the different types of stores, where the transport must stop, unload products, manage payments, and receive return of products in order to continue its journey. Thus, as Camagni (2011) argues, as the urban area grows, the logistics cost does not increase linearly (1 to 1) but exponentially, that is, the increase in logistics cost for each increase in density is greater than 1. In this context, the increase in the cost of supply is due to both the growing distances and the need for intermediation and storage as intermediate stages in the circulation between production and consumption.

These territorial limitations have a direct effect on the exclusion of small-scale and medium-scale traders, producers, or industries, since the scale of the metropolitan area limits their possibility of insertion, concentrating supply in supermarkets and large food companies. In any case, although there is a general tendency toward concentration and foreignization of the Argentine economy (Azpiazu et al., 2011), the characteristics of the low-density urban expansion configure a metropolis ordered territorially and sectorally around the real estate and food market impulses. In this context, the tension between the three logics proposed by Abramo (2012) is largely monopolized by these markets. Thus the urban planning and state regulatory instruments, in addition to the inter-jurisdictional metropolitan complexity, are subordinated to some small-scale initiatives, such as the fairs programs of both municipalities in the province and in the city of Buenos Aires. The most comprehensive initiatives, of regional or national scope, such as the installation of the Central Market of Buenos Aires in the early 1980s, one of the few metropolitan entities in Argentina, has been disarticulated in the framework of the deregulation of the 1990s and, despite having a great potential due to its location and availability of land, it has not been possible to redesign its role and promote its development. This food infrastructure, the most important in the country, has 540 hectares of developed and developable land for food logistics purposes according to the provisions of its expropriation decree. However, at present, most of the area is leased to large logistics companies, some of them food companies (Pérez Martín & Barsky, 2021). Finally, as a result of the increase in food prices, other marketing mechanisms have been developed, in some cases managed by social organizations, such as the Union of Land Workers (UTT) and its marketing nodes within the consolidated city, which seek to reduce the physical and operational distances suffered by both producers and consumers to improve accessibility to agroecological fresh food (Craviotti & Demicheli, 2023).

The flip side of the urban expansion of the AMBA, beyond the impact on the conditions of food circulation and commercialization in general, is the loss of very high-quality soils in productive terms, given their fertility, due to the installation of closed and private housing developments. Thus, in Greater La Plata, south of the AMBA, more than 3,000 new rural hectares have been urbanized between 2006 and 2016: 97% were destined for residential real estate development. In this regard, Baldini (2020) argues that vegetable production in Argentina is undergoing a strong transformation and retraction as a result of, among other factors, an urban expansion that pushes production not only to more remote areas with poorer quality and availability of logistics and commercial infrastructure but also to lower quality soils. A symptom of this phenomenon is that small-sized and medium-sized producers are being left out of this new production system, which, by moving away from the centers of consumption and to less suitable areas, must intensify the use of chemical inputs (fertilizers and agrochemicals) and greenhouses to improve productivity levels and sustain the activity. This production system requires greater investment and has higher costs, while it has environmental impacts due to the use of chemical inputs. In this sense, Baldini (2020) points out that between 1986 and 2015, the total urbanization of the district occupied about 16% of the territory, while horticulture occupied 10% of the peri-urban land. This activity gradually decreased until it represented less than 5% of the territory in 2015, while the urbanized territory increased to approximately 23%. In other words, while more than half of the urban area (51%) was settled on soils suitable for agriculture, horticultural productions both under greenhouses and outdoors were occupying soils with lower fertility levels. From this perspective, the logic of urban expansion for the purpose of extracting real estate income is displacing and limiting the production of fresh food from nearby areas.

Faced with this panorama, the first thing that can be observed is that a large part of land use decisions are made by local authorities, while planning decisions involving public investment are usually implemented at the provincial or national levels. This mismatch between resources and planning power in many cases generates few incentives for environmentally, socially, and economically sustainable territorial development and many incentives for *laissez faire land* use changes by the authorities. In particular, the impact of urban expansion on food production, circulation, and marketing has been limited to market practices, particularly real estate development, while state capacities in this area are limited under neoliberal urban policies.

Tensions over access to and use of urban land, both with the shift of the urban frontier toward the peri-urban and rural areas and toward the interior of the compact city, transcend the Argentine context and shape a regional scenario. This context is rooted in the type of urbanizations that, as mentioned earlier, have been developing since the 1970s, where the tension for spatial regulation and access to land is driven and organized by the action of the market, to the detriment of the role of the State and the necessity of the population, following the categories proposed by Abramo (2012). In this sense, the Declaration of Bogotá raised by the Pacto EcoSocial and Intercultural del Sur (2023) emphasizes on

> the elaboration and implementation of public policies that ensure new relationships between those who produce food and those who consume it, those who live in rural and urban areas, and guarantee fair prices, thus generating a decent income for those who produce in the countryside, as well as fair access to healthy food for consumers.

Bogota, the Colombian capital, is no exception to the type of *com-fusa* expansion referred to by Abramo (2012). Its growth, especially toward the north, has been constant in recent years, and it is estimated that between 2004 and 2019 almost 1,300 hectares have been urbanized in the surroundings of Bogota, a city located in a valley. In this context, González (2020) addresses the tension between this accelerated urbanization and the exclusion of farmers and agricultural production, precisely because they cannot afford to pay the price that the new rent for the already urbanized land generates. Thus, as urbanization expands over rural areas, the price of land rises; although agricultural productivity is not able to match the growth dynamics, farmers are forced to give up leasing or sell their land to urbanize, as in the case of the AMBA in Argentina. The issue of Bogotá's expansion is addressed by the local government, which has been trying to regulate urban sprawl with land-use planning instruments (Ballén-Velásquez, 2014). However, the tensions surrounding this process are present since urban expansion "ends up overflowing the objectives of land use plans" (González, 2020, p. 168), tilting the three logics in tension as proposed by Abramo (2012) in function of the market impulse.

Brazil's main urban agglomerates have also transformed their urbanization patterns, decreasing their population densities as a result of urban expansion toward the peripheries. In particular, São Paulo went from 12,180 inhabitants/km^2 to 9,377 inhabitants/km^2 between 1991 and 2020, a 23% reduction (Cruz-Muñoz, 2021). In this context, metropolization consolidated the growth of large supermarket chains that changed the form of food commercialization, as well as the shape of the territory itself (Cavalheiro Ribeiro da Silva & Mejía Artieda, 2021). This tension in terms of urban land use is clearly driven by supermarket companies, whose complementary strategy to the sale of food is the operation in the real estate market, as does the multinational Carrefour, which had a *real estate* business division since 2012 called Carrefour Property operating in Brazil. This division manages the group's real estate portfolio, both the rental of micro-spaces in supermarket branches and commercial premises in shopping malls, and the reservation of land for future branch opening and real estate development. Thus, as of 2024, the Carrefour Group operated 1,074 branches totaling 3.2 million square meters (m^2) and 3,000 stores totaling another 450,000 m^2 in shopping centers or shopping malls (Carrefour Group Brazil, 2024). The Carrefour Property Division accounts a land bank of 18 million m^2, that includes all the branches (3.2 million m^2) while the rest is vacant land (Carrefour Property, 2024). The destination of this land bank is, for example, real estate development in large-scale multi-use projects such as the recently developed "Complex Alto das Nações," which, taking advantage of the urban land of the first Carrefour hypermarket in Brazil, opened in 1975, multiplies the commercial area by five to seven times and develops area for luxury housing and office space (Exame, 2021). Something similar happens with the company Cencosud which, although it does not have a specific *real estate* division, beyond having supermarkets, shopping centers, and other retail stores, has 25 "unproductive" urban plots of land in Brazil totaling 386,476 m^2, while the more than 200 branches in that country total 566,466 m^2 (Cencosud, 2020, p. 192). In other words, in spatial terms, there is a potential for both food supply and real estate operations, thus blocking the possibility for the State to act as a territorial planner. In this sense, as argued by Ribeiro da Silva and Artieda (2021, p. 46) the modes of production of urban space—with the imprint of supermarkets—have repercussions not only on the commercialization of food but also "on the culture of food consumption, inequality of access to food and to the city, and an imbalance between the countryside and the city."

Final thoughts

It is impossible in the capitalist economies of Latin America to separate the commodification of urban land from that of food. That is to say, the modes of land production, both urban and rural, have a direct impact on the form of production, commercialization, and consumption of something as vital as food. This is not a cause–consequence relationship between two separate entities—the countryside and the city—but two expressions of the same problem that generate changes in both ways of relating to the territory. Increasingly, both urban and rural land appear in social relations as an exchange good that displaces its social function as a used good.

Beyond nuances and particularities, this is not a local problem, but rather a global one, with particularly serious consequences in economies that are not dominant on the global stage, such as those of Latin America. The Argentine case, but also the counterpoints mentioned for the Colombian and Brazilian cases, demonstrate this.

The first has to do with power dynamics, fundamentally with two of the most concentrated sectors: The deepening of commodification in twenty-first-century capitalism has consolidated the corporate sector, both in the real estate–financial complex that drives the low-density expansion of peri-urban areas and in the supermarket sector integrated with large food companies, at the expense of both small and medium farmers, food producers, and traders who can guarantee a diverse, quality, and accessible food supply. This growth also conquers governmental spheres and, in so doing, transforms the orientation of public policies. In other words, States continue to be actors with regulatory capacity and real power but are increasingly subordinated to the logic of the real estate and food market, to the detriment of collective welfare.

At this point, a second question arises as to what is the territory of these actors with real power: While the management of the conflict over access to land is settled within the national spheres, the larger corporate sectors are inserted in globalized dynamics that do not always respond nor must fully comply with the normative institutional framework of the territories they transform.

On the other hand, the question of counter-hegemonic globality remains valid, in the sense of to what extent it is possible (and necessary) for actors with the collective ability to dispute the urbanization model and the way in which food production and access to food are inserted to organize themselves beyond specific territories. Even without such a globalizing strategy, it is worth reflecting on the relations between sectors apparently split in their interests that, from this model of responsibility, can converge in some aspects of the interpellation to the ways in which the territory is being transformed. What connects the struggles of urban tenants with tenant farmers? What diversities are manifested by opening the category of food producers—or consumers? We even need to think of a broad cartography to understand the responsibility of organized forms of civil society such as transport unions that connect the dots in the food production chain. Ultimately, the question is who is *responsible for* this unjust territorial model and, therefore, *responsible for* its transformation.

Thinking in terms of who should be involved in public debate and decision-making about these issues constitutes a key line of approach to guide territorial planning and development in the face of public policy approaches that tend to divide the issue of access to food as a problem without considering the determining links with the land market throughout the supply chain. To the extent that actors operating in apparently independent circuits emerge with their conflicting interests regarding land use, the possibility of building fair transitions can only be considered from an integral perspective where the ways in which we feed ourselves are part of how we inhabit the territory.

Note

1 For instance, the EcoSocial and Intercultural Pact of the South (2023) was promoted in 2020 and brings together activists, militants, organizations, and social movements from Argentina, Colombia, Ecuador, and more recently, Brazil, Bolivia, Peru, and Venezuela. In this framework, the discussion focuses on the imbalances that are generating an unsustainable food regime that puts pressure on ecosystems and implies an undermining of the autonomy and sovereignty of the territories and their communities.

Bibliography

Abramo, P. (2012). La ciudad com-fusa: Mercado y producción de la estructura urbana en las grandes metrópolis latinoamericanas. *EURE (Santiago)*, *38*, 35–69. http://dx.doi.org/10.4067/S0250-71612012000200002

Azpiazu, D., Manzanelli, P., & Schorr, M. (2011). Concentración y extranjerización en la economía argentina en la posconvertibilidad (2002–2008). *Cuadernos del Cendes*, *28*, 97–119. http://hdl.handle.net/11336/192221

Baldini, C. (2020). *Territorio en movimiento: Las transformaciones territoriales del Cinturón Hortícola Platense en los últimos 30 años*. Universidad Nacional de La Plata.

Ballén-Velásquez, L. M. (2014). "Desbordando" la categoría de borde Reflexiones desde la experiencia bogotana. *Bitácora urbano territorial*, *24*(2), 131–140.

Barsky, A. (2005). El periurbano productivo, un espacio en constante transformación. Introducción al estado del debate, con referencias al caso de Buenos Aires. *Scripta Nova: revista electrónica de geografía y ciencias sociales*, *9*.

Barsky, A. (2010). La agricultura de "cercanías" a la ciudad y los ciclos del territorio periurbano. Reflexiones sobre el caso de la Región Metropolitana de Buenos Aires. En A. Svetlitza de Nemirovsky (Eds.), *Agricultura periurbana en Argentina y globalización. Escenarios, recorridos y problemas*. Ciudad Autónoma de Buenos Aires.

Berardo, M. (2019). Más allá de la dicotomía rural-urbano. *Quid 16: Revista del Área de Estudios Urbanos*, *11*, 316–324.

Brenner, N. (2016). *Critique of urbanization: Selected essays* (Vol. 156). Birkhäuser.

Brenner, N., Peck, J., & Theodore, N. (2011). After neoliberalization? En M. B. Steger & A. McNevin (Eds.), *Global ideologies and urban landscapes* (pp. 9–27). Routledge.

Camagni, R. (2011). *Economía urbana*. Antoni Bosch editor.

Carrefour Group Brasil. (2024). *Planilha de Resultados 1T24*. https://ri.grupocarrefourbrasil.com.br/informacoes-financeiras/apresentacoes

Carrefour Property. (2024). *Sobre nós*. https://www.carrefourproperty.com.br/faq

Cavalheiro Ribeiro da Silva, C., & Mejía Artieda, A. (2021). El consumo alimentario en la ciudad mercantilizada Dos casos en São Paulo (Brasil). *Bitácora Urbano Territorial, 31*, 45–58. https://dialnet.unirioja.es/servlet/articulo?codigo=7919359

Cencosud. (2020). *Memoria Anual Integrada 2019*. Chile. https://bit.ly/39kMuAq

Clichevsky, N. (2000). *Informalidad y Segregación Urbana en America Latina. Una aproximación*. Informe CEPAL, División de Medio Ambiente y Asentamientos Humanos.

Cordara, C., & Duarte, J. I. (Eds.). (2018). *¿Cómo crecen las ciudades argentinas? Estudio de la expansión urbana de los 33 grandes aglomerados*.

Craviotti, C., & Demicheli, J. C. (2023). Circuitos alternativos de alimentos: Prácticas y discursos en el abastecimiento mayorista de productos agroecológicos y orgánicos. *Mundo Agrario, 24*(55), e201. https://doi.org/10.24215/15155994e201

Cruz-Muñoz, F. (2021). Patrones de expansión urbana de las megaurbes latinoamericanas en el nuevo milenio. *EURE (Santiago), 47*, 29–49. http://dx.doi.org/10.7764/eure.47.140.02

Di Nucci, J. (2015). Concentración y uso corporativo del territorio en Argentina: La lógica territorial de Carrefour. *Cuadernos Geográficos, 54*(1), 186–208.

Di Nucci, J., & Lan, D. (2008). Globalización y modernización del comercio minorista argentino en la década de los noventa. *Huellas, 12*, 176–197.

Exame. (2021). *Carrefour Property e WTorre se unem para lançar um novo ícone para SP*. https://exame.com/negocios/carrefour-property-e-wtorre-se-unem-para-lancar-um-novo-icone-para-sp/

Found, W. (1971). *A theoretical approach to rural land-use patterns*. Edward Arnold.

González, J. I. (2020). Expansión urbana, dinámica de los precios del suelo rural y productividad agropecuaria (2008 y 2018)-Bogotá. En A. Smith Aranque Solano (Ed.), *Ordenamiento territorial y desarrollo regional*. Universidad Sergio Arboleda.

Harvey, D. (2012). *Rebel cities: From the right to the city to the urban revolution*. Verso Books.

Hernández Cordero, A., & Eneva, S. A. (2016). ¿Mercados, museos o malls? La gentrificación de los mercados municipales en Barcelona y Madrid. *EntreDiversidades, 6*, 143–173.

Jaramillo González, S. (2009). *Hacia una teoría de la renta del suelo urbano*. Ediciones Uniandes.

Jaramillo González, S. (2013). *Acerca de la investigación en mercados de tierra urbana en América Latina*. http://hdl.handle.net/1992/8409

Kozak, D. (2008). Assessing urban fragmentation: The emergence of new typologies in central Buenos Aires. En M. Jenks, D. Kozak, & P. Takkanon (Ed.), *World cities and urban form: Fragmented, polycentric, sustainable?* (pp. 239–258). Routledge.

Krausmann, F., & Langthaler, E. (2019). Food regimes and their trade links: A socio-ecological perspective. *Ecological Economics, 160*, 87–95. https://doi.org/10.1016/j.ecolecon.2019.02.011

López-Morales, E., & Klett, I. G. (2021). El complejo urbano financiero inmobiliario en América latina. Introducción. *Scripta Nova. Revista Electrónica de Geografía y Ciencias Sociales, 25*(1).

Mermet, A.-C. (2017). Global retail capital and the city: Towards an intensification of gentrification. *Urban Geography, 38*(8), 1158–1181. https://doi.org/10.1080/02723638.2016.1200328

Pacto EcoSocial e Intercultural del Sur. (2023). *Declaración de Bogotá. Hacia un pacto con la tierra: Geopolítica de las transiciones y re-existencias*.

Pérez Martín, J. (2021). *Abastecimiento de alimentos en el Área Metropolitana de Buenos Aires: Interacciones y configuración espacial de los entramados logísticos-comerciales en los sectores lácteo y frutihortícola*. Universitat Autònoma de Barcelona. http://hdl.handle.net/10803/671572

Pérez Martín, J. (2022). Los supermercados en el centro de la escena: Estrategia de negocios y formación de precios en el abastecimiento urbano de alimentos. *Realidad Económica, 52*(350), 9–38. https://ojs.iade.org.ar/index.php/re/article/view/205/174

Pérez Martín, J., & Barsky, A. (2021). La planificación del abastecimiento alimentario a la gran ciudad: Marchas y contramarchas del Mercado Central de Buenos Aires (1960–2019). *Mundo Agrario*, *22*(50-e172). https://doi.org/10.24215/15155994e172
Steel, C. (2013). *Hungry city: How food shapes our lives*. Vintage Books.
Vecslir Peri, L. (2011). Nuevas centralidades del ocio y del consumo: Ámbitos, modalidades e instrumentos de regulación de las grandes superficies comerciales en la Región Metropolitana de Buenos Aires. *Revista Iberoamericana de Urbanismo*, *5*, 31–44.
Von Braun, J. (2007). *Rural-urban linkages for growth, employment, and poverty reduction* (p. 22). IFPRI.

4

THE NEED OF LAND FOR PERI-URBAN AGRICULTURAL PRODUCTION AND ITS INCLUSION ONTO THE NATIONAL PUBLIC AGENDAS

Regional planning instruments to preserve green belts in Latin America

Andres Barsky

Introduction

In recent decades, the uncontrolled expansion of cities over the productive belts that surround them has become a global problem. In two projects coordinated by Angel et al. (2005, 2011), specialists from the World Bank and the Lincoln Institute studied for five years the growth patterns of 120 cities around the world, in both developed and developing countries. The results coincided in all cases: From the 1980s onward, and particularly since the 1990s, there has been an unprecedentedly large, fragmented, and low-density urban expansion. In other words, a disproportionate expansion of the periphery with high consumption of rural land. Another study, the document *"Urban sprawl in Europe: The ignored challenge"* (European Commission, 2006), warns how *urban sprawl* constitutes a serious danger for urban planning because it becomes extremely costly for the public treasury to expand infrastructures at the pace of, in Horacio Torres' terms, a true territorial *laissez faire* (Roitman, 1998, p. 2).[1] All these processes associated with a model of urban expansion that promotes an unrestricted growth of city's borders are drastically modifying the pre-existing relationship between the city and its productive environment: The peri-urban (Arellano Ramos, 2011). According to different authors, this has negatively exposed the role of the market as a vector of the organization of these types of spaces (Briano & Fritzsche, 2007; Aguilar, 2011).

In Latin American cities, spontaneous or "informal" urbanization—led by citizens and social organizations on often peripheral urban territories—is a difficult problem for public management at different levels because, as mentioned, in these cases the state apparatus must intervene in *faits accomplis* and make significant economic expenditures to complete it with the necessary infrastructure (Libertun &

DOI: 10.4324/9781003471929-7

Guerrero, 2017). The problem is further aggravated if urban growth acquires a diffuse character and takes place over large swaths of land, as is the case in many cities in Latin America. In places where the land is being urbanized with a dispersed pattern and the price of land rises sharply, lower-income sectors of the population are unable to access housing in central city areas and are pushed into marginal areas where they lack infrastructure and urban services. Beyond informal urbanization, expansion at urban peripheries also occurs through real estate development and the construction of public housing units. Regardless of the causes and form that urban expansion takes, its effect is often devastating for agricultural production in peri-urban areas, which are often the "green belts" that provide local and seasonal produce and goods for local markets.

The purpose of this chapter is to assess the current state of threats to and measures to protect agriculture around cities in Latin America, a continent that is known worldwide for being the fastest urbanizing continent (UNDESA, 2019).[2] The first section presents a general description and definition of some of the characteristics of peri-urban agriculture, highlighting especially the conditions of social and spatial vulnerability that agricultural production in proximity to cities presents and its increasing appearance on Latin American food and urbanistic agendas. It then provides several examples of strategies and experiences in Latin American cities related to the concrete management of peri-urban agriculture, whether through the institutionalization of relevant organizations, the enactment of specific laws, the implementation of programs aimed at small-scale production, or the generation of instruments for territorial intervention. Next, certain particularities of the Argentine case will be discussed with a discussion of policies in the Metropolitan Area of Buenos Aires (AMBA), a topic that the author has studied in depth (Barsky, 2013, 2018, 2022b). In the conclusions, and in accordance with the examples gathered in the paper, an argument is presented on the need to generate new public intervention instruments to preserve and design spaces of high productive and environmental value found in periurban areas.

The peri-urban complex as an interface territory and peri-urban agriculture as a mean of preserving land

The concept of the peri-urban refers to a *border territory* subjected to social and economic processes related to the capitalist valorization of space, as a consequence of the actual or potential incorporation of new lands into the city. When speaking of the peri-urban, we are speaking of an interface or border situation between two geographical types traditionally conceptualized as dichotomous or oppositional: The countryside and the city. It implies the identification of certain spaces where the transformation from rural to semi-rural and from semi-rural to urban is taking place, that is, their physical reconditioning for the purposes of urbanization, in which there is an intense anthropic pressures on the environment and an acute competition for access to land and other related resources. This translates into a land subdivision for real estate purposes, the location of primary-intensive enterprises, the establishment of industrial parks, and the settlement of housing developments of different socioeconomic origins, among other spatial manifestations. As an expanded periphery, the peri-urban can be understood as a space in which a series of imbalances and dysfunctions derived from diseconomies of agglomeration and processes of socio-spatial segregation typical of the city are externalized. In conclusion, the periurban area is presented as a heterogeneous contour of sharp social and productive contrasts (Barsky, 2005).

Therefore, the peri-urban edge constitutes a productive, residential, and service territory located in the space immediately adjacent to the physical area where cities are established. It develops when cities acquire certain dimensions, that is, when they form regional markets that need to be supplied from "nearby" (Azevedo da Silva, 2009). One of the most characteristic landscapes and social manifestations of periurban areas is the particular type of agriculture practiced there: The network of primary-intensive farms that make up the so-called *green belt*.[3] It is located in wedges, interstices, and vacant areas characteristic of these urban–rural interface spaces. Compared to other extensive or specialized agricultural systems that operate from other territories and manage significant volumes of production, the periurban green belt's essential competitive advantage lies in its proximity to the city (Barsky, 2010, 2022a; De Marco, 2020).[4,5]

In recent years, periurban agriculture has gained international recognition. In March 2012, the 32nd Regional Conference of the Food and Agriculture Organization of the United Nations (FAO) for Latin America and the Caribbean identified the promotion of urban and peri-urban agriculture as one of the priority areas for the region (FAO, 2012). In September 2015, the United Nations approved the "17 Sustainable Development Goals (SDGs) of the 2030 Agenda for Sustainable Development," among which are as follows: Zero hunger; sustainable cities and communities; and responsible production and consumption, among others. In October of that year, the Milan Urban Food Policy Pact was signed, involving European and worldwide municipalities, which recognized—among its recitals—that "family farming enterprises and small food producers (in particular women producers in different countries) play a key role in the food supply in cities and surrounding territories" (Milan Urban Policy Pact, 2015, p. 2). In 2016, the United Nations Conference on Housing and Sustainable Urban Development "Habitat III" included a discussion of the need to generate and coordinate "sustainable food security and agriculture policies in urban, peri-urban and rural areas" within the guidelines for a New Urban Agenda (United Nations, 2016, p. 36). Finally, last year the FAO—together with IFAD, UNICEF, WFP, and WHO—published the document "The State of Food Security and Nutrition in the World. Urbanization, food system transformation and healthy diets along the rural-urban continuum," called SOFI 2023. This report estimates that around 600 million people will be chronically undernourished in 2030 and focuses on the potential of functional linkages between rural, peri-urban, and urban areas to ensure access to healthy and affordable diets for the population.

The following systematization of Latin American experiences seeks to highlight different institutional initiatives that have incorporated peri-urban agriculture into the public agenda of different countries. The central question guiding this work is related to the implications of its promotion as a strategy for influencing land use planning and local food supply, in a context in which the dynamics of urbanization are strongly shaping the relationship between the city and its regional supply systems.

Experiences of peri-urban agriculture management in different Latin American countries

While periurban agriculture is a widespread phenomenon as old as cities themselves, in Latin America, the first country to have specific, state-led initiatives in urban and peri-urban agriculture was Cuba (FAO, 2004). Starting in 1987, the "Movement of organoponics and intensive vegetable gardens" was created, which became the Urban Agriculture Movement in 1997 and subsequently the Comprehensive Program for Urban and Suburban Agriculture in 2009, when it was institutionalized as such by the State.[6] This program, carried out under exceptional and continuous conditions of external trade blockade to the country, low average income, and within the framework of centralized planning, has been considered one of the most effective in Latin America in terms of the population involved, scope, and persistence over time[7] (Ávila Sánchez, 2005). In May 2012, the "International Seminar on Urban and Peri-urban Agriculture" was held in Cuba. It was sponsored by FAO and concluded with "The Havana Declaration on Urban and Periurban Agriculture" (FAO, 2013, p. 92).

With regard to Brazil, in July 2001, as a result of the actions of the Urban Reform movement, Federal Law No. 10.257, known as the "Statute of the City", was approved. This pioneering piece of Latin American urban law contemplates "the many and complex legal issues intrinsic to the process of *use, occupation and division of urban land, as well as providing adequate legal support to urban management practices*" (Fernándes, 2003), including edge zones.[8] Peri-urban agriculture projects, in particular, are explicitly defined and supported by the Ministry of Social Development.[9] Since 2004, the Urban and Peri-urban Agriculture Program has been institutionalized, whose guidelines were established in the document "Overview of urban and peri-urban agriculture in Brazil and policy guidelines for its promotion" (published in 2007 in conjunction with FAO). In addition, the Ministry of Agrarian Development has focused directly on the complex agenda of family farming, which includes peri-urban agriculture and which, as will be discussed later, had a decisive influence in Argentina in raising the public profile of peri-urban agriculture. Finally, some important regional programs stand out, such as the Urban and Periurban Agriculture Program (PROAURP) in the Metropolitan Region of São Paulo, the Policy to Support Urban Agriculture in Minas Gerais, and the Verticalization Program for Small Agricultural Production (Prove) in the Federal District of Brasilia, among others (Videiro Rosa, 2011).

In the case of Mexico, the active peri-urbanization processes taking place in different cities in the country have come up against the institutional complexity resulting from the land tenure regime that emerged from the Revolution (1910–1917). In recent years, the privatization of land in parceled ejido areas made possible as a result of the 1992 reforms to Article 27 of the Constitution, which enabled, for the first time, the possibility of selling ejido and communal land, led to the massive incorporation of social property into the urban real estate market. In 1993, the Program for the Certification of Ejido Rights and Titling of Urban Land (PROCEDE) was launched, whose administrative procedures were so complex that the State retained control over the ejidos during its first years. It was between 2006 and 2009 when the process reached a remarkable acceleration and "90% of the country's ejidos were titled, replacing community property with individual deeds," with devastating effects on agricultural production (Relli Ugartamendía, 2018, p. 42). On the other hand, as a consequence of said constitutional reform, the Secretariat of Agrarian Reform (SRA) deconcentrated the direction of the national agrarian registry, creating the National Agrarian Registry (RAN), the Agrarian Courts (TA), and the Agrarian Attorney's Office (PA), in order to make its operation more efficient. With regard to urban management, the Secretariat of Urban Development and Ecology (SEDUE) was transformed into the Secretariat of Social Development (SEDESOL) and, through the "100 Cities Program (P-100)," the idea of creating territorial reserves for urban development was taken up again. Based on the guidelines of the Agrarian Law, the General Law of Human Settlement, and PROCEDE, progress was made in the process of certifying ejido and communal land tenure until 1996, when a nationwide program called "Program for the Incorporation of Social Land into Urban Development (PISO)" was created, which has different procedures for incorporating ejido land into the city (Olivera Lozano, 2005). In recent years, there have been important institutional dynamics that articulate the urban and the rural, such as the incorporation of the historical Commission for the Regularization of Land Tenure (CORETT)—created in 1973 and which regularized 2.5 million irregular settlements in 30 years—into the Secretariat of Agrarian, Territorial, and Urban Development (SEDATU).[10]

In the Colombian case, in recent years the discussion on the new Law on Land for Development (Law 1,469 of June 30, 2011)—approved simultaneously with the new Organic Law on Territorial Planning—as well as the design of the "Master Plan for Food Supply and Food Security for Bogotá Capital District" (adopted in 2006) and the "Medellín Food Supply Plan" (approved at the end of 2011). The Land for Development Law is part of Colombia's important tradition of generating advanced legislation in the Latin American region.[11] It promotes the supply of land for development, popular housing macro-projects, the provision of road infrastructure, and public service networks that allow the urbanization and construction of land, as well as enabling management instruments for the capture of capital gains and the distribution of charges and benefits. On the other hand, the food supply plans of Bogotá and Medellín are design documents that include the discussion of food security for the urban population and the traceability of products entering from the regional environment of the cities, which includes different types of peri-urban agriculture. The implementation of these plans has not been free of debates about the consequences of these reordering initiatives on the small production chains that supply the so-called "marketplaces" (Planeta Paz, 2006) and the role of peasants in food production (Rodríguez Muñoz, 2004).

In the case of Venezuela, a country historically characterized by low fuel prices for its domestic market, there has been relatively little development of peri-urban agriculture. Nevertheless, in 2003 the Foundation for Innovation and Training for the Agrarian Revolution (CIARA) was institutionalized, which provided technical assistance to small individual and community production units (gardens) through the Project for the Development and Consolidation of Urban and Periurban Agriculture. This project was carried out in Caracas (Capital District) and different cities in the country. By 2012, the proposed radius of coverage was 10,000 units in 10 states, within the framework of the "Zero Hunger" plan. The work in the units was complemented by the contribution of unemployed people (Mission "Saber y Trabajo"[12]). In 2016, in a context of increasing economic difficulties following the fall in the price of a barrel of oil, the Ministry of Urban Agriculture was created (currently named "Ministry of Popular Power for Urban Agriculture") with the stated aims of managing peri-urban agriculture and supporting small-scale production, with the idea of taking advantage of the "physical enclaves of the country's urban spaces." In recent years, agro-productive brigades and independent producers have been defined as policy subjects, and Local Supply and Production Committees (CLAP) have been organized.

With respect to the case of Chile, it is worth mentioning a legal aspect that is of interest for periurban agriculture, since it has to do with the regulation of land use on the edges of the city. Decree Law 3,516, which has been in force for several decades, permits the subdivision of periurban rural land, provided that the Agricultural and Livestock Service (SAG) of the Ministry of Agriculture authorizes it. Likewise, requests for changes in land use are made to the Interministerial Commission formed by the Ministries of Housing and Urbanism and Agriculture (Naranjo Ramírez, 2007, p. 231). Beyond the fact that private sector agents can generally violate the regulatory framework by taking advantage of the institutional weaknesses characteristic of periurban areas, it is remarkable the role assigned to the Ministry of Agriculture in the preservation of periurban productive land and how a combined engineering between both portfolios has been considered.[13]

In the case of Peru, the Institute for the Promotion of Sustainable Development (IPES) has played a very important role in recent years as the Latin American headquarters of the Resource Center for Urban Agriculture and Reforestation (RUAF).[14] From there, publications, electronic debates, and various events have been generated that contribute to placing urban and peri-urban agriculture on the region's agenda. However, in recent decades, the national agenda has focused largely on the legalization of popular housing developments and pockets of rurality on public and private lands (the 1961 Slum Law and the Commission for the Formalization of Informal Property established in 1996, both of which had a strong territorial impact).

In the case of Ecuador, three significant events stand out in relation to urban and peri-urban agriculture. On the one hand, in 2001, the Urban Management Programme of the United Nations Centre for Urban Settlements, under the auspices of UNDP, held the International Seminar "Urban Agriculture in the Cities of the 21st Century" in Quito, where a large number of papers were presented and the "Quito Declaration" was issued, advocating the sustainable development of cities that incorporates urban and peri-urban agriculture into the political agenda and urban planning. On the other hand, in 2008 the "Right to the City" was included in the new Constitution of the Republic (Article 31).[15]

Finally, in 2016 the United Nations Conference on Housing and Sustainable Urban Development "Habitat III" took place, in which the guidelines for a New Urban Agenda were established which adopted (in point 123) the commitment to continue promoting "the integration of food security and nutritional needs of urban residents" and the "coordination of sustainable policies for food security and agriculture in urban areas, peri-urban and rural areas, in order to facilitate the production, storage, transport and marketing of food to consumers in appropriate and affordable ways and thereby reduce food losses and prevent and reuse food waste" (United Nations, 2016: 36).

In recent years, in the Metropolitan District of Quito, the Participatory Urban Agriculture (AGRUPAR) instrument has helped promote gardens identified as urban, peri-urban, and small-scale rural.

Finally, with regard to Bolivia, in the last decade, the State has established a national planning system called SISPLAN, which encourages the establishment of rural communities and provides special resources for the construction of infrastructure, both social and productive. Land management plans in rural areas seek to influence types of agricultural production, according to national and local development priorities (Ministry of Federal Planning, 2015, p. 64). In recent years, the Ministry of Productive Development and Plural Economy implemented the National Urban and Peri-urban Agriculture Program (PNAUP) aimed at local projects located in Municipal Technical Units dependent on Municipal or Departmental Autonomous Governments.

Particularities of the Argentine case in peri-urban agriculture management

The chapter now turns to a more detailed analysis of trends, management, and challenges in periurban agriculture in Argentina. In keeping with growth trends in other Latin American urban areas over the last 20 years, Argentina's largest cities in the country show a marked decrease in average density (Lanfranchi et al., 2019). That is, urban expansion in these areas is characterized by low density, dispersion, and discontinuity, leaving wide gaps subject to real estate speculation. Among the modalities that drive the expansion, the existence of residential complexes and gated communities is particularly salient. A series of conflictive problems emerges from this type of urbanization, including encroachment on productive rural land, pressure on protected natural areas, and the presence of marked social dualisms, spatial segregation, and inequality. In short, such urbanization patterns, similar to those of other Latin American contexts, represent a form of structurally deficient development pattern with high economic, environmental, and social costs (Blanco, 2013, pp. 14–15).[16]

In this context, periurban agriculture has emerged as an issue in conjunction with the advance of Family Farming on the country's political and social agenda. This is largely due to the fact that as of 2004, Brazil began to put pressure on the other MERCOSUR trade zone members to incorporate Family Farming as an issue on their state agendas. As a result, the National Forum for Family Farming (FoNAF) was institutionalized in Argentina in 2005, at which time the State coordinated with various trade and agricultural associations to advance the initiative. The institutionalization process continued to deepen until 2008, when the government experienced a major political conflict with the agro-export sector over the collection of taxes on foreign trade. From that moment onward, the FoNAF became linked to the periurban producers of the Metropolitan Area of Buenos Aires (AMBA)—until then invisible or undifferentiated from the rest—as a new type of family farmers on whom initiatives aimed at small-scale production could focus.

Periurban agriculture also began to appear on the national agenda in different capacities starting in the early 2000s, as a response to major local economic and food crises. Starting in those years, a series of municipal, provincial, and national public policies was implemented in the AMBA. These included the creation of the Municipal Institute for Local Economic Development (IMDEL) of the Municipality of Moreno, the Institute for Local Development (IDEL) of the Municipality of Florencio Varela, the Program for the Promotion of Sustainable Agriculture (PRO.A.A.S.) of the Municipality of Pilar, the Agreement between the National Secretariat of Agriculture and the municipalities of the AMBA to subsidize peri-urban agriculture, and the creation of the Peri-urban Agriculture Directorate in the Province of Buenos Aires. Subsequent to the 2008 agro-export conflict, the National Periurban Agriculture Program of the Ministry of Agriculture of the Nation was consolidated. Meanwhile, an experimental agency for urban and periurban agriculture of the National Institute of Agricultural Technology called "INTA AMBA"—the first of its kind in Latin America—was institutionalized, and the Secretariat of Territorial Development and Family Agriculture was created within the Ministry of Agriculture. Through these initiatives, various public agents became involved with small producers in the metropolitan periurban area (mostly of Bolivian nationality, see Chapter 10 of this volume) in order to help them improve their production practices, set up wholesale and retail markets, inform them how to regularize their undocumented status, etc. As a result, peri-urban agriculture gained significant visibility on the national public agenda with the National Peri-urban Agriculture Plan reaching 112 municipalities in 13 provinces and the provincial and municipal administrations of different regions of the country engaging in an active process of institutionalizing specialized units.

Despite the marked support that periurban agriculture has received through different policies, including in the form of subsidies, training, and other inputs, the sector continues to face significant challenges. Indeed, the implementation of the different programs enumerated earlier coincided with a new cycle of urban expansion in recent decades that has affected the productive belts of the country's main cities and threatened the livelihoods of producers (Lanfranchi et al., 2019). Despite official attention and support, therefore, periurban producers continue to be highly vulnerable to macroeconomic oscillations and capital cycles, and the technical capacities of the state to guide and influence land use planning are inadequate in dealing with the resultant pressures faced by producers. In this sense, it is important to recognize that periurban belts require a specific set of territorial and economic planning measures to sustain production, which is threatened by the advance of urbanization as a result of a subtle "interplay of forces." In short, the implementation of policies aimed at protecting green belts has its limits. The Argentine State has significant operational difficulties in designing and implementing planning policies with effective impact on the territory and with continuity over time (Barsky, 2013).

Periurban agriculture is also vulnerable to shifts in the political terrain. In recent years in Argentina, with changes in the federal government in 2015 and 2023, neoliberal economic administrations took office. These governments promoted neo-modernizing discourses, which claim to promote, through increasing economic deregulation, an increase in *commodity* exports in order to transform Argentina into "the supermarket of the world" (recreating a new foundational myth with respect to the one that maintained that the country had been the "breadbasket of the world" between 1880 and 1930). In this context, family farming—which drives the agenda of peri-urban agriculture—has recently lost its position in national governmental agricultural planning and decisions. In 2018, in the context of a major financial crisis that led the country to ask the International Monetary Fund (IMF) for help, there was a profound restructuring in the organization of the national administration: The Ministry of Agriculture lost its ministerial rank (acquired in 2008) and became a secretariat. Likewise, in recent years, the Family Farming area was deactivated, which essentially eliminated the work of territorial technicians who had worked on the ground with producers and agricultural communities around the country. Nevertheless, as a result of the diverse relationships generated among stakeholders in previous years, the peri-urban agricultural agenda continues to be active through its presence in various provincial and municipal jurisdictions. Likewise, a number of social movements linked to peri-urban production (Unión de Trabajadores de la Tierra, Movimiento de Trabajadores Excluidos, etc.) have gained public visibility in recent years through demonstrations in the city of Buenos Aires (known as "*verdurazos*") that demand government support and raise awareness about local production and agroecological practices. Likewise, community-supported agriculture initiatives have multiplied and food bank networks are once again gaining prominence. In a context of growing political conflict, food insecurity, and economic uncertainty, the peri-urban agriculture agenda continues to be present today through various fields of public action.

Conclusion

Peri-urban agriculture is a common feature of cities throughout Latin America which provides an important source of food for urban consumers, yet it is threatened by increasing rates of urbanization and requires governmental protection and support in order to be able to flourish. This chapter has provided a synthesis of the diverse institutional mechanisms created in different Latin American countries through which the problem of sustaining peri-urban agriculture has been addressed. Undoubtedly, at the turn of the century, the region has seen important initiatives linked to the search for a more socially sustainable mode of urbanization and the preservation of agriculture that is visualized and revalued by the city. As we have seen in the examples provided in this chapter, there are a wide range of interventions with varied results.

Brazil and Colombia have the most developed land regulatory legislation in the region, while Mexico and Bolivia have the most complex institutional arrangements for managing it. The issue of peri-urban agriculture in Brazil is part of the country's important tradition of working with family farmers, while Colombia has an important body of legislation and there have been initiatives linked to the modernization of urban food supply in Bogota and Medellin, where a city-led food governance design has been discussed in relation to its regional environment.[17] Chile has instituted a land authority defined as the Ministry of Agriculture, which acts in conjunction with the Ministry of Urban Planning and Housing to determine new land uses in peri-urban areas; while Argentina has recently encouraged the creation of action areas linked to family farming and has national programs aimed at peri-urban production: The National Peri-urban Agriculture Plan, a large experimental agency for the Metropolitan Region of Buenos Aires specializing in urban and peri-urban agriculture (INTA-AMBA) and the Secretariat of Territorial Development and Family Agriculture. All these initiatives emerged from the political context following the economic crisis of 2002 and the political crisis of 2008, and are currently being reformulated.

Within the framework of serious economic restrictions and shortages, Venezuela works in urban and peri-urban agriculture in an undifferentiated manner through agricultural production missions (small-scale family gardens) and grants ministerial status to urban agriculture, while Cuba promotes urban and peri-urban agriculture through hydroponic gardens and intensive gardens. Peru has promoted the dissemination of peri-urban agriculture in the region through IPES and, in Ecuador, the "Quito Declaration" established relevant guidelines for urban and peri-urban agriculture in Latin America, and the issue was highlighted at the "Habitat III" event organized by the United Nations. In addition, the country currently has a chapter on the "Right to the City" in its recently created Magna Carta.

In taking these diverse experiences into consideration, it is clear that the preservation of peri-urban agriculture in Latin American cities must combine existing land management instruments, adapted to the complex socioeconomic and environmental dynamics of interface spaces, where urban and rural or neo-rural logics intermingle. There is a need for intergovernmental information systems in Latin America on the institutional land regulatory bodies that have been developed in recent years (land laws, land authorities at different levels) as well as on the territorial figures of preservation of the peri-urban edge (horticultural parks, urban containment reserves, etc.) or other instrumental procedures (construction of new urban areas, etc., or other instrumental procedures (construction of land banks, determination of special zones of social interest, creation of progressive land taxes to curb the speculative use of urban land, etc.), which are generally limited or partially developed initiatives in the region. Protecting horticultural green belts, "circumventing" cities with production spaces that strengthen their food security and sovereignty, is part of the complex exercise of projecting the future evolution of Latin American cities.

Notes

1 The urban sprawl of our times

> no longer manifests itself as a continuous growth, in an oil slick, but rather as a dispersion of urban processes on a regional scale. This dispersion leads us to think that the European city model, more compact from the physical point of view and equitable in terms of social appropriation, is giving way to the American city model, more dispersed and structured in 'islands' connected through highway networks.
>
> *(Subsecretaría de Urbanismo de la Provincia de Buenos Aires, 2007, p. 151)*

> Likewise, Fernández Maraschio argues—based on Chambers and Castells—that from the expansion and diffusion of communication technologies, the countryside and the outskirts of cities increasingly constitute the *locus* of a shared and commonly modeled world. . . . The post-fordist city grows in an expanded manner from the intangible networks of the information society. *Exopolis* are thus formed, where the growth of 'external' cities predominates and exogenous forces gain importance in shaping the urban space.
>
> *(2012, p. 99)*

2 According to the Food and Agriculture Organization of the United Nations (FAO), agriculture in urban and peri-urban areas currently provides food for about 700 million city residents, i.e., a quarter of the world's population living in agglomerations. And it stresses that population growth between now and 2030 will be concentrated in the urban areas of developing countries. It should also be noted that the urban population represented 30% of the world's population in 1950, rising to 57% in 2021, and is estimated to reach 68% of the total by 2050 (FAO, 2002, FAO et al., 2023).

3 In Argentina, the term "green belt" refers to the peri-urban space made up of a network of family farms or orchards—and others with more entrepreneurial characteristics—

surrounding large cities, whose production is mainly of leafy and seasonal vegetables. The location pattern of these highly intensive activities in the use of production factors (land, labor, and capital) responds to their geographic proximity to large urban centers. From an economic point of view, the "green belt" fulfills the function of providing food for the city's population (Barsky, 2005).

4 According to a recent systematization (Feito & Barsky, 2020), the notion of *peri-urban* emerged in the mid-twentieth century in Western Europe, as part of a sequence of conceptual elaborations that sought to account for the growing urbanization processes deployed in rural areas. In 1915, Patrick Geddes mentioned the *conurbations* that, since the end of the 19th century, were generating the accelerated suburbanization or dispersion of English urban centers. In 1918, Charles Galpin introduced the term *rurbanity in* the face of the advance of industrialization to the detriment of the rural world, an issue that had already been raised by Frédéric Le Play during the nineteenth century (Galimberti & Cimadevila, 2016). In the 1920s and 1930s, the Chicago School of Human Ecology devoted itself to the sociological study of the processes of geographical expansion of cities in the United States, using terms of biological origin such as *succession, invasion, assimilation*. In 1934, Robert Redfield referred to the *folk-urban continuum* when he studied peasant societies that were increasingly urbanizing in Mexico (Barros, 1999). In 1937, Thomas Lynn Smith used the concept of *urban fringe* to describe the area located outside the administrative boundaries of urban municipalities, which was to be called *rural-urban fringe* by G. S. Wehrwein and L. A. Salter in 1940. In 1954, Edward Ullman used the concept of *amenity migrants* to characterize those who are the protagonists of city-countryside migratory movements in search of alternative life projects (Trimano, 2019), constituting the antecedent of the so-called *neo-rural migrants* (neo-ruralism), a notion widely used since the 1980s in Europe and whose beginnings were reported by Joan Nogué. In a similar sense, in 1955 Auguste C. Spectorsky defined as *exurbanites* those who moved their residence to the *exurbia* (beyond the *suburb*), *a* term widespread in the United States. From the 1960s onward, a large number of academic contributions appeared, especially in England and France. The concept of *peri-urban*, with a spatialist imprint, was used by French geographers such as Bernard Kayser (1960) and Jean Bernard Racine (1967) and took root decisively in the following decades in European and Latin American academic and governmental circles.

5 Continuing with the main conceptual contributions in this field (Feito & Barsky, 2020), it is worth noting that in 1966 Raymond Edward Pahl referred to the *urban-rural continuum* and, in the mid-1970s, Hugh D. Clout to the *urbanization of the countryside* or *diffuse urbanization* (later conceptualized by Giuseppe Dematteis as *dispersed city* or *diffuse city*). In 1974, Harold Carter incorporated the *urban-rural interface zone* into his studies on American cities. In 1976, Gérard Bauer and Jean-Michel Roux referred to *rurbanization* or *rurubano* to refer to new residential phenomena in the areas surrounding the oldest French cities, also characterized as *ville éparpillée*. In the same year, Brian Berry developed the concept of *counter-urbanization* (taken up again in the mid and late 1980s by Paul Cloke and Anthony Gerard Champion) to refer to the new arrival of the wealthy classes on the outskirts of the city. In recent decades, the concept of *city-region* (the idea that the city commands or dominates a regional environment that includes or subordinates rural areas), attributed to John Friedmann in the early 1980s (Boissier Etcheverry, 2006), has been strongly imposed in urban planning, although some works place its origin in the contributions of Robert Dickinson in 1947 (Davoudi, 2010). Likewise, from the field of environmental studies, certain concepts from ecology focus on rural–urban relations. In the mid-1980s, Eugene Odum and Ramón Margaleff stated that a city can only be considered a complete ecosystem if the input and output environments are fully included in it. Since the mid-1990s, Jorge Morello has focused on the study of *neo-ecosystems* and *agrosystems* in the *urban-rural frontiers*.

6 "The direction and coordination of this program is the responsibility of the National Urban Agriculture Group, made up of seven ministries and 17 scientific and/or development

institutions, with the participation of 14 provincial groups and 169 municipal groups. The program is structured into 12 crop sub-programs, 17 livestock sub-programs and 9 support sub-programs related to technical production issues" (FAO, 2004, p. 25).

7 "During the crisis of the 1990s and the collapse of the socialist camp, in addition to the historical situation of the economic blockade, food production in the cities contributed significantly to alleviate shortages and shortages. In approximately 15 years of development of urban agriculture, it has become a generalized practice in the main Cuban cities" (Ávila Sánchez, 2005, p. 39).

8 "There is a shift from a centralized and technocratic vision to a recognition of planning as a technical-political process in which a permanent negotiation is established between states and municipalities to agree on common lines of action in relation to territorial and urban development issues. This consensus process is still under development. . . .The Ministry of Cities consolidates this change through a new legal and administrative scaffolding focused on the fulfillment of human rights that prevents practices of forced evictions of informal populations and, instead, allocates resources and priorities to those agencies that promote the settlement and rooting of the population, granting property titles and various forms of land tenure security" (Ministry of Federal Planning, Public Investment and Services, 2015, p. 62).

9 According to the Ministry of Social Development of Brazil, "UPA (Urban and Periurban Agriculture) is a multidimensional concept that includes the production, transformation, commercialization and provision of services, in a safe way, to generate agricultural products (vegetables, fruits, medicinal plants, ornamental plants, cultivated or derived from agro-extractivism, etc.) and livestock (small animals) for self-consumption or commercialization, (re)using, in an efficient and sustainable way, the resources and livestock (small animals), for self-consumption or commercialization, (re)using, in an efficient and sustainable way, the resources and insecticides (pesticides, herbicides and herbicides), for self-consumption or commercialization.) and livestock (small animals) destined for self-consumption or commercialization, (re)utilizing, in an efficient and sustainable way, local resources and inputs (soil, water, waste, labor, knowledge, etc.). These activities can be practiced in intra-urban, urban, or peri-urban spaces, being linked to urban dynamics or metropolitan regions and articulated with the territorial and environmental management of the cities" (Ministério Do Desenvolvimiento Social E Combate A Fome, 2007, p. 6).

10 For a recent balance of the situation of peri-urban agriculture in Mexico and other Latin American countries, see Ávila Sánchez (2015, 2018), respectively.

11 Law 388 of 1997 of Colombia includes among the principles of land use planning 'the social and ecological function of property', 'the prevalence of the general interest over the particular', 'the distribution of the burdens and benefits of urban development' (art. 2 of Law 388/97 and art. 9 of the draft law). With regard to the social and ecological function of property, the formula used by the Political Constitution of Colombia establishes that 'Property is a social function that implies obligations. As such, it has an inherent ecological function' (Article 58). Regarding land categories, it establishes the following classification: urban land, urban expansion land and rural land (Articles 30 to 35) (Maldonado, 2010).

12 The brigadista mission work system began in 2003 and was inspired by the Cuban model.

13 In recent years, the SAG has issued provisions to address the rustic land subdivisions occurring on the outskirts of several cities, causing a change of use (from agricultural to housing purposes). Ministerial Ordinary No. 637/2022, endorsed by Circular No. 471/22.

14 In 1996, the Resource Center for Urban Agriculture and Reforestation (RUAF), a center sponsored by the International Support Group on Urban Agriculture funded by the Netherlands and Canada, was created within the framework of the Strategic Initiative for Urban and Peri-Urban Agriculture (CGIAR-SIUPA). This organization has become one of the world's leading references on the subject.

15 On experiences in peri-urban agriculture in Guyana, Paraguay, Uruguay, and Central American or Caribbean countries, see FAO documents (2012 and 2013).

16 In 2011 and 2012, the Ministry of Agriculture presented the Strategic Food and Agroindustrial Plans (PEA) 1 and 2 and the Bases for the Management of the Argentine Rural Territory, focusing mainly on production projections and the area planted with extensive agriculture for the coming years.

17 Citing Kevin Morgan and Roberta Sonnino, specialist Margaret Pasquini states that "given urbanization trends, the evident vulnerability of urban areas to price fluctuations and persistent diet-related public health problems, it is not surprising that cities are emerging as significant actors in the transformation of agri-food systems through initiatives to re-engineer their supply systems. For Johannes Wiskerke, these urban food strategies are part of a new model of food governance associated with the emergence of a new integrated and territorial agro-food geography that seeks to "re-anchor" production systems in the territory by basing them on the socio-cultural and environmental qualities and characteristics of a region, "re-connect" actors in a regional food network and "intertwine" food production with other rural activities such as conservation, landscape management, agro-tourism, education, etc." (CIDER, 2012).

Bibliography

Aguilar, Marta. (2011). *De los planes de embellecimiento a los lineamientos estratégicos metropolitanos: ¿qué hay de nuevo?* Buenos Aires: Instituto del Conurbano, Universidad Nacional de General Sarmiento, 2 de junio.

Angel, Shlomo; Sheppard, Stephen; Civco, Daniel; Buckley, Robert; Chabaeva, Anna; Gitlin, Lucy; Kraley, Alison; Parent, Jason; & Perlin, Micah. (2005). *The Dynamics of Global Urban Expansion*. Transport and Urban Development Department. World Bank. http://documents.worldbank.org/curated/en/138671468161635731/The-dynamics-of-global-urban-expansion

Angel, Shlomo; Parent, Jason; Civco, Daniel; & Blei, Alejandro. (2011). *Making Room for a Planet of Cities*. Cambridge: Lincoln Land Institute. https://www.lincolninst.edu/publications/policy-focus-reports/making-room-planet-cities/

Arellano Ramos, Blanca. (2011). *El urban sprawl: Un modelo de urbanización insostenible*. Tesis doctoral. Barcelona: Universidad Politécnica de Cataluña. http://www-cpsv.upc.es/tesis/PT11_arellano.pdf>

Ávila Sánchez, Héctor. (2018). "Agricultura urbana y periurbana: Reconfiguraciones territoriales y potencialidades en torno a los sistemas alimentarios urbanos." *Investigaciones geográficas*, N° 98, abril. http://dx.doi.org/10.14350/rig.59785. https://www.scielo.org.mx/pdf/igeo/n98/2448-7279-igeo-98-9.pdf

Ávila Sánchez, Héctor (comp.) (2005). *Lo urbano-rural: ¿Nuevas expresiones territoriales?* Cuernavaca: CRIM-UNAM. http://biblioteca.clacso.edu.ar/subida/Mexico/crim-unam/20100503120801/Lo_urbano_rural. pdf

Ávila Sánchez, Héctor (Coord.). (2015). *La ciudad en el campo. Expresiones regionales en México*. Cuernavaca: CRIM-UNAM.

Azevedo Da Silva, Clecio. (2009). "La configuración de los circuitos de proximidad en el sistema alimentario. Tendencias evolutivas." *Documents d'Anàlisi Geogràfica*, 1(54), 11–32. http://www.raco.cat/index.php/DocumentsAnalisi/article/download/139967/191146

Barros, Claudia. (1999). "De rural a rururbano: Transformaciones territoriales y construcción de lugares al sudoeste del Área Metropolitana de Buenos Aires." *Scripta Nova*, 51(45). https://bit.ly/2ZdvYgS

Barsky, Andrés. (2005). El periurbano productivo, un espacio en constante transformación. Introducción al estado del debate, con referencias al caso de Buenos Aires. *Scripta Nova*, 194(36). http://www.ub.edu/geocrit/sn/sn-194-36.htm

Barsky, Andrés. (2010). La agricultura de "cercanías" a la ciudad y los ciclos del territorio periurbano. Reflexiones sobre el caso de la Región Metropolitana de Buenos Aires." En: Svetlitza De Nemirovsky, Ada (Coord.), *Agricultura periurbana en Argentina y globalización. Escenarios, recorridos y problemas*. Buenos Aires: Facultad Latinoamericana de Ciencias Sociales, 15–30. http://www.flacso.org.ar/uploaded_files/Noticias/agriculturaperiurbana.pdf

Barsky, Andrés. (2013). *Gestionando la diversidad del territorio periurbano desde la complejidad de las instituciones estatales. Implementación de políticas públicas para el sostenimiento de la agricultura en los bordes de la Región Metropolitana de Buenos Aires (2000–2013)*. Tesis Doctoral. Barcelona: Universidad Autónoma de Barcelona. http://www.tdx.cat/handle/10803/129121

Barsky, Andrés. (2018). "La gestión del Estado en los bordes de la ciudad Análisis de las políticas públicas para el sostenimiento de las producciones agrícolas periurbanas en la Región Metropolitana de Buenos Aires (2000–2017)." En: Daniela Soldano, Alicia Novick, Cristina Cravino y Andrés Barsky (compiladores). *Pobreza urbana, vivienda y segregación residencial en América Latina*. Buenos Aires: Editorial Universidad Nacional de General Sarmiento.

Barsky, Andrés. (2020). "La necesidad de protección de las pequeñas producciones agrícolas alrededor de las ciudades. Una aproximación al estado del debate en América Latina." En: González Maraschio, Fernanda y Villarreal Federico (Coords.), *La agricultura familiar entre lo rural y lo urbano*. Luján: Editorial de la Universidad Nacional de Luján.

Barsky, Andrés. (2022a). "La producción alimentaria en los bordes de la ciudad y la gravitación política de una agenda territorial periurbana. El AMBA como caso de referencia." En: Tania Porcaro, Esteban Salizzi, Juan Luis Martirén y Sol Lanteri (Compiladores), *Fronteras: Aportes para la consolidación de un campo de estudios*. Teseo, Buenos Aires: Grupo de Estudios sobre Fronteras y Regiones (GEFRE), Instituto de Geografía, Universidad de Buenos Aires. https://www.teseopress.com/fronterasaportesparalaconsolidaciondeuncampodeestudios/chapter/la-produccion-alimentaria-en-los-bordes-de-la-ciudad-y-la/

Barsky, Andrés. (2022b). "Periurbano y abastecimiento metropolitano. Pensar en la gobernanza alimentaria y sus actores intervinientes." En: *Gobernar espacios metropolitanos. Un análisis federal sobre los continuos urbanos en Argentina*. Buenos Aires: Instituto de Capacitación Parlamentaria. Secretaría Parlamentaria, HCN, Editorial Teseo. https://www.teseopress.com/gobernarespaciosmetropolitanos/chapter/pensar-en-la-gobernanza-alimentaria-y-sus-actores/

Blanco, Jorge. (2013). "Sistema urbano y dinámica de urbanización en Argentina: tendencias y perspectivas en el marco del Plan Estratégico Territorial." En: *IX Jornada de Extensión en Geografía de la Universidad Nacional de Luján*. San Miguel: Centro Regional San Miguel, Universidad Nacional de Luján, 12 de agosto: 13–15.

Boissier Etcheverry, Sergio. (2006). Algunas reflexiones para aproximarse al concepto de ciudad–región. *Estudios Sociales*, 14(28) México jul./dic. https://bit.ly/3eU1OpL

Briano, Luis y Fritzsche, Federico (2007). "Transformaciones industriales en el borde metropolitano de Buenos Aires. Pilar como distrito representativo." *Scripta Nova*, 245(45). http://www.ub.edu/geocrit/sn/sn-24545.htm>

CIARA. (2013). *Proyecto de Desarrollo y Consolidación de la Agricultura Urbana y Periurbana*. Caracas: Fundación de Innovación y Capacitación para la Revolución Agraria. www.ciara.gob.ve

CIDER. (2012). *Sistemas alimentarios urbanos y desarrollo regional*. Margaret Pasquini. Bogotá: Centro de Estudios Interdisciplinarios sobre Desarrollo, Universidad de Los Andes.

Davoudi, Simin. (2010). "Defining the city-region." En: R. Kitchin y N. Thrift (Eds.), *International Encyclopedia of Human Geography*. Oxford, Inglaterra: Elsevier.

De Marco, Celeste. (2020). "Los extramuros productivos. Un balance en el estudio de espacios periurbanos en Argentina." En: Graciela Mateo y Juan Cerdá (Compiladores), *La ruralidad en tensión*. Buenos Aires: Teseo. https://www.teseopress.com/ruralidad/chapter/los-extramuros-productivos-un-balance-en-el-estudio-de-espacios-periurbanos-en-argentina/

European Commission. (2006). *Urban sprawl in Europe: The ignored challenge*. Copenhague: European Environment Agency. http://www.eea.europa.eu/publications/eea_report_2006_10

FAO. (2002). "Seguridad alimentaria urbana." En: *Enfoques, Departamento de Agricultura y Protección del Consumidor*. Roma: Organización de las Naciones Unidas para la Agricultura y la Alimentación. http://www.fao.org/ag/esp/revista/0206sp2.htm

FAO. (2004). *Experiencias en agricultura urbana y periurbana en América Latina y el Caribe. Necesidades de políticas e involucramiento institucional*. Reynaldo Trevinio (consultor). Santiago de Chile: Oficina Regional para América Latina y El Caribe. http://www.umoar.edu.sv/biblio/agricultura/agricultura% agricultura%20urbanaFAO.pdf

FAO. (2012). *XXXII Conferencia Regional de la FAO para América Latina y el Caribe*. Roma: Organización de las Naciones Unidas para la Agricultura y la Alimentación. http://www.rlc.fao.org/es/agenda/xxxii-conferencia-regional/

FAO. (2013). "Memorias del Seminario Internacional de Agricultura Urbana y Periurbana." La Habana, 14 al 17 de mayo de 2012. Roma: Organización de las Naciones Unidas para la Agricultura y la Alimentación. http://www.fao.org/alc/file/media/pubs/2013/aupCuba.pdf

FAO, IFAD, UNICEF, WFP y WHO. (2023). *The State of Food Security and Nutrition in the World 2023. Urbanization, agrifood systems transformation and healthy diets across the rural–urban continuum*. Roma: FAO. https://doi.org/10.4060/cc3017en

Feito, Carolina y Barsky, Andrés. (2020). "Concepto de periurbano (entrada). En co-autoría con Carolina Feito." En: Alejandra Salomón y José Muzlera (Eds.), *Diccionario del agro iberoamericano* (segunda versión). Buenos Aires: Editorial Teseo.

Fernándes, Edésio. (2003). "Del Código Civil al Estatuto de la Ciudad: Algunas notas sobre la trayectoria del Derecho Urbanístico en Brasil." *EURE*, 29(87), 63–76. http://www.scielo.cl/scielo.php?pid=S0250-71612003008700005& script=sci_arttext

Fernández Maraschio, María Fernanda. (2012). "Identidades y conflictos en territorios de frontera rural-urbana." *Eutopía*, 3. Quito: FLACSO-CEDET, noviembre.

Galimberti, S., y Cimadevila, G. (2016). "La máquina de ilusionar. Rurbanidad, intervención sociotécnica y condiciones de vulnerabilidad." *Redes*, 22(43). Quilmes, Argentina: Universidad Nacional de Quilmes. https://bit.ly/2VohUzR

Gutman, Pablo, Gutman, Graciela y Dascal, Guillermo. (1987). *El campo en la ciudad. La producción agrícola en el Gran Buenos Aires*. Buenos Aires: Centro de Estudios Urbanos y Regionales (CEUR), Informes de Investigación, Nº 6.

Kayser, Bernard. (1960). "Economie et mobilité de la population dans les villages péri-urbains de la Côte d'Azur." *Revue Économique*, 11(3), 380–394. http://www.persee.fr/web/revues/home/prescript/article/reco_0035-2764_1960_num_ 11_3_40 7414

Lanfranchi, Gabriel, Cordara, Christian, Duarte, Juan Ignacio, Giménez Hutton, Tobías, Rodríguez, Sol y Ferlicca, Francesca. (2019). *¿Cómo crecen las ciudades argentinas? Estudio de la expansión urbana de los 33 grandes aglomerados*. Ciudad Autónoma de Buenos Aires: CIPPEC. https://bit.ly/3ldvnpw

Libertun, Nora y Guerrero, Roberto. (2017). ¿Cuánto cuesta la densificación? La relación entre la densidad y el costo de proveer servicios urbanos básicos en Brasil, Chile, Ecuador y México. *EURE (Santiago)*, 43(130), 235–267. https://doi.org/10.4067/s0250-71612017000300235

Maldonado, Melinda Lis. (2010). "Hacia una Ley Nacional de Ordenamiento Territorial: Reflexiones a partir de tres propuestas normativas." *Café de las Ciudades*, 9(96). http://www.cafedelasciudades.com.ar/planes_96_1.htm

Milan Urban Policy Pact. (2015). "Milan urban food policy pact." *Milán, Agosto*. https://www.foodpolicymilano.org/wp-content/uploads/2015/10/Milan-Urban-Food-Policy-Pact-_SPA.pdf

MinisterioDe Planificación Federal, Inversión Pública Y Servicios. (2015). *Lineamientos para la planificación territorial de la República Argentina. Plan Estratégico Territorial (Avance III)*. Buenos Aires: Subsecretaría de Planificación Territorial de la Inversión Pública.

https://www.mininterior.gov.ar/planificacion/pdf/Lineamientos-planificacion-territorial-(2015).pdf

MinistérioDo Desenvolvimiento Social E Combate A Fome. (2007). *Seleção de Proponentes para apoio a projetos de Agricultura Urbana e Periurbana*. Brasilia: Secretaria Nacional de Segurança Alimentar e Nutricional. http://www.mds.gov.br/segurancaalimentar/editais/editais-anteriores/2007/arquivos/edit al-01.2007.pdf

Naciones Unidas. (2016). *Nueva agenda urbana. Hábitat III*. Conferencia de las Naciones Unidas sobre la Vivienda y el Desarrollo Urbano Sostenible. Quito: 17 al 20 de octubre. habitat3.org/wp-content/uploads/Brochure-Español-Web-final.pdf

Naranjo Ramírez, Gloria. (2007). "Expansión metropolitana en el periurbano de Santiago. Implicancias territoriales en la Provincia de Chacabuco." En: Carlos De Mattos e Rodrigo Hidalgo (Eds.), *Santiago de Chile: Reconfiguración metropolitana y movilidad espacial*. Santiago: Instituto de Estudios Urbanos y Territoriales e Instituto de Geografía, Pontificia Universidad Católica.

Olivera Lozano, Guillermo. (2005). "La reforma al artículo 27 constitucional y la incorporación de las tierras ejidales al mercado legal de suelo urbano en México." *Scripta Nova*, 194(33). http://www.ub.edu/geocrit/sn/sn-194-33.htm

Pacto De Política Urbana De Milán. (2015). *Milán, agosto*. https://www.foodpolicymilano.org/wp-content/uploads/2015/10/Milan-Urban-Food-Policy-Pact-_SPA.pdf

Planeta, Paz. (2006). *Bogotá: autonomía agroalimentaria. Diálogos y controversias*. Forero Álvarez Román y otros. Bogotá: Ediciones Antropos. http://planetapaz.org

Racine, Jean Bernard. (1967). "Exurbanisation et métamorphisme périurbain: introduction à l'étude de la croissance urbaine au sud du Saint-Laurent." *Revue de Géographie de Montreal*, 21(2), 313–342.

Relli Ugartamendía, Mariana. (2018). "Política de regularización del hábitat popular urbano: Provincia de Buenos Aires y partido de La Plata, 1983–2015" (Tesis Doctoral). Ensenada: Secretaría de Posgrado, Facultad de Humanidades y Ciencias de la Educación, Universidad Nacional de La Plata.

Rodríguez Muñoz, Bladimir. (2004). "Bogota sin hambre: Una oportunidad para reconocer el papel central de los campesinos en la construcción de Colombia." En: Varios autores. *Región, espacio y territorio en Colombia Conferencias en geografía*. Bogotá: Centro Editorial Facultad de Ciencias Humanas, Universidad Nacional de Colombia. http://www.bdigital.unal.edu.co/1534/10/09CAPI08.pdf

Roitman, Sonia. (2008). "Planificación urbana y actores sociales intervinientes: El desarrollo de urbanizaciones cerradas." *X Coloquio Internacional de Geocrítica*. Barcelona, 26–30 de mayo. http://www.ub.edu/geocrit/-xcol/78.htm

Subsecretaría De Urbanismo Y Vivienda De La Provincia De Buenos Aires. (2007). *Lineamientos estratégicos para la Región Metropolitana de Buenos Aires*. La Plata: Subsecretaría de Urbanismo y Vivienda, Dirección Provincial de Ordenamiento Urbano y Territorial. http://www.mosp.gba.gov.ar/sitios/urbanoter/ofmetro/mapasgeo.php

Trimano, Luciana. (2019). ¿Qué es la *neorruralidad*? Reflexiones sobre la construcción de un objeto multidimensional. *Territorios*, 49. Bogotá, Colombia: Universidad del Rosario. Recuperado el 18/04/2020 de https://bit.ly/2BMTGse

UNDESA. (2019). *World urbanization prospects: The 2018 revision*. United Nations Department of Economic and Social Affairs, Population Division.

United Nations. (2016). *Nueva agenda urbana. Hábitat III*. Conferencia de las Naciones Unidas sobre la Vivienda y el Desarrollo Urbano Sostenible. Quito: 17 al 20 de octubre. habitat3.org/wp-content/uploads/Brochure-Español-Web-final.pdf

Videiro Rosa, P. P. (2011). "Políticas públicas em agricultura urbana e periurbana no Brasil." *Revista Geográfica de América Central*, 2, 1–17.

SECTION II

Mobilities

5

ON THE WAY TO THE CITY

Food transportation in short marketing circuits in Mexico City

Ayari G. Pasquier Merino and Simone Buratti

Introduction

Food systems in Latin America have been profoundly transformed by the advanced rates of urbanization in the region, the incorporation of agribusiness-driven technological packages in the agricultural sector, the internationalization of commercial food transactions, and the growing control of food chains by supermarkets (Bisang & Gutman, 2005). These processes have generated significant challenges, such as food price volatility, the prevalence and accessibility of ultra-processed products in food environments, the marginalization of small producers, and precarious labor conditions along the supply chain, as well as various negative impacts on the environment. In contrast to these trends, social movements have emerged throughout the region that demand the right of peoples to decide about their food, promote agroecology as a reference for responsible production, and strive for a fairer distribution of the profits generated in commercial exchanges. These movements converge, in one way or another, with the growing importance given to the sustainability of food systems in the international cooperation and development agenda, as can be seen in the 2030 Agenda (UN, 2015).

In this context, local initiatives that seek to generate more socially and ecologically responsible food production, distribution, and consumption options have multiplied. The sale of agroecological products from peri-urban areas, distributed through short commercialization circuits (CCC, for its Spanish acronym Cadenas Cortas de Consumo), is possibly one of the most tangible strategies for food sustainability in contemporary cities. Their number has increased significantly in the last two decades, first in what is known as the Global North, and more recently also in Latin America (Levidow et al., 2023) and other regions of the world, gaining visibility for certain spheres of the urban population. Short circuits were the main food

DOI: 10.4324/9781003471929-9

distribution scheme until relatively recently, when the industrial transformation of food and the modernization of transportation and distribution logistics enabled the development of long chains, boosting the international market and the development of economies of scale (Reardon, 2015). In some regions, local trade remains important for the food security of populations living in precarious economic conditions.

In this text we are interested in those CCCs that have emerged in recent decades as an alternative to conventional food systems, where geographical proximity, low or no intermediation, and relational proximity (Marsden et al., 2000; Renting et al., 2003) are identified as factors of social responsibility and become relevant in the generation of product value. This phenomenon has developed in a context marked by growing uncertainty about the safety of food from agroindustrial production and the dissatisfaction of some social sectors with the supply of conventional food markets due to their lack of diversity, quality and/or traceability, and their environmental impacts. These initiatives usually share an interest in minimizing the environmental impacts of agroindustrial food systems, generating profits for small-scale producers, supplying healthy food to the urban population, and raising consumer awareness of the problems generated by conventional food systems. In some cases, these spaces evolve into platforms for activism, promoting participatory governance of urban food systems (Pasquier Merino et al., 2022). However, there is a great diversity among these strategies, making it difficult to generalize, being a phenomenon that combines elements of agroecological management, solidarity economy, and citizen activism, with dynamics of gentrification, gourmetization, and other exclusionary processes common in the cities of the Global South, which acquire greater or lesser importance depending on the case.

Literature developed around CCCs and other related concepts, such as short marketing chains and alternative food networks, has tended to emphasize their positive qualities, especially in terms of their social and environmental contributions (Paciarotti & Torregiani, 2021). However, a critical line of this phenomenon has also been developed, discussing the limits of the re-localization of food chains (DuPuis & Goodman, 2005) and the direct interaction between producers and consumers (Goodman, 2004), and documenting the exclusionary nature of many of these initiatives (Guthman, 2008; Mastronardi et al., 2015). The environmental efficiency of CCCs has also been questioned, showing contrasting results regarding the lower generation of greenhouse gasses associated with transportation due to the multiplication of private trips for distribution purposes (Paloviita, 2010; Kulak et al., 2015).

In this text, we are interested in the logistical aspects of CCCs and, in particular, in the transportation of goods—a topic that has received little attention in both the literature (Blanquart et al., 2015; Paciarotti & Torregiani, 2021) and the practical development of this type of strategy, which usually prioritizes agricultural management and the opening of marketing spaces. Transportation is one of the major contributors to the generation of greenhouse gasses, so one line of promotion of CCCs has been related to their utility as a mitigation strategy in the face of climate change. However, studies on life cycle analysis have shown that food transportation has a marginal contribution and CCCs may have the opposite of intended effects by not benefiting from the efficiency achieved by logistics developed in large-scale food distribution (Wakeland et al., 2012; Accorsi et al., 2022). Studies analyzing transportation in CCCs identify it as a crucial aspect in the development of this type of initiative (Nsamzinshuti et al., 2017; Ljungberg et al., 2013), especially in urban centers "characterized by space shortages, street congestion, lack of loading and unloading infrastructure, and delivery times and access rules, which limit the efficiency and quality of urban logistics operations" (Nsamzinshuti et al., 2017, p. 101).

With regard to CCC distribution strategies in urban areas, existing studies have distinguished three CCC primary schemes, with differentiated economic and environmental impacts: (i) direct distribution, in which producers use their own means to bring their products to consumers; (ii) collaborative distribution, in which a group of producers organizes to optimize distribution (Lacombe, 2013; Blanquart et al., 2015), a strategy with the potential to optimize distribution, but which depends on trust relationships and agreement generation capabilities; and iii) the inclusion of an external actor providing logistics service (Nsamzinshuti et al., 2018). The discussion of this last distribution scheme highlights the potential of the participation of non-profit associations that make infrastructure, logistical design, and execution capabilities available to the CCCs to solve packaging, bulking, transportation, and storage activities (Horst et al., 2011). This strategy has proven successful in some cases, however, it is suggested that it tends to have little stability and expertise, given that it depends on external funding and/or volunteer labor (LeBlanc et al., 2014; Jablonski et al., 2016; Klein & Michas, 2014). This scheme can also have a more entrepreneurial form that usually gains in efficiency; however, there is a risk that commercial control prevails over the social interests of the CCCs and affects producers' profits (Izumi et al., 2010; Bloom & Hinrichs, 2010). Some experiences of this type of strategy have introduced the use of electric vehicles in order to reduce their carbon footprint (Galati et al., 2021).

This text focuses on the logistics and conditions of transporting goods from peri-urban production areas to marketing spaces generated by CCCs in Mexico City (CDMX). It contributes to literature and visualizes areas of opportunity to consolidate the contributions of CCCs to the construction of fairer and more sustainable food systems (Blanquart et al., 2015; Nsamzinshuti et al., 2017). The research is qualitative and is based on 60 interviews with the heads of production and transformation projects in three municipalities located in the conservation land area of Mexico City (Milpa Alta, Tlalpan, and Xochimilco), a discussion workshop on transportation issues with producers and CCC facilitators, in-depth interviews with various CCC managers, and visits to production and distribution spaces in the city, carried out in the period 2020–2023. The productive projects included in the study were identified based on directories generated by government programs that seek to promote the transition to agroecology in what is known as the conservation land area of the CDMX and from visits to various CCCs operating in the city. All of the documented projects are small-scale initiatives of artisanal food production and/or transformation; however, there are some differences among them regarding the type of ecosystem in which they work (wetland or highland), access to irrigation, the time they have been operating, the type of products, and their distance from the city.

The text begins with an overview of the urban development of CDMX, the characteristics of peri-urban agriculture, and the development of CCC in recent years. In the second section, there is a discussion of the general conditions of mobility and transportation in the city and the strategies of goods transportation in CCC. The closing section contains final reflections on the question of transport and logistics for CCCs.

Urban growth, peri-urban agriculture, and CCC in Mexico City

Mexico City has been an important urban center since precolonial times, historically concentrating much of the region's political and economic power. In the 1930s it began to experience significant demographic growth as a result of the migratory flows of rural residents seeking opportunities for social mobility. This growth was accentuated after 1950. Initially, its territorial expansion was concentrated in the industrial center of the north and east of the city, surpassing the limits of the territorial demarcation of what was then known as the "Federal District"—today CDMX. The high rates of population growth and territorial expansion continued in the second half of the twentieth century, forming what is currently known as the "Metropolitan Zone of the Valley of Mexico," which includes the territory of the CDMX, 59 municipalities in the state of Mexico and one in the state of Hidalgo (see Figure 5.1). Currently, this metropolitan area has almost 22 million inhabitants, which corresponds to approximately 20% of the national population, despite occupying only 3% of the territory, being the second most populated urban area in Latin America (Sobrino, 2012).

The territorial expansion of the CDMX occurred within a context characterized by the absence of territorial planning, inadequate investment in infrastructure and services, and the irregular occupation of land. This is a common dynamic observed in other Latin American cities (Navarro & Moctezuma, 1989). This generated strong inequality in access to services and housing conditions (Garza, 2007), long daily commutes in precarious transportation for an important part of its population (Negrete & Paquette, 2011), and important environmental deterioration processes linked to soil sealing, overexploitation of aquifers, and atmospheric pollution (Capps et al., 2016). In the late 1970s, the city government identified the need to curb urban growth, which was beginning to expand southward, in order to maintain the ecosystem services provided by this area to the city, declaring 88,442 hectares as "conservation land," corresponding to 59% of the CDMX (PAOT, 2002). This area is located in the municipalities of Tlalpan, Milpa Alta, Tláhuac, and Xochimilco, and some fragments of the municipalities of Cuajimalpa de Morelos, Magdalena Contreras, Álvaro Obregón, Gustavo A. Madero, and Iztapalapa.

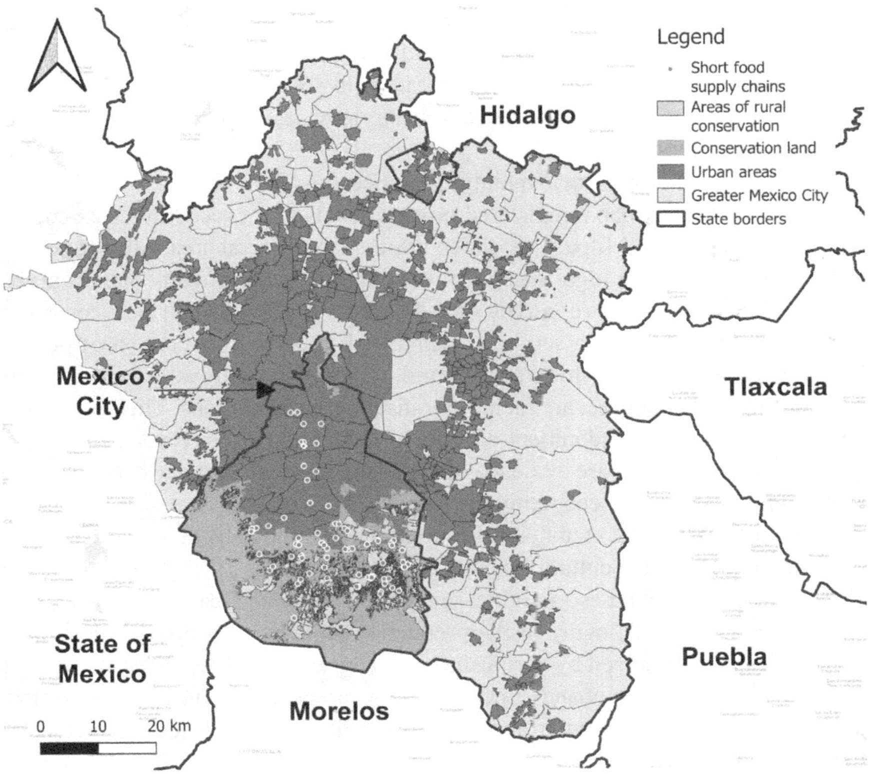

MAP 5.1 Metropolitan Zone of the Valley of Mexico

Source: Own elaboration with data from Agencia Digital de Innovación Pública del Gobierno de la Ciudad de México, 2023, and Centro de Investigación en Ciencias de Información Geoespacial CONAHCYT 2021.

It is important to note that the designation of this area as 'conservation land' (see Figure 5.1) was an institutional decision imposed by the government of the then Federal District on the ancestral territory of native peoples, who still maintain, to a certain extent, their organizational, cultural, and productive traditions. Notably, 70% of this land is classified as social property (PAOT, 2002), meaning that ejidatarios (members of agrarian communities with collective land tenure) or comuneros (holders of communal land rights), depending on the case, have use rights over collectively owned areas regulated by community assemblies. Thus, since its origin, the area included settlements and areas for agricultural use on hillsides and wetlands, which cover 22,800 hectares and correspond to one-third of the conservation land—mainly in the municipalities of Tlalpan, Milpa Alta, Tláhuac, and Xochimilco (SEDEMA, 2016).

This area is currently highly fragmented, resulting in a landscape composed of "patches" of ecosystems with varying degrees of conservation, including forests, meadows, rocky areas, pastures and wetlands, agricultural areas, villages where the families of the original settlers live, and "irregular settlements" where families have occupied land over the last few decades. In socioeconomic terms, this area has precarious conditions and scarce housing services, especially in the case of irregular settlements.

In 2020, the alcaldías that mainly comprise this area—Milpa Alta, Tláhuac, Tlalpan, and Xochimilco—registered poverty levels that exceed the Mexico City average, especially in Milpa Alta, which has the largest rural area. Among poverty indicators, not only do high rates of poverty and extreme poverty stand out, but also the lack of essential resources such as access to food, health services, social security, and basic housing services (CONEVAL, 2020). This context of poverty is part of a scenario in which agricultural activities, traditionally central to the local economy and culture, are facing significant transformations. The reduction of cultivated land, the abandonment of plots of land, and the conversion of land for unregulated tourist uses are evidence of a profound change in the way of life of the inhabitants. Despite the economic pressure that drives many to seek livelihoods outside the agricultural sector, local production continues to be a pillar both for food supply and for the cultural identity of the community.

Despite the fact that these activities are carried out in an area formally cataloged as "conservation land", many of the production units have integrated the technological packages endorsed by agribusiness and agrarian policies in recent decades. This has resulted in the abandonment of native seeds and in an intensive utilization of inputs with strong environmental implications. Testimonies gathered in the framework of this research show that, since the 1990s, some producers critical of this trend began to work on the recovery of traditional forms of agriculture and the incorporation of other agroecological techniques, in alliance with actors linked to academia and civil society organizations. Until recently, however, this process was marginal and little known. Gradually, more social projects have emerged around agroecological production and eco-business initiatives interested in the trade of "organic" food, diversifying the profile of producers (Bertran Vilà et al., 2022) and making the issue more visible in academic and public policy forums. In recent years, the local government has introduced programs to promote the agroecological transition in the area, including a certification system—known as "Green Seal", the delivery of compost generated from the treatment of urban solid waste, and the organization of producers' fairs in cultural and recreational spaces in the city. It is worth noting that both social and institutional initiatives emphasize their ecological contributions and support for small producers, yet they often overlook the provision of healthy food. This is particularly striking in a city where 60.8% of households experience some degree of food insecurity (ENSANUT, 2022), and 76% of adults are overweight or obese (ENSANUT, 2018).

The production units visited in this research project are aimed for sale at the market, with a minority of production destined for self-supply. In most cases, their organization is family-based, although they usually include some employees in production and distribution tasks. In all cases, the low economic profitability of agricultural activities forces families to supplement their income, either by having some members work in the city's tertiary sector or by relying on the financial and labor contributions of retired family members. Some producers have ventured into processing as a strategy to add value to their products, increase their market supply, and avoid shrinkage. In the most successful cases, this strategy has managed to generate employment for other members of the household or the locality; however, it represents a considerable workload that is not always profitable. Some projects have explored ecotourism or environmental education initiatives to supplement their income; those who have been able to better articulate these types of strategies comment that they periodically provide more income than the sale of agricultural products. There were also some cases with a business profile and operational organization, as well as initiatives led by civil society organizations that prioritize the demonstrative nature of their activities within the framework of broader environmental education projects.

In Mexico City, as in many other cities worldwide, the push for agroecology aligns with a growing interest among urban consumers in accessing organic food—free of potentially harmful inputs—while also supporting local economies. However, marketing remains one of the major challenges faced by producers. This has to do to a large extent with the fact that the reduced ecological footprint and social benefits of small-scale agroecological production are neither distinguished nor remunerated in conventional distribution channels. In response to this, several initiatives have emerged in the city that seek to make visible the contributions of agroecological projects in conservation land and promote fairer economic exchanges with urban consumers based on CCCs. These distribution initiatives are mainly located in the southern part of the city, in middle-class areas, and operate through different strategies, including specialized stores, producers' markets, cooperatives, consumer groups, and online purchasing systems promoted by social actors, and fairs and markets promoted by the local government. The products offered include vegetables, legumes, and some traditionally processed foods such as bread, corn products, dairy products, cold meats, and handmade cosmetics.

The research on which this chapter draws has documented that many of the city's CCCs depend, at least in part, on the voluntary or low-paid work of urban youth who participate in these spaces out of conviction, or as a form of activism, and who serve as "managers." In recent years the teams in charge of their management have accumulated significant operational experience; however, there is no professionalizing trajectory. It should also be noted that many of these initiatives operate outside tax, labor, and health regulations. They are not, however, usually identified as part of "informal commerce," associated for example with street food vendors, nor does this informality generally represent a problem in a context where the informal economy occupies 54.9% of the Gross Added Value (INEGI, 2023), although it can limit their participation in some sales spaces.

The promoters of the city's CCCs typically have an explicit intention to develop "alternative" distribution strategies, which are defined in opposition to "conventional" agrifood systems. These strategies are often characterized as unfair and unsustainable. Among producers, there is a greater diversity of perspectives on this matter. Some of them sell their products in local markets and various CCCs, as well as to intermediaries who market their products in supermarket chains, where organic products are already part of their regular offering. The recent recognition of the CCCs by the local government has created opportunities for their development, with initiatives such as organizing fairs or producers' markets in public spaces and cultural events. So far, no institutional strategies have been developed to integrate agroecological producers from conservation land into the city's conventional food distribution systems. These include more 'traditional' networks—centered around the central wholesale market, street fairs, and local markets—as well as supermarket chains operating across the city. Despite their increase, to date the contribution of the CCCs to the distribution of food in the city is marginal, in terms of the number of both consumers and food distributed and producers involved and the area of cultivation involved.

Logistics and freight forwarding at CCC

Mexico City has experienced a remarkable change in its demographics and urban structure in the last 80 years, marked by a decrease in the population of the central part and accelerated growth of peripheral areas, especially in the conurbation municipalities of the State of Mexico (Schteingart & Ibarra, 2016). This has had a significant impact on mobility and urban planning. Dependence on private cars has had a sharp increase, with an almost 13-fold increase in the number of vehicles per 100 inhabitants between 1959 and 2005 (Schteingart & Ibarra, 2016); microbuses and combis have become the main means of public transport (Schteingart & Ibarra, 2016), while the use of high capacity and low environmental impact modes of transport has decreased. This has led to an imbalance in the transportation system, favoring less sustainable and efficient options, as well as a considerable time investment in transportation with precarious conditions for a large part of the population. Despite multiple proposed plans, the city has not managed to significantly improve its public transport system or reduce dependence on private cars, posing ongoing challenges to urban mobility.

Urban mobility conditions in Mexico City have a significant impact on various economic activities, as the efficiency and accessibility of transportation directly influence the operation and profitability of businesses. In the context of CCCs, where proximity and speed are key factors, mobility limitations and possibilities become critical determinants. Traffic conditions, the availability of efficient means of transport, and distribution routes directly affect the logistics and distribution of products within these circuits. A local producer from Milpa Alta shares his direct experience in this regard, pointing to pragmatic adaptations in the absence of specialized transport systems for agricultural products:

> *In reality, there is no specialized system. If anything, for vegetables, what we do manage to do is to wet them and transport them wet. Fruit, no. We try to harvest in the mornings and afternoons, avoiding the hot hours for transportation.*
> *(Interview with a producer from Mexico City, 2021)*

The necessity for innovative approaches to logistics in order to offset the detrimental impact of urban mobility on the freshness and quality of agricultural products is indicative of the ingenious ways in which producers are adapting to urban conditions in order to maintain the viability of their operations. These conditions impact the profile of producers and consumers participating in the city's CCCs. Producers may be constrained or favored by their proximity to easily accessible areas, affecting their ability to participate in these circuits. The reality of these challenges is illustrated by multiple producers who, when asked about the main obstacles to commercialization, clearly identified them as *transportation* and access to desirable and viable points of sale.

On the consumers' side, mobility conditions affect their preferences and purchasing patterns; those with easy access to marketing points may opt more for local products, while those with mobility difficulties may rely more on traditional or large-scale purchasing options, including those that provide home delivery as many supermarkets do today. Traffic congestion, access conditions for producers, and the availability of efficient public transportation are relevant factors that should be taken into account when deciding where to establish markets or delivery points. However, few CCCs in the city have these characteristics, as their location obeys other types of parameters, mainly the opportunity to access spaces, already complex in itself in highly concentrated urban spaces, such as Mexico City.

Generally, producers engage in different marketing strategies, seeking to maximize their sales possibilities. However, few CCCs in the city meet these characteristics, as their location is primarily determined by the availability of space—already a complex issue in a highly dense urban environment like Mexico City. One producer shares:

> *In this case, the only thing we do at home is to put a wet blanket on the boxes or sometimes we soak them in water, the whole vegetable because it is only for the next day or the same day.*
> *(Interview with a producer from Mexico City, 2021)*

Fairness in price redistribution also presents a challenge. Although some producers have found a balance in local markets, as the same producer points out: *"Here we already have this little market, many customers from 3, 4 years ago . . . the price is fair for us"* (Interview with a producer from Mexico City, 2021).

However, exploring more lucrative markets could double their income. The barrier to expanding into these new markets is not only saturation but also the need for investment to establish their own premises, as one Xochimilco producer suggests: *"that is what we are looking at as a network, already having our own premises. . . . But, we need the investment to put a store in that area"* (Interview with producer in Mexico City, 2021).

Only sales to supermarkets are made through an intermediary who visits the production sites; the rest of the strategies only manage the sales spaces and ask the producers to deliver the products to a specific point and, in many cases, to stay for several hours to be directly in charge of the sale. In the tasks of liaising for CCC groups and sales, women often play a central role. Faced with logistical and economic challenges, such as the scarcity of opportunities and the high cost of transportation, collaborative strategies emerge as practical and effective solutions. This collective approach not only alleviates the financial burdens associated with product distribution but also fosters a network of mutual support among producers. By sharing resources and strategies, these women strengthen their presence and effectiveness within the CCCs, as one of them comments: *"That's what we do. To reduce transportation costs, we get together. We get to know other compañeritas, we also invite them or we see how we can get together"* (Interview with a producer from Mexico City, 2021).

The direct relationship between producers and consumers is often described as an added value of the CCCs, particularly in their scheme of producers' markets, being spaces for exchange and, ideally, for building reciprocal relationships. However, in many cases these exchanges are limited to commercial transactions and become time-consuming tasks for producers, adding to their already long working hours. However, there are experiences that challenge this dynamic, promoting a closer and more meaningful relationship between producers and consumers. A producer from Xochimilco shares his perspective on his connection with the market:

> *"In this case of the network, yes, they are pure people, we don't call them clients, we call them allies. We know that part because we consider them as allies because they know what they are eating and we know that it goes directly to the families."*
>
> *(Interview with producer in Mexico City, 2021)*

Mobility conditions in the city, access to means of transportation by producers, and access to points of sale are central factors in the viability of both productive projects and the CCCs themselves. Mobility conditions vary significantly between different areas of the city depending on the characteristics of the territory and the available transportation infrastructure. In the CDMX, production units located in wetland areas face particular logistical challenges. Although these areas offer advantages such as the possibility of natural irrigation and high productivity, allowing up to three planting cycles per year, the logistics of getting production out of these lands is complex. Before produce can be loaded onto a vehicle, it must be transported by canoe and wheelbarrow. This unique process is further complicated by limitations in conventional transportation. An interviewee from Xochimilco shares her personal experience in this regard:

> *When you have to move the product, how do you do it? By car. . . . That's another big issue, that I don't have transportation to walk. So it's public transportation. Cab. From here to Coyoacán, from here to Tlalpan it's 100 pesos one way, 100 pesos back. . . . Sometimes sales were not good.*
>
> *(Interview with a producer from Mexico City, 2021)*

The additional financial burden that transportation represents for producers, especially when they are forced to rely on means such as cabs to bring their products to market, can significantly erode their profit margins, especially on days of low sales. These conditions evidence the limits of the definition of proximity by distance, without considering the morphological and demographic characteristics of the territories (Paciarotti & Torregiani, 2021). Those who work on hillsides face fewer difficulties in transporting their production but require vehicles that can travel along roads that are not always in good condition, especially during the rainy season.

As previously stated, the agroecological production and artisanal transformation projects developed in the conservation land area of Mexico City exhibit a diversity of profiles, which translates into a differentiated capacity for investment and access to infrastructure (Bertran Vilà et al., 2022). Among the producers interviewed, 35 own a car (25 own a pickup truck and 10 own a standard car), three rent a pickup truck or car, two only sell by delivery and charge the client for courier services, one borrows a car from relatives, nine pay for a cab, four use a bicycle, five use public transportation (RTP or metro), carrying their merchandise in a backpack, two are transported on foot, and only one participates in collection routes of initiatives that distribute the products. Those who handle dairy and meat products use a cooler, but none have a refrigerated vehicle. Vegetables and fruits are usually covered with tarps and wet rags to preserve their freshness and protect them. It was also documented that many producers have difficulty in accounting for transportation costs and do not usually consider them as part of their production costs. In addition to the limited availability of vehicles, the study identified several other issues related to transportation. These included the time required for loading and unloading, which was found to be excessive due to a lack of adequate space. Other studies on the subject document similar situations, highlighting the generation of negative environmental impacts and the high costs for producers due to the lack of attention to the issue (Moustier, 2017; Nsamzinshuti et al., 2017, 2018; Paciarotti & Torregiani, 2021).

Almost all the people interviewed in this regard identified access and transport conditions as an area of opportunity. Logistics emerges as a strategic area of cooperation in the CCCs, capable of addressing some of the limits identified by literature, such as high costs and the generation of market niches, the small variety of products, the difficulties in constantly supplying public institutions, high transportation costs, the lack of economies of scale, the difficulties to reach points of sale, and the saturation of the people involved (Paciarotti & Torregiani, 2021). In this regard, a producer interviewed in Tlalpan offers a practical perspective on diversification in means of transport adapted to the specific needs of fresh produce production:

> *In the case of fresh produce production, for example, what is the means of transportation of the products? Right now we use almost everything. If they are close by, we already have bikes. If it is very far away and we are not asked for much, there is a guy who delivers our products on a motorcycle. The biggest ones always go by car or van. We try to make it a car to save money. We took the back seat off, put it flat and then we put all these coolers on it. We bring the milk by truck. We transport it in milk drums. It arrives, we put it in here and the next day we work it.*
>
> *(Interview with a producer from Mexico City, 2021)*

This adaptability in logistics, from the use of bicycles for short distances to the modification of vehicles to maximize efficiency, illustrates how innovative transportation strategies can significantly contribute to overcoming logistical challenges while promoting sustainability and efficiency in the distribution of fresh produce. The challenges of transporting goods and the limited feasibility of direct sales in CCCs have led to the emergence of intermediaries who are not formally recognized as such. These individuals often produce some goods themselves while making agreements with neighboring producers to expand the variety of products at their stalls—using arrangements similar to what the literature describes as 'collaborative distribution'. This situation is known by many of the managers of the CCCs, but it is not usually openly discussed. The lack of visibility of this problem, and the consequent lack of options to support producers in the transportation of their goods, operates as a filter for the type of producers who participate in these spaces, a particularly relevant factor when considering the social precariousness of many of the producers of the conservation land and the low profitability of agricultural activities. The focus of the CCC on this issue could help to strengthen the governance of these initiatives. It could also help determine the distribution of benefits and ensure that producers continue to benefit from these schemes.

The results of this study show that the infrastructure for transporting goods and expertise in distribution logistics[1] are an essential node for the successful integration of small producers in the peri-urban area to the distribution spaces in the city, and a condition for enhancing the benefits obtained by producers and the expansion of access to fresh, healthy food from sustainable schemes to other consumer sectors in the city.

Final thoughts

Urbanization is one of the most important demographic phenomena of the last century and imposes major challenges for the present and the future (UN-Habitat, 2022). Food security and sustainability of food systems are formally recognized as priorities in the international development agenda (UN, 2015). Urban and peri-urban agriculture, small producers, and short marketing circuits are identified as key elements to strengthen food security in cities and the sustainability of food systems (FAO, 2021; MUFPP, 2023). And yet, the initiatives that work to articulate these elements remain as "alternative" spaces, relying largely on voluntary work and facing great daily management challenges, remaining on the margins of food distribution strategies in the city, and leaving out an important part of the producers and almost all consumers.

In the Latin American context, marked by strong socioeconomic inequality (Oxfam, 2015) and a strong presence of the triple burden of malnutrition (Gómez et al., 2013), CCCs face even greater challenges to consolidate, replicate, and/or scale and may eventually become more of a new link in urban food landscapes, segmented and exclusionary, restricted to a narrow group of consumers with socio-environmental claims, than drivers of the transformation of urban food systems.

The conditions of mobility and transportation of goods in the CCCs show some of the limits of these initiatives to promote fundamental transformations and consolidate their multiple environmental and social contributions, showing an important field of opportunity in the articulation of intermediation schemes to make the distribution of food produced in the conservation land area of Mexico City more efficient and inclusive. Literature shows that cooperation among actors makes it possible to build innovative and efficient logistics models, increasing the success of CCCs, sharing costs among the actors involved, and opening wider markets (Paciarotti & Torregiani, 2021). But participation has a cost for social actors that defines participation capacities and sometimes excludes the most vulnerable actors (Pasquier Merino, 2017).

The conservation land area of Mexico City is facing a process of strong socio-environmental deterioration and producers have to face day by day the pressure of urban growth, the lack of economic profitability, the difficulties of generational change, the conflict in the spaces of local territorial management, and growing insecurity. In this context, growing food and betting on agroecological transition becomes, for many of its actors, an act of resistance and a space for activism, with an uncertain future. Considering the importance of the environmental services of the conservation land area for Mexico City and the multiple challenges it faces, the articulation of distribution strategies for food produced in this area could benefit significantly from public policy that respect and complement the strategies proposed by civil society, following what De Schutter and Dedeurwaerdere (2022) characterize as "facilitating policies." Their absence compromises the agroecological transition in Mexico City's conservation land, limiting the number of producers that can benefit from these circuits and, therefore, the area planted with this type of management achieves a certain economic viability. This has an impact not only on the profile of producers who have access to these networks but also on the profile of consumers with access to food distributed from these circuits, losing an important potential to address the problems of food insecurity and nutritional health faced by a significant part of the city's population.

Note

1 The definition proposed in CSMP, 2013 is taken as a reference, where it is described as the "Process of planning, implementing and controlling procedures for the efficient and effective transportation and storage of goods, including services and related information, from the point of origin to the point of consumption, in order to meet customer requirements. This definition includes inbound, outbound, internal and external movements" (CSCMP, 2013: 117bi).

References

Accorsi, R., Cholette, S., Guidani, B., Manzini, R., Ronzoni, M. (2022). Sustainability assessment of transport operations in local Food Supply Chain networks. Transportation Research Procedia, 67, 1–11. https://doi.org/10.1016/j.trpro.2022.12.049

Bertran Vilà, M., Pasquier Merino A. G., Villatoro Hernández G. (2022). Food producers in the peri urban area of Mexico City: A study on the linkages between social capital and food sustainability. Sustainability, 14, 15960. https://doi.org/10.3390/su142315960

Bisang, R., Gutman, G. E. (2005). Acumulación y tramas agroalimentarias en América Latina. Revista de la CEPAL, 87, 115–129. https://doi.org/10.18356/e8691f11-es

Blanquart, C., Gonçalves, A., Raton, G., Vaillant, L. (2015). Vecteurs et freins d'une logistique plus durable dans les circuits courts: le cas du Nord – Pas-de-Calais. ASRLDF. Montpellier, France. Available in: https://hal.science/hal-01176784/document

Bloom J. D., Hinrichs C. C. (2010). Moving local food through conventional food system infrastructure: Value chain framework comparisons and insights. Renewable Agriculture and Food Systems, 26(1), 13–23. https://doi.org/10.1017/S1742170510000384

Capps, K. A., Bentsen, C. N., Ramírez, A. (2016). Poverty, urbanization, and environmental degradation: Urban streams in the developing world. Freshwater Science, 35(1), 429–435.

CONEVAL. (2020). Medición de la pobreza por entidades federativas y municipios 2020. Consejo Nacional de Evaluación de la Política de Desarrollo Social. Available in: https://www.coneval.org.mx/Medicion/Paginas/Pobreza-municipio-2010-2020.aspx

CSCMP – Council of Supply Chain Management Professionals. (2013). Supply chain management terms and glossary. Available in: https://cscmp.org/CSCMP/Educate/SCM_Definitions_and_Glossary_of_Terms.aspx

De Schutter, O., Dedeurwaerdere, T. (2022). Social innovation in the service of social and ecological transformation: The rise of the enabling state. Routledge Focus.

DuPuis, E. M., Goodman, D. (2005). Should we go "home" to eat?: Toward a reflexive politics of localism. Journal of Rural Studies, 21, 359–371. https://doi.org/10.1016/j.jrurstud.2005.05.011

ENSANUT. (2018). Encuesta Nacional de Salud y Nutrición. Instituto Nacional de Salud Pública. Consultada en https://www.inegi.org.mx/programas/ensanut/2018/

ENSANUT. (2022). Encuesta Nacional de Salud y Nutrición. Instituto Nacional de Salud Pública. Consultada en https://ensanut.insp.mx/encuestas/ensanutcontinua2022/descargas.php

FAO. (2021). FAO's strategic framework 2021. Food and Agriculture Organization of the United Nation. Rome. October 2021. Available in: https://www.fao.org/3/cb7099en/cb7099en.pdf

Galati, A., Giacomarra, M., Concialdi, P., Crescimanno, M. (2021). Exploring the feasibility of introducing electric freight vehicles in the short food supply chain: A multi-stakeholder approach. Case Studies on Transport Policy, 9, 950–957. http://dx.doi.org/10.1016/j.cstp.2021.04.015

Garza, G. (2007). La urbanización metropolitana en México: normatividad y características socioeconómicas. Papeles de Población, 13(52), 77–108. Available in: https://www.scielo.org.mx/scielo.php?script=sci_arttext&pid=S1405-74252007000200004

Gómez, M. I., Barrett, C. B., Raney, T., Pinstrup-Andersen, P., Meerman, J., Croppenstedt, A., Carisma, B., Thompson, B. (2013). Post-green revolution food systems and the triple burden of malnutrition. Food Policy, 42, 129–138. https://doi.org/10.1016/J.FOODPOL.2013.06.009

Goodman, D. (2004). Rural Europe redux? Reflections on alternative agro-food networks and paradigm change. Sociol Ruralis, 44(1), 3–16. https://doi.org/10.1111/j.1467-9523.2004.00258.x

Guthman, J. (2008). Bringing good food to others: investigating the subjects of alternative food practice. Cultural Geographies, 15, 431–447. Available in: https://journals.sagepub.com/doi/pdf/10.1177/1474474008094315

Horst, M., Ringstrom, E., Tyman, S., Ward, M. K., Werner, V., Born, B. (2011). Toward a more expansive understanding of food hubs. Journal of Agriculture, Food Systems, and Community Development, 2(1), 209–225. http://dx.doi.org/10.5304/jafscd.2011.021.017

INEGI. (2023). Mediciones de la Economía Informal Trimestral por Entidad Federativa. Segundo trimestre de 2023. Comunicado de prensa N. 746/23, 28/11/2023, Instituto Nacional de Estadística y Geografía. Available in: https://www.inegi.org.mx/contenidos/saladeprensa/boletines/2023/MEITEF/MEITEF2023_11.pdf

Izumi, B. T., Wright, D. W., Hamm, M. W. (2010). Farm to school programs: Exploring the role of regionally-based food distributors in alternative agrifood networks. Agriculture and Human Values, 27, 335–350.

Jablonski, B. B. R., Schmit, T. M., Kay, D. (2016). Assessing the economic impacts of food hubs on regional economies: A framework that includes opportunity cost. Agricultural and Resource Economics Review, 45(1), 43–172. http://dx.doi.org/10.1017/age.2016.9

Klein, K., Michas, A. (2014). The Farm Fresh Healthcare Project: Analysis of a hybrid values-based supply chain. Journal of Agriculture, Food Systems, and Community Development, 5(1), 57–74. http://dx.doi.org/10.5304/jafscd.2014.051.003

Kulak, M., Nemecek, T., Frossard, E., Chable, V., Gaillard, G. (2015). Life cycle assessment of bread from several alternative food networks in Europe. Journal of Clean Production, 90, 104–113. https://doi.org/10.1016/j.jclepro.2014.10.060

Lacombe, C. (2013). Organiser la collaboration logistique dans les circuits alimentaires de PROXIMITE: quelle place pour le réseau Cuma et la coopération agricole de production? Ecole Supérieure d'Agriculture d'Angers. Available in: http://www.cuma.fr/sites/default/files/rapport_camille_lacombe_final.pdf

LeBlanc, J., Conner, D., McRae, G., Darby, H. (2014). Building resilience in nonprofit food hubs. Journal of Agriculture, Food Systems, and Community Development, 4(3), 121–135. https://doi.org/10.5304/jafscd.2014.043.005

Levidow, L., Sansolo, D., Schiavinatto, M. (2023). Territorialising local food systems for an agroecologial transition in Latin America. Land, 12(8), 1577. https://doi.org/10.3390/land12081577

Ljungberg, D., Juriado, R., Gebresenbet, G. (2013). Conceptual model for improving local food supply chain logistics. Proceedings of the 13th world conference on transport research. Rio de Janeiro, Brazil. http://dx.doi.org/10.1080/14783360902924325

Marsden T., Banks J., Bristow G. (2000). Food supply chain approaches: Exploring their role in rural development. Sociologia Ruralis, 40(4), 424–438. https://doi.org/10.1111/1467-9523.00158

Mastronardi, L., Marino, D., Cavallo, A., Giannelli, A. (2015). Exploring the role of farmers in short food supply chains: The case of Italy. International Food and Agribusiness Management Review, 18(2), 109–130. Available in: https://www.ifama.org/resources/Documents/v18i2/Mastronardi-Marino-Cavallo-Giannelli.pdf

Moustier, P. (2017). Short urban food chains in developing countries: Signs of the past or of the future? Natures Sciences Sociétés, 25, 7–20. https://doi.org/10.1051/nss/2017018

MUFPP. (2023). Framework for action. Milan Urban Food Policy Pact. Available in: https://www.milanurbanfoodpolicypact.org/framework-for-action/

Navarro, B., Moctezuma, B. P. (1989). La urbanización popular en la ciudad de México. Universidad Nacional Autónoma de México, Instituto de Investigaciones Económicas, Editorial Nuestro Tiempo, S.A., México D.F.

Negrete, M. E., Paquette, C. (2011). La interacción entre transporte público y urbanización en la zona metropolitana de la Ciudad de México: un modelo expansivo que llega a sus límites. Territorios, 25, 15–33. Available in: https://revistas.urosario.edu.co/index.php/territorios/article/view/1872

Nsamzinshuti, A., Janjevic, M., Rigo, N., Ndiaye, A. B. (2017). Logistics collaboration solutions to improve short food supply chain solution performance. Proceedings of the World Conference on Supply Chain Management, 2(1), 57–69. http://dx.doi.org/10.17501/wcosm.2017.2106

Nsamzinshuti, A., Janjevic, M., Rigo, N., Ndiaye, A. B. (2018). Short supply chains as a viable alternative for the distribution of food in urban areas? Investigation of the performance of several distribution schemes, sustainable freight transport. In V. Zeimpekis, E. Aktas, M. Bourlakis, I. Minis (Eds.), Theory, Models, and Case Studies. Springer, pp. 99–119.

OXFAM. (2015). Privilegios que niegan derechos. Desigualdad extrema y secuestro d ela democracia en América Latina y el Caribe. Available in: https://www-cdn.oxfam.org/s3fs-public/file_attachments/reporte_iguales-oxfambr.pdf

Paciarotti, C., Torregiani, F. (2021). The logistics of the short food supply chain: A literature review. Sustainable Production and Consumption, 26, 428–442. https://doi.org/10.1016/j.spc.2020.10.002

Paloviita, A. (2010). Consumers' sustainability perceptions of the supply chain of locally produced food. Sustainability, 2(6), 1492–1509. https://doi.org/10.3390/su2061492

PAOT. (2002). Regulación del suelo de conservación del Distrito Federal y acciones para sancionar obras o actividades ilícitas. Procuraduría Ambiental y del Ordenamiento Territorial del D.F. Available in: http://centro.paot.org.mx/documentos/paot/informes/informe2003_borrame/2002/informe/anexos/cap4/conservacion.pdf

Pasquier Merino, A. G. (2017). Connotaciones y paradojas en torno a la participación de los actores locales en iniciativas de desarrollo rural. LiminaR, 15(1), 112–127. https://doi.org/10.2536/liminar.v15i1.498

Pasquier Merino, A. G., Torres Salcido, G., Monachon D. S., Villatoro Hernández, J. G. (2022). Alternative food networks, social capital, and public policy in Mexico City. Sustainability, 14(23). https://doi.org/10.3390/su142316278

Reardon T. (2015). The hidden middle: the quiet revolution in the midstream of agrifood value chains in developing countries, Oxford Review of Economic Policy, 31(1), 45–63. http://dx.doi.org/10.1093/oxrep/grv011

Renting H., Marsden T. K., Banks J. (2003). Understanding alternative food networks: Exploring the role of short food supply chains in rural development. Environment and Planning, 35, 393–411. http://dx.doi.org/10.1068/a3510

Schteingart, M., Ibarra, V. (2016). Desarrollo urbano-ambiental y movilidad en la Ciudad de México. Evaluación histórica, cambios recientes y políticas públicas. El Colegio de México.

SEDEMA. (2016). Suelo de Conservación. Secretaría del Medio Ambiente. México. Available in: https://www.sedema.cdmx.gob.mx/storage/app/media/Libro_Suelo_de_Conservacion.pdf

Sobrino, J. (2012). La urbanización en el México contemporáneo. Notas de Población, 94, 93–122. CEPAL. Available in: https://www.cepal.org/sites/default/files/events/files/jaime_sobrino.pdf

UN. (2015). Transforming our world: The 2030 Agenda for Sustainable Development, Resolution adopted by the General Assembly on 25 September 2015, A/RES/70/1, United Nations.

UN-Habitat. (2022). World Cities Report 2022. Envisaging the future of cities. United Nations Human Settlements Programme. Available in: https://unhabitat.org/sites/default/files/2022/06/wcr_2022.pdf

Wakeland, W., Cholette, S., Venkat, K. (2012). Food transportation issues and reducing carbon footprint. In J. I. Boye, Y. Arcand (Eds.), Green Technologies in Food Production and Processing. Food Engineering Series. Springer.

6

MOBILE INFRASTRUCTURES

The appification of the urban food delivery

Dhan Zunino Singh and Erick Alejandro Ferrer Sánchez

Introduction

Urban food delivery services through digital platforms are an example of the emergence of new patterns of trade and consumption that have gained increasing economic and social importance worldwide in recent years. Almost one-third of the global population order food through the Internet, and the frequent customers (those who order one or more times per week) are increasing (Kantar, 2022). Due to this demand, total market[1] revenues have increased significantly from US$171.06 billion in 2019 to US$394.4 billion in 2023 (Statista, 2023). It is estimated that approximately 1.9 billion people order food online through digital platforms or apps (DoorDash, Uber Eats, Grubhub, and so on), and this number is expected to reach around 2.5 billion users by 2028 (Statista, 2024b).

Latin America follows these trends. In Brazil, for example, people order food delivery once every two weeks, while in Mexico the average is once every three to four weeks and in Argentina four out of ten app users ask for food once a week. Additionally, in the region, the category of customers consuming food through delivery apps at least once a week grew by 66% from 2020 to 2022 (Kantar, 2022). In 2022, the earnings generated by online food delivery services reached a value of US$6.13 billion (a 63% increase compared to earnings generated in 2019) (Statista, 2024a). Latin American entrepreneurs have created their own apps (PedidosYa or Rappi) becoming leaders in the region, and the image of thousands of young people, from lower classes or migrants, pedaling to carry food is now an entirely everyday part of the Latin American cityscapes.

Urban food delivery is not new, of course, but what is novel is its appification. Appification, or the related concepts of platform capitalism and "platform urbanism," highlight how e-commerce or digital platforms are changing or reshaping

DOI: 10.4324/9781003471929-10

socio-spatial practices and the urban environment. In dialogue with emerging studies that point to the rising importance of different digital platforms in mediating access to urban services and spaces in Latin America, this chapter turns its attention to understanding how food delivery platforms in particular establish particular relationships between digital spaces, urban spaces, and the actors and objects in motion in both of these. Given the nascent state of the field of research, the chapter primarily aims to synthesize and analyze existing studies on the appification of food delivery in Latin American cities. Drawing on this literature as well as secondary sources (statistics, reports, and press), it also offers a mobile and infrastructural perspective to conceptualize urban food delivery. The embodied practice of delivery as well as the materiality of food, in this digital regime, implies the emergence of what we will call a *mobile urban infrastructure* that mediates, like other food infrastructures, the reproduction of urban space. To consider food delivery applications as a mobile urban infrastructure allows us to highlight the vital importance of food for urban life, attention to how food circulates, and the materiality of e-commerce. We conclude with a discussion on why this is important in thinking about food provisioning and consumption in Latin America more broadly.

The urban space in platform capitalism

Following the international financial crisis of 2008–2009, various platform companies for mobility, accommodation, delivery, and messaging which emerged primarily in San Francisco have begun to operate in most major cities worldwide. These companies have driven the expansion of "platform capitalism" (Srnicek, 2021), characterized by the intensive use of information technology, data, and the Internet in innovating forms of production and exchange of goods and services, labor flexibilization, and deregulation. They have also led to the emergence of digital platforms as companies that can be understood as "sociotechnical intermediaries and commercial arrangements aimed at automating market exchanges and mediating social action" (Sadowski, 2020, p. 449).

Platform capitalism is often portrayed as neutral, as a collaborative or sharing economy, in which digital platforms merely act as intermediaries between individuals (customers and suppliers) exchanging goods and services. However, this supposed neutrality conceals the management and exploitation functions that these companies perform on space, objects, and people (Martínez Sordoni, 2020, p. 13). Platform capitalism represents a new way of organizing social relations of production, emphasizing "the technological mediations of the relationship between companies, workers, and consumers, as well as the emergence of new forms of corporate power and surveillance" (Radetich, 2022, p. 11). In line with the ideas of Lefebvre (2013), who highlighted that social space is both a means of production and domination and a social product, platform capitalism thus implies a new form of production of space.

The concept of "platform urbanism" (Sadowski, 2020; Rossi, 2022) emphasizes that digital platforms are inherently linked to urban space, enabling them to produce an appropriate value (money/data) while also shaping urban space (physical/digital), affecting the social, economic, and political dynamics of urban life. Digital platforms require technological infrastructure as well as physical space to operate, benefiting from population density, spatial proximity of businesses and consumers, market diversity and size, urban residents' education levels and incomes, worker availability, and the use of publicly funded urban infrastructure, all the while evading taxes and many local regulations. They also influence the production of physical space, for instance, housing rental platforms contribute to the gentrification and touristification of certain urban areas (Brossat, 2019), while delivery service platforms contribute to increased traffic congestion and pollution levels and exacerbate inequality in resource distribution among different social groups (Artioli, 2018). Platform-mediated exchanges facilitate the digital representation of the city through mediating experiences between people and places, through discursive constructions and images, these digital representations of urban life, in turn, influence users' decisions in the urban environment. Already with the impact of telematics on urban space, Amin and Thrift noticed that the former did not signify the end of "older forms of technological and human communication, or the dematerialization of the city into a space of bit and flows but," following Mike Crang, they "produce a new form of space-time" a "real-time cityspace" that allows a "distanced economy" (2010, pp. 66–67).

One way in which urban space is being transformed by platforms is the reshaping of urban freight transport services. E-commerce, the buying and selling of products or services over the Internet, has become an indispensable form of global retail trade, especially with the proliferation of smartphones and more recently due to the experience of the COVID-19 pandemic. The increased online orders entail a higher demand for "instant delivery" services, known as last-mile delivery (Mohammad et al., 2023), a growing market that has been exploited and modified by the management of orders and deliveries through digital platforms, which, as intermediaries, connect businesses and consumers with a third party responsible for the delivery service.

Thus, new digital goods delivery platforms have emerged, which according to Dablanc et al. (2017, p. 2), can be defined as: "Instant delivery services that provide on-demand delivery within two hours—by private individuals, independent contractors, or employees—by connecting consignors, couriers, and consignees via a digital platform." In this definition, the authors emphasize the short time span between order and delivery, as well as access to data through smartphones. Finally, the use of the adjective "instant" refers to the urban consumer's need for instant gratification. This definition is relevant for developing a proposal for delivery platforms from a mobility perspective, as will be discussed later.

Immediate delivery services operate in many urban logistics chains, but food delivery services are the most popular. These are not a new phenomenon in platform urbanization, but prior to the Internet becoming a mediator between businesses and consumers, the available food offerings were limited to local businesses, which handled this service themselves. The most iconic example is pizza restaurants. With the emergence of instant delivery services via the Internet, consumers have gained access to a wider range of food offerings, including high-quality restaurants and products. Delivery and personal shopper for supermarkets as well as the emergence of 'black kitchen' or stores where the apps have their own stock of products are also part of these new spaces and practices that are reshaping cities.

Food delivery in Latin America

The origins of online food delivery service platforms in Latin America can be traced between 2009 and 2015 with the creation of the Uruguayan company *PedidosYa*, which was acquired by the German company Delivery Hero in 2014, and the creation of *Rappi* in Colombia in 2015. However, it was not until recent years that online food delivery platforms began to acquire a significant and widespread presence in the region. Companies like iFood, Rappi, Uber Eats, and Glovo began operating in Brazil in the mid-2010s. In Mexico, PedidosYa appeared in 2014, followed by Uber Eats and PostMates in 2016; and by 2022, there were around 13 applications operating in this territory with about 50,000 workers, with Uber Eats and Rappi being the largest in terms of the number of delivery drivers in their fleets. In Colombia, the context of labor informality (a widespread situation in the region) and Venezuelan migration has allowed Rappi to become the main food delivery platform since its creation in 2015, although other platforms have also been favored in this country, incorporating around 25,000 delivery drivers. Glovo and Rappi appeared in Peru in 2017 and 2018, respectively, while in Ecuador, they appeared in 2018 and 2019. In Argentina, Rappi, Glovo, and PedidosYa began operations in 2018 (Miguez & Diana Menendez, 2023). After the pandemics, PedidosYa and Rappi remained the leading companies in Argentina, gathering about 50,000 deliveries.

The rapid growth of these companies in the Latin American context, characterized by the precariousness and informality of labor markets, the relatively low cost of the service, the promise of self-regulation of time, and the entrepreneurial character of this commercial activity of transporting food within the city, has prompted a growing body of research on the subject. Generally, the research on food delivery and application in Latin America can be divided into three main lines of inquiry. The first and most prominent of these emerges from labor studies and is concerned with delivery workers, their work and living conditions, and the implications of food apps for labor more generally. Research in Mexico (Alba Vega et al., 2021), Brazil (Abílio et al., 2020), and Argentina (Haidar, 2020; Palermo & Ventrici, 2020; Madariaga et al., 2019), for example, describe the sociodemographic profile and working conditions of delivery workers through surveys and in-depth interviews.

These studies concur that delivery workers are predominantly young men, in many cities they are immigrants, who work between nine and ten hours a day, and are vulnerable to accidents, theft, harassment, and discrimination. They also note that schedule flexibility is a valued quality for workers. Yet, under this flexibility, that many workers appreciate, there is a rigid regime of control through the apps that penalize workers when they do not want to accept an order (Haidar, 2020). Thus work hours are not entirely free; they are actually determined by peak order demand times and by platform algorithms that assign orders to riders based on their ranking.

Labor studies help understand the precarious conditions of work in this new economy that promises a self-regulation of time. Strikes against these companies, fights for labor rights, and attempts of creating working unions are well known. These rose during the Covid-19 pandemics, but they started before. Based on interviews with activists from different delivery driver movements in various Latin American countries, Gutiérrez Crocco and Atzeni (2022), Ortega Erreguerena (2023), Miguez and Diana Menendez (2023) focus on the forms of resistance, solidarity, and political organization of the drivers to consolidate themselves as social movements or formal unions demanding better working conditions, recognition of their rights, and platform regulation. They also examine the experiences of international strikes and the forms of repression exerted by the platforms. In 2019, one of the earliest strikes in Buenos Aires consisted in "hacking" the system (of the company called Rappi): In a synchronized manner, workers accepted orders and then waited 30 minutes—which is the maximum waiting time permitted by the application—and then "liberated" (refused) the order. Thus, they ultimately created a stoppage in deliveries for two hours in an action largely coordinated through WhatsApp groups. Due to the lack of delivery people and high demand, this also caused an increase in the cost of the application.

Other kinds of protests or ways of dealing with the unequal relations or forms of exploitation, imposed by the owners of the apps, have been studied to understand the type of worker that this digital economy is producing but also workers' tactics of resistance that include the knowledge and use of digital technology as well as of space. WhatsApp has served, in this sense, as a mediation of care politics among workers (Diz et al., 2023). Overall, the labor studies agree that despite the spatial dispersion of the workers, solidarity among delivery drivers and communication through social networks have allowed the consolidation of forms of organization and collective action at the local level and, since the pandemic began, there has been a process of international protest coordination.

Another line of existing research shifts the focus of analysis from the delivery drivers to the platforms themselves. This type of study is mainly exploratory and descriptive, aiming to characterize the design and content of the platforms through statistical information. Piggato et al. (2017) analyze the design of 30 food delivery platforms in Brazil, for example, by examining the presence or absence of variables regarding the clarity of language and instructions on platform operation, information accuracy, ease of navigation, the company's willingness to address inquiries, payment methods, prices, waiting times, interaction between companies and customers, among others. The authors conclude that ease of navigation is one of the features that platforms need to improve, as users who regularly use these services seek convenience when ordering food, but if they encounter difficulties in its operation, they will likely stop using it.

The content on digital food delivery platforms, such as food offerings and marketing strategies, has been a subject of research in literature addressing the digital food environment. These studies consider that the digital food environment influences consumers' food and nutrition decisions through social media, digital marketing, online food retail, and digital health promotion interventions (Granheim et al., 2022). Very few studies of this kind have been conducted in Latin America, mainly focusing on Brazil. For example, Horta et al. (2021) analyze the food offerings on the iFood platform during the COVID-19 pandemic in Brazil. They examine a sample of 1,750 advertisements on the platform, categorizing foods according to their degree of processing and analyzing marketing strategies such as the use of images, combos, discounts, free delivery, and slogans about economy, pleasure, or health. The authors conclude that Brazil's digital food environment is obesogenic because it promotes unhealthy eating habits, with a higher presence of ultra-processed foods compared to minimally processed foods. Matos et al. (2023), meanwhile, conducted a study in which they gathered information from 3,339 establishments advertised on the Rappi platform in nine cities across Latin America (Buenos Aires, São Paulo, Santiago de Chile, Bogotá, San José, Quito, Mexico City, Lima, and Montevideo). They classify these establishments based on the keywords used in their platform advertisements and analyze the marketing strategies employed. They conclude that in most of the cities, the 'snack' category is the most frequent, although the categories of 'typical food' and 'meat and fish' were very common in four of them. Meanwhile, the "healthy" category is the least frequent in most cities. The authors acknowledge that using keywords from descriptions as analysis categories may be misleading, as restaurants can advertise their products as healthy or as typical cuisine without necessarily being true. Another critique of this type of literature is that it does not explain the mechanisms by which certain restaurants are advertised more than others.

Considering that one of the primary features of food delivery applications is that of mobility, it is perhaps surprising that few studies in Latin America have focused on this new labor relationship paying attention to the fact that this work is carried out on the move. A mobility perspective is needed considering that the experience of cycling, along with the self-management of time, is one of the main advantages promoted by the apps (Maulat, 2021). In Santiago de Chile, Vecchio et al. (2022) have stressed the spatial dimension of delivery applications, the mobility strategies of the workers, and, particularly, inequalities or mobility injustice shaped by the relation between customer and worker. Jirón and Ulriksen Moretti (2022) have conceptualized this kind of activity as "digital mobile work," highlighting the spatial reconfiguration of the workplace and timework, and how the city is used as an infrastructure.

Urban food delivery, carried out mainly by bicycles, can be considered a sustainable mobility since last-mile food transport has always been considered a problem due to gas emissions and congestion (Mohammad et al., 2023). Apps highlight this kind of benefit of their service. However, this kind of mobility involves perils or vulnerability for those who are in motion because, on the one hand, of frequent accidents (provoked by the violence of motor-based traffic, due to the way in which delivery workers move, the lack of lights or the quality of the bicycle) and robbery—in the night or in dangerous districts—which is very common in Latin American cities, where levels of crime (and fear about crime and insecurity) are extremely high. In this vein, Vecchio et al. (2022) have shown how vulnerable delivery people were during the Covid-19 pandemics in Santiago de Chile. Under those circumstances, being immobile (stay at home) was considered a safety measure, whereas circulation was perceived as a dangerous practice (Zunino Singh, 2021).

Urban food delivery as human and mobile infrastructure

Urban food delivery connects distant places to transport things through a socio-material network that has an infrastructural shape and function. Infrastructures compose networks that make possible the circulation of people, information, commodities, resources, water, money, and waste, among other many things, within the city, shaping the circulatory systems that make possible the urban metabolism (Swyngedouw, 2006). The infrastructure of food transport is part of these systems of circulation and the study of supply chains gives an account of how they are vital to feeding cities. Deener (2020) has pointed out that under certain historical conditions, the social and technical components of food transportation mutually reinforce each other, constituting an *infrastructural regime of feeding cities*. This regime allows actors to connect agricultural production sites with urban demand contexts and achieve economic gains by controlling product qualities, coordinating distribution timelines through storage and transportation, and shaping consumer expectations about the high volumes and varieties of products available in markets. These regimes have an interdependent character that encompasses how companies make money from food distribution as well as the manner and place where people buy food; they assess product quality and how people experience access to these products in their daily lives.

It might be difficult to see a group of thousands of bikers with big boxes on their backs and using apps through mobile phones as an infrastructure since it does not resemble those physical and fixed spaces that are usually recognized as infrastructures—such as, conducts, roads, routes, pipes, canals, cables, bridges, aerial routes and airports, ports and rivers, rails, tunnels—or large technological systems such as communication, electrical services, sanitary works, railway networks, and so on. However, the STS and mobilities studies literatures (Leigh Star, 1999; McCallum & Zunino Singh, 2022) have approached infrastructure from a new perspective that allows us to conceive it beyond the idea of a physical and neutral support and highlight they are socio-technological networks that mediate mobilities. This section argues that urban food delivery has infrastructural characteristics and shows the peculiarities of this urban food infrastructure, taking into consideration several theoretical propositions.

Hybridity

Influenced by the ANT, infrastructure is conceived as an assemblage of heterogeneous actants, humans, and non-humans. This hybrid network is composed of a hardware aspect which involves materialities that usually are named as infrastructure such as pipes, cables, streets, and so on. But, today, "soft" aspects of the infrastructure that include human work, skills, and knowledge as well as the role of formulas, information, codes, timetables, science, and so on may also be considered part of the hybrid network. In order to consider something as an infrastructure, we should assess to what extent the object has infrastructural characteristics since infrastructure can be used as a metaphor or as a concept. An infrastructural perspective can conceive of an infrastructure as many other things that, at first sight, we cannot name them as such, such as groups of people, rivers, plants, or certain animal activity that may play infrastructural roles, for example. The notion of "humans as infrastructure" (Simone, 2004) helps go beyond traditional approaches and objects to stress the importance of social networks and human activities. In this sense, the skills, physical effort, knowledge, and body of the delivery workers or the embodied practice of moving food plays a significant role and it is not merely a by-product of the digital platform. Similarly, as Hayden (2022) has argued regarding the role of street vendors in Mexico City, we can see those groups of people transporting food by bicycles are the core of the delivery service. They compose a socio-technological gathering made of young (men and women) people, bicycles, mobile phones, boxes, and apps that connect, on a large-scale, distant places (shops or black kitchens with houses or workplaces, for example).

(Im)mobility

Infrastructure, since its origin, is closely related to mobility because the term was created in the railway industry to name rails, stations, and signals (the fixed physical space and materiality that allow the movement of trains). The centrality of mobility is recognized by scholars who do not belong to the mobilities studies field. Larkin (2013), for example, points out that infrastructures are things that move other things, connecting distant places. For mobilities studies, any flow occurs or is possible through a physical space that is called "moorings" (Sheller & Urry, 2006). This notion makes mobility and immobility two sides of the same coin. Moreover, most infrastructures produce friction since, although they make movement possible, they also block, segregate, regulate, or control flows. Some mobility scholars, based on processual philosophy, have criticized the emphasis on the immobility of the moorings or spaces of mobilities. Although streets, tunnels or rails, and stations look fixed, they are also mobile in the sense they transform over time. Moreover, the notion of maintenance and repair (Graham & Thrift, 2007), as a constant human work needed to keep an infrastructure alive, highlights how infrastructure can decay due to the lack of investment and human work. In this sense, Schabacher

(2013) has coined the term *infrastructuring* to stress that infrastructure is a process and, thus, is mobile. In the case of food delivery, the neologism is more than a metaphor, this human infrastructure is actually on the move. This mobile infrastructure, in turn, relies upon other fixed infrastructure such as streets (including bike lanes and traffic signals) and communication, bank or monetary and electrical systems. Sidewalks, squares, and certain public spaces of the city are significant places for this activity as they work as waiting times. This overlapping is another attribute of infrastructures, as Graham and Marvin (2001) point out.

Therefore, to see these people who carry boxes on their backs while pedaling on the streets as a socio-technological assemblage, which transports food on a large scale, making possible urban life, is to begin making them visible as an urban mobile infrastructure. Now it is important to explore what kind of mobility the appification of urban delivery produces. From the customer's perspective, the experience is limited to their interaction with the app interface, which, on one hand, turns restaurants into *non-places*, as places that apparently exist only in the form of a digital menu. On the other hand, the platforms present themselves to the consumer as providers of convenience, but they invisibilize the things that need to be moved and the delivery drivers, who are the ones actually providing this convenience through their work, which involves their corporality, takes time, and occupies a place in the urban space.

Infrastructure of fast delivery food: Relational and embodied mobility

Food, everywhere in the world, is a matter that needs to be physically transported (Hayden & Zunino Singh, 2020). This basic fact allows us to highlight the significant role of the "digital mobile workers," their bodies, skills, and material devices. However, the appification and the food consuming pattern involve a particular rhythm to be analyzed: This type of food circulation is marked by the hypermobility of the worker and immobility of the consumer. This hypermobility is not only a matter of distance and number of journeys but speed. A rapid and direct connection between the supplier and the customer to dispatch food or other items has been a long dream in modern times. For example, air-compressed pipes or pneumatic tube systems were created and used in the late nineteenth century for mail dispatch, even conceived for moving people. Many projects imagined a large network of tubes connecting big shops with houses. Yet, that dispatch took place through a fixed infrastructure that avoided street traffic. On the contrary, urban food delivery is a mobile infrastructure on the street.

Looking at the delivery based on cycling, in particular, this work requires, apart from the bicycle, energy and bodily effort defined by the time of pedaling. Time and distance are two aspects that usually deliver workers point out in their discourses. One of the companies that operated in Buenos Aires, Pedidos.ya [Order. now], launched an ad on YouTube called "Volá con Pedidos.ya" [Fly with Pedidos.

ya] in which a delivery boy moves through the city overcoming physical obstacles and making acrobatics movements—some of them impossible—to transport the order as quickly as possible. This ad expresses the spirit of these food transport companies, which is not only about connecting or being intermediaries between supply and demand but about comfort and speed. Clients do not need to move to buy things, they receive their orders (in the ad not only food is delivered but also other items like condoms or medicine) from a young man who pedals day and night, using a vehicle which is versatile to cross the city.

The rhythm—time, distance, physical effort, and energy (Lefebvre, 2004)—of delivering by bicycle was depicted by a journalist in Buenos Aires, who did this job for a few months to tell his experience, as an experience of discomfort, annoyance, a negative effort (Gullo, 2018). Pedaling was an unhappy experience, unlike how apps advertise this kind of job in terms of "the joy of pedalling." Maulat (2021) identifies that those who enjoy pedaling are workers who used to be cyclists before starting to deliver. Nonetheless, many studies agree that delivery people complain about how time and space are regulated by the apps because the algorithms have become forms of subordination and control (through reward and punishment): To refuse an order because in terms of time–space is not convenient can produce a reduction of orders or block the user. One of the most common practices is not to accept an order at the end of the day that is too far from the worker's home because then the time and distance of the last trip is too long. This last journey is part of his/her commuting.

Speed becomes not only the rhythm of this activity but shapes a mobility regime—as characterized by the term "instant delivery" or some names of the apps: Rappi or PedidosYa. This regime forces workers to cross the city -to cross, rather than moving through, because the worker has to find the fastest way to accomplish the job: Shortcuts, not to respect the traffic signals, to go in the wrong direction, to cycle on the sidewalks, and other risky movements to speed-up. Their spatial practices, the mobility in urban space, are governed by time—and, more precisely: Waiting time (Jirón & Ulriksen Moretti, 2022). What these delivery companies are offering is not only the immobility of the client—for whom immobility means comfort—but promising a rapid transport which implies a commodification of waiting. Time is economically valued and a key attribute of this service, even if the delivery time is far from what the advertising promises.

In terms of relational mobility, therefore, speed—the acceleration of food transport and, therefore, the hypermobility of the worker—is closely related to the waiting time of the (immobile) client. Moreover, the faster each journey is done, the more deliveries per day. From the perspective of the worker, speed is translated into the number of those deliveries—the income depends on this—and the reduction of waiting time. The survey conducted by Haidar (2020) during the pandemics in Buenos Aires shows how the amount of work per day increased in that context without working more hours: On the same day more deliveries were carried out and the waiting time (between orders) was highly reduced -this was also observed by Beccaria et al. (2020).

In short, this acceleration is signed by immediacy and based on a hypermobility/immobility relationship. Immediacy is an effect of the digital platform because the client can order without physically moving through his/her mobile phone. Someone else will make the physical effort to materially transport the order. Once the order is maiden, waiting time for the client begins—a time that needs to be reduced. The hypermobility of the worker is, moreover, tracked (controlled) by the client and the company. This unequal relational mobility is based on different bodily experiences between the relaxed waiting time of the client (comfort) and the bodily exhausting experience of pedaling of the worker.

Final considerations

To conceptualize urban food delivery as a mobile urban infrastructure allows us to have another analytical approach that stresses the vital importance of feeding the city and how the way of feeding involves social and material relationships in motion that, in turn, affect the (re)production of urban space. To approach the appification of food delivery only from the labor conditions or the asymmetric relationship between people and apps may overlook this infrastructural character. This type of food delivery is part of the larger supply chains, like other modes of transport that shape logistics systems. Infrastructures produce connections between distant places and mediations. Delivery work is, hence, more than a by-product of a digital platform. Velho and Ureta (2019) claim infrastructures are not solid but "frail", particularly in Latin America where stabilization is critical due to recurrent economic and institutional crises. The appification of food delivery has become massive, even under these frail labor conditions. The constant friction between the tyranny of the apps and the workers' resistance might be part of the frail character of this infrastructure, but it is not an impediment to mediating and sustaining this new pattern of food consumption.

Infrastructures move things, but infrastructures can also be mobile. Urban food delivery is a good example of not only how humans can act as an infrastructure but also how this is not always fixed. The mobility perspective also highlights how delivery work mediates this new pattern of food supply and consumption becoming an infrastructure of "hurry" (Dennis et al., 2018). Instant delivery is a mobility regime, part of a long process of acceleration, time–space compression, that has characterized modern transport and cities. Such acceleration takes place within the asymmetric relationship between the immobile consumer and the hypermobile intermediary.

Note

1 This market is subdivided into (1) Grocery delivery, which includes unprepared food products, personal hygiene, and household cleaning items, usually delivered by the store's own service; and (2) Meal delivery, which includes prepared and ready-to-eat foods. Meal delivery can be of two types: (a) the restaurant delivers the order through its own service (Restaurant delivery); (b) the delivery is provided by a digital platform for restaurants that do not have their own delivery service (Platform delivery).

References

Abílio, L. C., Almeida, P. F., Amorim, H., Cardoso, A. C., Fonseca, V. P., Kalil, R. B., & Machado, S. (2020). Condições de trabalho de entregadores via plataforma digital durante a Covid-19. *Revista Jurídica Trabalho E Desenvolvimento Humano, 3*. https://doi.org/10.33239/rjtdh.v.74

Alba Vega, C., Bensusán, G., & Vega, G. (2021). *El trabajo del futuro con derechos laborales. Diagnóstico y estrategia de política pública para el reconocimiento de derechos laborales de personas trabajadoras por plataformas digitales*. México: Colmex. https://ces.cdmx.gob.mx/storage/app/media/publicaciones2020/Estudio_derechos_laborales.pdf

Amin, A., & Thrift, N. (2010). *Cities: Reimagining the urban*. Cambridge: Polity.

Artioli, F. (2018). *Digital platforms and cities: A literature review for urban research*. Cities are Back in Town Working Paper 1. Sciences Po Urban School. Paris, France. https://sciencespo.hal.science/hal-02385137

Beccaria, L., Lopez Mourel, E., Mercer, R., & Vinocur, P. (2020). *Delivery en pandemia: el trabajo en las plataformas digitales de reparto en Argentina. Nota técnica*. Buenos Aires: OIT.

Brossat, I. (2019). *Airbnb. La ciudad uberizada*. Spain: Katakrak.

Dablanc, L., Morganti, E., Arvidsson, N., Woxenius, J., Browne, M., & Saidi, N. (2017). The rise of on-demand 'instant deliveries' in European cities. *Supply Chain Forum: An International Journal, 15*. http://dx.doi.org/10.1080/16258312.2017.1375375

Deener, A. (2020). *The problem with feeding cities: The social transformation of infrastructure, abundance, and inequality in America*. Chicago: The University of Chicago Press.

Dennis, R., Mackintosh, P., & Holdsworth, D. (2018). *Architectures of hurry-mobilities, cities and modernity*. London: Routledge.

Diz, C., González Granados, P., & Prieto Arratibel, A. (2023). Reaprendiendo a trabajar: saberes que cuidan en el manejo de algoritmos entre riders. *Revista de Antropología, 78*(1), e001d.

Graham, S., & Marvin, S. (2001). *Splintering urbanism: Networked infrastructures, technological mobilities and the urban condition*. London: Routledge.

Graham, S., & Thrift, N. (2007). Out of order: Understanding repair and maintenance. *Theory, Culture & Society, 24*(3), 1–25.

Granheim, S. I., Løvhaug, A. L., Terragni, L., Torheim, L. E., & Thurston, M. (2022). Mapping the digital food environment: A systematic scoping review. *Obesity Reviews, 23*(1). http://dx.doi.org/10.1111/obr.13356

Gullo, E. (2018). Capitalismo con tracción a sangre. *Anfibia*. www.revistaanfibia.com/capitalismo-traccion-sangre/

Gutiérrez Crocco, F., & Atzeni, M. (2022). Entre precarización, control algorítmico y movilización. Efectos de la pandemia de COVID-19 en las y los repartidores de plataformas en Argentina y Chile. *Revista Internacional del Trabajo, 141*(3), 489–511. https://doi.org/10.1111/ilrs.12206

Haidar, J. (2020). La configuración del proceso de trabajo en las plataformas de reparto en la Ciudad de Buenos Aires. Un abordaje multidimensional y multi-método (julio/agosto de 2020). *Informe de coyuntura, 11*, 1–96.

Hayden, T. (2022). Movilidad y Alimentos. In D. Zunino Singh, P. Jirón, & G. Giucci (Eds.), *Nuevos términos clave para los estudios de movilidad en América Latina* (pp. 259–272). Buenos Aires: Teseo.

Hayden, T., & Zunino Singh, D. (2020). Food and mobility. *Journal of Transport History, 41*, 278–288.

Hayden, T. B. (2021). Street food as infrastructure: consumer mobility, vendor removability and food security in Mexico City. *Food, Culture & Society, 24*(1), 98–111. https://doi.org/10.1080/15528014.2020.1859920

Horta, P. M., Matos, J. D., & Mendes, L. L. (2021). Digital food environment during the coronavirus disease 2019 (COVID-19) pandemic in Brazil: An analysis of food advertising in an online food delivery platform. *British Journal of Nutrition, 126*, 767–772. https://doi.org/10.1017/S0007114520004560

Jirón, P., & Ulriksen Moretti, C. (2022). Trabajos móviles digitales. In D. Zunino Singh, P. Jirón, & G. Giucci (Eds.), *Nuevos términos clave para los estudios de movilidad en América Latina* (pp. 259–272). Buenos Aires: Teseo.

Kantar. (2022). *Dining out at home. How meal delivery is transforming foodservice*. https://kantar.turtl.co/story/foodservice-2022-p

Larkin, B. (2013). The politics and poetics of infrastructure. *Annual Review of Anthropology, 42*, 327–343.

Lefebvre, H. (2004). *Rythmanalysis: Space time and everyday life*. London Continuum.

Lefebvre, H. (2013). *La producción del espacio*. Spain: Capitán Swing.

Leigh Star, S. (1999). The ethnography of infrastructure. *American Behavioral Scientist, 43*, 377–391.

Madariaga, J., Buenadicha, C., Molina, E., & Ernest, C. (2019). *Economía de plataformas y empleo: ¿cómo es trabajar para una app en Argentina?* Argentina: CIPPEC-BID – OIT.

Martínez Sordoni, L. (2020). Prólogo a la edición en castellano. In S. Abdelnour & D. Méda (Eds.), *Cuando tu jefe es una app* (pp. 11–21). Spain: Katakrak.

Matos, J. D., Julião, K. C., & Horta, P. M. (2023). Characteristics of food establishments registered with a meal delivery app in Latin America. *British Journal of Nutrition, 130*, 2155–2161. https://doi.org/10.1017/S0007114523001368

Maulat, J. (2021). Being a bicycle delivery rider: Passion or exploitation? *Mobile Lives Forum*. https://en.forumviesmobiles.org/project/2020/12/14/being-bicycle-delivery-rider-passion-or-exploitation-13525?utm_source=nl_en&utm_medium=email&utm_campaign=2906_Deliv

McCallum, S., & Zunino Singh, D. (2023). Infraestructura de movilidad. In D. Zunino Singh, P. Jirón, & G. Giucci (Eds.), *Nuevos términos clave para los estudios de movilidad en América Latina* (pp. 153–165). Buenos Aires: Teseo.

Miguez, P., & Diana Menendez, N. (2023). Trabajo y plataformas. Desafíos para la organización de trabajadores de plataformas en América Latina. *Trabajo y Sociedad, XXIV*(40). https://www.unse.edu.ar/trabajoysociedad/40%20L_T%20MIGUEZ-DIANA%20MENENDEZ.pdf

Mohammad, W. A., Nazih Diab, Y., Elomri, A., & Triki, C. (2023). Innovative solutions in last mile delivery: concepts, practices, challenges and future directions. *Supply Chain Forum: An International Journal, 24*(2), 151–169. https://doi.org/10.1080/16258312.2023.2173488

Ortega Erreguerena, J. (2023). Resistencias frente al capitalismo de plataformas: paros internacionales de los repartidores en América Latina. *Acta Sociológica, 90*, 241–269. https://doi.org/10.22201/fcpys.24484938e.2023.90.86279

Palermo, H., & Ventrici, P. B. (2020). Creativos, divertidos, emprendedores y meritocráticos El trabajo en contexto de las tecnologías de la información. *Cuadernos De antropologia Social, 52*. https://doi.org/10.34096/cas.i52.6905

Piggato, G., Machado, J. G., Negreti, A. D., & Machado, L. M. (2017). Have you chosen your request? Analysis of online food delivery companies in Brazil. *British Food Journal, 119*(3), 639–657. https://doi.org/10.1108/BFJ-05-2016-0207

Radetich, N. (2022). *Cappitalismo. La uberización del trabajo*. Mexico: Siglo XXI.

Rossi, L. S. R. (2022). Ciudades, comunicación digital y pospandemia: de las smart cities al urbanismo de plataformas. *Universitas-XXI, 37*, 123–146. https://doi.org/10.17163/uni.n37.2022.05

Sadowski, J. (2020). Cyberspace and cityscapes: On the emergence of platform urbanism. *Urban Geography, 41*(3), 448–452. https://doi.org/10.1080/02723638.2020.1721055

Schabacher, G. (2013). Mobilizing transport: Media, actor-networld, and infrastructures. *Transfers: Interdisciplinary Journal of Mobility Studies, 3*(1), 75–94.

Sheller, M., & Urry, J. (2006). The new mobilities paradigm. *Environment and Planning A*, *38*(2), 207–226.
Simone, A. M. M. (2004). People as infrastructure: Intersecting fragments in Johannesburg. *Public Culture*, *16*(3), 407–429.
Srnicek, N. (2021). *Capitalismo de plataformas*. Buenos Aires: Caja Negra.
Statista. (2023). *Ingresos del mercado de reparto de comida en línea a nivel mundial de 2017 a 2027, por canal*. https://es.statista.com/estadisticas/1273125/ingresos-del-mercado-de-entrega-de-comida-online-a-nivel-mundial/
Statista. (2024a). *Ingresos de servicios de envío de comida en línea en América Latina de 2017 a 2027, por segmento*. https://es.statista.com/previsiones/1309487/ingresos-de-servicios-online-de-entrega-de-comida-en-america-latina
Statista. (2024b). *Number of users of the online food delivery market worldwide from 2018 to 2028, by segment*. https://www.statista.com/forecasts/891088/online-food-delivery-users-by-segment-worldwide
Swyngedouw, E. (2006). Circulations and metabolisms: (Hybrid) natures and (cyborg) cities. *Science as Culture*, *15*(2), 105–121.
Vecchio, G., Tiznado-Aitken, I., Albornoz, C., & Tironi, M. (2022). Delivery workers and the interplay of digital and mobility (in)justice. *Digital Geography and Society*, *3*, 100036.
Velho, R., & Ureta, S. (2019). Frail modernities: Latin American infrastructures between repair and ruination. *Tapuya: Latin American Science, Technology and Society*, *2*(1), 428–441.
Zunino Singh, D. (2021). *Immobility is healthy. Risky mobility of the delivery service in Buenos Aires during the pandemic (and beyond)*. Conference Paper Presented at Entangled Im/Mobilities. Perspectives from the Humanities and Social Sciences, University of Vienna.

7

MIGRATION AND URBAN FOOD SYSTEMS IN LATIN AMERICA

Tiana Bakić Hayden, Mercedes Eguiguren and Yolanda Alfaro

Introduction

Urbanization and migration are interlinked phenomena. As cities around the world expanded throughout the twentieth century, urbanization took place at an especially rapid tempo in Latin America, fueled largely by industrialization and changing agricultural technologies and regimes which drew (or pushed) large numbers of people from rural areas to cities. Indeed, the question of migration (especially rural–urban migration) was central to the development of urban policies and to urban studies in the region and has contributed to shaping the social and political contours of the contemporary Latin American city (Germani, 1969; Roberts, 1980; Gorelik, 2022). While extensive studies exist on the ways that migration has shaped urban economies, territorial development, housing, infrastructure, language, and culture, the relationship between migration and the development of urban food systems and cultures is relatively underdeveloped in Latin America. Yet studies focused on the history of urban food systems in other parts of the world, in cities such as London (Steel, 2013), New York (Baics, 2016; Ray, 2016); Chicago (Cronon, 1992), and Philadelphia (Deener, 2020), have shown that migration is always intimately tied to the development of food-related infrastructures, networks, and practices. In Latin America, Jeffrey Pilcher's (1998, 1999, 2005) work stands out in highlighting the role of migrants in shaping cuisine and culinary infrastructures in Mexico. Collectively, these works show that migrants, whether from rural areas or from other countries, often seek work as food merchants, vendors, producers, or restaurateurs, thus bringing to urban food systems ingredients, recipes, commercial practices, and social networks, which shape the way that food is made, sold, prepared, and experienced in their new homes.

This chapter outlines the insertion of international migrants into the food systems of different Latin American cities and points to the need for a research agenda

DOI: 10.4324/9781003471929-11

on contemporary international migration and urban food systems in the region. By urban food systems, we refer to the constellation of places, people, institutions, regulations, and activities that exist within a particular urban context, which connect food production, processing, distribution, consumption, and waste management.[1] Our focus on contemporary international migration is justified by the fact that Latin American cities are increasingly destinations for refugees and migrants from other countries, due to a combination of factors including repressive border regimes and anti-immigrant policies in the United States (and elsewhere), heightened economic and political instability or violence in countries such as Venezuela, Haiti, and throughout Central America, and climate change-related crises, especially in rural areas. We consider this new reality against the backdrop of the continent's history as a node of global mobility, both as a destination of migrants and other mobile groups of European, Asian, and African origins, and, more recently, as the origin of transnational migration to the Global North. With this in mind, and following studies that suggest that international migrants play key roles in shaping urban food systems in other parts of the world, we ask as follows: What is the role of newly arrived groups in markets, fields, and kitchens in Latin America? How does this vary in different national and regional contexts in the continent? What types of jobs or roles in food systems do newcomers seek today? What patterns can be observed? What conditions and challenges do migrants face in these roles?

Rather than providing comprehensive and detailed responses to these questions, in this text we aim to provide a general overview of what existing scholarly literature allows us to understand about the insertion of migrants in food systems. Our objective is to shine a light on the fact that the very systems and infrastructures through which we feed ourselves in Latin America are dependent upon, and shaped by, the labor of people who have come to cities from all over the world, and we give a preliminary sense of how this is occurring differently in cities in the region. To that end, the chapter is organized as follows: First, we provide a brief summary of the ways in which scholarship from other areas of the world has discussed the urban–food–migration nexus, in order to identify potential questions and areas of interest for Latin America. We then provide a review of how Latin American scholarship on urbanization and migration has evolved over the last century, and where food systems have appeared (or failed to appear) in this work. We then survey scholarly and media coverage so as to provide a brief overview of contemporary international migration in two Latin American capitals, Quito and Buenos Aires, in relation to food-related spaces, actors, or processes in the city. We conclude with some thoughts on how a focus on migration can help develop a more robust understanding of cities and food systems in the region.

Migration, food, and cities

Throughout the world, the contemporary global food system, characterized by industrialized food production concentrated in the hands of a small number of corporations, depends on the inexpensive, flexible, and precarious labor of migrant workers. There is a very large body of scholarly work that deals with the reliance of global food systems on migrant labor, but the majority of it looks at agricultural workers, surely due in part to the fact that in many areas of the Global North migrants represent the backbone of rural economies. Thus, for example, in the United States in the 2018–2020 period, immigrant workers (the majority hailing from Latin America, but representing nationalities from around the world) made up nearly 70% of the farmworker population and are central to the operation of large-scale industrial farms, "family" farms and organic farms alike[2] (Holmes, 2013; Blanchette, 2020). In Europe, meanwhile, migrants from Bangladesh, Nepal, and elsewhere in Asia and the Middle East plow and tend the fields from Spain to the United Kingdom, often in the absence of legal status or protections. Although these workers are often employees on farms who labor under highly exploitative conditions, immigrant agricultural workers may also bring experience and expertise from their home countries. For example, despite the threats to small farms in the United States, today immigrant farmers from Cuba, Southeast Asia, Honduras, and elsewhere have brought new farming techniques and varieties of plants to farms in the United States (Imbruce, 2007). Historically, migrant farmers from Eastern Europe, Italy, Germany, and other countries shaped the types of vegetables that were grown in green belts surrounding many major American cities (Gabaccia, 2000; Deener, 2020; Baics, 2016). Indeed, as Donna Gabaccia (2000) argues in her sweeping history of the contribution of immigrants (and settlers) to food cultures in the United States, newly arrived populations over the last 200-plus years successively brought with them agricultural techniques and knowledge from countries of origin, effectively shaping the land and market on "American" food cultures. Even today, as Valerie Imbruce argues in her study of Southeast Asian and Honduran farmers in the United States, immigrant farmers, and the urban networks that they provision, represent an alternative food system which brings new types of plants to market, and pushes against the homogenizing tendencies of the contemporary food regime (Imbruce, 2016).

In this sense, scholarship on migrant involvement in the production side of food systems invites us to pay attention not only to exploitation and marginalization—undeniably crucial topics for anyone interested in just food systems—but also to look at how migrants may participate in shaping *supply*, both in terms of types of ingredients and in the commercial systems in which they participate. This, accordingly, brings us to the question of the *urban*, since both supply and distribution networks are ultimately oriented toward supplying cities. Thus, immigrants may bring specific growing techniques or seeds to a new place—which evolves in relation to the demands of urban markets—, but they also often take on an important role in urban supply networks, including in wholesaling, retail, and food preparation. One need only take a stroll through some of the most bustling food markets in most global cities, or read up on the history of urban commerce, to see that the names of businesses, employees, and products on sale speak to waves of migration, past and present.

Scholarship on migration and urban economies has described the prevalence of migrants in urban food systems through concepts of "ethnic" economies, businesses, enclaves, and labor networks, generally within disciplines such as urban economics, geography, or sociology. These works show that migrants integrate into local economies often through transnational networks, where local brokers and kin networks assist in finding jobs in destination countries, often in low-paying industries with few protections, such as the food industry (Lindquist et al., 2012; Guérin, 2013; McCollum & Findlay, 2018). Migrants in much of the world may also seek employment not as waged laborers but rather as entrepreneurs and in informal economies, including food markets, street vending, or restaurant kitchens (Imilan & Millaleo, 2015,). Historically in the United States and in Europe, where much of this research has concentrated, migrants played an important role in the development of urban wholesale and fresh markets. In the United States, for example, Italian, German, and Eastern European migrants in the late nineteenth and early twentieth centuries found success in both urban food markets and periurban agricultural production, often linking the two (see Deener, 2020; Gabaccia, 2000). Today, Latin American and Asian migrants may be found working in small produce stores, large markets, and as street vendors and restaurant workers throughout the United States (Ray; Vázquez-Medina; Devlin).

Throughout the Global South, meanwhile, there is evidence that migrants play an important role in urban food systems. In contemporary South Africa, for example, migrants from Zimbabwe, Angola, and other African nations often find employment in the informal economy, especially as food vendors, thus providing affordable food to both migrant and local populations, and introducing dishes from different countries (Crush et al., 2015). In India, similarly, migrants from Tibet, Nepal, and other parts of India often turn to food vending, bringing their specific dishes and flavors to cities such as Delhi and Mumbai (Baviskar, 2021). In the United States, cities such as New York and Chicago have seen their streets filled with the flavors and sounds of street vendors from various waves of incoming migrant groups over the past century, from Jewish to Italian to Chinese to Mexican (Ray, 2016; Gabaccia, 2000). Taking stock of this literature in the United States, Krishnendu Ray argues in his book *The Ethnic Restaurateur,* that waves of "ethnic" or migrant populations—from small-scale peddlers to elite restaurateurs—have thus shaped taste itself as they cook for diverse urban populations, frequently mixing ingredients, recipes, and approaches in heterodox ways. Thus, he argues, migrant cooks are usually overlooked but crucial actors in the production of *taste*. Yet, Ray suggests that not all migrant groups shape national cuisines in the same manner since social mobility (whose ease is facilitated due to a range of factors including educational status, race, and transnational network) leads certain groups to be able to leave the precarious and difficult world of food systems work for better jobs in other fields and industries, thus giving them less time to effectively leave their mark on national cuisines.

Regardless of the particular staying power of, say, sushi versus bhel puri, the broader point is that processes of human mobility—including colonization, rural–urban migration, and transnational migrations—produce local and national cuisines and tastes, even as the idea of 'authentic' or timeless national cuisines denies the very syncretism of cuisine. Furthermore, cities, as the primary destination for contemporary migrants, are precisely sites where taste is produced "from below" by migrant cooks, vendors, and consumers (Zanoni, 2018; Ray, 2016). We might thus say, following the anthropologist David Howes, that the social (or in this case, demographic) revolution of planetary urbanization entails as well a revolution in the senses (2006). Yet how has this played out in the Latin American context? How might theories of the urban in Latin America open up pathways for understanding the role of migrants in the region's urban food systems?

Migration, urbanization (and food?) in Latin America

While literature on the link between migration and urbanization in Latin America is abundant—indeed, Latin American urbanization was central to urban studies and demography's development (see also Gorelik)—and while there is a growing, although still relatively small literature on social studies of food in the region, which has linked migration and food practices (Pilcher, 1998; Vázquez-Medina, 2016), there is still little work that explicitly connects these discussions, and most of the existing research is concentrated in Argentina and Chile. Nevertheless, certain discussions in urban studies and migration studies in Latin America are instructive in beginning to think about migrant involvement in food systems.

First are studies of Latin American urbanization which have had as one of their main concerns the understanding of the causes and persistence of urban informality (Quijano, 1972; Pachano, 1988; De Oliveira & Roberts, 1993). These types of studies, which emerged in the region since the 1940s in countries such as Mexico and Argentina, and then in other national contexts throughout the second half of the twentieth century, stem from a line of work focused on understanding the dynamic growth of Latin American cities and observing its implications for urban planning. Issues such as the growth of informal neighborhoods, the inadequacy of public services, and the expansion of the informal economy are crucial problems for this literature (Deler, 1988). In this line of urban studies, rural migration (from the countryside) is associated with the growth of peripheral neighborhoods and informal urbanization (in both housing and labor), often understood as "subsistence strategies" of poor migrants. In recent decades, rather than seeing informality as an urban problem, some scholars point out that the formal sector is sustained by low-cost services provided by the informal sector, which are also vital to the urban economy (De Oliveira & Roberts, 1993; Kirshner, 2010; Arizpe, 1989). All of this scholarship is useful in pointing to the importance of recognizing "the informal" in urban food systems, and the way that migration and mobility shape these spaces. It also opens the door to understanding how food emerges in relation to other "informal" urban spaces and systems. Nevertheless, literature has generally failed to address *food specific* dimensions of this economy, although there is a growing interest in the role of street food in local cultures and economies (see Hayden & Farah, this volume for a review of this literature).

Another relevant body of literature for understanding the migration–city–food nexus are more recent studies examining urban food systems and international migration, respectively. Most of these works emerge in the first two decades of the twenty-first century, and their objects of study respond to both new research interests and the economic, social, and demographic transformations occurring since the 1990s. In literature developed on urban food systems, for example, internal migrants are usually recognized as important actors, but there is little consideration of how international migration plays into food systems, or why the particular cultural, economic, and political dimensions of different groups might have effects on the systems of trade, commerce, and consumption (Hollenstein, 2019, 2020; Rodríguez & Hollenstein, 2020).

In migration studies, on the other hand, we find a field that has expanded considerably in the last 20 years throughout Latin America and where the question of immigration *to* countries such as Ecuador, Peru, Bolivia, or Mexico, Chile, and beyond is present (see Álvarez Velasco, 2022; Gómez & Herrera, 2022; Blouin & Zamora Gómez, 2022; Alfaro & Ramírez, 2019; Masferrer et al., 2023). Although the links between foodscapes and migration have not been the most prioritized topic in Latin American migration studies, when attention has been paid to this topic (although, see Hayden, 2024; Orjuela-Grimm et al., 2022), it has been primarily from cultural and historical studies, amidst broader interests in identity dynamics, relations with local populations, and transnational practices. In general terms, case studies predominate, and a combination of groups of different origins and historical periods have been examined.

Thus, there have been some historical works interested in the arrival and establishment of immigrant "colonies" of diverse origins since the early twentieth century, such as Chinese, Italians, Germans, Spaniards, Lebanese, and Syrians, primarily not only in countries such as Argentina and Brazil but also in Mexico, Ecuador, Colombia, and Peru (Campos & Martínez, 2020; Nobrega, 2008; Novick, 2008; Delgado, 2018; Zapata, 2019). Although there were varied routes and motives that brought European and Asian migrants at the turn of the twentieth century, as varied as their forms of settlement and incorporation into local societies, in general, the Latin American region has a history of settlement of mainly Italians, Spaniards and Chinese, with a significant presence as owners and employees of restaurants and warehouses, stores, or supermarkets (Martínez Esquivel, 2007; Chan & Strabucchi, 2019; Zapata, 2019; Campos, 2020; Brauner, 2020). Jeffrey Pilcher's work stands out in centering the role of human mobility in the transformation of "culinary infrastructures" in Mexico (Pilcher, 2016).

Regarding immigration in Latin American cities, we find a greater interest and breadth of academic production on the different manifestations of migrant presence in cities such as Buenos Aires and Santiago, where the role of international migrants is visible in areas such as the sale of agricultural products, stores and markets selling processed and fresh food, and the sale of prepared dishes (Stefoni, 2008; Garcés, 2011; Margarit & Bijit, 2015; Ortale & Santos, 2021; Brauner, 2020; Medina Flores & Basfi-fer Obregón, 2018; Imilan & Millaleo, 2015; Chan & Strabucchi, 2019; Pinto et al., 2022). These flows have diversified food practices and transformed public spaces and informal economic networks in these countries. These studies have shown that migrants not only enrich the local culinary culture by introducing new ingredients and dishes but also establish transnational networks that allow them to maintain and adapt their traditional food practices in the new environment. In addition, these studies show the dynamics of integration and exclusion that migrants face, affecting their access to food and other basic resources.

In the Andean region, in contrast, there are fewer comparable studies, due, on the one hand, to the fact that, in these countries, the migrant presence in food systems continues to come mainly from within the country (Kirshner, 2010; Jaramillo & Jácome, 2019; Maglia et al., 2019), and on the other hand, that these countries were characterized until the beginning of this century, by their international emigration movements, and not for being large-scale recipients of population. However, there is now a growing interest in the Andean countries toward understanding migrants' food practices and meanings as well as in food vending as an economic activity performed by migrants (Vélez, 2022; Larrea et al., 2020; Martens, 2024; Pastor, 2018; Alfaro & Ramírez, 2019).

In the research from the Andes and Southern Cone, two theoretical approaches have predominated in this field. On the one hand, by focusing on the study of migration as a social process, emphasis is placed on both the economic, social, and cultural strategies involved in the insertion into food businesses or informal sales and the "ethnic enclaves" that have often given rise to the sale of foods characteristic of the migrants' place of origin (*"comidas típicas"*) or the marketing of food products also associated with the place left behind (Yagüe, 2014; Vélez, 2022; Larrea et al., 2020). On the other hand, there is an approach focused on investigating patterns of economic insertion from the dynamics of the labor market, highlighting the labor and social precariousness to which the migrant population is forced (Herrera Mosquera & Cabezas Gálvez, 2020; Blouin & Freier, 2019; Chan & Strabucchi, 2019; Alfaro & Ramírez, 2019).

Much more recently, work performed through apps and digital platforms, such as home delivery of food and other products and private transportation, has begun to generate interest. In these studies developed mainly by the sociology of labor, with the interest of understanding the gig economy phenomenon in its local manifestation, migrants residing in various Latin American cities "appear" as a sector of the urban precariat to which labor studies had not necessarily paid attention before (Negri, 2020; Hidalgo Cordero & Valencia Castro, 2019). Particularly in the midst of the vast academic production dedicated to understanding the social transformations generated during the COVID-19 pandemic, sociology of migration and labor scholars focused on what was already evident: The ongoing movement of motorcycles or bicycles of migrant delivery workers who circulated through the

Latin American cities semi-paralyzed by the pandemic, carrying prepared food or supermarket purchases mainly to the urban middle and upper classes, who in general could stay at home during the confinements (Herrera, 2021).

Finally, though beyond this chapter's scope, we highlight emerging literature on global mobilities and urban transformations dedicated to capturing local changes due to "lifestyle" migration (Hayes, 2018, 2013) from the global North to the South. In small-sized or medium-sized Ecuadorian cities like Cuenca or Cotacachi, or neighborhoods of Mexico City, the arrival of North American retirees and "digital nomads" brings changes in food supply, types of outlets, price increases, and even the introduction of English-only menus and signage (Hayes, 2018; see Cordero & Vázquez-Medina, this volume). These changes cater to the demands of these new residents, differing from traditional local tastes and often exceeding the purchasing power of local neighbors.

As can be seen, we have found a dispersed literature that responds to heterogeneous study interests, which is also remarkably vast; addressing different historical moments, types of mobility, and forms of involvement and interrelationship between migratory, circulatory, and production logics of urban food systems. We argue that, in order to understand these complex interrelationships, it is necessary to highlight the key roles played by migrants and their ways of inhabiting urban space, and, by doing so, to identify their ways of making and belonging to urban food systems and to cities more broadly. We now turn to the case of two cities, Quito and Buenos Aires, to discuss further the way in which migrants have shaped the food systems.

Migrant insertion in food systems in two Latin American cities

Quito, Ecuador

Ecuadorian cities have been fed by continuous flows of internal migrants whose departure from the countryside is due to the confluence of several factors, among them, the so-called destructuring of rural societies, the deterioration of living conditions in the countryside, the advance of modernization processes that favored the concentration of resources in the cities, among others (Martínez, 1984). Among the work and livelihood that peasants and indigenous migrants have found in cities, the sale of food in markets and on the streets stands out, which has been studied especially in Ecuador and Bolivia (Barragán, 2009; Kirshner, 2010; Azogue, 2012; Medeiros et al., 2013). Indeed, indigenous and peasant migrants, and especially women, play a leading role in the provision of food in city markets, thus becoming part of the *popular* sector of food marketing and production (Maglia et al., 2019; Barragán, 2009).

Ecuador has been receiving a significant number of regional migrations in the Andes since the early 2000s, mainly from Colombia and Peru at the beginning of this century, and later from Cuba, Haiti, and Venezuela (Gómez & Herrera, 2022; Álvarez Velasco, 2022). Indeed, by the second half of the 2010s, the most visible immigrant presence across the region was precisely that of the Venezuelan diaspora, which, since then, has arrived mainly in Colombia, Peru, Chile, and Ecuador, and, on a smaller scale, in several other countries across the continent, including Bolivia (Alfaro & Ramírez, 2019; Gandini et al., 2019).

In Ecuador, and the Andean region more broadly, the participation of migrants in food economies cannot be understood as a succession of stages over time, rather, what we find is an overlapping of forms of mobility that leads in certain cases to the repetition of similar patterns of involvement in food systems. Thus, in the same way that the circuits of transport and marketing of agricultural products from the countryside to the cities have been sustained by itinerant traders and migrants across national territories (Ibarra, 2008; Kingman, 2014; Yagüe, 2014), in cross-border areas the same logics of circulation and networks extend to the sides of the borders for the supply of food and goods of various kinds (Tassi & Poma, 2020; Casparrino et al., 2021; Jiménez et al., 2019).

In urban contexts, most international migrants find their source of income in the informal sector. The occupations performed vary depending on the city and, in some cases, gender. To a lesser extent, level of education, social networks, and migratory status have an influence. In the midst of regional variations in labor insertion, the food sector stands out as a place of economic activity, whether in businesses selling prepared food such as restaurants and cafeterias, or in the sale of fresh or processed products, such as in markets and informal street vending (Alfaro & Ramírez, 2019).

Ortega and Ospina (2012) show that this was the case of the internationally displaced population from Colombia who increasingly sought refuge in Ecuador since the early 2000s. Studying their main urban destinations, Quito and Guayaquil, the authors show that food commerce was crucial in their economic insertion. Food commerce and work in restaurants, cafeterias, and bars made up more than 20% of Colombian refugees' and asylum seekers' occupations in Quito around 2010. A much lower percentage were owners, with one of the three main business types being bakeries. This could be confirmed by anyone walking through Quito's streets in the early 2000s, when *panaderías colombianas* (most of them featuring the colors of the Colombian flag, the country's name, or a *sombrero vueltiao* on their facades) seemed ubiquitous. Equally distinctive was *Avena Polaca*, a Colombian oatmeal-based drink available in these bakeries. The labor market insertion of Colombian displaced people as food vendors, or bakery or restaurant employees, reflects inequalities of migrant labor in food commerce in two ways: One, evidences common downward social mobility paths of migrants with higher levels of education or professionalization, whom, nonetheless, start selling food in the streets or find jobs in restaurants because of the difficulties associated with continuing their professional trajectories. Two, the socioeconomic inequalities among migrant groups of the same origin. It was not uncommon for more recently arrived Colombians to find jobs with more established and wealthier migrants from their own country (Ortega & Ospina, 2012).

The food landscape in Quito in recent years has continued to evolve toward a more cosmopolitan offer and image, a phenomenon in whose emergence the diversification of migrant origins in the city has played no small role (Martens, 2024). Pastor's study (2018) explores the business of shawarma restaurants, which are quite successful among Quito's middle-class youth. Inquiring into the conditions of migration of Afghans in the city, Pastor examines the insertion of these migrants in shawarma businesses,[3] where their national identity blends in with that of other Middle Eastern migrants, and with the orientalizing stereotypes of Quiteños toward the "Arab," a term that in this Andean city is used as a generic to designate everything perceived as of Middle Eastern or West Asian origin. Pastor's work shows the strategic role of imaginaries, symbols, and identities in migration and in the sale of ethnic foods. Although Afghans have no traditional relationship with shawarma, in Quito, the popularity of this food provides them a livelihood in a context where institutional regulations, language, and social perceptions are adverse to them. In terms of the relationship between migration and food trade, works such as this also challenge the idea of a natural, linear relationship between migrants and the production of "ethnic" foods.

By contrast, in spaces traditionally occupied by Indigenous urbanites, such as markets and street food sales, international migrants are now also found. In the case of Quito's San Roque market, which has been a center of reception and reorganization of economic and social strategies of indigenous people from the country's highlands (Azogue, 2012), Rojas-Galindo et al. (2024) find that the presence of Venezuelan migrants selling on the periphery of the market and working as *cargadores* generates new encounters, relationships of coexistence and tensions between the more established vendors and recent migrants. Between exclusion and recognition, local merchants identify the "shopping cart system" as an innovation brought by Venezuelan immigrants to San Roque, and value it, while at the same expressing certain rejection to the newcomers, because of the competition between the formalized sector of the market and the informal one, whose growth local vendors associate with the increase of international migrants (Rojas-Galindo et al., 2024).

Indeed, Venezuelan migrants in their wide dispersion throughout the length and breadth of the continent have found in the sale of street food one of the few alternatives, if not the only one, to earn income and survive (Alfaro & Ramírez, 2019), and, in exceptional cases, they have created businesses, by both offering gastronomy which is relatively new to cities like Quito, Cochabamba, or Mexico (Alfaro & Ramírez, 2019) and the incursion into new forms of local foodscapes, as described by Martens (2024) in her original work on food trucks in Quito. This is how *arepas* and *tequeños* have become the visible symbol of the new Venezuelan migration and its transcontinental character as well as a way for migrants to articulate to the urban economy.

Buenos Aires, Argentina

Argentina may be the country with the most significant body of research dealing with the question of transnational migration and its insertion in the food system, although, again, in the majority of cases, food is not the explicit focus of the research. The vast majority of these studies focus on Buenos Aires, and what we learn is that migrants play an undeniably important role in the capital's food system. Widespread migration from Italy in the nineteenth century left its mark on the Spanish-dominated and beef-dominated cuisine in the form of the ubiquity of pasta, pizza, canelone, gelato, and other Italian favorites in the urban foodscape. The success of Italian immigration in effectively reshaping Argentina's foodways may be understood as a product of the sheer fact that Italians outnumbered other migrant groups in a significant manner and that they were able to position themselves as a familiar "other" in comparison with more racialized groups (such as Jews or Arabs) (Zanoni, 2018). Yet it also has to do with the fact that Italians during this key period of national identity formation came to occupy key places in the food system, including as vendors in the *abasto* wholesale market district, as importers of Italian products, as restaurateurs, and small-scale food vendors (Zanoni, 2018). Syrian, Lebanese, Armenian, and Eastern European Jewish and non-Jewish populations also migrated in this time period, but their respective cuisines are more "niche" than the Italian, perhaps due to their relatively reduced numbers or perhaps to the different forms of social mobility which the communities experienced over subsequent generations.

More recent migrations in the twentieth century play a central role in contemporary food provisioning. On the one hand, there are *supermercados chinos*, Chinese-owned and Taiwanese-owned supermarkets which have become important in the city since the 1980s (see Pérez Martín, this volume, also Marrero, 2016; Grimson et al., 2016). These grocery stores emerged starting in the 1970s, when waves of Taiwanese immigrants came to Argentina, and continued in the early 2000s with new waves of migration from mainland China (Rolando & Segui, 2015; Denardi, 2016). Unlike other groups, who inserted themselves into Buenos Aires' food system through public fresh markets or wholesale districts, the Chinese community entered directly into grocery stores, selling primarily packaged foodstuffs and home foods. A study by Denardi (2016) suggests that this may in part be attributable to explicit efforts on the part of the Chinese state to foment migration and entrepreneurialism among its departees, as well as the (related) existence of organized migrant merchant associations who act collectively in purchasing and negotiations. Grimson et al. suggest that the saturation of the Chinese grocery market in Buenos Aires has contributed to the migration to other parts of Argentina, where there are new markets. In addition, Chinese ready-made eateries, featuring takeaway buffets of both Asian and Argentine/mixed fare, have appeared throughout Buenos Aires, part of a new venture which caters to the ever-growing need for eating out, but capitalizes on the associations and entrepreneurial structure and networks of the Chinese community (Denardi, 2016). In any event, this shows that the question of country and historic moment are keys to understanding *how* and *where* newcomers might seek work in food systems.

If overseas migration from Italy, Spain, and China is visible throughout Buenos Aires, the role of regional migration from nearby countries, especially Bolivia and

Peru, is overwhelmingly visible in the city's produce trade and periurban greenbelt production. Throughout Buenos Aires, fruit and vegetables are usually sold in *verdulerías,* small greengrocers often run by families from Bolivia, and in some cases, Peru. Bolivians, who only started appearing in the 1980s in significant numbers first as agricultural workers in the "green belts" around Buenos Aires and other urban centers, have become the dominant actors in the fresh produce production, commercialization, and supply system. Within the "ethnic enclave," labor contracting occurs through local intermediaries and depends on family employment, where all members of families, including children and women (who are considered to be skilled merchants in the Bolivian community) participate (Benencia, 2012, 2006; Benencia & Quaranta, 2006). Peruvians, similarly, have been analyzed in terms of the kinship networks that permit them to find employment in Buenos Aires, and although there is little analysis of food systems *in particular*, many of the examples of jobs in which they work are in produce markets and shops (Herrera Jurado, 2022; Lapenda, 2021). One of the key results of this concentration of produce in the hands of the Bolivian community is that gender dynamics have been shifting, with women taking on more prominent and visible roles in the food system, especially as merchants.

Finally, in recent years a key new player in urban food systems in Buenos Aires (and throughout Latin America and the world) are digital applications for food delivery, including grocery and restaurant. Migrants, who face barriers to accessing more formal or network-dependent work options, represent a ready labor pool for these applications, with studies suggesting that they make up the majority of workers across delivery apps (see Zunino & Ferrer, this volume; Negri, 2020). In Buenos Aires, for the delivery application *Rappi*, for example, migrants have been found to comprise over 83% of delivery workers, the majority of those hailing from one place: Venezuela (Madariaga et al., 2019). The presence of Venezuelans, many of whom hail from urban contexts, in delivery apps contrasts with Bolivian and Peruvian communities, who often come from rural areas and make use of extensive kin and social networks to seek employment and constitute important and powerful economic groups in the Argentine food system.

Conclusions: toward a research agenda

While much of the scholarship and policy approaches to food systems recognize that there are different stakeholders, or actors, involved in ensuring that urban consumers have access to food, to date there has been relatively little consideration of the ways in which processes of migration contribute to shaping the spaces, practices, and networks involved in feeding cities. Yet a closer look at urban food systems, as we have very briefly illustrated in our discussion of the cases presented earlier, shows that migrant flows, and the translocal and transnational networks, forms of discrimination, and inequality associated with these, play a major role in constituting much of the urban food system. Food systems, especially retail and distribution spaces, often provide important early points of insertion into local economies. This is in keeping with the need to keep food prices low in order to placate urban consumers. At the same time, migrants begin to infuse local restaurants and food landscapes with their recipes, flavors, and ingredients, with implications for ways of eating in the cities.

This chapter represents a first effort to draw connections and commonalities between different fields of study, with the purpose of illuminating future research agendas at the intersection between migration, urbanization, and food systems in Latin America, with a special focus on the Andean region and the Southern Cone in South America. The intense mobility that the region is currently experiencing is a timely moment to take stock of what we know, and what remains to be known in this area.

First, it is clear that Latin American urban foodscapes continue to be shaped by new migrants arriving in these spaces. The novelty is that this is no longer only a characteristic of traditional receiving countries, such as Argentina, but now includes the new regional destinations of international migration. The predominant focus at the moment is on Venezuelan migrants, yet, as we have shown in the chapter, other internal and international migrants, whether newly arrived or with longer trajectories of settlement, also converge in urban food systems.

The heterogeneous presence of migrants of diverse origins in the spaces of production, circulation, and sale of food demonstrates the multi-layered reality of migration in Latin America. In the future, it will be important to pay attention to the similarities and differences between the established businesses of older migrants and the new ventures of more recent arrivals. In countries such as Argentina, for example, there seems to be a clear segmentation between Chinese supermarkets (established and profitable businesses with fixed premises), Bolivian *verdulerías*, which rely on dense networks and cross-border circulation, and the livelihood spaces of Venezuelan delivery workers, dependent on constant circulation, regulated at a distance by digital platforms, and where value extraction is more extreme. In the Andes, on the other hand, Venezuelan street vendors, as well as app-delivery workers, share and dispute informal trade spaces with local urbanites, their compatriots from other parts of the country, and other immigrants. In these cases it is worth asking about the reconfiguration of class, race, and gender hierarchies within the social organization of food systems.

In addition, in both the Southern Cone and the Andean region, we believe it is important to look more broadly into the interactions and relationships between different migrant groups, including internal and international migrants of different nationalities, and returnees, as they unfold in local foodscapes. This would contribute to more nuanced understandings of the daily formation of social relationships and ongoing city-making processes. In terms of both types of studies and geographic areas of interest, we observe that most of the scholarly work concentrates on capitals and large cities. Ethnographic case studies need to be complemented by comparative studies that include middle-size cities, regions, and different countries.

Notes

1 See Smit et al. (1996) and Smit (2016) for further discussion of UFS definitions.
2 See the Farm Labor report of the Economic Research Service US Department of Agriculture (link)
3 Shawarma restaurants in Quito generally are a combination of fast-food style and "ethnic" eateries. They frequently sell French fries and burgers as well.

Bibliography

Alfaro, Y., & Ramírez, A. (2019). Arepas venezolanas a la orden. La presencia cada vez menos silenciosa de la migración venezolana en Cochabamba, Bolivia. In L. Gandini, F. Lozano, & V. Prieto (Coords.), *Crisis y migración de población venezolana. Entre la desprotección y la seguridad jurídica en Latinoamérica* (pp. 185–208). SUDIMER-UNAM.

Álvarez Velasco, S. (2022). Between hostility and solidarity: The production of the Andean Region – Southern Cone transit migratory corridor. In G. Herrera & C. Gómez (Eds.), *Migration in South America: IMISCOE regional reader* (pp. 51–76). Springer. https://doi.org/10.1007/978-3-031-11061-0

Arizpe. L. (1989). *La mujer en el desarrollo de México y de América Latina*. Universidad Nacional Autónoma de México; Centro Regional de Investigaciones Multidisciplinarias.

Azogue, A. (2012). El barrio de San Roque . . . Lugar de acogida. In E. Kingman (Coord.), *San Roque: indígenas urbanos, seguridad y patrimonio* (pp. 21–36). Quito: FLACSO Sede Ecuador – HEIFFER Ecuador.

Baics, G. (2016). *Feeding Gotham: The political economy and geography of food in New York City, 1790–1860*. Princeton University Press.

Barragán, R. (2009). Más allá de lo mestizo, más allá de lo aymara: organización y representaciones de clase y etnicidad en el comercio callejero en la ciudad de La Paz. In E. Kingman Garcés (Comp.), *Historia social urbana: Espacios y flujos* (pp. 293–323). Quito: FLACSO Ecuador; Ministerio de Cultura del Ecuador.

Baviskar, A. (2021). Street food and the art of survival: Migrants and places in Delhi, India. *Food, Culture & Society*, *24*(1), 142–155. https://doi.org/10.1080/15528014.2020.1859903

Benencia, R. (2006). Bolivianización de la horticultura en la Argentina. Procesos de migración transnacional y construcción de territorios productivos. In *Migraciones regionales hacia la Argentina. Diferencias, desigualdad y derechos* (pp. 66–95). Prometeo.

Benencia, R. (2012). Predominio de inmigrantes bolivianos en los eslabones estratégicos de la cadena agroalimentaria de la horticultura en fresco de la Argentina. *Política y Sociedad*, *49*(1). https://doi.org/10.5209/rev_POSO.2012.v49.n1.36521

Benencia, R. R., & Quaranta, G. J. (2006). *Mercados de trabajo y economías de enclave: La "escalera boliviana" en la actualidad*. https://ri.conicet.gov.ar/handle/11336/74706

Berg, U. D. (2015). *Mobile selves: Race, migration and belonging in Peru and the U.S.* Nueva York y Londres: New York University Press.

Blanchette, A. (2020). *Porkopolis: American animality, standardized life, and the factory farm*. Duke University Press.

Blouin, C., & Freier, L. F. (2019). Población venezolana en Lima: entre la regularización y la precariedad. In L. Gandini, F. Lozano, & V. Prieto (Coords.), *Crisis y migración de población venezolana. Entre la desprotección y la seguridad jurídica en Latinoamérica* (pp. 157–184). SUDIMER-UNAM.

Blouin, C., & Zamora Gómez, C. (2022). Institutional and social Xenophobia towards Venezuelan migrants in the context of a racialized country: The case of Peru. In G. Herrera & C. Gómez (Eds.), *Migration in South America: IMISCOE regional reader* (pp. 169–190). Springer. https://doi.org/10.1007/978-3-031-11061-0

Brauner, S. (2020). Migraciones chinas, identidades y prácticas alimentarias: los restaurantes chinos y locales de comida rápida en la Ciudad Autónoma de Buenos Aires (1970–2018). In I. V. Campos & R. Martínez (Eds.), *Los chinos de ultramar: Sabor, cultura alimentaria y prácticas culinarias* (pp. 177–200). México: Palabra de Clío.

Campos, I. V. (2020). Entre cafés de chinos y buffet, del barrio a la plaza comercial: manifestaciones de la cultura alimentaria china en la Ciudad de México. In I. V. Campos & R. Martínez (Eds.), *Los chinos de ultramar: Sabor, cultura alimentaria y prácticas culinarias* (pp. 87–116). México: Palabra de Clío.

Campos, I. V., & Martínez, R. (2020). *Los chinos de ultramar: Sabor, cultura alimentaria y prácticas culinarias*. México: Palabra de Clío.

Casparrino, C., Guizardi, M., & Tamborino, F. V. (2021). Escenas de un protagonismo: migrantes aimaras bolivianas en el Agro-mercado de Arica (Chile). *Diario de Campo Cuarta Época, 5*(12), 108–133.

Chan, C., & Strabucchi, M. M. (2019). Creating and negotiating "Chineseness" through Chinese restaurants in Santiago, Chile. In *American Chinese Restaurants* (pp. 3–25). Routledge.

Cronon, W. (1992). *Nature's metropolis: Chicago and the Great West* (3rd print). Norton.

Crush, J., Chikanda, A., & Skinner, C. (2015). Migrant entrepreneurship and informality in South African cities. In *Mean streets: Migration, Xenophobia and informality in South Africa* (pp. 1–24). Cape Town: SAMP, ACC and IDRC.

De Oliveira, O., & Roberts, B. (1993). La informalidad urbana en años de expansión, crisis y reestructuración económica. *Estudios Sociológicos, XI*(31), 33–58.

Deener, A. (2020). *The problem with feeding cities: The social transformation of infrastructure, abundance, and inequality in America*. University of Chicago Press.

Deler, J.-P. (1988). Barrios populares y organización del espacio de las metrópolis andinas. Ensayo de modelización. *Bulletin de l'Institut Français d'Études Andines, 17–1*, 239–250.

Deler, J.-P. (1992). Ciudades andinas: Viejos y nuevos modelos. En E. Kingman (Comp.), *Ciudades de los Andes: Visión histórica y contemporánea* (pp. 351–374). Quito: Centro de Investigaciones CIUDAD.

Delgado, S. V. (2018). Exploring Middle Eastern immigration: History and contemporary diaspora of Middle Eastern immigrants to Latin America and culinary practices influenced by their culture. *UC Merced Undergraduate Research Journal, 10*(2). https://escholarship.org/uc/item/4rp7q2c5

Denardi, L. (2016). Casetes, redes y banquetes. Prácticas comerciales de chinos, taiwaneses y argentinos en Buenos Aires. *Etnografías Contemporáneas, 2*(2).

Gabaccia, D. R. (2000). *We are what we eat: Ethnic food and the making of Americans*. Harvard University Press. https://doi.org/10.4159/9780674037441

Gandini, L., Lozano, F., & Prieto, V. (Coords.). (2019). *Crisis y migración de población venezolana. Entre la desprotección y la seguridad jurídica en Latinoamérica*. SUDIMER-UNAM.

Garcés, A. (2011). Comercio inmigrante y economías étnicas: síntesis y críticas de los debates vigentes. *Polis. Revista Latinoamericana*, no. 29 (August), 1–20. https://journals.openedition.org/polis/1928?lang=en

Germani, Gino. 1969. *La sociología de la modernización*. Buenos Aires: Paidós.

Gómez, C., & Herrera, G. (2022). State and "Mixed Migrations": Migration policies towards Haitians, Colombians and Venezuelans in Ecuador. En G. Herrera & C. Gómez (Eds.), *Migration in South America: IMISCOE regional reader* (pp. 77–98). Springer.

Gorelik, A. (2022). *La ciudad latinoamericana: Una figura de la imaginación social del siglo XX*. Siglo XXI Editores. https://books.google.com/books?hl=en&lr=&id=1oxlEAAAQBAJ&oi=fnd&pg=PT6&dq=gorelik+%22la+ciudad+latinoamericana%22&ots=0fNLsA6CSU&sig=sQU__lzjgvOtUy-66OYL6xz3frI

Grimson, A., Ng, G., & Denardi, L. (2016). Las organizaciones de inmigrantes chinos en Argentina. *Migración y Desarrollo, 14*(26), 25–73.

Guérin, I. (2013). Bonded labour, Agrarian changes and capitalism: Emerging patterns in South India. *Journal of Agrarian Change*, *13*(3), 405–423.
Guerrero, A. (1983). *Haciendas, capital y lucha de clases andina*. Quito: El Conejo.
Hayden, T. B. (2024). Incomplete documentation, social isolation, and culinary estrangement: Factors affecting food security among urban migrant populations in Mexico. *Global Food Security*, *42*, 100779.
Hayes, M. (2018). *Gringolandia: Lifestyle migration under late capitalism*. Minneapolis, MN: University of Minnesota Press.
Hayes, M. (2013). Una nueva migración económica: el arbitraje geográfico de los jubilados estadounidenses hacia los países andinos. *Boletín AndinaMigrante*, *15*, 2–13.
Herrera, G. (2021). Migraciones en pandemia: nuevas y viejas formas de desigualdad. *Nueva Sociedad*, *293*, 106–116.
Herrera, G., & Cabezas, G. (2019). Ecuador: de la recepcion a la disuasión. Políticas frente a la población venezolana y experiencia migratoria 2015–2018. In *Crisis y migración de población venezolana. Entre la desprotección y la seguridad jurídica en Latinoamérica* (pp. 125–156). Mexico: Universidad Nacional Autónoma de México.
Herrera, G., & Gómez, C. (2022). Introduction: Emergent issues of South American migrations. In *Migration in South America: IMISCOE regional reader* (pp. 1–23). Cham: Springer International Publishing.
Herrera Jurado, B. B. (2022). *Conseguir trabajo y vivienda: La solidaridad étnica de los trabajadores peruanos en la Ciudad de Buenos Aires (1990–2021)*. https://ri.conicet.gov.ar/handle/11336/201083
Herrera Mosquera, G., & Cabezas Gálvez, G. (2020). Los tortuosos caminos de la migración venezolana en Sudamérica: tránsitos precarios y cierre de fronteras. *Migración y Desarrollo*, *18*(34), 33–56.
Hidalgo Cordero, K., & Valencia Castro, B. (2019). *Entre la precarización y el alivio cotidiano: las plataformas Uber Eats y Glovo en Quito*. Friedrich-Ebert-Stiftung Ecuador-Instituto Latinoamericano de Investigaciones Sociales.
Hollenstein, P. (2019). *¿Están en riesgo los mercados y ferias municipales?: aprovisionamiento de alimentos, economías populares y la organización del espacio público urbano de Quito*. Friedrich-Ebert-Stiftung Ecuador-Instituto Latinoamericano de Investigaciones Sociales.
Hollenstein, P. (2020). El mercado agroalimentario ecuatoriano: hacia un programa de investigación. *Ecuador Debate*, *110*(Agosto), 145–159.
Holmes, S. M. (2013). *Fresh fruit, broken bodies: Migrant farmworkers in the United States*. University of California Press.
Howes, D. (2006). Charting the sensorial revolution. *The Senses and Society*, *1*(1), 113–128. https://doi.org/10.2752/174589206778055673
Ibarra, H. (2008). Ferrocarril, redes mercantiles y arrieros en la Sierra central ecuatoriana. En H. Ibarra (Comp.), *El camino de hierro. Cien años de la llegada del ferrocarril a Quito* (pp. 51–81). Quito: FONSAL.
Imbruce, V. (2007). Bringing Southeast Asia to the Southeast United States: New forms of alternative agriculture in Homestead, Florida. *Agriculture and Human Values*, *24*, 41–59.
Imbruce, V. (2016). *From farm to canal street: Chinatown's alternative food network in the global marketplace*. Cornell University Press. https://doi.org/10.7591/9781501701238
Imilan, W. A., & Millaleo, A. (2015). Comer a lo peruano. Lugares de la migración gastronómica. In W. A. Imilan, F. Márquez, & C. Stefoni (Eds), *Rutas migrantes en Chile: Habitar, festejar y trabajar* (pp. 99–120). Santiago: Ediciones Universidad Alberto Hurtado.
Jaramillo, O., & Jácome, V. (2019). From a popular economy to a popular and solidarity economy in Quito: A case of indigenous urban immigrants in the San Roque neighborhood. *CIRIEC-Espana Revista de Economia Publica, Social y Cooperativa*, *96*, 155–187.
Jiménez, R., Bachmann, P. F., & Loza, N. (2019). Ferias informales y migración laboral comercial. Apuntes para el debate del corredor fronterizo peruano-chileno. *Estudios Fronterizos*, *20*, e037, 1–29. https://doi.org/10.21670/ref.1916037

Jurado, B. H. (2022). Los pliegues de la racialización. Los trabajadores peruanos en la Ciudad de Buenos Aires (1990–2021). *PACHA. Revista de Estudios Contemporáneos Del Sur Global*, *3*(8), e21098.

Kingman, E. (1992). Ciudades de los Andes: Homogenialización y diversidad. In E. Kingman (Comp.), *Ciudades de los Andes. Visión histórica y contemporánea. Travaux de l'Institut Français d'Études Andines 72*. Quito: IFEA; CIUDAD.

Kingman, E. (2014). Oficios y trajines callejeros. In E. Kingman & B. Muratorio (Eds.), *Los trajines callejeros. Memoria y vida cotidiana. Quito, siglos XIX–XX* (pp. 27–112). Quito: FLACSO Sede Ecuador; Instituto Metropolitano de Patrimonio; Fundación Museos de la Ciudad.

Kirshner, J. (2010). Migration, informalization and public space in Santa Cruz, Bolivia. *Bolivian Studies Journal*, 150–190.

Lapenda, M. (2021). Migración Peruana, Identidad y Lógicas Residenciales En Un Espacio Suburbano Del Área Metropolitana de Buenos Aires (AMBA), Argentina. *ODISEA. Revista de Estudios Migratorios*, no. 8, 154–182.

Larrea, M. D. L., Aulestia, C., Moncayo, G. N. C., & Zurita, J. D. A. (2020). Migración cubana: ¿Influencia en la oferta de establecimientos de alimentos y bebidas en Quito? *Revista de Investigación Enlace Universitario, 19*(1), 1–15.

Lindquist, J., Xiang, B., & Yeoh, B. S. (2012). Opening the black box of migration: Brokers, the organization of transnational mobility and the changing political economy in Asia. *Pacific Affairs*, *85*(1), 7–19.

Madariaga, J., Buenadicha, C., Molina, E., & Ernst, C. (2019). *Economía de plataformas y empleo:¿ cómo es trabajar para una app en Argentina?* (Vol. 718). Inter-American Development Bank.

Maglia, G., Lipski, J., Mina, J., & Cuenu, Y. (2019). Transacciones discursivas, economía simbólica y cocinas de la Afromemoria en la Plaza de Mercado de Cali. *Middle Atlantic Review of Latin American Studies*, *3*(1), 35.

Margarit, D., & Bijit, K. (2015). Los negocios de inmigrantes sudamericanos: una aproximación a las estrategias de instalación e integración socioterritorial en la comuna de Santiago de Chile. In M. Guizardi (Ed.). *Las fronteras del transnacionalismo. Límites y desbordes de la experiencia migrante en el centro y norte de Chile* (pp. 63–83). Santiago: Universidad de Tarapacá; Ocho Libros Editores.

Marrero, D. (2016). *El rol de los supermercados chinos en la integración social de la población china en Buenos Aires/The role of chinese supermarkets in the social integration of the Chinese population in Buenos Aires*. https://digitalcollections.sit.edu/isp_collection/2428/

Martens, C. (2024). Migration, cultural and class boundaries in Quito's food truck scene. In, J. Crush, A. Chikanda, & S. Ramachandran (Eds.). *New directions in South-South migration*. Cham: Springer.

Martínez, L. (1984). *De campesinos a proletarios: cambios en la mano de obra rural en la sierra del Ecuador*. Quito: El Conejo.

Martínez Esquivel, R. (2007). *Los chinos de ultramar*. Palabra de Clío.

Masferrer, C., Pedroza, L., Covarrubias, A., García-Guerrero, V. M., Gil Everaert, I., González, G., Rodríguez, O., Yúnez-Naude, A., & Zepeda, B. (2023). Considerations for a new research agenda on migration and refugee studies: Lessons from studying migration and foreign policies in Mexico. *Journal of Immigrant & Refugee Studies*, *21*(4), 566–580. https://doi.org/10.1080/15562948.2022.2137268

McCollum, D., & Findlay, A. (2018). Oiling the wheels? Flexible labour markets and the migration industry. *Journal of Ethnic and Migration Studies*, *44*(4), 558–574.

Medeiros, C., Rodríguez-Carmona, A., Ferrufino, G., & Tassi, N. (2013). Ensanchando los intersticios. Institucionalidades y estrategias económicas del comercio popular. *T'inkazos. Revista Boliviana de Ciencias Sociales, 33,* 27–46. https://www.redalyc.org/articulo.oa?id=426141576003

Medina Flores, G., & Basfi-fer Obregón, K. (2018). Desafíos y oportunidades en la venta de comida callejera por migrantes en Santiago, Chile. *Cuadernos Médico Sociales*, *58*(4), 77–84. https://cuadernosms.cl/index.php/cms/article/view/333

Negri, S. (2020). El proceso de trabajo y la experiencia de los trabajadores en las plataformas de delivery en la Argentina. *Estudios Del Trabajo*, *60*, 26–55.

Nobrega. R. (2008). Migraciones y modernidad brasileña: Italianos, nordestinos y bolivianos en San Pablo. In S. Novick (Comp.), *Las migraciones en América Latina. Políticas, culturas y estrategias* (pp. 113–131). Buenos Aires: Catálogos; CLACSO.

Novick, S. (2008). Migración y políticas en Argentina: tres leyes para un país extenso (1876–2004). In S. Novick (Comp.), *Las migraciones en América Latina. Políticas, culturas y estrategias* (pp. 131–151). Buenos Aires: Catálogos; CLACSO.

Orjuela-Grimm, M., Deschak, C., Aragon Gama, C. A., Bhatt Carreño, S., Hoyos, L., Mundo, V., . . . & Infante, C. (2022). Migrants on the move and food (in) security: A call for research. *Journal of Immigrant and Minority Health*, *24*, 1–10.

Ortale, S., & Santos, J. (2021). Etnicidad y comida . . . más allá de la alimentación familiar. Estudio en una comunidad peruana de Ensenada (Pcia. de Buenos Aires, Argentina). Dossier Alimentación y Cocinas En Las Américas. Grupo de Trabajo, 22.

Ortega, C., & Ospina, O. (2012). Capítulo III. Condiciones y estrategias de vida. In C. Ortega & O. Ospina (Eds.), *"No se puede ser refugiado toda la vida . . .": refugiados urbanos: el caso de la población colombiana en Quito y Guayaquil* (pp. 125–172). Flacso-Sede Ecuador.

Pachano, Simón. (1988). Los estudios sobre migración, población y empleo en el Ecuador. En S. Pachano (Comp.), *Población, migración y empleo en el Ecuador* (pp. 197–224). Quito: ILDIS.

Pastor, J. M. (2018). *Negociando la identidad en la migración. El caso de los afganos en Ecuador y su estrategia de supervivencia en torno al negocio del "Shawarma"* [Tesis de Especialización Superior, FLACSO Ecuador].

Pilcher, J. (1998). *Que Vivan Los Tamales: Food and the making of Mexican identity*. University of New Mexico Press.

Pilcher, J. M. (2005). Industrial Tortillas and Folkloric Pepsi: The nutritional consequences of hybrid cuisines in Mexico. In J. L. Watson & M. A. Caldwell (Eds.), *The cultural politics of food and eating*. Blackwell.

Pilcher, J. M. (2016). Preface: Culinary infrastructure. *Global Food History*, *2*(2), 101–104. https://doi.org/10.1080/20549547.2016.1214897

Pilcher, J. M., & Laudan, R. (1999). Chiles, chocolate, and race in new Spain: Glancing backward to Spain or looking forward to Mexico? *Eighteenth Century Life*, *23*(2), 59–70.

Pinto Baleisan, C., Colin, C., & Eria Madariaga, L. M. (2022). Negociaciones en la puesta en escena del país de origen. Un estudio transnacional sobre restaurantes extranjeros en Gran Valparaíso, Chile. *Migraciones Internacionales*, *13*. https://doi.org/10.33679/

Quijano, A. (1972). La Constitución del "Mundo" de la Marginalidad Urbana. *EURE: Revista de Estudios Urbano Regionales*, *2*(5), 89–106.

Ray, K. (2016). *The ethnic restaurateur*. Bloomsbury Academic, an imprint of Bloomsbury Publishing, Plc.

Rivera Sánchez, L. (2004). Transformaciones comunitarias y remesas socioculturales de los migrantes mixtecos poblanos. *Migración y desarrollo*, *2*, 62–81.

Rivera Sánchez, L. (2017). De la migración interna a la migración internacional en México. Apuntes sobre la formación de un campo de estudio. Íconos. *Revista de Ciencias Sociales*, *58*, 37–57.

Roberts, B. R. (1980). *Ciudades de campesinos: La economía política de la urbanización en el tercer mundo*. México: Siglo XXI.

Rodríguez, A., & Hollenstein, P. (2020). Searching for alternatives to oligopolistic modernisation: Food provisioning, social organisation and interculturality in Quito's urban markets. In G. V. Raphael Hoetmer & M. M'Barek (Eds.), *Cities of dignity: Urban transformation around the world* (pp. 122–141). Rosa Luxemburg Stiftung.

Rojas-Galindo, M., Unda-Padilla, M., & Pacheco, A. (2024). Entre la informalidad y la inseguridad: nuevas dinámicas alimentarias y comerciales en el mercado San Roque de Quito. *Íconos: Revista de Ciencias Sociales*, *79*, 99–117.

Rolando, E. S., & Segui, V. R. (2015). Chinos en Buenos Aires: Una mirada sobre la actividad de los supermercados. *Latino-Americanas*, *90*.

Smit, J., Ratta, A., & Nasr, J. (1996). *Urban agriculture. Food, Jobs and Sustainable Cities,* Publication Series for Habitat II, Vol. 1.

Smit, W. (2016). Urban governance and urban food systems in Africa: Examining the linkages. *Cities*, *58*, 80–86.

Steel, C. (2013). *Hungry city: How food shapes our lives*. Vintage.

Stefoni, C. (2008). Gastronomía peruana en las calles de Santiago y la construcción de espacios transnacionales y territorios. In S. Novick (Comp.), *Las migraciones en América Latina. Políticas, culturas y estrategias* (pp. 211–228). Buenos Aires: Catálogos; CLACSO.

Tassi, N., & Poma, W. (2020). Los caminos de la economía popular: circuitos económicos populares y reconfiguraciones regionales. *Temas Sociales*, *47*, 10–35.

Vázquez-Medina, J. A. (2016). *Cocina, nostalgia y etnicidad en restaurantes mexicanos de Estados Unidos*. https://www.torrossa.com/it/resources/an/3181302

Vélez, C. A. G. (2022). Tequeños en Bogotá, consumo nostálgico de comida y migración venezolana. *Ciencias Sociales y Educación*, *11*(22), 96–119. https://doi.org/10.22395/csye.v11n22a5

Yagüe, B. (2014). Hacer "comestible" la ciudad. Las redes como estrategias alimentarias de los indígenas urbanos de Leticia, Amazonía colombiana. *Revista Colombiana de Antropología*, *50*(2), 141–166.

Zanoni, E. (2018). Migrant marketplaces: Globalizing histories of migrant foodways. *Global Food History*, *4*(1), 3–21. https://doi.org/10.1080/20549547.2018.1423828

Zapata, A. (2019). Los chinos de Cuba y del Perú: revisión historiográfica. *Investigaciones sociales*, *22*(42), 131–154. https://doi.org/10.15381/is.v22i42.17485

8

EATING ON THE MOVE

Metro stations as care infrastructure in the city of Santiago

Paola Jirón, Juan Antonio Carrasco, Walter Imilan, Inés Figueroa, Adriana Brinck and Francisca Basaure

Introduction

The implementation of the integrated public transportation system Transantiago[1] in 2007 generated an exponential increase in the use of the Metro in Santiago, Chile. Fare integration implied that, with the same fare payment, people could access the urban bus system and connect without additional payment to the metro system. Since then, Santiago residents have had to learn to adapt, modify, innovate, and resist the old ways of traveling, incorporating new modes, spaces, people, schedules, charges, and access, among many daily practices in order to move around the city in light of the new mobility infrastructures (Jirón et al., 2016). These transformations have also generated transfer areas, especially between buses and metro stations, where waiting and passenger exchange provide ideal spaces for street commerce.

The Santiago metro system has 136 stations distributed across 26 districts of the capital of Chile[2] (see Metro Santiago Map in the following https://www.metro.cl/el-viaje/plano-de-red). With the main purpose of connecting the city's travelers with their multiple destinations, the metro stations were designed to make the connection and flow more efficient and to privilege speedy and smooth circulation. Their design did not take into account, however, the alternative and informal spaces and practices that could emerge in the areas surrounding the stations, including the presence of street commerce. Yet in various parts of the city, commerce around subway stations including the sale of prepared food, clothing, fruits and vegetables, telephone accessories, and a range of products, is widespread. Indeed, in many cases, the spaces near entryways, exits and transit points around public transportation hubs have become food courts of sorts, with food offerings of different types, prices, quality, and type. For more than two million daily users of the Santiago

DOI: 10.4324/9781003471929-12

metro, in fact, these food stalls comprise an integrated part of their experience of public transit and their daily mobility.

This chapter analyzes the use and appropriations that occur of the public spaces in and around Santiago's subway system for the purposes of feeding and eating in order to argue that these constitute parts of networks of care. Foodwork–which implies the planning, procuring, preparation, serving, and clean-up related to food—is a central form of gendered care work, as feminist scholars have argued (Beagan et al., 2008). By approaching the food practices of Santiago's residents through the lens of care, it becomes possible to understand how urban infrastructures are inserted in the complex field of the daily lives of the city's inhabitants, and the ways in which they do, and don't, meet their needs.

The argument developed here on the relationship between mobility infrastructures and care draws on and contributes to two bodies of academic scholarship. First, it draws on studies that emphasize the socio-material condition of infrastructures. Infrastructures in such an approach are understood as assemblages between materialities and the everyday lives of inhabitants, who through their practices create and transform infrastructures (Latham & Wood, 2015). Second, the chapter draws on the notion of the feminist ethic of care, which emphasizes that care relations and care practices are not exclusive to individuals (Held, 2005). Such an approach implies understanding care as a product of relationships between humans as well as between human and non-human agents. This means expanding the idea of care beyond its conventional understanding as the relationship between those who care (often women) and those who are cared for, to a definition that encompasses the way in which society as a whole provides (or fails to provide) care for different groups and individuals. In this sense, we suggest that infrastructures, including mobility infrastructures, can be understood as part of care networks, and that they might in fact be conceived as *infrastructures of care*, regardless of the specific objectives for which they were designed. This argument points to the need for urban planning practices, including mobility and transport planning, to incorporate a care perspective into the way that they create policies and infrastructures.

Based on a mobile ethnographic approach,[3] this chapter explores how the relationship between the spatial configuration of subway stations, informal food buying and selling practices, and informal work strategies is part of the complex phenomenon of eating on the move in Santiago, Chile. The ethnographic work[4] consisted of two phases: In the first phase, 118 metro stations[5] were analyzed according to the type of food for sale, the hours of operation of stalls, their arrangement in the space around the stations, as well as the identification of vendors, flows, and schedules. In the second phase, specific stations and types of products that were identified as relevant to observe were selected. The former include stations with high flow in the morning (in central areas of the city and in areas with high passenger traffic) or in the afternoon (areas with high traffic at the end of the workday, terminal, and intermodal stations). The fieldwork consisted of interviews and a day of ethnographic shadowing (Jirón, 2010), to accompany the vendors of different foodstuffs in the process of preparation, sale, and post-sale of their products. The empirical section, focused on the description of food vending strategies and their diverse practices, is followed by a reflection on care and mobility infrastructures, advocating a broad understanding of the spatial dimension of daily life that invites us to recognize the multiple relationships that emerge between informal economies, health, and infrastructures in the city.

Food environments in subway exits: street food and informal labor

Food environments are the physical, economic, political, and sociocultural contexts that frames the interaction of consumers with the food system with a view to the acquisition, preparation, and consumption of food (GTOP, 2022). Together with socioeconomic standings, food environments are key elements that affect the food practices of urban populations. The public street is one of the five main types of food environments, and it refers to the purchase and sale of food in public spaces such as streets, squares, and transportation sites, among others (Cerda et al., 2016, p. 21). In cities in many parts of Latin America, as in other parts of the world, street food vendors are an important presence which shapes the food routines of many people (Hayden, 2021; Giglia, 2022; Imilan et al., 2015; Garcia, 2011).

The sale and consumption of food in public spaces in Chile are a relatively recent practice, unlike in other large Latin American cities. In the early 2000s, the use of public space for the sale of food took on a new dimension thanks to migrants, especially from Peru. New economic practices developed by migrants have gained visibility in the field of food since the first decade of this century (Imilan, 2015). Indeed, in central places in the city, public space is transformed through the street food trade. Certainly, in Santiago, food was sold in public spaces from before the arrival of Peruvian migrants, but it had previously been limited to very specific places, such as bus stops or busy intersections, and to certain products such as coffee and sandwiches, or to specific temporalities of the day such as early weekday mornings or late weekend nights. At present, although the migrant population maintains an important participation in street food, it is no longer an activity exclusively linked to migration, and the product offerings and commercial strategies are expanding. In the context of the expanding and integrating public transport system, subway stations in particular had become sites where informal food markets were growing.

The rise of street food in general in Santiago can be linked to several overlapping processes which are common to diverse cities in Latin America and other parts of the Global South. In general, eating outside of the home is a growing phenomenon in many Latin American cities (Hayden, 2024). One reason has to do with the radical changes in the organization of daily life. For example, the incorporation of women into the labor force has meant a transformation in the way households function, with less time available to cook every day, families living away from home for a large part of the day, and the need to feed themselves outside the home. Cerda et al. (2016) argue that, due to various socioeconomic and demographic phenomena, including internal and international migration, urban expansion, the increase in underemployment and unemployment, the magnitude and complexity of the commute between home and work, as well as the difficulty of finding affordable food outlets along the way, have led to the intensification of the sale of food in public spaces, mainly in the context of informal work. Currently, this type of food constitutes a relevant option to satisfy a growing demand for both food and work for working and immigrant populations in large cities and can be seen as key to the food security of mobile urban populations (Cerda et al., 2016; Duhau & Giglia, 2007; Hayden, 2021). On the other hand, the dynamics of flexible and remote work, as well as the changes in commuting times imposed by new mobility systems such as Transantiago, have driven the rise of food-on-the-go practices as an increasingly important part of informal commerce (Jirón & Imilan, 2015).

In the city of Santiago, the surroundings of metro stations have become privileged spaces for the food trade in recent years. The establishment of the subway as the structural axis of the mass transit system has boosted the emergence of these new urban landscapes. In this sense, the offerings of street food in subway stations generate employment and an important source of income for a significant proportion of the population. This is particularly true in times of economic crisis and also with the increase of migrant population to cities such as Santiago. Although street food vending represents a food alternative for millions of people, as well as a source of employment for both women and migrant population—90 and 70% of the total number of vendors, respectively (Cerda et al., 2016)—this sector also shows problematic aspects related to hygiene and nutrition.

Spatial transformation and culinary offerings

The metro has become for many a *mobile place* (Jirón et al., 2016), a space designed for mobility and that people signify as they pass through or stay in it. Despite the lack of intentional design for such purposes, through their mobility practices, people provide meaning to mobility infrastructures in different ways, including metro cars, platforms, stairs, ticket offices, access and connector spaces, bus stops, seats, lights, streets, sidewalks, walkways, street crossings, among many others. They may sit, rest, kiss, talk, take a lunch break, read, or do any other number of things in these places. In Santiago, one of the favorite spaces which have been re-signified for food purposes are metro exits.

From early in the morning, prior to the subway's opening, until several hours after the stations close, you can see stalls with lights, seats, awnings, tables, fairground carts, or handkerchiefs laid out on the ground, ready for the thousands of customers who come to shop. The objects with which they set up to sell include dollies,[6] plastic boxes, coolers,[7] plastic stools, plastic bags, elastic straps,[8] supermarket carts, folding tables, sunshades, or various carts. The arrangement of the

IMAGE 8.1 Sales stalls at the subway exit

Source: Own elaboration—FONDECYT Regular N° 1171113

stalls is strategic according to the particular design and access of each station. The stalls in fact shape access to the subway, creating pathways that guide travelers into the stations (see Image 8.2). As foods represent a significant percentage of the things on sale at the entrance to the subway, we can see a food environment emerging in these locations.

Different foods can be found in the stalls surrounding the subways exists: There are stalls that specialize in a single product, such as natural juices, croissants, desserts in a glass, or *tequeños*.[9] These usually work a couple of hours a day. Some stalls offer more sophisticated, varied foods, including vegan dishes, Arabic food, *hot dogs*, Chinese food, traditional lunches, sandwiches, sushi with multiple fillings, among others.

There are different rhythms to the food commerce around subway stations. At breakfast time, sandwiches, *sopaipillas*,[10] fruit, yogurt with jam or cereal, hard-boiled eggs, cakes, croissants, tequeños, arepas,[11] natural juices, coffee, or hot tea are the most common. The food varies according to the season; more fruit in the summer, more sandwiches in the winter. At lunchtime, meanwhile, some stalls offer packed lunches, which can easily be taken away. Some products are prepared in advance by the vendors or their distributors, whereas others are prepared on-site, including natural juices, sopaipillas, empanadas, or some sandwiches (Image 8.5). In the

IMAGE 8.2 Rodrigo de Araya Metro Station

Source: Own elaboration—FONDECYT Regular N° 1171113

evening, as many workers return home, prepared foods which can be eaten on the spot or taken home and served to the family are commonly found, especially in terminal or more peripheral stations. The smell of grilled meat and fried food fills the air in many stations starting at around 17:00 or 18:00 hours. There are stations offering grilled meats (Chilean, Peruvian, or Colombian style), sopaipillas (with various sauces), French fries, churros, *hot dogs* (with a variety of sauces and fillings for all tastes), pizzas, arepas,[12] stuffed potatoes, sushi, and *handrolls*,[13] among others. The different temporalities of foods speak to how important eating out has become as an everyday practice in all meals and moments of the day in Santiago, as in other cities, and also shows how street food vendors become part of what Hayden (2021) has called people's *mobile food routines*.

Systematic observation shows that the vendors take ownership of their selling places; they are usually located in the same places each day. Each vendor's space is negotiated over time and respected by the other vendors, both explicitly and implicitly, who, in addition to competing among themselves, also support each other in the face of common difficulties, as is common with street vendors throughout Latin America's cities (see Hayden & Farah, this volume for an overview). This is especially relevant when dealing with the police or enforcement officials. In the communes of Santiago, enforcement has different intensities. According to the vendors themselves, in some municipalities the authorities negotiate so that the space does not look "disorderly", demanding awnings and location in certain pre-established spaces, while other municipalities simply ignore the situation. But there are also more severe authorities, who dismantle the facilities, issue fines, and confiscate the merchandise.

The work of selling in the stalls around the metro is hard work and requires preparation and scheduling. The vendors improve their offerings as conditions improve, as in the cases of Veronica and Jacinta subsequently. In the event of an inspection, vendors remain alert to the arrival of municipal officials or police officers:

> *Veronica and her daughter live near the station where they sell sushi from a cart. Veronica had it made with wheels, which seem to make a great effort to resist the weight of the metal structure. She works without a permit, but with the intention of becoming a formalized worker. To do so, she needs to comply with a series of requirements, including a "professional" cart with a capacity of 100 liters of water, with lights and everything, which costs around $600,000 pesos.*
>
> *Veronica buys most of her cooking products from an importer. Nearby she buys pots, plastics, etcetera. She rides her bicycle to shop, as everything is close by. She prepares the rolls at home and fries the breaded sushi at the moment before serving. Along with the sushi, she offers soy sauce or sweet and sour sauce, which she delivers in a transparent bag. She also offers cakes with decorations.*
>
> *She only attends the station on Tuesdays, Wednesdays and Thursdays, because she is not on leave—she says. She arrives around 19:00 and leaves at 23:00. On Saturdays she sells at the market. He has a few regular customers. Each roll, individually, is priced at $2,000, and in a 3x5 promotion. She delivers them whole or cut, according to the customer's taste. She uses her finger as a measure for the cuts. As she tries to handle the money as little as possible, when she is paid she asks the customer to deposit the money under a tray. Hygiene is important to her. She used to have a water can, and wash her hands there, but it broke recently, so now she uses a bottle. Her short hair is uncovered, as are her hands. She wears a face mask, however, this seems to be rather decorative. She uses a fork to move the roll in the boiling oil, and with a strainer she removes the remains of fried breading left in the oil.*[14]
>
> *Jacinta sells sopaipillas and cheese empanadas at the west exit of the station. There she places her cargo bike; a large square folding table with a white cover on the right side of the bike; some plastic containers; a couple of large colored plastic boxes. Above the cargo area of the motorcycle is the kitchen. The kitchen is part of an old cart that Jacinta disassembled, but the water and wheels failed. From the old cart she salvaged the kitchen area, a gas stove. It lacks the knob, but she deftly moves the "pituto*[15] *"that is visible, lighting and extinguishing the fire with a few matches when she needs to heat the oil to refill the sopaipillas and empanadas she cooks on the spot. She buys gas in the neighborhood immediately behind the place where the cart is located. To the left, on the frame of*

the motorcycle, a small sign shows a picture of a sopaipilla and an empanada. It is printed, but the prices are handwritten, in marker. Sopaipillas are $200 and empanadas are $250.

The stand has tea and instant coffee on the folding table, where there are also white plastic spoons inside a transparent plastic bag. Another jar contains white sugar. In one of the plastic boxes there are individual tea bags. In addition, on the table there are different candies: large chocolates of different brands. In addition, there are cleaning products: bottles of detergent, toilet paper of different brands. The sopaipillas are made with dehydrated pumpkin, which gives them a color and flavor unmistakably reminiscent of homemade sopaipilla, even though they are made in a factory and not personally by her.

Below the stove, in the storage space of the motorcycle, there are trays of plastic film where the cheese empanadas are stored waiting to be prepared.

The cases of Veronica and Jacinta illustrate several elements of selling food at metro exits. First, that this is a job that requires planning, organization, and a willingness to meet the goals they set for themselves in terms of sales. Street selling is, after all, an entrepreneurial activity, as many neoliberal supporters of small commerce have pointed out (De Soto). On the other hand, since the space is not adequate for sales, vendors literally have to assemble the physical elements with which they organize their business: stalls, objects, and elements for serving, cooking, and cleaning are all part of what vendors need to take to and from their space on the street each day. The process of perfecting their stalls is something that generally develops as they establish themselves in each place of sale. Just like Verónica and Jacinta, thousands of vendors have been setting up along the mobility infrastructure in the City of Santiago, to generate income and provide the millions of Santiago residents with important sources of daily food.

Food as a care practice

Within transportation studies, many of the scholarships that link health and mobility have been focused on the role of urban environmental and travel behaviors on physical activity and sedentary lifestyles, especially in relation to obesity (Carrasco et al., 2019). This line of study has been taken up by mobility scholars interested in understanding and promoting policy interventions linked to active modes of travel such as cycling and walking. Thus, infrastructures linked to "active" modes of transit, including bicycle lanes, pedestrian paths, and pedestrianization have been analyzed. Metros and public transport hubs are generally less present in research related to health and consumption, and they are certainly not considered in relation to their role as spaces of consumption.

Meanwhile, within scholarship that attempts to link built environments to food consumption patterns, there is likewise a tendency to privilege questions of obesity, rather than food security more broadly, or to look at how certain spaces constitute "obesogenic" environments (Llamas, 2018; Mustieles Granell et al., 2023). In this sense, Bastías García (2018) points out that for the city of Santiago, the built environment has a special influence on unhealthy eating practices by favoring both higher caloric consumption and lower energy expenditure. Among the environmental factors that promote higher caloric intake is the availability of a wide variety of processed foods with high energy density, low price, and magnified taste in specific territories. Despite the existence of free markets[16] in lower-income sectors in the city of Santiago, Bastías García (2018) posits that the presence of establishments with mixed or unprocessed food supply in low socioeconomic sectors suggests that such establishments generate differentiated food environments according to socioeconomic context. This means that the food offerings in low-income sectors hinder regular access to healthy food in the city of Santiago. This could indicate the existence of "food deserts", that is, low-income places where residents are unable to buy affordable and healthy food (Cummins, 2014; Reyes-Puente et al., 2022; Pinheiro et al., 2022).

Nevertheless, work related to the spatial accessibility of food and food environments which uses concepts, such as "food deserts" or "food oases," rarely takes the question of transport and mobility into consideration and too often focuses narrowly on ingredients purchased in supermarkets rather than the totality of spaces and elements of daily food practices (Shannon, 2016). Understanding the type of food accessed, and where and how eating practices are linked to daily routines is fundamental to addressing the issue. Regarding the type of food, it is not only relevant to consider what is sold in supermarkets and neighborhood stores. It is also necessary to address the type and location of food, formal and informal, that is accessed on a daily basis during daily activities, including the analysis of daily mobility in relation to the type of food that is acquired on the move throughout the day (Hayden, 2021; Bosco et al., 2017). The case of proliferating street foods outside of metro stations in Santiago presented here invites us to explore how mobility affects food consumption patterns, in terms of thinking about both urban consumers as necessarily mobile subjects whose meals occur often far from home and how the infrastructures for transport themselves act as micro-food environments. In this view of the built environment, mobility infrastructures, such as metro stations, should be seen as fundamental components of food environments.

If we think of mobility infrastructures as elements of food environments, the next step is to ask how this relates to the theory of care which we introduced in the introduction of this chapter. Tronto and Fisher proposed a useful definition of care for the purposes of our discussion in 1990: A species activity that includes everything we do to maintain, continue and repair our 'world' so that we can live as well as possible. That world includes our bodies, ourselves, our environment, all that is sought to be woven into a complex web of life support" (Tronto and Fisher 1990: 40).

This means that care practices refer to those activities necessary to reproduce the totality of life and not only include those linked to the upbringing and care of the sick, disabled, or elderly but also include practices of communication, hygiene, physical and mental health, rest, education, play, grooming, self-care *and feeding*, among many others. These practices require an organization that involves support and care chains (Jirón & Gómez, 2018; Solar-Ortega, 2020), people, and multiple elements, including infrastructures, that facilitate it. These are embodied practices and therefore, where it is the bodies that exercise mobility, in the case of feeding, it is the bodies that are affected by this practice. Foodwork, in other words, is a key form of caring, but it is one that we need to recognize as taking place not only in the home, between women and their families, as is often proposed, but something which must necessarily occur at different scales and in different places throughout the city as people engage in their daily lives.

Given this understanding of food as care, it becomes clear that the informal sale of food is thus part of an infrastructure of care. Jacinta, Verónica, and other men and women like them who have set up stands, tables, and carts near the exits of Santiago's metros emerge in response to changes in a mobility infrastructure, where there is a failure of planning to anticipate needs and desires of travelers to eat, rest, and other elements. They become, in other words, part of an infrastructure of care, even as they face numerous challenges in their roles as informal workers.

This brings us to the question of nutrition and health in relation to care. Namely, to what extent do the foods that people are able to buy on the street supportive of their bodies and wellbeing? While street foods are part of people's daily routines, for example, they may not necessarily be the source of healthy foods which contribute to bodily well-being. Indeed, some studies of street foods suggest that they are high in calories and do not necessarily offer balanced meal options. However, improving access to healthy food does not necessarily mean eliminating *street food*, as this can significantly affect the food options of many Santiago city dwellers with limited time and money. Indeed, as Hayden (2021) argues, it is important to recognize street food in relation to the daily mobilities of consumers and thus, as part of the food security of low-income and middle-income groups and as urban infrastructure more broadly. However, it is important to look for ways in which food intake along the city's multiple journeys is not only healthy, but available in the same journeys and nearby food environments, and also affordable. The food sold at the exits of metro stations must therefore first be recognized as the source of daily food that it is, in order to be able to develop strategies to support those people, like Jacinta and Verónica, who sell it. Incorporating street food into planning—for both mobility and public space—is important not only because of its abundant presence in a large part of the metro network but also because it constitutes a considerable source of income for a segment of the population.

Conclusion

As Power (2019) has argued, infrastructures are not inert objects, but rather dynamic patterns that are the basis of social organization, as sociotechnical systems. This view allows us to analyze how infrastructure shapes social life and to identify the values that are selectively encoded, thus reproducing social differences through their use. Thus, as infrastructure changes, as has been the case with the transportation infrastructure in the city of Santiago, so do the daily practices of traveling, eating, and caring. We have seen in other works the impact that mobility has on care practices (Jirón & Gómez, 2018), particularly for women. In this chapter, we see how transformations in mobility infrastructures generate changes in forms of traveling, congregating, and consuming. In this sense, we can see how infrastructures allow us to take care of or neglect people's nutrition.

This chapter has shown how the impacts of transformations in public transport policies and infrastructures in Santiago, Chile, generate changing forms of spatial appropriation, place-making, and forms of everyday life. In particular, the chapter has drawn attention to the proliferation of street food vending practices around metro stations as attending to the needs of mobile urban populations and has suggested that it is useful to think about these spaces of sales in relation to care. Street food stands provide foods for mobile populations, filling a need which transport and urban planning has poorly accounted or provided for. In this sense, we need to think of mobility infrastructures as related to broader systems of care, where people need to be fed.

This argument has far-reaching implications in terms of how we think about and plan cities, where food security becomes something that needs to be incorporated into planning on multiple scales and sites. Access to healthy foods throughout the city, including through markets, urban gardens, and prepared food venues, thus becomes an imperative that needs to be considered in relation to people's daily journeys, and in relation to the diverse infrastructures upon which urban life depends. How the city supports or restricts the ways in which individuals, families, and communities take care of themselves will be crucial when thinking about ways to plan for the future. This would imply, in the case of food, thinking not only about the quality of food, its distribution capacity, and accessibility but also about the way in which infrastructures, in this case of mobility, promote more or less healthy and sustainable ways of taking care of ourselves and feeding ourselves. In terms of planning mobility infrastructures, taking foodwork and care into consideration means that we need to consider various aspects, from the design of metro stations, provision of eating areas, cleaning areas (toilets, for example), hygiene and health control, among many others. More broadly, this chapter is an invitation to think about how mobility infrastructures in Latin American cities collaborate or detract from territorial approaches to care.

Notes

1 Currently Red Transport System.
2 Designed as the backbone of Santiago's public transportation system, it was inaugurated in 1975 and, since then, the system has been considerably expanded to seven lines currently in operation. In addition, there is a new line under construction and several extensions underway, as well as two new lines planned for the year 2030.
3 The work team consisted of four anthropologists and two urban planners.

4 The ethnographic work is part of FONDECYT Regular Research Project No. 1171113 "Understanding the relationship between people's mobility and food patterns, and the role of attitudes and social networks."
5 The research was conducted prior to the inauguration of Metro Line 3.
6 Manual loading trolley with two wheels on its base for displacement.
7 Container that maintains the temperature.
8 Elastics with hooks to hold objects.
9 A popular Venezuelan fried flour dough stuffed with cheese.
10 Popular Chilean fried flour and pumpkin dough.
11 Corn flour fried dough, usually stuffed with various fillings.
12 Roasted or fried corn dough.
13 Fried rice rolls with different fillings.
14 Ethnographic story.
15 Elongated and protruding portion of an object.
16 Food retail markets, mainly fruits and vegetables, located a few days a week in the open air, mainly in the streets.

Bibliography

Bastías García, M. (2018). *Entorno Alimentario Comunitario y Obesidad en Santiago Urbano, Chile* [Tesis de Doctorado en Salud Pública, Facultad de Medicina, Universidad de Chile].

Beagan, B., Chapman, G. E., D'Sylva, A., & Bassett, B. R. (2008). 'It's just easier for me to do it': Rationalizing the family division of foodwork. *Sociology*, *42*(4), 653–671. https://doi.org/10.1177/0038038508091621

Bosco, F. J., Joassart-Marcelli, P., & O'Neal, B. (2017). Food journeys: Place, mobility, and the everyday food practices of young people. *Annals of the American Association of Geographers*, *107*(6), 1479–1498.

Carrasco, J., Jirón, P., & Imilan, W. (2019). *Movilidades y alimentos: Aproximaciones a espacios y vidas cotidianas en Santiago, Chile*. Trabajo presentado en Conferencia ALAS 2019 – Lima, Perú. GT 02. Ciudades Latinoamericanas en el Nuevo Milenio.

Cerda, R., Egaña, D., Espinoza, P., & Masferrer, D. (2016). *Marco conceptual sobre los factores condicionantes de los ambientes alimentarios en Chile*. Facultad de Medicina Universidad de Chile y Ministerio de Salud Junio.

Cummins, S. (2014). Food deserts. In W. C. Cockerham, R. Dingwall, & S. Quah (Eds.), *The Wiley Blackwell encyclopedia of health, illness, behavior, and society*. https://doi.org/10.1002/9781118410868.wbehibs450

Duhau, E., & Giglia, A. (2007). Nuevas centralidades y prácticas de consumo en la Ciudad de México: del microcomercio al hipermercado. *EURE (Santiago)*, *33*(98), 77–95. https://dx.doi.org/10.4067/S0250-71612007000100005

Garcia, D. (2011). Una etnografía económica de los tacos callejeros en México. El caso de Monterrey. *Estudios Sociales* (Hermosillo, Son.), *19*(37), 31–63.

Giglia, A. (2022). De los Suburbios Residenciales a los Conjuntos Cerrados: Espacio Local y Prácticas de Consumo. En A. Aguayo y A. Zirión (Comp.), *Habitar y comprender el espacio urbano. Escritos de Angela Giglia sobre la Ciudad de México*. Universidad Autónoma Metropolitana, Unidad Iztapalapa/División de Ciencias Sociales y Humanidades, Departamento de Antropología.

Gómez, M. J. (2017). *Estaciones de metro: espacio público desde el diseño y la experiencia de movilidad. Casos de estudio: estaciones Francisco Bilbao y Elisa Correa*. Seminario de Investigación, Carrera de Arquitectura, Facultad de Arquitectura y Urbanismo, Universidad de Chile.

GTOP. (2022). *Policy brief "Recomendaciones para la consideración del ambiente alimentario doméstico en las intervenciones alimentario-nutricionales." Grupo Transdisciplinario para la Obesidad de Poblaciones (GTOP)*. Santiago, Chile: Universidad de Chile.

Hayden, T. B. (2021). Street food as infrastructure: Consumer mobility, vendor removability and food security in Mexico City. *Food, Culture & Society*, *24*(1), 98–111. https://dx.doi.org/10.1080/15528014.2020.1859920

Hayden, T. B. (2024). Incomplete documentation, social isolation, and culinary estrangement: Factors affecting food security among urban migrant populations in Mexico. *Global Food Security*, *42*, 100779. https://doi.org/10.1016/j.gfs.2024.100779

Held, V. (2005). *The ethics of care: Personal, political, and global*. Oxford University Press.

Imilan, W. (2015). Performing national identity through Peruvian food migration in Santiago de Chile. *Fennia: International Journal of Geography*, *2*, 227–241. https://doi.org/10.11143/46369

Imilan, W., y Millaleo, A. (2015). Comer a lo peruano, lugares de la migración gastronómica. En W. Imilan, F. Márquez, y C. Stefoni (Eds.), *Rutas migrantes en Chile: Habitar, festejar y trabajar* (pp. 99–120). Santiago: Ediciones Universidad Alberto Hurtado.

Jirón, P. (2010). On becoming "la sombra/the shadow." In M. Büscher, J. Urry, & K. Witchger (Eds.), *Mobile methods* (pp. 36–52). London: Taylor & Francis Books.

Jirón, P., y Gómez, J. (2018). Interdependencia, cuidado y género desde las estrategias de movilidad en la ciudad de Santiago. *Tempo Social*, *30*(2), 55–72.

Jirón, P., & Imilan, W. A. (2015). Embodying flexibility: Experiencing labour flexibility through urban daily mobility in Santiago de Chile. *Mobilities*, *10*(1). https://doi.org/10.1080/17450101.2013.848583

Jirón, P., Imilan, W. A., y Iturra, L. (2016). Relearning to travel in Santiago: The importance of mobile place-making and travelling know-how. *Cultural Geographies*, *23*(4), 599–614. https://doi.org/10.1177/1474474015622141

Jirón, P., Solar-Ortega, M., Rubio, D., Cortés-Morales, S., Cid, B., y Carrasco, J. (2022). La espacialización de los cuidados. Entretejiendo relaciones de cuidado a través de la movilidad. *Revista INVI*, *37*(104), 199–229. https://doi.org/10.5354/0718-8358.2022.65647

Latham, A., & Wood, P. R. H. (2015). Inhabiting infrastructure: Exploring the interactional spaces of urban cycling. *Environment and Planning A: Economy and Space*, *47*(2), 300–319. https://doi.org/10.1068/a140049p

Llamas, C. R. (2018). *Ciudades obesogénicas y mujeres vulnerables: salud urbana y exclusión socioespacial en South Bronx, La Courneuve y Lomas del Sur*. ITESO.

Metro Santiago. (2023). *Red Metro de Santiago*. https://www.metro.cl/el-viaje/plano-de-red

Mustieles Granell, F., Petzold-Rodríguez, A., Gilarranz Runge, C., & Schumacher González, M. (2023). Ciudades: sedentarismo y obesidad. *Inter disciplina*, *11*(31), 247–271. Epub 10 de noviembre de 2023. https://doi.org/10.22201/ceiich.24485705e.2023.31.83500

Pinheiro, A. C., Quintiliano-Scarpelli, D., Flores, J. A., Álvarez, C., Suárez-Reyes, M., Palacios, J. L., Quevedo, T. P., & de Oliveira, M. R. M. (2022). Food availability in different food environments surrounding schools in a vulnerable urban area of Santiago, Chile: Exploring socioeconomic determinants. *Foods*, *11*(7), 901.

Reyes-Puente, A. L., Peña-Portilla, D. G., Alcalá-Reyes, S., Rodríguez-Bustos, L., & Núñez, J. M. (2022). Changes in food environment patterns in the metropolitan area of the valley of Mexico, 2010–2020. *International Journal of Environmental Research and Public Health*, *19*(15), 8960.

Shannon, J. (2016). Beyond the supermarket solution: Linking food deserts, neighborhood context, and everyday mobility. *Annals of the American Association of Geographers*, *106*(1), 186–202.

Solar-Ortega, M. (2020). *Espacialidades del cuidado. Develando las prácticas espaciales de mujeres cuidadoras en Santiago de Chile* [Tesis de Magíster en Hábitat Residencial, Facultad de Arquitectura y Urbanismo, Universidad de Chile, Santiago].

Tronto, J. C., & Fisher, B. (1990). Toward a feminist theory of caring. In E. Abel & M. Nelson (Eds.), *Circles of care* (pp. 36–54). SUNY Press.

SECTION III
Governance

9

SUPERMARKET EXPANSION STRATEGIES IN LATIN AMERICA

Impacts on urban economic structure and food environments

Joaquín Pérez Martín

Introduction

Supermarkets have expanded in the food trade, becoming key players in urban life and agrifood systems in Latin America, precisely because of their great capacity to mediate the supply networks that link the countryside with the city. Although the first experiences of this type of commerce appeared in the 1950s, the great investment and expansion of this sector, mainly through multinational companies, began in the 1970s, generating concrete effects in the 1980s and 1990s, when a strong expansion took place (Reardon & Berdegué, 2002). The introduction of supermarkets[1]—also known as the *modern channel*—in food retailing has displaced traditional businesses and small traders, while it has been transforming the economic dynamics of food supply and, in particular, the characteristics of food environments.

In terms of the impact on the urban economic structure, the expansion of supermarkets and the displacement of small retailers increases the scale of logistic-commercial operations, generating higher levels of efficiency due to economies of scale, but with higher costs, which creates a significant barrier to entry, reducing the number of players and generating high and increasing levels of concentration (Pérez Martín, 2022; Richards & Pasirayi, 2023). This is why the market share of supermarkets correlates globally with the increase in population income, middle-class sizes, and urbanization rates (OCDE, 2015; Torres, 2011). Thus it is that supermarkets choose to settle initially in large cities: that is, they settle and begin their expansion process where they find an agglomeration of consumption that, given certain income levels, can absorb a higher aggregate logistic-commercial operation cost. In Latin America, this process takes place in a context in which States, at different scales, have been losing their capacity

DOI: 10.4324/9781003471929-14

to regulate, coordinate, or intervene in commercial activity, leading to a process of privatization and liberalization of the food supply, in line with the neoliberal imprint that has been consolidating in the region since the 1970s.

On the other hand, the growth of supermarkets and the displacement of small stores have modified both agrifood systems and their supply networks throughout Latin America (Minten & Reardon, 2008; Pérez Martín, 2022). They have configured food environments[2] that condition access to healthy and nutritious diets, in part due to the fact that the massiveness of supermarkets' operations, seeking to maximize profitability over their three main costs (the inventory of products displayed and stored, the square meters of branches, and the cost of labor), affects the quality and diversity of the food offerings (Baker et al., 2020; Hawkes, 2008, 2009). In addition, because supermarkets direct their own supply to large agrifood suppliers, the circulation of small and medium-sized enterprises (SME) food producers on the streets of each of the cities is reduced, so that small retailers are limited in their ability to access suppliers in line with their scale of operation, affecting their competitive capacity. The exclusion of SME food suppliers from supermarkets is at the same time directly linked to the consistent unilateral implementation of commercial practices and payments to suppliers that transfer profitability in a debatably legal manner from the agrifood sector to the supermarkets.[3]

Although different countries in Latin America have different rates of supermarket dominance and consolidation, in all places *modern* and traditional channels of food commercialization coexist, albeit with different levels of market share and sectoral specializations. Throughout the region, supermarkets are exploring strategies to expand, stabilize, and gain market share, displacing traditional channels. Thus, according to the socio-economic conditions of each country and city, supermarkets diversify the format of their branches—a strategy commonly known as the *omni-channel*, boost the articulation with *e-commerce*, develop their own brands, and implement promotions and discounts, among other strategies. Identifying and analyzing them comparatively on a regional scale allows us to understand the role of the major players in food marketing in the urban economy and food environments in order to delineate the potential for complementation or competition with small-sized and medium-sized retailers and their supply chains, mainly on the basis of public–private strategies (Gasca & Torres, 2014).

The objective of this chapter is to analyze the expansion of supermarkets on a regional scale and the different strategies being implemented to delineate the potential effects on urban food environments and food access. In order to analyze the expansion strategies of supermarkets in the countries of the region, a three-stage segmentation is proposed according to the levels of market share and their stability over time: installation, expansion, and consolidation. In particular, the focus of this chapter is on those countries with the greatest presence of supermarkets. The case of Chile will be addressed first, as the only country where supermarkets are in a consolidation phase, followed by the cases of Argentina, Brazil, and Mexico, countries where supermarkets are going through their expansion stage (for further in-depth discussion of the case of Brazil, see Smalley Soares Pereira, this volume). The paper is based on a mixed methodological strategy, including interviews with key actors, spatial analysis, and basic statistics that the author has been developing since 2017.

Supermarket expansion in Latin America

Supermarkets have a long history of operating in Latin American countries, with the four countries discussed in this chapter standing out as the ones where they were installed earliest (Reardon & Berdegué, 2002) and which also have the largest market share currently. Latin American countries are becoming increasingly urbanized, with ever larger cities and populations with levels of income and inequality that, although they have improved substantially in recent decades, still have considerable proportions of the population living in poverty. Given the levels of income and expenditure, the weight of food purchases in household budgets is significant, between 14% (Brazil) and 30% (Mexico), which, together with their large populations, creates food markets of considerable size for the expansion of supermarkets.

Chile has the particularity of being the country in the region where supermarkets have achieved the highest market share—68% in 2023, according to Kantar (2024b)—and is the only country identified as being in the consolidation stage. Unlike the rest of the countries, where the most intense expansion came from multinational investments, such as those of the French Carrefour and the North American Walmart, in this case growth was strongly driven by local firms. Such is the case of Cencosud and D&S, the latter finally acquired in 2009 by Walmart. This expansion was driven by a significant growth in real per capita income (between 1984 and 1998, it grew steadily at an average annual rate of 5%), growing urbanization rates and increasingly populated cities, a greater incorporation of women into the dynamics of formal work outside the home, and the massive adoption of household equipment, such as refrigerators and freezers (Faiguenbaum et al., 2002). As these authors point out, the growth of supermarket participation in Chile was concentrated mainly in high-income areas of large cities during the 1970s and 1980s, while from the 1990s onward, the expansion reached intermediate cities and middle and low-income neighborhoods. During the years 2000 and 2010 supermarkets reached market share levels in Chile comparable to European countries, where the role of supermarkets covers between 60% and 90% of the household food market: 60% in 2000, 75% in 2018, and, finally, decreasing post-pandemic again to reach 60% in 2022 and then rebounding to 68% in 2023 (FNE, 2007; Kantar, 2024b). Chile took 18 years (between 1998 and 2016) to consolidate the three elements that the consulting firm Kearney (2017) identifies as essential for the expansion of *retailers*: the growth of the middle classes, consumers' appreciation of the "organized" conditions of supermarkets, and the deregulation of some "restrictions".

This strong expansion of the supermarket sector led to a still greater concentration as a result of mergers and acquisitions, particularly led by Cencosud, which expanded both within Chile and in the region, based on its experience in the retail sector and developing new complementary businesses: real estate and finance (Calderón Hoffmann, 2007). In this way, Cencosud has become one of the main regional players, together with Carrefour, Walmart, the French Casino, and the Mexican companies Oxxo and Chedraui, standing out globally as the 83rd retail company in terms of turnover, and the second in Latin America, according to the ranking elaborated by Deloitte (2023). Cencosud's presence in the region is materialized through five business units (supermarkets, department stores, home improvement, shopping centers, and financial services) and in five countries (Argentina, Colombia, Peru, Chile, and Brazil), through 938 supermarkets, which generate 74% of total revenues. Since 2022, it has also been operating in the United States (USA) through the acquisition of Fresh Market supermarkets (Cencosud, 2023).

The development of supermarkets in Argentina, meanwhile, can be divided into four stages (Pérez Martín, 2022; Ciccolella, 2000). From the opening of the first supermarket in 1950 until 1981, income conditions and a series of political events did not allow a significant expansion of supermarkets. By the early 1980s, when Carrefour and Cencosud set up in Argentina, there had already been a wide diffusion and adoption of the new commercial system by consumers, who had adopted the new patterns of modernization of the food retail trade, although this had not materialized in a significant growth in market share. Between 1982 and 2002 there were two other stages in the spread and expansion of supermarkets, which differed basically in the intensity of the process. Even though, during the 1980s the economic situation was not good (per capita income decreased by an average of 2% per year between 1980 and 1989), with hyperinflation and a complex political context, Carrefour arrived on the scene in 1982, while the Dutch company SHV (Makro) did the same in 1988.

Starting in 1989, a new Argentine government started introducing a series of neoliberal reforms, whereby policies for deregulation, privatization, and liberalization of investment, production, and trade were implemented. These changes, which picked up steam in the early 1990s, changed the social and economic scenario and promoted the expansion of supermarkets. Thus, Walmart arrived in 1995, the French Promodès in 1996 and Auchan in 1997, the Spanish Dia also in 1997, and finally Casino and the Dutch Royal Ahold in 1998. The arrival of all these companies, mainly European, took place through the opening of new branches, as well as mergers and acquisitions, which led to a growth in market share of 22 percentage points between 1993 and 1999, when the maximum historical share of supermarkets in Argentina was reached (57%). The 2001/2002 crisis marked the beginning of the fourth stage of supermarket development in Argentina. The depth of the crisis caused a drop in income, as well as an increase in poverty and inequality, substantially affecting consumption patterns. Since 2002, supermarkets have been losing market share until reaching 32% in 2006. From then on, supermarkets slowly recovered their role until reaching 45% market share in 2023 (Kantar, 2024b). This loss of market share was basically transferred to the "Chinese" supermarkets,[4] which have established themselves as the main competition of the supermarket chains until today (see Hayden et al., this volume).

In the case of Brazil, the first supermarkets were installed in the early 1950s, from transformations of local companies such as Sirva-se (in 1953), Pão de Açúcar (in 1959), and Zaffari (in 1960), which incorporated the various innovations that were spreading from the USA and Europe, adopting a new business model, *layout* of the branches, and equipment. (GPA, 2024; Grupo Zaffari, 2024; Monteiro et al., 2014). During the 1970s, the commercial structure was dominated by small-sized and medium-sized family businesses that were growing in the number of branches and diversifying their formats. However, the early arrival of foreign investments generated a momentum of opening branches, acquisitions, mergers, and increased competition: SHV (Makro) arrived in 1972 and Carrefour in 1975 (Aguiar, 2009; da Rocha & Dib, 2002). Since 1966, Brazil had 15 years of uninterrupted economic growth (at an average annual rate of 6%) in the so-called "Brazilian economic miracle," which took place during the dictatorial regime in power. Although the per capita income was lower than that shown by Argentina or Mexico, by the mid-1970s it already had seven cities with more than one million inhabitants that, totaling a market of 25 million people, doubled the urban population of these two countries (UNDESA, 2018; World Bank, 2024). In this way, Brazil would gradually become a major destination for international investments in the retail sector. During the 1980s, the expansion of supermarkets continued, mainly in the hands of local companies, with the entry of Promodès in 1983 and the Portuguese company Sonae in 1989.

During the 1990s, the application of the Real Plan increased income and stabilized inflation levels, affecting consumption patterns. In tune with the times, Brazil also entered a stage of deregulation and liberalization, reinforcing the attractiveness of the Brazilian market for the massive entry of multinational companies, consolidating supermarkets, and its foreignization (Monteiro et al., 2014). Thus, Walmart entered in 1995, Royal Ahold in 1996, the Portuguese Jerónimo Martins in 1997 and Casino in 1999, acquiring the main local company Companhia Brasileira de Distribuição, being constituted years later as GPA. The market share of supermarkets in Brazil declined from 1994 to 2000, coinciding with a drop in revenues, and then rebounded to 44% in 2002 (Farina, 2002; Farina et al., 2005). Between 1995 and 2007, the concentration process intensified, with 89 merger and acquisition operations, which increased the supermarkets' share in the food trade and concentrated the sector (Monteiro et al., 2012). In this context, in 2007 Cencosud entered the Brazilian market, consolidating its expansion at the regional level. In 2014 supermarkets reached a market share of 58%. (Kantar, 2016) while the latest available data (Kantar, 2024b) drops to 45% of the household food retail market.[5] Currently, the main players are Carrefour (which in 2015 became the first and only supermarket company to have a presence in all Brazilian states), Assaí (which in 2021 spun off from the Casino group), Grupo Mateus, GPA, and Supermercados BH.

The development of supermarkets in Mexico can be characterized in three stages (Schwentesius & Gómez, 2002). The first began in the late 1940s with the opening of the first self-service branches of Sumesa and Calimax, both located outside the country's capital. Then, toward the end of the 1950s and during the 1960s the new commercial type was installed in Mexico City with the opening of the branches of Aurrera, Grupo Gigante, and Comercial Mexicana (Casado Izquierdo, 2018; Chavez, 2002). In 1976, 7-Eleven, a chain specialized in convenience stores, was installed. Two years later, the first branch of Oxxo opened, another company oriented to convenience businesses, a new business unit of FEMSA, the local bottler of Coca-Cola. Oxxo is the Latin American's most important retail company, with sales of more than US$15.3 billion and almost 20,000 branches in Mexico and with more than 2,000 branches in other countries of the region, as well as in Spain and the USA (Deloitte, 2023). The second stage of supermarket expansion began in 1981 and it was the period when the North American chains Walmart and Safeway entered the country, acquiring minority stakes in Mexican supermarkets (Futurama and Casa Ley, respectively), which constituted the beginning of the foreignization and the entry of large global retail players. Until 1985, the food supply in Mexico depended on a regulatory framework that established broad state participation and coordination, particularly in retail trade, through a massive network of public markets (see Téllez Contreras chapter on this Section) and supermarkets, such as Diconsa (Gasca Zamora, 2015). In line with the neoliberal reforms of the time, in the early 1980s foreign investment and commercial activity were deregulated, enabling the arrival of foreign companies in the supermarket sector. As pointed out by Gasca and Torres (2014, p. 135), the food supply network began to be defined as "multi-scalar structure of branches and corporations."

In 1990 Mexico began negotiations to join the Free Trade Agreement between Canada and the United States, which had been signed two years earlier, thus beginning the third stage of supermarket development. With the beginning of the negotiations, North American companies accelerated their landing in Mexico: Walmart bought 50% of CIFRA supermarkets (in 1991), expanding its participation in the country, while HEB supermarkets and Fleming arrived in 1991 and 1992, respectively. During the 1990s, after Mexico formalized its entry into the North American Free Trade Agreement (NAFTA), more foreign supermarkets arrived: the North American Kmart (in 1993), Carrefour (in 1994), Auchan (in 1995), and the North American Costco (in 1995) (Durand, 2007). The combination of Mexico's incorporation into the free trade agreement and the massive arrival of North American supermarkets led to increased food imports, affecting local producers: while in the five-year period 1986–1990 imports represented 10% of the volume of food consumed locally, between 2000 and 2004 the weight of foreign products increased to 19% (FAO, 2024). In 2003 the market share of supermarkets reached 33% of the market, while in 2015 it had grown to 54% (Gasca Zamora, 2015) falling to 50% nowadays (Kantar, 2024b).

Impact of supermarket expansion strategies on urban economic structure and food environments: a comparative look at a regional scale

In the Latin American context, where socio-spatial fragmentation prevails (Janoschka, 2002), supermarket expansion strategies seek to ensure, above all, diversity and adaptability in order to sustain and gain market share, a strategy that the retail sector has termed *omni-channel*. In this context, the three largest countries in the region (Brazil, Mexico, and Argentina) have undergone similar supermarket expansion processes, which, despite the different time periods, show similar market shares today: between 45% and 50%. These three countries account for 69% of the population and 63% of the cities with more than one million inhabitants of all countries in the region as of 2020 (UNDESA, 2018) while, after Chile, they are the countries with the highest per capita income. For its part, in Chile, unlike the rest of the countries, the expansion was more consistent and early and did not come from investments by multinationals, but with a strong impulse from local firms. The concentration of the Chilean population in the only city with more than one million inhabitants (the capital, Santiago de Chile), together with the long history of market opening and liberalization policies, initially promoted by the dictatorship and later by democratic governments, are two key elements that explain the current context of supermarkets in this country, where they have a 68% market share.

In each of the countries of the region, the scenario is also fragmented in terms of consumption. On the one hand, the conditions of income, poverty, and, above all, multiple and informal employment of a large part of the population create a socio-economic context that restricts access to food at the household level. This leads to low-volume, low-spending and high-frequency consumption patterns, with visits to multiple types of supermarket branches and other type of stores in order to find the greatest possible diversity of prices, offers, and payment methods. On the other hand, these socio-economic conditions are complemented by minority proportions of the population, from the middle-income and high-income sectors, with food purchase and consumption patterns without major restrictions. However, the number of types of stores visited does not vary substantially between different income levels, it is a cross-cutting consumption practice in the countries of the region: while low and middle-income households visit an average of 9 types of stores, high-income households visit 9.4 types of stores, as analyzed by the consulting firm Kantar (2024a). In other words, although this multiplicity of stores visited makes up food environments that indicate, a priori, some level of competition and complementarity, supermarkets capture consumption in several of these types of stores under their *omni-channel* strategy.

A comparative analysis of the current state of the *omni-channel* strategy, as can be seen in Figures 9.1, shows that the market share of supermarkets in each of the countries is achieved with a particular composition for each type of branch, which affects the type of food environment that is formed. For example, the three countries with market shares of between 45% and 50% have a very different

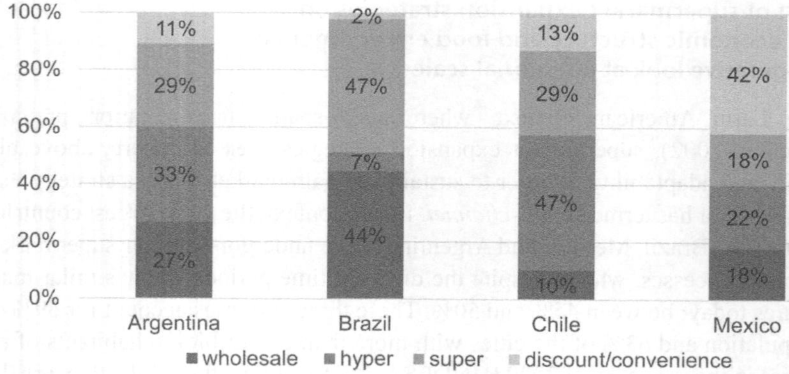

FIGURE 9.1 Share of supermarket sales by type of branch in the different countries
Source: Own elaboration based on Kantar (2024b)

composition: in Argentina the share by type of outlet is divided approximately in thirds between wholesale (27%), hyper (33%), and supermarket (29%); in Brazil, it is divided approximately in halves between wholesale (44%) and supermarket (47%); in Mexico, it has the largest proportion of discount or convenience stores (42%), while the remaining share is divided into thirds between the remaining types of branches. Finally, in Chile, the market share of supermarkets is mainly distributed among hyper (47%) and, to a lesser extent, supermarkets (29%).

In this context, at the regional level there has been a notable expansion, on the one hand, of convenience stores and discount or local supermarkets (Kantar, 2024a), which enter into the circulation of those purchases with a low level of expenditure and quantity of products (less than 10) both for households and for the consumption of food on the street. This type of expansion also operates as an infrastructure that offers a limited stock but is accessible in a wide time range and massively spread throughout the urban fabric for interaction with online platforms (see Zunino & Ferrer chapter in the previous section). In particular, in the case of Mexico, in the post-pandemic period convenience stores have been the fastest-growing type of commerce (Kantar, 2023). In this context, the company Oxxo has expanded its number of branches by more than 70% in the last 10 years, reaching more than 21,000 stores in Mexico alone (Ameth, 2015; Flores, 2023).

The other type of trade that has expanded significantly is that of wholesale supermarkets (Kantar, 2024a), where households make on average one purchase per month, with a higher level of spending and types of products (fewer than 20). This expansion pattern expanded in the post-pandemic with a focus on accessing lower prices and making purchases with low frequency avoiding agglomerations and possible contagions. However, it is a segment oriented to the middle and upper classes that have the possibility of making large purchases since they have high and regular incomes. This growth is mainly explained by the case of Brazil, where the operation of wholesale supermarkets has the highest level of market share in the region, mainly in the hands of Carrefour and Casino, as Smalley Soares Pereira points out in the chapter later. In 2023, the expansion was driven mainly through investments for the acquisition of branches of other companies, with the impact this brings on sector concentration, and to a lesser extent for the construction of new branches (ABRAS, 2023).

In the case of Argentina, despite showing a scenario of thirds, the expansion strategy of supermarkets has been reconfiguring food environments. Thus in the last decades, between 1997 and 2016, the total number of branches and commercial area increased, although the operation was concentrated, given that both the commercial area (112%) and the average number of branches (207%) per company increased. This growth occurred with a decrease in the average size of branches, particularly due to the strong expansion of proximity supermarkets in the hands of Carrefour, with its Express format, and Dia% (Pérez Martín, 2022).

On the other hand, Cencosud's expansion strategy in Chile is clearly based on large branches: in the last decade, the number of hypermarket branches increased by 59% and only 3% of supermarkets. The novelty is that in 2021 the company launched a new type of convenience branches (Spid) with its own online platform and the potential to develop logistics services using these branches as dark stores. They currently have 34 branches in total, which represents 14% of the company's total stores in Chile (Cencosud, 2014, 2024).

Thus, during the 1980s and 1990s, the expansion of supermarkets occurred almost exclusively with the opening of medium and large branches, installed in areas of low and medium population density, which required significant investments in urban land. In many cases the larger branches have been transformed into wholesale formats or new ones are opened in areas of lower peri-urban population density, often driven by the growth of the urban sprawl articulated around the expansion of highways, as has been studied by Vecslir Peri (2011) for Argentine cities. Since the 2000s, and massively in the last decades, expansion patterns have diversified with the opening of branches of different dimensions, layouts, and types of commercial operations. As mentioned, particularly in the cases of Argentina, Chile, and Mexico, expansion strategies incorporate, with greater or lesser impact on market share, the opening of a large number of small branches in the most densely populated areas.

In terms of the food environments that are shaped by the emergence of the different types of supermarket branches, expansion into smaller stores offers less product and supplier diversity, as well as higher cost and price structures. In contrast, as branch size increases and the operation transitions from retail to wholesale, the trend is reversed: supply increases in terms of products and suppliers, while the operation is more efficient and can offer lower prices. Broadly speaking, however, these types of branches do not compete with each other, but complement each other due to the effect of different locations, types of food products offered, and buying patterns absorbed by each type.

The pattern of small branch expansion has a more costly operating structure, as pointed out by Aalto-Setälä (2000) and Guy et al. (2005) mainly in terms of the weight of labor and urban land cost components. Although in this expansion pattern the weight of urban land is computed mainly through rent payments or franchise contracts, the price per square meter of urban land is multiplied up to four or five times by the effect of location in the case of the Buenos Aires Metropolitan Area (Subsecretaría de Planeamiento, 2016), compared to the branches of large stores that are located in areas of lower population density and on the urban fringes. In turn, this expansion model demands a more intense logistic operation for the supply of hundreds of branches in each city or metropolitan area, where the time of circulation, unloading, and commercial management in each of the branches is the main limitation to massively supply a commercial network as dense as this one. This type of expansion substantially restricts the number of suppliers given the limited shelf space in the branches and the high operating cost of supply. On average, the assortment of these branches has between 3,500 and 4,500 SKUs supplied by around 100 companies, regardless of whether the brand is the supplier's or the supermarket's (private label). Since the last mile supply is generally operated by the supermarket itself from a logistics center located on the outskirts of the cities, suppliers are excluded from urban circulation, limiting the capacity to supply other types of businesses that compete with supermarkets. In addition, the saturation of branches within the urban fabric generates an impulse of competition and displacement of small traditional stores, which, as studied by D'Andrea et al. (2006), sustain their business dynamics on different operational elements.

On the other hand, as the size of the branches increases and the format changes from retail to wholesale, efficiency increases in terms of the size of purchases and the incidence of labor and urban land costs, due to the location of the branches in areas of lower population density and urban fringe. This type of expansion demands a more massive supply scheme and requires high and regular incomes from consumers, as well as time and, preferably, access to motorized mobility (Guy et al., 2005). Thus, the impact of supermarket expansion on food environments combines the aggregate effects at the level of each branch, where the transaction with the consumer takes place and from where the operational scheme of supermarkets is transferred to the other types of stores conditioning there functioning and sustainability.

Although the main cost component of the supermarket operation is the stock available on the shelves, regardless of the size of the branch, the long deferral of the supermarket's payment terms to its suppliers dilutes its effect. Thus, since the stock is provided by the suppliers, the supermarkets' profitability will depend on the balance between sales level and the most important cost components: labor and commercial urban land. That is why product assortment planning and the pricing strategy together with the promotions and discounts offered by supermarkets are key elements of supermarket to adjust and increase sales margin, even though strongly influence the configuration of food environments. Promotions and discounts account for between 15% and 25% of the volume of purchases made in the region.

In Mexico, for example, 96% of households shop in supermarkets using promotions (Kantar, 2021a, 2021b). Thus, while these commercial practices affect the patterns of food purchase and consumption (Hawkes, 2009), they also restrict the transparent dissemination of prices, affecting competition with other commercial types. Following what Camargo et al. (2020) and Elorriaga et al. (2023) observed for the cases of Brazil and Argentina, respectively, the assortment of foods available on the shelves shapes food environments that diverting them from nutritional recommendations.

Final thoughts

The expansion of supermarkets in recent decades in Latin America has had an impact on the logistical and commercial functioning of cities, affecting the characteristics of food environments, particularly in the countries analyzed here. So far, expansion has been driven by acquisitions, mergers, and the installation of new branches of different sizes, layouts, types of operations, and sector specializations. With the evolution of the population's income, the urbanization of metropolitan areas, and the implementation of deregulations, supermarkets reached market shares between 45% and 68% (Kantar, 2024b), while the remaining portion is held by other small and medium scale commercial types (grocery stores, bakeries, greengrocers, among others). These smaller businesses, meanwhile, find themselves trying to compete and adapt in a supermarket-dominated food system, through strategies of productive restructuring, innovation, and investment.

The imprint of "rapid expansion" proposed by Reardon and Berdegué (2002) in the early 2000s, based on the global phenomenon of the modernization of food trade that reached the "emerging" markets of Latin America, was sustained on the one hand by deregulation, liberalization, and the growth of foreign direct investment in the region (CEPAL, 2015), especially between the 1990s and 2000s. In turn, this macro context was aligned with the expansive strategy of large global supermarkets that sought to internationalize their operation in search of new sources of income for the expansion of their businesses (Baud & Durand, 2012). However, these drivers seem to be already exhausted, so that, regardless of the growth that supermarkets may have from now on, what seems to be clear is that the food market will continue to be distributed in significant proportions with the structure of traditional small and medium-sized stores. In other words, none of the countries analyzed seems to be on the way to relegating their food markets to supermarkets to a greater extent, especially given the recent trajectories described: Argentina reached its maximum market share level in 1999, Chile recently recovered market share lost during the pandemic, Mexico has a deeply rooted structure of small-sized and medium-sized stores and the growth of supermarkets was late, while Brazil has lost market share in recent years.

Given the financial capacity and scale of operation, the *omni-channel* strategy of supermarkets is effective in permeating atomized urban economic structures, such as those that are expanding in the countries of the region, with small-sized and medium-sized stores that have a highly diversified supply. The great challenge then, in order to build food environments that promote healthy and accessible diets, is to maintain this mix with a significant presence of small-scale and medium-scale multi-stakeholder networks. In this context, *online* platforms, although they bring other types of impacts, have expanded, articulating logistically, commercially, and financially with traditional stores, boosting their sustainability vis-à-vis supermarkets and complementing the supply network.

The power of supermarkets vis-à-vis consumers and suppliers has had a substantial impact on the configuration of food networks, while governments have lost their regulatory capacity. For this reason, it is essential to innovate, on the one hand, in effective regulations aimed at supermarkets that limit and control their market power, in fiscal or transactional matters, for example. On the other hand, it is vital to strongly promote the development of food infrastructure that promotes public–private articulation as a governance and coordination scheme for small-sized and medium-sized businesses at two scales: urban food markets and multi-sector peri-urban logistics platforms. The development of these two types of infrastructures articulated through streets, roads, and highways, mostly, provides the necessary support to foster the inclusion of small and medium farmers, industries, and businesses in food environments.

So far, regardless of the trajectories of each of the countries and the apparent stagnation, supermarkets have expanded in all countries that have increased their levels of urbanization and income. This is relevant not only for the countries analyzed, where supermarkets are in stages of expansion and consolidation, beyond the limits they are encountering for their growth, but especially for those where their presence is even less relevant. Beyond the characteristics of supermarket expansion and its impact on urban food environments in the region, there are other elements that could be expanded in future research to support (or not) what is proposed here. Some, in particular, are mentioned, such as the disruptive growth of online platforms that complement but also compete with supermarkets. Also, the impact of supermarkets on food environments and the type of access they shape through both pricing strategies and the type of food products. Finally, the potential of new regulatory strategies, no longer on trade, but intervening in packaging with front seals, for example—and the invigoration and relocation of food issues in cities.

Notes

1 Supermarkets include those large-scale commercial or retail sector players that operate a significant number of branches and commercial space with different characteristics in terms of size (generally speaking, from 50 to 15,000 m^2), product diversity, and type of operation (wholesale, retail, convenience, discount, proximity, etc.). The following commercial types are considered: hyper, super, discount store, and wholesaler, identified by Kantar (2024b).

2 The food environment is understood as the interface—physical or virtual—where people interact with urban supply networks for food acquisition and consumption (Turner et al., 2018).

3 In Argentina, a significant differential time window has been found between supermarkets actually collecting their sales from consumers (considering the participation of each of the means of payment, which have different crediting times) and paying their suppliers, which ranges between 50 and 80 days (Pérez Martín, 2021).
4 "Chinese" supermarkets are small stores that have been established in Argentina since the 1980s. Although they originally came from Taiwan, nowadays they mainly migrate from Fujian province, China, constituting a small-scale investment scheme that, once in Argentina, specializes almost exclusively in the supermarket sector. These traders act mostly individually at the level of each branch. The growth in the scale of operation that has been identified reaches no more than five to ten branches, so it is a largely decentralized sector, unlike large supermarket companies. At present, "Chinese" supermarkets have an aggregate market share of between 15% and 20% at the national level (Pérez Martín, 2021).
5 There is a methodological divergence between the data presented in this chapter and those included by Smalley Soares Pereira below in this section. The data used in this chapter for the four countries analyzed refer to the same source (Kantar, 2024b) and originate from household-level surveys. The data used by Smalley Soares Pereira are provided by the Brazilian Supermarkets Association (ABRAS) based on a survey by Nielsen, the market consulting firm, where the sales of supermarket companies are surveyed. Belik (2020) and Reardon and Berdegué (2002) warn about some methodological issues in the ABRAS data; however, it has been widely used, which opens intriguing future debates.

Bibliography

Aalto-Setälä, V. (2000). Economies of scale in grocery retailing in Finland. *Journal of Retailing and Consumer Services*, *7*(4), 207–213. https://doi.org/10.1016/S0969-6989(00)00018-7

ABRAS. (2023). *Superhiper ABRAS.*

Aguiar, D. (2009). The case of Brazil. En K. W. Stiegert & D. H. Kim (Eds.), *Structural changes in food retailing: Six country case studies*. University of Wisconsin-Madison, Department of Agricultural and Applied Economics, Food System Research Group. https://EconPapers.repec.org/RePEc:ags:uwfssc:60674

Ameth, E. (2015). *Las cadenas comerciales que más crecieron en 2014*. https://www.forbes.com.mx/las-cadenas-comerciales-que-mas-crecieron-en-2014/

Baker, P., Machado, P., Santos, T., Sievert, K., Backholer, K., Hadjikakou, M., Russell, C., Huse, O., Bell, C., Scrinis, G., Worsley, A., Friel, S., & Lawrence, M. (2020). Ultra-processed foods and the nutrition transition: Global, regional and national trends, food systems transformations and political economy drivers. *Obesity Reviews*, *21*(12), e13126. https://doi.org/10.1111/obr.13126

Baud, C., & Durand, C. (2012). Financialization, globalization and the making of profits by leading retailers. *Socio-Economic Review*, *10*(2), 241–266. https://doi.org/10.1093/ser/mwr016

Belik, W. (2020). *Estudo sobre a Cadeia de Alimentos*. Ibirapitanga, Instituto Clima e Sociedade, Imaflora. https://bit.ly/3ZdodZ7

Calderón Hoffmann, A. (2007). El modelo de expansión de las grandes cadenas minoristas chilenas. *Revista de la CEPAL*, *2006*(90), 151–170. https://doi.org/10.18356/c888e53b-es

Casado Izquierdo, J. M. (2018). Supermercados en México: Expansión y espacios de inserción. *Estudios Geográficos*, *79*(284), 167. https://doi.org/10.3989/estgeogr.201807

Cencosud. (2014). *Memoria Anual Integrada 2013*. Chile.

Cencosud. (2023). *Memoria Anual Integrada 2022*. Chile.

Cencosud. (2024). *Memoria Anual Integrada 2023*. Chile.

CEPAL. (2015). *La Inversión Extranjera Directa en América Latina y el Caribe 2015*. Comisión Económica para América Latina y el Caribe.

Chavez, M. (2002). The transformation of Mexican retailing with NAFTA. *Development Policy Review*, *20*(4), 503–513. https://doi.org/10.1111/1467-7679.00186

Ciccolella, P. (2000). Distribución global y territorio. Modernización y concentración comercial en Argentina en los años noventa. *Economía, Sociedad y Territorio*, *2*(7), 459–496.

da Rocha, A., & Dib, L. A. (2002). The entry of Wal-Mart in Brazil and the competitive responses of multinational and domestic firms. *International Journal of Retail & Distribution Management*, *30*(1), 61–73. https://doi.org/10.1108/09590550210415266

de Camargo, A. M., de Farias, J. P., Mazzonetto, A. C., Dean, M., & Fiates, G. M. R. (2020). Content of Brazilian supermarket circulars do not reflect national dietary guidelines. *Health Promotion International*, *35*(5), 1052–1060. https://doi.org/10.1093/heapro/daz100

D'Andrea, G., Lopez-Aleman, B., & Stengel, A. (2006). Why small retailers endure in Latin America. *International Journal of Retail & Distribution Management*, *34*(9), 661–673. https://doi.org/10.1108/09590550610683184

Deloitte. (2023). *2023 Global powers of retailing*.

Durand, C. (2007). Externalities from foreign direct investment in the Mexican retailing sector. *Cambridge Journal of Economics*, *31*(3), 393–411. https://doi.org/10.1093/cje/bel046

Elorriaga, N., Cavallo, A. S., Moyano, D. L., Torres, V., Faye, M., & Irazola, V. (2023). Propiedades saludables, procesamiento y descuento de precios de los alimentos anunciados en los volantes de supermercados en Buenos Aires, Argentina. *Revista Española de Nutrición Humana y Dietética*, *27*(4).

Faiguenbaum, S., Berdegué, J. A., & Reardon, T. (2002). The rapid rise of supermarkets in Chile: Effects on dairy, vegetable, and beef chains. *Development Policy Review*, *20*(4), 459–471. https://doi.org/10.1111/1467-7679.00183

FAO. (2024). *FAOSTAT – Food balance sheets*. Roma: FAO. https://bit.ly/30084XF

Farina, E. M. M. Q. (2002). Consolidation, multinationalisation, and competition in Brazil: Impacts on horticulture and dairy products systems. *Development Policy Review*, *20*(4), 441–457. https://doi.org/10.1111/1467-7679.00182

Farina, E. M. M. Q., Nunes, R., & Monteiro, G. F. de A. (2005). Supermarkets and their impacts on the agrifood system of Brazil: The competition among retailers. *Agribusiness*, *21*(2), 133–147. https://doi.org/10.1002/agr.20039

Flores, M. (2023). *OXXO: cuántas tiendas existen y quién es su actual dueño*. https://www.infobae.com/mexico/2023/07/15/oxxo-cuantas-tiendas-existen-y-quien-es-su-actual-dueno/

FNE. (2007). *Análisis Económico de la Industria de Supermercados en el marco de la Causa Rol N° 101/2006*. Santiago de Chile: Fiscalía Nacional Económica – Gobierno de Chile.

Gasca, J., & Torres, F. (2014). El control corporativo de la distribución de alimentos en México. *Problemas del Desarrollo*, *45*(176), 133–155. https://doi.org/10.1016/S0301-7036(14)70853-3

Gasca Zamora, J. G. (2015). *Tensión en los modelos de comercialización y consumo en la Ciudad de México a partir de la expansión de supermercados y plazas comerciales*. Presentado en 20° Encuentro Nacional sobre Desarrollo Regional en México.

GPA. (2024). *Nossa história*. https://www.gpabr.com/pt/conheca-o-gpa/historia-e-premios-do-gpa/

Grupo Zaffari. (2024). *Linha do tempo*. https://www.grupozaffari.com.br/grupo-zaffari/linha-do-tempo/

Guy, C., Bennison, D., & Clarke, R. (2005). Scale economies and superstore retailing: New evidence from the UK. *Journal of Retailing and Consumer Services*, *12*(2), 73–81. https://doi.org/10.1016/j.jretconser.2004.03.002

Hawkes, C. (2008). Dietary implications of supermarket development: A global perspective. *Development Policy Review*, *26*(6), 657–692. https://doi.org/10.1111/j.1467-7679.2008.00428.x

Hawkes, C. (2009). Sales promotions and food consumption. *Nutrition Reviews*, *67*(6), 333–342. https://doi.org/10.1111/j.1753-4887.2009.00206.x
Janoschka, M. (2002). El nuevo modelo de la ciudad latinoamericana: Fragmentación y privatización. *EURE (Santiago)*, *28*(85), 11–20.
Kantar. (2016, junio 21). Consumer insights – LATAM 2016 (Q1 2016). Recuperado 30 de mayo de 2019, de https://bit.ly/37yaBwG
Kantar. (2021a). *Desafiando el futuro: Analizando datos y anticipando tendencias.*
Kantar. (2021b, julio 7). ¿Quiénes son los compradores de promociones? Recuperado 13 de abril de 2024, de https://bit.ly/3TYTGK9
Kantar. (2023). *OMNICHANNEL REPORT. Latam 2023 1st edition.*
Kantar. (2024a). *Desafiando el futuro: Analizando datos y anticipando tendencias.*
Kantar. (2024b). *Omnichannel. Reporte 2024: Decodificando 25 millones de elecciones de los consumidores de toda Latinoamérica.* https://www.kantar.com/latin-america/campaigns/kwp/2024/omnichannel-report-2024
Kearney. (2017). *The 2017 global retail development index: The age of focus.* https://bit.ly/3UvBklO
Minten, B., & Reardon, T. (2008). Food prices, quality, and quality's pricing in supermarkets versus traditional markets in developing countries. *Review of Agricultural Economics*, *30*(3), 480–490. https://doi.org/10.1111/j.1467-9353.2008.00422.x
Monteiro, G., Farina, E., & Nunes, R. (2012). Food-retail development and the myth of everyday low prices: The case of Brazil. *Development Policy Review*, *30*(1), 49–66. https://doi.org/10.1111/j.1467-7679.2012.00559.x
Monteiro, G., Nunes, R., & Farina, E. M. (2014). Food retail strategy and policy in Brazil: Heterogeneous retail formats and competition. En *Retailing in emerging markets* (pp. 124–156). Routledge.
OCDE. (2015). *Documento de base elaborado por la Secretaría de la OCDE.* Presentado en Foro Latinoamericano de Competencia: Sesión III – Cuestiones de competencia en el sector de la venta de productos de alimentación: Prestando atención a la conducta empresarial, Montego Bay, Jamaica. Montego Bay, Jamaica. https://www.oecd.org/competition/latinamerica/2015-latin-american-competition-forum.htm
Pérez Martín, J. (2021). *Abastecimiento de alimentos en el Área Metropolitana de Buenos Aires: Interacciones y configuración espacial de los entramados logísticos-comerciales en los sectores lácteo y frutihortícola.* Universitat Autònoma de Barcelona, Barcelona, España. http://hdl.handle.net/10803/671572
Pérez Martín, J. (2022). Los supermercados en el centro de la escena: Estrategia de negocios y formación de precios en el abastecimiento urbano de alimentos. *Realidad Económica*, *52*(350), 9–38. https://ojs.iade.org.ar/index.php/re/article/view/205/174
Reardon, T., & Berdegué, J. A. (2002). The rapid rise of supermarkets in Latin America: Challenges and opportunities for development. *Development Policy Review*, *20*(4), 371–388.
Richards, T. J., & Pasirayi, S. (2023). Food retailing in developing economies: Review of empirical insights and new directions. *Agribusiness*. https://doi.org/10.1002/agr.21867
Schwentesius, R., & Gómez, M. Á. (2002). Supermarkets in Mexico: Impacts on horticulture systems. *Development Policy Review*, *20*(4), 487–502. https://doi.org/10.1111/1467-7679.00185
Subsecretaría de Planeamiento. (2016). *Distribución territorial del precio de oferta de terrenos en la Región Metropolitana de Buenos Aires.* Ministerio de Desarrollo Urbano y Transporte – Gobierno de la Ciudad Autónoma de Buenos Aires. https://bit.ly/3hEfRR7
Torres Torres, F. (2011). El abasto de alimentos en México hacia una transición económica y territorial. *Problemas del desarrollo*, *42*(166), 63–84.
Turner, C., Aggarwal, A., Walls, H., Herforth, A., Drewnowski, A., Coates, J., Kalamatianou, S., & Kadiyala, S. (2018). Concepts and critical perspectives for food environment

research: A global framework with implications for action in low- and middle-income countries. *Global Food Security*, *18*, 93–101. https://doi.org/10.1016/j.gfs.2018.08.003
UNDESA. (2018). *World urbanization prospects: The 2018 revision.* United Nations Department of Economic and Social Affairs – Population Division. https://bit.ly/3f2VRFZ
Vecslir Peri, L. (2011). Nuevas centralidades del ocio y del consumo: Ámbitos, modalidades e instrumentos de regulación de las grandes superficies comerciales en la Región Metropolitana de Buenos Aires. *Revista Iberoamericana de Urbanismo*, *5*, 31–44.
World Bank. (2024). *World Bank, poverty and inequality platform* [Data set]. Washington, DC. https://bit.ly/3hENqTe

10

CONCENTRATION AND CENTRALIZATION OF CAPITAL IN BRAZILIAN FOOD RETAIL

Economic strategies, territorial expansion, and the production of urban space in medium-sized cities

Cláudio Smalley Soares Pereira

Introduction

On March 17, 2017, in an interview published in an important Brazilian corporate newspaper, a high-ranking representative of Carrefour spoke about the company's operations around the world, particularly in Brazil, in the context of the company's restructuring on a global scale. Georges Plassat, the company's CEO at the time, was emphatic when he said "Brazil is a beautiful business that gives you enthusiasm." At the time, Brazil accounted for 16% of the company's global turnover, and of the 14.5 billion euros in revenue from Latin America, 12 billion came from Brazil. This means, in percentage terms, approximately 80% (Fernandes, 2017). According to the same article, the company executive showed confidence in the recovery of the national economy, which at that time, after the parliamentary coup against former President Dilma Rousseff of the Workers' Party (2011–2016), seemed to be moving toward political and economic stability.

The mood for economic recovery pervaded the retail sector as a whole, including food retail, as well as a large part of the productive sectors. On the other hand, there has been growing political and economic instability since the fall of Rousseff. With Michel Temer (2016–2018) and Jair Bolsonaro (2018–2022), neoliberal reforms in the economy, in an attempt to create a new business environment more favorable to *laissez-faire* and market logic, became the norm. In 2020, the country ended with a 13.5% unemployment rate, the highest since 2012, with growing rates of hunger. For the first time in 17 years, more than half of the population had no guarantee of food on the table, which means 116.8 million people were food insecure, affecting more poor people, women, and the Black population (Almeida, 2021). At the same time, the concentration of the food retail market in the hands of supermarkets was 92.9%[1] (Belik, 2020), among the types of retailers included in the survey

DOI: 10.4324/9781003471929-15

of the Nielsen consultancy that the Brazilian Supermarkets Association (ABRAS) presents every year. Although 2017 through 2022 were difficult years for a large percentage of the population, in other words, large retail corporations increased their profits and expanded their activities in the territory. The supermarket industry, in particular, recorded good economic figures, especially in 2019 and, albeit to a lesser extent, during the SARS-Cov-2 pandemic (2020–2021). Since then, it has posted positive figures. In 2022, it represented 7.03% of the national gross domestic product (GDP), according to ABRAS (SuperHiper, 2023). The movements seen in the economy signal a growing monopolization, revealed by the concentration and centralization of capital in the sector. In the same context, in 2020 and 2021, Carrefour, the largest retailer in Brazil today, acquired stores from the Dutch company Makro and bought Grupo Big, formerly Walmart, in two operations that cost R$9.4 billion.

This chapter seeks to analyze the process of concentration and centralization of capital within the food retail sector in Brazil from a geographical perspective. The strategies employed by companies such as Carrefour and Casino in Brazil's socio-spatial formation over the last few decades consist of extending their territorial dominance by expanding a new format—the *atacarejo*—that mixes retail and wholesale. This commercial format has large dimensions (around 5,000 m^2 of sales area), carries out retail and wholesale transactions with a low price policy as its main economic strategy, and targets in particular poor consumers. The new strategy of large internationalized retailers in Brazil combines, on the one hand, the closure of hypermarkets and supermarkets and, on the other, the territorial expansion of *atacarejos* in the country. This strategy has a clear impact on the production of urban spaces. In this process, Brazil's medium-sized cities have become a target for the expansion of these large commercial areas, aligned with the new production and consumption logics of globalized retail.

Concentration and centralization of capital

Following Lefebvre's (1973) line of argument, we can say that capitalism has survived through the production of space. The dynamics of capitalism involve a space–time that is necessary for understanding how it works. In this sense, according to Swyngedouw (2020, p. 299), "the various geographies of accumulation are space-forming and space-dependent," from eighteenth-century and nineteenth-century colonialism to contemporary globalization, "they confirm the spatial constellations and geographical contradictions inherent in capitalism."

The concentration of capital and the centralization of capital refer to the social process and, therefore, to the reproduction of capital, which has geographical dimensions (Smith, 2020; Lencioni, 2008; Sposito, 2017). They are concepts that refer to different things. The concentration of capital is "the process that expands the means of production and workers, thus broadening the base of accumulation and confusing itself with it" (Lencioni, 2008, p. 11), including the purchase of machinery and hiring more workers. On the other hand, the centralization of capital "occurs when two or more independent capitals are combined into a single capital" and which "leads to a more rapid expansion in the scale of production (and potentially a rapid increase in the productivity of labor), than could be achieved by the simple concentration of capital in existing units" (Smith, 2020, p. 166). The centralization of capital, which occurs directly through merger or incorporation, or indirectly through the credit system (Smith, 2020, p. 166), is a redistribution of the ownership of existing capital (Marx, 2013, p. 702), which is increasingly concentrated in fewer hands, and is not directly related to the accumulation or growth of social capital (Smith, 2020; Lencioni, 2008). As Marx (2013) argued in Book I of *Capital,* "If here capital grows in the hands of one man until it reaches great masses, it is because there it is lost in the hands of many other men. This is centralization itself" (Marx, 2013, p. 702).

Both processes have a spatial dimension and imply considering their role in the production of space at various scales (Smith, 2020; Lencioni, 2008; Sposito, 2017). They are even more important in the current context of globalization and economic restructuring, as they reveal the unity of the socio-spatial process that seeks to understand the movement of capital (Lencioni, 2008). From the point of view of both social capital and the spatial dimension, concentration and centralization can be analyzed from various aspects, ranging from the productive, monetary, and commercial capital, to the formation of productive regions and urban centralities.

Commercial capital is that which is located between productive capital and consumer capital (Ducatel & Blomley, 1990), that is to say, it refers to the circulation of commodities and is therefore linked to commerce and consumption at the same time as it is tied to the broader dynamics of capital accumulation. Retail capital is thus an expression of commercial capital, which is divided into both "commodity capital" and "money capital" (Marx, 2017; Ducatel & Blomley, 1990; Harvey, 2014, pp. 141–165). It is therefore a fraction of the total social capital responsible for circulation and interested in the accumulation of capital through the exchange of commodities.

In the contemporary world, food retail capital has expanded its power, redefined power relations with productive capital (Ducatel & Blomley, 1990; Senauer & Reardon, 2010; Peres & Matioli, 2020), and intensified the exploitation of labor, with supermarkets (and the food supply chain as a whole) being responsible for driving inequality and hunger (Oxfam, 2018; Elias, 2021). This is why it is crucial to "unravel the role that commercial capitalists like Walmart, Ikea and Carrefour play in the political economy of our times" (Harvey, 2014, p. 21).

The concentration and centralization of retail capital expanded considerably after the Second World War, resulting in a "restructuring of retail" with spatial and urban impacts (Ducatel & Blomley, 1990). The emergence of supermarkets and their consolidation, in the context of the 1929 crisis in the United States, favored the uneven expansion, in space and time, of this commercial form, making it increasingly central to food retailing (Senauer & Reardon, 2010).

It is possible to identify that in contemporary capitalism, retail is changing and, in this context, the concentration and centralization of capital is increasing. According to Coe and Wrigley (2018), the new economic geography of globalization makes it possible to situate a "retail revolution" that has two interconnected aspects. On the one hand, there has been a wide-ranging transformation of the agricultural and manufacturing sectors, within the food and consumer goods sector. On the other hand, the international expansion of retail companies has transformed market structures, retail, and local supply networks, associated with changes in regulatory frameworks, consumption patterns, and a multitude of aspects of "socio-spatial formations" (Santos, 1977). In this sense, the deepening of "retail restructuring" (Ducatel & Blomley, 1990) has spatial and urban implications. In the case of Brazil, this process is expressed in the concentration of the supermarket sector, which has expanded in recent decades associated with a logic of territorial expansion (Sposito & Sousa, 2022).

The transformations of food retail capital in Brazil

The last three decades have seen intense spatial and economic processes that have changed the geographical dynamics of retail companies, in terms of both expansionist strategies and relations involving other capitals, the state, and economic agents. Transnational corporations have thus taken the lead from the point of view of the production of space in the context of globalization, reproducing business units in many socio-spatial formations, new distribution formats, the insertion of retail on different platforms such as the Internet, and altering the market structure of the sector. In the case of Brazil, and similarly in Latin America (Reardon & Berdegué, 2002), the expansion of commercial capital in the food retail sector took place between the 1960s and 1980s, exploding in the 1990s.

According to the Brazilian Society of Commerce and Consumption (SBVC, 2023), in its latest report on the 300 largest Brazilian retail companies, the supermarket sector accounts for 49.6% of total sales, which amounted to R$519.1 billion. Of the total number of companies analyzed, 152 (50.7%) are in the supermarket sector, which had a turnover expansion of around 16.2% between 2021 and 2022. Of the ten largest, four are supermarket companies (Carrefour, Assaí, Mateus, and GPA Alimentar).

The first supermarkets in Brazil appeared between the late 1940s and mid-1950s, inspired by the US model and located in the city of São Paulo. The spatial expansion of this commercial format began at the end of the 1960s, due to the economic and political situation, with the role of the state under the military dictatorship. The late 1960s and early 1970s, known as the "economic miracle,"[2] favored both the expansion of stores and companies and the expansion of the scale of those that existed. At this time, a process of capital centralization began (Gomes, 2022b). It was also at this time that the first units of foreign companies were set up in Brazil, like Makro in 1972 (from The Netherlands), Carrefour in 1975 (from France),

Sonae in 1989 (Portugal), and Walmart in 1995 (from the United States), among others (Sposito & Sousa, 2022).

The late 1970s to the 1980s were a period of capital crisis (Soja, 1993), which affected Latin American countries and Brazil, but this did not affect the supermarket sector, which grew and consolidated its dominant position in the sale of food products, at around 85% in the 1980s (Gomes, 2022a, p. 34). Until the mid-1990s, national economic instability contributed to the decline in growth that had been seen in the previous decade, which resulted in companies redefining their strategies through organizational changes, such as reducing store sizes, increasing productivity, and seeking to maximize profits. From 1997 onward, there was a reversal of the trend, with an increase in the number of stores, sales areas, and many investments, involving, since 1995, "a marked process of internationalization, led by some of the world's largest supermarket groups" (Gomes, 2022a, pp. 38–39).

In the 2000s, Brazil was the country in Latin America with the largest share of supermarkets in the food retail trade, accounting for 75%, compared to Argentina (57%), Panama (54%), Chile and Costa Rica (50%), and Mexico (45%) (Reardon & Berdegué, 2002, p. 374). This brief account is useful to prepare our demonstration of the contemporary moment. Over the last 40 years, the trend has been toward greater centralization of capital, involving internationalized retail capital, as shown in Figure 10.1.

The scenario at the start of the twenty-first century consolidated the trend that had been showing itself at the end of the 1990s. In the last 20 years, however, two periods can be identified: (a) the one from 2004 to 2014; and (b) another from 2015 to the present. The process of concentration and centralization of capital has advanced since the 1980s and has been consolidated, resulting in substantial transformations

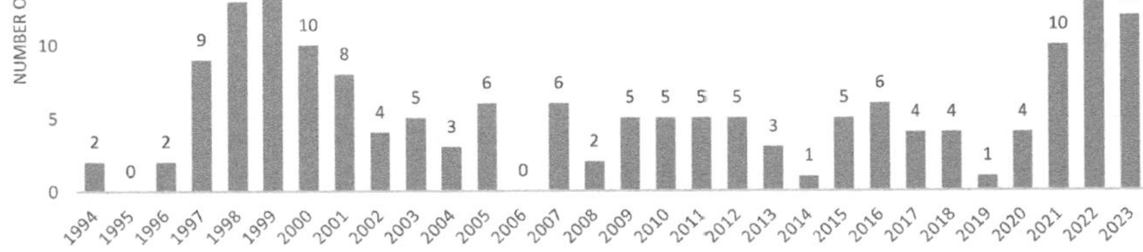

FIGURE 10.1 Brazil: Mergers and acquisitions in the supermarket sector between 1994 and 2023

Source: KPMG (2023)

in Brazilian socio-spatial formation, so that the entire territory has become a target for international commercial capital companies in the food retail sector.

As far as the period between 2004 and 2014 is concerned, there is a systemic dynamic involving a number of factors. This period was the focus of two reports by the consultancy Deloitte (2009, 2014), which analyzed Brazilian retail from the point of view of macroeconomic dynamics and the recent history of retail since the turn of the twentieth century, looking at the situation in the face of the 2007–2008 crisis and the outlook for the following years. For Deloitte (2009, 2014), the wage bill, social policies for income distribution and deconcentration, combined with the creation of formal jobs, credit expansion, and the *commodities boom*, contributed significantly to the expansion of retail and *shopping centers* in the period, in all regions, despite the inequalities and differences in this expansion in regional terms. It is important to mention that the state was an important agent in the production of space at this time, as public investments in housing programs ("Minha Casa, Minha Vida", with an initial target of one million homes), as well as the Growth Acceleration Program (PAC), which involved urban mobility and infrastructure works due to the mega-events (2014 Fifa World Cup and 2016 Olympics), reveals extensive spending on investment and consumption. It was in this context that important mergers and acquisitions of large retail companies took place, such as the purchase of Atacadão by Carrefour, Assaí by Grupo Pão de Açúcar, and GBarbosa by the Chilean Cencosud.

From 2015 onward, the scenario changed. The economic and political crisis begins to take shape, with the "June 2013 protests" (Maricato et al., 2013) as a highlight. At this juncture, rising unemployment, inflation rates, and falling purchasing power, as well as the articulation of the right in political power, caused the fall of President Dilma Rousseff in 2016. From then on, a more openly liberal logic triumphed in economic policy, with various neoliberal reforms (labor, social security, etc.). Faced with a decline in the consumption power of the middle and working classes, supermarket companies began to invest heavily in strategies that combined the concentration and centralization of capital with territorial expansion. A large part of this movement resulted in the expansion of the *atacarejos.*

To give an idea of the degree of concentration, "in October 1999, the five largest chains accounted for 40% of the segment's gross sales, while in 1994 this share was 23%" (Saab & Gimenez, 2000, p. 110). In 2022, according to Abras (SuperHiper, 2023), the five largest accounted for 44.17% of the entire industry's turnover, of which three (equivalent to 36.5%) are foreign-owned (Carrefour with 21.2%, Assaí with 11.7%, and GPA with 3.6%, respectively, in first, second, and fourth place). In this ranking of the five largest, foreign-owned companies account for 88.8% of turnover. If we look at the ten largest (Table 10.1), concentration jumped from 40.3% in 2020 to 47.8%. This shows that, as the number of stores has grown from 55,000 in 1999 to 94,706 in 2022 (SuperHiper, 2023), there has been concentration in the hands of fewer and fewer companies.

Those responsible for this growth in supermarket companies over the last decade have been the *cash and carry stores,* which, together with real estate investments

TABLE 10.1 Brazil: Top 10 supermarket companies in 2022

Companies	*Ranking*	*UF*	*Turnover in R$*	*Sales area*	*No. of stores*	*No. of Check Mite*	*No. of employees*
Carrefour	1	SP	108.052.000.000	1.512.045	1.203		150.000
Assaí Wholesale	2	SP	59.700.000.000	1.306.723	263	7.487	76.024
Mateus Supermercados S.A	3	MA	24.602.821.000	495.445	232	3.506	45.335
GPA	4	SP	18.531.000.000	1.059.620	658	-	52.981
Supermercados BH Comércio de Alimentos S.A	5	MG	14.011.918.334	325.468	262	3.205	29.191
Irmãos Muffato & Cia. Ltda	6	PR	12.044.330.26	303.685	88	2.166	18.418
SDB Comércio de Alimentos Ltda.	7	SP	11.223.995.000	254.031	81	1.585	12.83
Cencosud Brasil Comercial S.A	8	SP	11.115.723.771	529.860	218	2.405	19.367
Mart Minas wholesale and Retail & Dom Wholesaler	9	MG	8.322.471.834	371.000	70	1.567	13.134
DMA Distribuidora S.A	10	MG	7.661.273.203	383.142	185	2.599	17.724
Top 10	–	–	275.265.533.409	6.541.019	3.260	24.520	435.004

Source: Own elaboration based on Abaas (2023) and SBVC (2023)

and the opening of small format stores, have expanded their scope of action in the territory, mobilizing capital to places and regions where they had previously had little presence. In this context, several cities experienced large-scale commercial format stores for the first time.

The so-called *atacarejos* have gained prominence and importance (territorially and economically) since the crisis of 2015. A 2022 report revealed that "Wholesaling went from 47% to 67% . . . in terms of consumer penetration. This came from the middle and upper classes, as well as other classes that were already customers. Since the crisis of 2015 and 2016, consumers have been looking to save money" (Cardoso, 2022). All the strategies of international capital companies, especially Carrefour and Casino, began to incorporate this format as the central focus of their actions, which involved redefining their economic and spatial strategy.

Some major economic moves with spatial repercussions have taken place in the last decade. The first was the purchase of Walmart Brasil by the *Advent* Investment Fund in 2018, which restructured the company's operations in Brazil, renaming it Grupo Big; the second was the purchase of 30 Makro stores by Carrefour in 2020 for R$1.95 billion; the third was the split between Assaí and GPA in 2021, which began to operate separately, albeit under the same parent company. The fourth move, and perhaps the largest, was Carrefour's purchase of the Big Group in 2021 for R$7.5 billion. Finally, the fifth move was the sale of Assaí shares belonging to Cassino, in 2023, thus leaving control of the *atacarejo* chain. These moves had very clear geographical impacts, altering the commercial geography of food retail in the country and the dynamics of urban spaces.

The territorial and urban dimension of food retail strategies in Brazil

From a historical point of view, in Latin America, the logic behind the installation of these forms of commerce took place mainly in large metropolitan areas, and only since the 1990s have they expanded to medium and small towns (Reardon & Berdegué, 2002). As the concentration and centralization of capital advances, territorial expansion beyond the most dynamic region of Brazilian socio-spatial formation (the South and Southeast) is consolidated. Expansion over the last few decades has allowed for greater penetration into various regional spaces, with a particular impact on medium-sized cities (Sposito & Sousa, 2022).

A large part of the incorporation of the poor into "modern" circuits of consumption in Brazil, and the transformations in the commercial geography of the cities has been due to the role played by department stores, especially *atacarejos*, which have grown substantially in the last two decades. These large-scale stores have become the fundamental strategy of food retail commercial capital over the last 20 years but with greater intensity in the last decade. In 2008, the article "Grandes redes trocaram o tradicional hipermercado pelo novo *'atacarejo'*" (Big chains swap the traditional hypermarket for the new *'atacarejo'*), published in the newspaper Valor Econômico (Abras, 2008), showed that the three biggest retail chains operating in Brazil had started to invest in the *atacarejo* format. Walmart bought Sonae's operations in 2005, including Maxxi Atacado, and in 2007 Pão de Açúcar (CBD) bought Assaí and Carrefour bought Atacadão. These operations were worth R$1.7 billion, R$207 million, and R$2.2 billion, respectively. The article revealed that "the three big retailers—Carrefour, Wal-Mart and Grupo Pão de Açúcar—are converting conventional hypermarkets to their *'atacarejo'* brands, a typically Brazilian format aimed at the low-income population" (Abras, 2008).

Graph 2 should be interpreted on the basis of this process, in which companies have entered the wholesale business through mergers and acquisitions, while over the last 15 years they have intensified their actions by opening stores and converting super and hypermarkets into wholesale stores. Of the 387 Grupo Big stores acquired by Carrefour, 48% were in the Northeast, 34% in the South, and 18% in the Southeast (Carrefour, 2021). From 2021 to 2023, Carrefour opened 110 stores, of which 92 were conversions to the *atacarejo* format, and of the stores acquired from the Big Group, 129 were converted (Figure 10.2) and 76 became Atacadão units (Carrefour, 2023b). This expanded the company's presence in the territory. Assaí, for its part, reported that "at the end of 2023, 64 hypermarket conversions were in operation. The number of converted stores has . . . a sales multiple in line

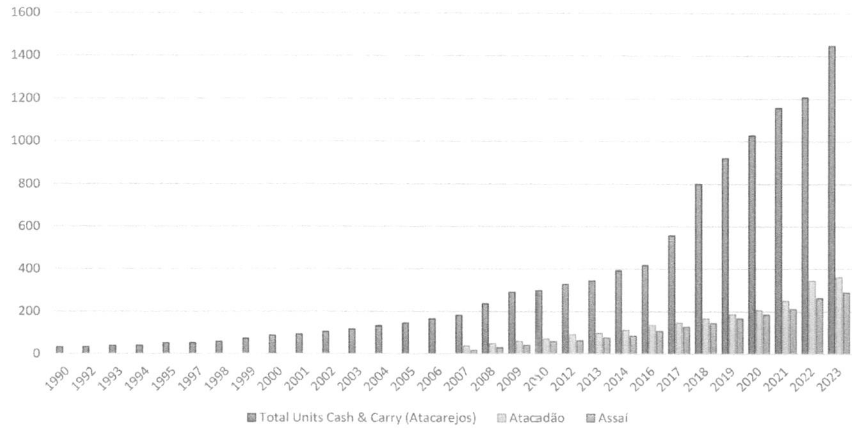

FIGURE 10.2 Brazil: Expansion of cash and carry in the last 25 years

Source: Own elaboration based on ABAAS (2023), Assaí (2024a) and Carrefour (2023a).

with the project's objectives (3x vs. hypermarket format)" (Assaí, 2024b, p. 5). This made it possible to expand into medium-sized cities that were unfamiliar with large foreign-owned stores of this nature (Pereira, 2020a, p. 193).

According to Abras (SuperHiper, 2023), wholesalers accounted for most of the supermarket sector's turnover, with 66.7%; in terms of revenue, the figure is 47.3%, followed by conventional supermarkets and hypermarkets, with 38.6% and 7.8%, respectively. Atacarejos received the most investment (48.1%), followed by super and hypermarkets (44.4%). Atacadão represents 70% of Carrefour's sales in Brazil (Carrefour, 2023b). The success of this format in Brazil has encouraged its internationalization, as Carrefour has announced the implementation of the first Atacadão unit in France, still in 2024, in Aulnay-sous-Bois, northwest of Paris, with an investment of 10 million euros (approximately R$ 53 million), but has been facing resistance from the French (Finotti, 2024).

Territorial insertion is one of the significant transformations in the context of the "retail revolution," through the mobilization of a set of strategies involving the culture of places of consumption, real estate planning, and land use (Coe & Wrigley, 2018). This implies the "capitalist use of territory" (Calabi & Indovina, 1992), essentially linked to the relations of production and reproduction that articulate the production, circulation and valorization of capital, and, finally, the reproduction of the workforce. These capitalist uses of territory also involve the real estate strategies that retailers have been developing in recent decades, which have enabled supermarket companies to transform land and real estate into an economic asset to generate profitability[3] (Mérenne-Schoumaker & Nappi-Choulet, 2014; Pereira, 2020a, 2020b) in a global context of redefined power relations with financial agents (Baud & Durand, 2012; Benquet & Durand, 2016).

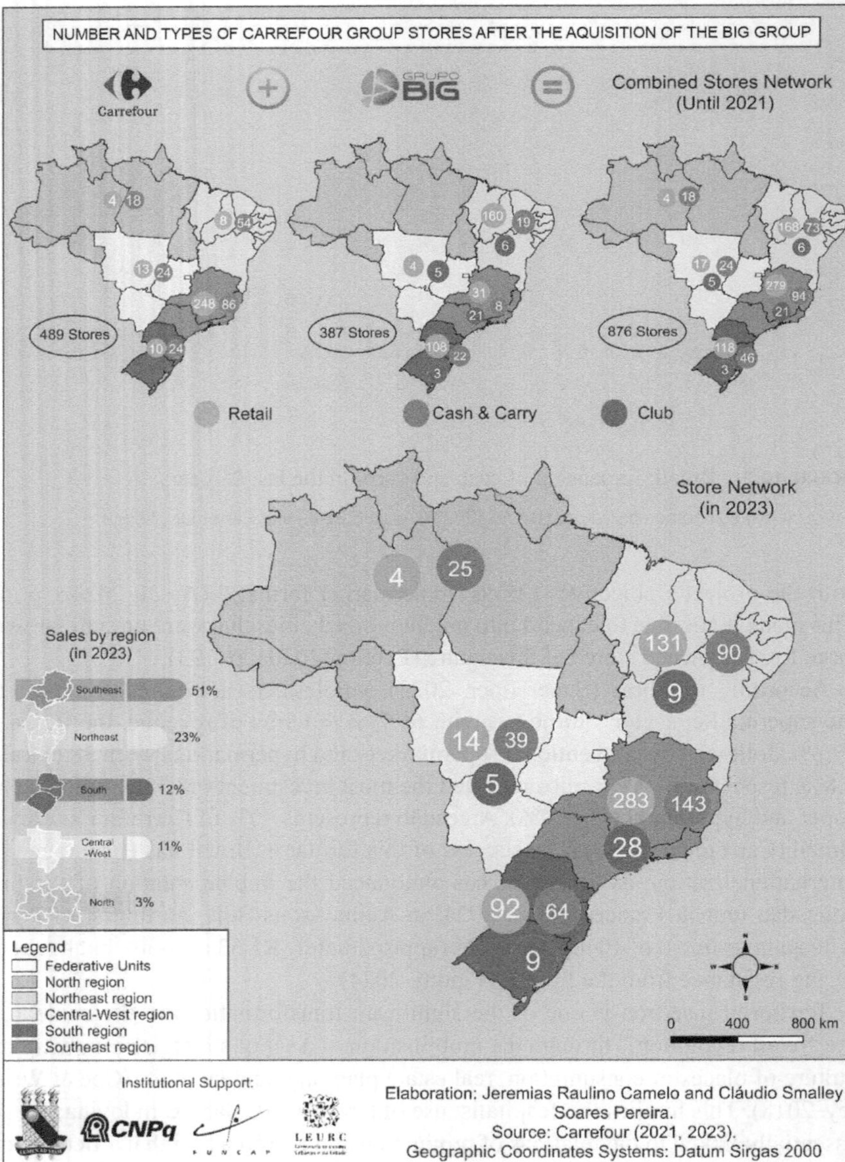

MAP 10.1 Location, number, and types of Carrefour stores after the acquisition of the Big Group

Source: Own elaboration based on Carrefour (2021, 2023a)

Since the territorial dynamics of retail expansion are anchored in cities, it is essential to situate the impacts of this process on the production of urban space. The relationship between commerce and the city is a historical one, and a considerable part of it stems from the role played by food consumption spaces. Thus, fairs, markets, and supermarkets play an important role in understanding the logics and processes of urban transformation (Pereira, 2020a). In this sense, one could argue in favor of a link between a "restructuring of retail" (Ducatel & Blomley, 1990), with urban restructuring (Soja, 1993; Sposito, 2007) that substantially modifies the relationship between the city and commerce (Salgueiro & Cachinho, 2009; Mermet, 2017; Pereira, 2020a) and can lead to processes of socio-spatial fragmentation (Caprón, 2000; Sposito & Sposito, 2020).

Table 10.2 and Map 10.2 show the urban dimension of the *atacarejos* of the three largest companies in the sector in Brazil (Abaas, 2023; Silva, 2023). It can be seen that they are spatially concentrated in the metropolises, which have 46.5% of commercial units. In second place, the regional capitals, with an average population of between 300,000 and 1.4 million inhabitants, account for 39% and the rest, 14.5%, are in municipalities with an average of between 12,500 and 120,000 inhabitants. This indicates that despite the country's territorial expansion, the atacarejos are concentrated in just a few urban centers, which are home to more than half the country's population.

Medium-sized cities, as they have been analyzed in Brazil, are spaces that mediate between large metropolitan areas and small towns and rural areas (Sposito, 2007). In recent decades, these areas have become important for the analysis of Brazilian urbanization, as they are the target of migratory processes, public and private investment, and economic dynamics. They are also spaces where socio-spatial inequalities are blatant. Commercial activities and the role of consumption have produced important transformations in urban morphologies and the social division of space. Medium-sized cities basically refer to the urban centers included as "regional capitals" in Table 10.2, but not all regional capitals are medium-sized cities.

The capitalist use of territory linked to commercial activities reflects the process of capital valorization and the search for new spaces to expand and make a profit. In the case of Brazil, this process has meant the incorporation of cities into the production and reproduction dynamics of international retail capital, especially in the North and Northeast regions, where supermarkets and hypermarkets used to exist only in the metropolises. The capillarity of the companies expanded, deconcentrating units, expanding organically (with new units) or via conversions, replacing supermarkets and hypermarkets, and opening *atacarejos* in their place.

Cities such as Juazeiro do Norte, Petrolina, Mossoró, Juazeiro da Bahia, and Sobral, all in the northeast of Brazil, have seen the arrival of large commercial areas that have redefined the urban spatial dynamics of retail trade. In the

TABLE 10.2 Brazil: Presence of cash and carry brands Atacadão, Assaí, and Mateus according to the national urban hierarchy until August 2022

Level in the urban network	*Sub-level in the urban network*	*Number of urban centers*	*Demographic aspects**	*No. of Atacadão*	*No. of Assaí*	*No. Mix Mateus*	*Percentage of attacks*
Metropolis	Major National Metropolis	1	Population arrangement of Sao Paulo, with 21.5 million inhabitants	113	125	6	46.5
	National Metropolis	2	Brasilia (3.9 million inhabitants); Rio de Janeiro/RJ (12.7 million inhabitants)				
	Metropolis	12	The average population of three million				
Regional Capitals	Regional Capitals A	9	Range from 800,000 to 1.4 million inhabitants	109	77	19	39
	Regional Capitals B	24	Average population 530 thousand inhabitants				
	Regional Capitals C	64	Average population of 300 thousand inhabitants				
Sub-regional centers	Subregional centers A	96	Average population of 120 thousand inhabitants	27	18	25	13
	Subregional centers B	256	National average of 70 thousand inhabitants				
Zone Centers	Zone A centers	147	Average population of 30 thousand inhabitants	0	0	3	1,5
	Zone B centers	251	Average population of 30 thousand inhabitants				
Local Centers	–	4.037	Average population of 12.5 thousand inhabitants	1	0	4	
Total	–	5.570	–	250	220	57	100

Note: *The average population of each study unit is considered only as an approximation, since the urban centers at each level of the hierarchy vary due to their location in the territory, according to the regions and the proximity and distance relationships they establish with other urban centers.

Source: Own elaboration based on IBGE (2020) and Silva (2023, p. 42).

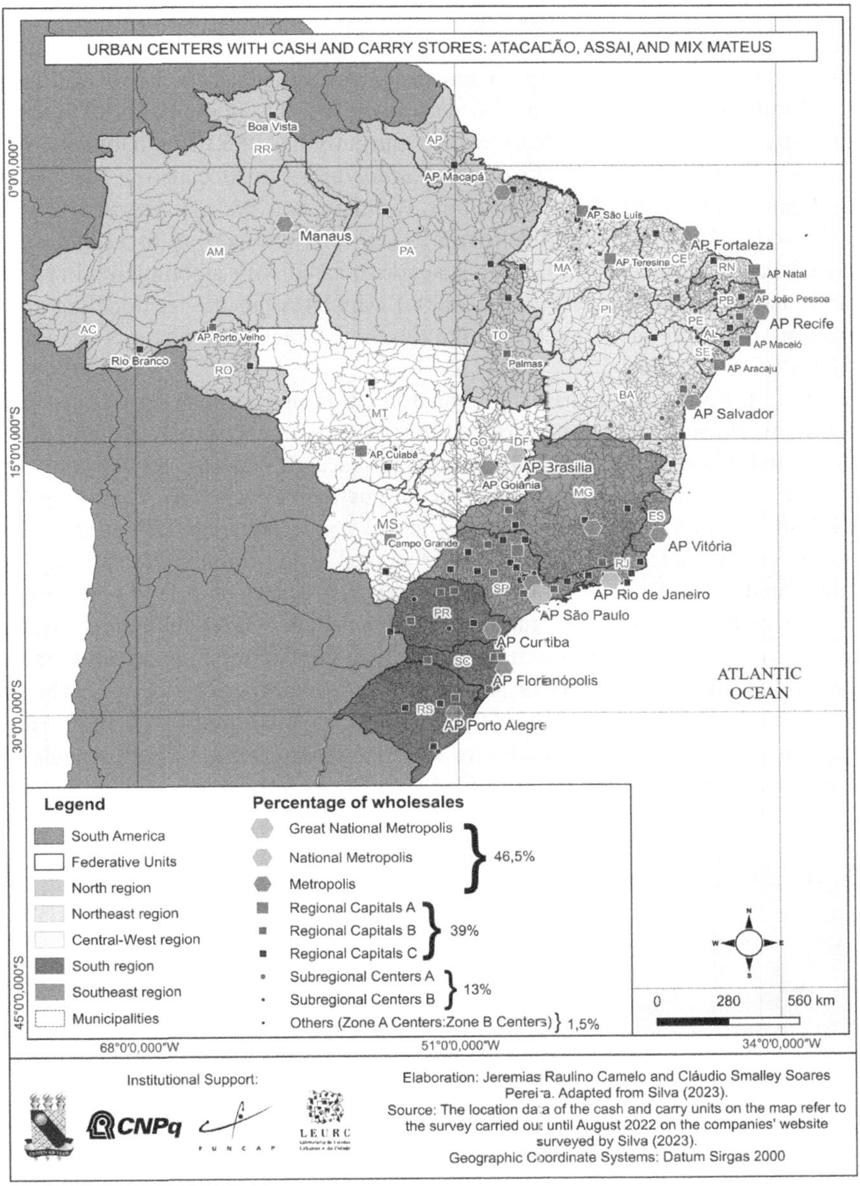

MAP 10.2 Brazilian urban centers with atacarejos: Atacadão, Assaí, and Mix Mateus

Source: Own elaboration based on Silva (2023)

medium-sized cities of the south and southeast of the country, *atacarejos* have added to the already strong presence of hypermarkets (Pereira, 2020a; Miyazaki, 2022). The cost of setting up an *atacarejo* unit ranges from R$30 million to R$40 million. To give an idea of what this means, the municipality of Juazeiro do Norte, in the interior of Ceará, which currently has 286,120 inhabitants, 96% of whom live in the city, received three *atacarejos* (an Atacadão, a Maxxi, and an Assaí, respectively, from Carrefour, Walmart, and Pão de Açúcar) between 2009 and 2013, which together cost R$95 million and add up to 11,900 m² of sales area. A restructuring of urban space associated with a commercial restructuring has become evident (Pereira, 2020a), which reveals the "remodeling of the geographies of production and consumption in the image and likeness of capital" (Harvey, 2021, p. 80).

The implications in terms of the transformation or restructuring of cities cannot be overlooked and are of various kinds. My summary is more general and is based mainly on Pereira (2020a) and recent research I have been carrying out.[4] I would highlight three aspects. First, the production of a *new social and economic division of urban space* was evident. The *atacarejos* have contributed to changing the classic patterns of urban land use as well as imprinting new marks on the urban landscape. The spatial location strategy is, when possible, a combination of large areas with available land that can support large-scale equipment (usually on the outskirts of cities), proximity to highways and fast communication routes (car use is crucial here), and a location close to working-class neighborhoods, which are the main beneficiaries of these companies' facilities (Figure 10.3). However, in some cases, it is possible to see that some of these developments are associated with urban expansion vectors aimed at high incomes (middle class and

FIGURE 10.3 Assaí Unit in the city of Petrolina, state of Pernambuco, inaugurated in 2022

Source: Assaí. Available at: https://www.assai.com.br/inauguracoes/assai-petrolina#galeria-2

FIGURE 10.4 View of the city center (verticalized) from the northwest sector of the city of Mossoró, state of Rio Grande do Norte, with an Atacadão unit on the left

Source: Field research, 2022.

elite), which points to an urban dynamic aligned with socio-spatial fragmentation (Figure 10.4).

The second aspect is the significant impact of these large companies on the *traditional food retail trade*. Small retail spaces such as street markets, public markets, and neighborhood shops have been affected. Although the small food trade has not been completely destroyed, its capillarity has diminished, since the spatial concentration of goods of all kinds, from fresh to processed, combined with low prices, has meant that international commercial capital has come to dominate and reorient consumption practices in medium-sized cities. This had a regional impact, as countless consumers and traders from nearby small towns began to stock up at the *atacarejos*, making its spatial reach clear on a regional scale.

Finally, the combination of new location strategies and food consumption practices has strengthened (and in some cases has been decisive in) the *redefinition of the urban center-periphery structure*. The need for large areas to be set up, combined with communication routes, meant that *atacarejo* units were set up on the urban peripheries, redefining consumption practices and reducing the economic power of city centers. These areas still concentrate a significant portion of the retail trade in medium-sized cities, but in relation to the food retail trade, the peripheries have better accommodated the demands of international commercial capital, which has brought roads to their vicinity, interfered in the circulation of public and private transport (even on a regional scale), and has imprinted an urban structure associated with the multiplication of commercial centralities (Pereira, 2020a).

Conclusion

This chapter sought to examine the process of concentration and centralization of commercial retail capital in Brazil. The focus in terms of economic activity was the supermarket sector. The historical perspective of the emergence of supermarkets in Brazil was outlined, and the growing role of international commercial capital in Brazilian food retail was highlighted. In particular, we looked at atacarejos, which are large-scale stores that sell both wholesale and retail. Large international food retail companies began to invest in this sector from the first decade of the twenty-first century as an economic strategy to increase their surplus value and expand their presence geographically in Brazil's socio-spatial formation.

In a country like Brazil, one of the most unequal in the world, this whole process has spatial and urban implications. To the extent that the food trade is concentrated in large, foreign-capitalized chains, traditional shops experience instability, their importance in the economic life of cities diminishes, and many of them disappear. The production of urban space becomes a key element for commercial spaces, since cities have an intimate relationship with commercial activity.

The new large-scale formats have an impact on the urban structure, redefining the content of what is the center and the periphery and modifying the patterns of urban land use, with clear repercussions on the costliness of urban life in a context permeated by neoliberalism associated with the precariousness of work and where hunger, inequality, and food security are still present. This is a challenge still to be faced, a contradiction that reveals the perversity of capital's control over food systems.

Notes

1 There is a methodological divergence between the data presented in this chapter, and those included by Pérez Martín previously in this section. The data used in this chapter are provided by the Brazilian Supermarkets Association (ABRAS) based on a survey by Nielsen, the market consulting firm, where the sales of supermarket companies are surveyed. While the data used by Pérez Martín are based on Kantar (2024), which implements household-level surveys. Belik (2020) and Reardon and Berdegué (2002) warn about some methodological issues in the ABRAS data; however, it has been widely used, which opens intriguing future debates.

2 Between 1968 and 1973, Brazil's gross domestic product grew by 11% a year, with relatively low inflation rates (Gomes, 2022a, p. 32).

3 "Acquisition of the BIG Group brought geographic complementarity and R$7 billion in real estate assets" (Carrefour, 2023b, p. 15). Investments in land and real estate, as well as the formation of *land banks,* have become an economic and spatial strategy for retail companies, as Pereira (2020b) analyzed.

4 Research project "Socio-spatial fragmentation and Brazilian urbanization: scales, vectors, rhythms and forms," coordinated by Maria Encarnação Beltrão Sposito (FAPESP—Process: 18/07701-8) and "Atlas of the social and environmental dynamics of Petrolina and Juazeiro/BA," coordinated by me (CNPq—Process: 409930/2021-0).

References

Abaas. (2023). A evolução do atacarejo no Brasil. Revista Abaas, ano 6, n. 17, 2023. Disponível em: https://abaas.com.br/wp-content/uploads/2023/09/book_abaas_17.pdf. Acesso em 6. mai. 2024.

Abras. (2008). Grandes redes trocam o tradicional hipermercado pelo novo "atacarejo". 25 set. 2008. Disponível em: https://www.abras.com.br/clipping/geral/1249/grandes-redes-trocam-o-tradicional-hipermercado-pelo-novo-atacarejo. Acesso em: 08 mai. 2024.

Almeida, C (2021). Fome cresce pela primeira vez em 17 anos, mais da metade da população não tem garantia de comida na mesa. O Globo, Economia. 06/04/2021. Disponível em: https://oglobo.globo.com/economia/fome-cresce-pela-1-vez-em-17-anos-mais-da-metade-da-populacao-nao-tem-garantia-de-comida-na-mesa-24956620. Acesso: 07 mai. 2024.

Assaí. (2024a). Apresentação institucional. Assaí Atacadista, abril de 2024, 45p.

Assaí. (2024b). Divulgação de resultados 4T23 e 2023. Fevereiro de 2024, 18p.

Baud, C; Durand, C. (2012). Financialization, globalization, and the making of profits by leading retailers. Socio-Economic Review, n. 10, p.241–266.

Belik, W. (2020). Estudo sobre a Cadeia de Alimentos (Relatório de pesquisa).

Benquet, M; Durand, C. (2016). La financiarisation de la grande distribution. Restructuration de l'actionnariat et déclin économique du groupe Carrefour (1999–2013). Revue Française de Socio-Économie, n. 16, p.37–59.

Calabi, D; Indovina, F. (1992). Sobre o uso capitalista do território. Orientação, São Paulo, n. 9, p.37–66.

Caprón, G. (2000). Fragmentation et polarisation urbaine: le rôle des hypermarchés dans les restructurations territoriales de l'aire métropolitaine de Buenos Aires. Bulletin de l'Association de géographes français, ano 77, p.106–116.

Cardoso, D. H. (2022). Atacarejo é nova aposta da classe alta para driblar inflação. Estado de Minas, Economia e Negócios, 16/04/2022. Disponível em: https://www.em.com.br/app/noticia/economia/2022/04/16/internas_economia,1360371/atacarejo-e-nova-aposta-da-classe-alta-para-driblar-inflacao.shtml. Acesso em: 16 mar. 2023.

Carrefour. (2021). Aquisição do Grupo Big, março de 2021. Apresentação institucional, 29p.

Carrefour. (2023a). Relatório anual de sustentabilidade, 2023, 153p. https://www.grupocarrefourbrasil.com.br/sustentabilidade/.

Carrefour. (2023b). Investidor Morning 2023, Grupo Carrefour Brasil. 28/11/2023. Disponível em: https://ri.grupocarrefourbrasil.com.br/. Acesso 9 mai. 2024.

Coe, N. M; Wrigley, N. (2018). Towards new economic geographies of retail globalization. In: Clark, G. L; Feldman, M. P; Gertler, M. S; Wojcik, D; Kaiser, A. (eds.) The New Oxford Handbook of Economic Geography. New Edition ed. Oxford: Oxford Univeristy Press, p.427–447.

Deloitte. (2009). Análise setorial varejo. Um setor em grandes transformações. Deloitte Touche Tohmatsu, 26p.

Deloitte. (2014). Os Poderosos do Varejo Global: o varejo além de todos os limites. Deloitte Touche Tohmatsu, 32p.

Ducatel, K; Blomley, N. (1990). Rethinking retail capital. International Journal of Urban and Regional Research, n. 14, p.207–227.

Elias, D. (2021). O alimento-mercadoria e a fome no Brasil. Boletim Goiano de Geografia, v. 41, n. 1, p.1–35.

Fernandes, D. (2017). O Brasil é "um belo negócio" para o Carrefour. Valor Econômico, Empresas. 10/03/2017. Disponível em: http://www.valor.com.br/empresas/4894472/brasil-e-belo-negocio-para-o-carrefour. Acesso em: 17 abr. 2017.

Finotti, I (2024). Ainda sob ataque, Atacadão troca de cidade e vai inaugurar 1ª loja na Grande Paris. Folha de São Paulo, 8/01/2024. Disponível em: https://www1.folha.uol.com.br/

mercado/2024/01/ainda-sob-ataque-atacadao-troca-de-cidade-e-vai-inaugurar-1a-loja-na-grande-paris.shtml. Acesso em: 24.mai. 2024.
Gomes, V. B. (2022a) A origem do ramo supermercadista em diferentes localidades. In: Miyazaki, V. K; Gomes, V. B; Sposito, M. E. B; Sousa, G. M. (Org.) As lógicas econômicas e espaciais do ramo supermercadista. Rio de Janeiro: Consequência, p.17–51.
Gomes, V. B. (2022b). O ramo supermercadista brasileiro no período recente. In: Miyazaki, V. K; Gomes, V. B; Sposito, M. E. B; Sousa, G. M. (Org.) As lógicas econômicas e espaciais do ramo supermercadista. Rio de Janeiro: Consequência, p.53–138.
Harvey, D. (2014). Para entender o Capital, livros II e III. São Paulo: Boitempo.
Harvey, D. (2021). O espaço e o tempo do valor. RDP, Brasília, v. 18, n. 97, p.77–102.
Ibge. (2020). Regiões de influência das Cidades 2018. Rio de Janeiro.
Kantar. (2024). Omnichannel. Reporte 2024: Decodificando 25 millones de elecciones de los consumidores de toda Latinoamérica.
KPMG (2023). Fusões e aquisições. 2° trimestre de 2023. 53p. Disponível em: https://assets.kpmg.com/content/dam/kpmg/br/pdf/2023/11/KPMG_FA2.trim.2023v.4.pdf.
Lefebvre, H. (1973). La survie du capitalisme: la re-production des rapports de production. Paris: Anthropos.
Lencioni, S. (2008). Concentração e centralização das atividades urbanas: uma perspectiva multiescalar. Reflexões a partir do caso de São Paulo. Revista de Geografía Norte Grande, núm. 39, p.7–20.
Maricato, E. *et al.* (2013). Cidades rebeldes: passe livre e as manifestações que tomaram as ruas do Brasil. São Paulo: Boitempo.
Marx, K. (2013). O Capital, livro I. São Paulo: Boitempo.
Marx, K. (2017). O Capital, livro III. São Paulo: Boitempo.
Mérenne-Schoumaker, B; Nappi-Choulet, I. (2014). Commerce et opérateurs immobiliers: um marche na voie de financiarisation. In: Gasnier, A; Lemarchand, N. (eds.) Le commerce dans tous ses états. Rennes: Presses Universitaires de Rennes, p.197–204.
Mermet, A.-C. (2017). Global retail capital and the city: towards an intensification of gentrification. Urban Geography, v. 38, n. 8, p.1158–1181. https://doi.org/10.1080/02723638.2016.1200328.
Miyazaki, V. K. (2022). O ramo supermercadista nas cidades médias. In: Miyazaki, V. K; Gomes, V. B; Sposito, M. E. B; Sousa, G. M. (Org.) As lógicas econômicas e espaciais do ramo supermercadista. Rio de Janeiro: Consequência, p.207–301.
Oxfam (2018). Hora de Mudar: desigualdade e sofrimento humano nas cadeias de fornecimento dos supermercados.
Pereira, C. S. S (2020a). A nova condição urbana. Espaços comerciais e de consumo na produção e reestruturação da cidade. Curitiba: Appris.
Pereira, C. S. S. (2020b). The production of space and the transformations of contemporary capitalism: real estate strategies of retail companies. Mercator, v. 19, p.1–15. https://doi.org/10.4215/rm2020.e19004.
Peres, J.; Matioli, V. (2020). Donos do Mercado: Como os grandes supermercados exploram trabalhadores, fornecedores e a sociedade. São Paulo: Elefante.
Reardon, T., & Berdegué, J. A. (2002). The rapid rise of supermarkets in Latin America: Challenges and opportunities for development. Development Policy Review, v. 20, n. 4, p.371–388.
Saab, W. G. L.; Gimenez, L. C. P. (2000). Aspectos atuais do varejo de alimentos no mundo e no Brasil. BNDES Setorial, Rio de Janeiro, n. 11, p.101–121.
Salgueiro, T. B; Cachinho, H. (2009). As relações cidade-comércio. Dinâmicas de evolução e modelos interpretativos. In: Carreras, C; Pacheco, S. M. M. (Org.) Cidade e Comércio: a rua na perspectiva internacional. Rio de Janeiro: Armazém das Letras, p.9–40.
Santos, M. (1977). Society and Space: social formation as theory and method. Antipode, vol. 9, n. 1, p.3–13.
SBVC. (2023). As 300 maiores empresas do varejo brasileiro. Ranking do Varejo SBVC Curitiba: Posigraf.

Senauer, B; Reardon, T. (2010). The global spread of modern food retailing. In: Petrovic, M; Senauer, B; Hamilton, G. G. (eds.) The market makers: How retailers are reshaping the global economy. Oxford University Press, p.271–290.
Silva, M. L. (2023). Produção do espaço e uso do território no Brasil dos atacarejos: novas faces do capitalismo dependente? Relatório de Qualificação (Doutorado em Geografia). Instituto de Filosofia e Ciências Humanas. Universidade Federal do Pará, Belém-PA, 2023, 108p.
Smith, N. (2020). Desarrollo desigual. Naturaleza, capital y la producción del espacio. Madrid: Traficantes de Sueños.
Soja, E. W. (1993). Geografias pós-modernas: a reafirmação do espaço na teoria social crítica. Rio de Janeiro: Zahar.
Sposito, M. E. B. (2007). Cidades médias: reestruturação das cidades e reestruturação urbana. In: Sposito, M. E. B (Org.) Cidades médias: espaços em transição. São Paulo: Expressão Popular, p.233–253.
Sposito, M. E. B. (2017). Concentração e centralização. In: Sposito, E. S. (Org.). Glossário de Geografia Humana e Econômica. São Paulo: Edunesp, p.1–65.
Sposito, M. E. B; Sousa, G. M. (2022). Concentração econômica e expansão territorial: lógicas espaciais do ramo supermercadista. In: Miyazaki, V. K; Gomes, V. B; Sposito, M. E. B; Sousa, G. M. (Org.) As lógicas econômicas e espaciais do ramo supermercadista. Rio de Janeiro: Consequência, p.139–206.
Sposito, M. E. B; Sposito, E. S. (2020). Sociospatial fragmentation. Mercator, v. 19, p.1–13.
SuperHiper. (2023). Ranking Abras 2023. Maio 2023, ano 49, n. 558, 204p.
Swyngedouw, E. (2020). Geografia. In: Fine, B; Saad-Filho, A. (Org.) Dicionário de economia política marxista. São Paulo: Expressão Popular, p.299–305.

11

FAIR TRADE AND AGROECOLOGY

Emerging tools to strengthen commercial strategies of family farmers organizations

Julián Monkes

Introduction: peri-urban agriculture and its relationship to agroecology

According to UN data (2018), 55% of the world's population lives in cities, a number which is projected to reach 68% by 2050. In the case of Argentina, that percentage is currently 92%. The increase in population and demand for agricultural products implies changes in dietary habits and strong pressure on agricultural production, promoting the phenomena of expansion and intensification of natural ecosystems (Hasegawa et al., 2019). In turn, the hegemonic agrifood model deepens the impacts on health due to the difficulty for many sectors of the urban population in accessing healthy food. Indeed, in Latin America and the Caribbean in general, there are 48 million undernourished people and 205 million that suffer moderate or severe food insecurity (FAO et al., 2020).

The unsustainability of the intensive production model has become visible as a result of the growing negative impact of certain practices of modern and industrial agriculture in Latin America (Gazzano et al., 2021). In fruit and vegetable production, the high rate of dependency on inputs and the technification of the production systems make them economically viable in the short term for the most capitalized producers, but ecologically and socially unsustainable in the long term (Marasas, 2012). In particular, the different peri-urban productive territories are shrinking in area and number of producers, and/or relocating to greater distances from their nearby urban markets. This represents a problem since these have a strategic character for the diet of urban consumers and for the socioeconomic development of rural producer families (Mitidieri, 2015, see Barksy, this volume). To a large extent, this phenomenon is due to the dispersed expansion of the urban frontier for speculative and real estate purposes (Cordara et al., 2017; Barsky, this volume).

DOI: 10.4324/9781003471929-16

The horticultural belt of La Plata, Argentina (CHLP), is located in the humid pampas and contains one of the oldest and most consolidated agrarian areas of the region (Benencia, 2012). It represents the main source of fresh foods for the Buenos Aires metropolitan area (García, 2012). In most farms in this area, production is intensive, technified, and requires high inputs (Simonatto, 2000). Moreover, the productive area is decreasing in La Plata as a result of an urban frontier due to real estate developments (Carballo, 2013), which is produced by the lack of planning and management of land use and access to land for productive purposes in peri-urban areas (Feito, 2014; Granero et al., this volume). As a result, rising land rents have forced the relocation of producing families to areas with cheaper rents, which are located outside available irrigation infrastructures, with greater ecological fragility and/or which are surrounded by extensive monoculture production areas (Giobellina et al., 2017).

In this context, agroecological production has emerged as a key strategy to avoid rural–urban migration and to halt the advance of the hegemonic production model (Feito, 2014). Although agroecology emerged in the 1970s, it is only in the last decade that the term has been massified in the public and political agenda, where it has been promoted as a path toward food security and sovereignty (Manzanal & González, 2010; Gliessman, 2013). In La Plata, agroecological horticultural production has promoted collective and associative strategies among producers and has been linked with territorial interventions that support family farming (Ambort, 2017). In the region, the adoption of agroecological practices has been found to allow producer families to improve the sale of their production in multiple ways (Monkes & Easdale, 2023). On the one hand, by incorporating bio-inputs that allow fertilization and prevent pests and diseases, they reduce the purchase of dollarized inputs, making their production more competitive by lowering relative costs. On the other hand, working with an agroecological perspective requires diversifying production to recover the ecological functions that allow for regulating and reducing the impact of pests and diseases; this, in turn, allows for greater stability in production. Finally, agroecology requires the construction of a community network with the rest of the producers in the area, since the production of bioinputs, the purchase of organic waste for composting, and the sale of production are only viable in economic terms if it acquires the necessary scale. Agroecology thus appears not only as an alternative strategy when raising claims and demands for public policies but also as a way to facilitate access to technical information, provide encouragement among producers, and enhance alternative marketing channels. This provides producers with better possibilities of facing market instability, greater power in determining prices, and support for establishing alternative commercial links (Souza Casadinho, 2013; Ambort, 2017).

Despite the promise of agroecology, however, family farms continue to face challenges in the commercialization and distribution of their products (Lazarte et al., 2020). This is due, on the one hand, to the lack of integration or coordination between small-scale producers, which does not allow them to generate the necessary scale to sell their products to wholesalers at a good price. On the other hand, most family farms lack the capacity to sell their products directly from the farm, which generates a dependence on intermediaries who appropriate a large percentage of the final price of the food, leaving farmers with extremely low-profit margins. In turn, the decentralization of wholesale markets in the Buenos Aires Metropolitan Area—into 41 markets—may negatively affect price formation since decentralization actually promotes the formation of longer supply chains with additional intermediaries, which drives up prices for consumers without improving payout to producers (Pérez Martín, 2022). The combination of all these factors generates a very low-profit margin for people working in fruit and vegetable production in the CHLP, which is why different organizations are deploying mechanisms to eliminate intermediaries and move toward short marketing chain schemes (López García, 2012).

This chapter analyzes the use of cooperative and associative strategies by small-scale family farmers in La Plata. Drawing on extensive ethnographic fieldwork conducted between 2018–2022 with the producers' association "Federación Rural para la Producción y el Arraigo" (FRPA), the analysis suggests that such strategies are effective in addressing commercialization challenges, in promoting the adoption of agroecology, and in improving the well-being and stability of family farms.

The organizational development of family farming: the case of the "federación rural para la producción y el arraigo" (rural federation for production and rooting)

Cooperativist and associativist organizations promote a varied agenda in search of solutions to the agricultural sector's problems related to issues such as access to land, training, financing, and marketing, among others. Politically speaking, organizing collectively allows agriculturalists to have a presence in spaces of negotiation with government agencies. Economically, collective strategies allow small producers to scale up and assert themselves in terms of setting prices and negotiating conditions with buyers and intermediaries. In Argentina, as elsewhere in Latin America, collective organizational strategies are linked to the promotion of agroecological strategies.

Cooperativism and associativism have enjoyed significant success as organizational strategies in the La Plata area in recent years. While Bolivian horticulturists, in particular, have long engaged in forms of collective organization along ethnic lines (García, 2014), in recent years the number of agricultural associations has multiplied and expanded more broadly among producers of other origins. Many of the producers with whom fieldwork was conducted reported that they began to organize in order to defend their territories against the encroachment of urban and real estate developments, as well as to access resources. Before organizing, producers report that *"there was no culture of struggle . . . nor did I know that organizations existed. We were like animals, alone in the field"* (producer from Los Hornos, 2019). As time went by, they began to improve their production conditions by associating among groups of families and gaining access to different incentive programs from provincial and national governments.

The greatest leap in terms of the rise of the collective organization took place in 2016 with a "quintero strike." This strike was due to the devaluation of the Argentine peso—which multiplied the price of agro-inputs whose value is dollarized—and the tariff hikes in public services, caused a nearly 1000% increase in the cost of electricity and fuel (Lazarte et al., 2020). One producer narrated that historical moment in these terms:

> *The rent increased to 30% of what I was producing, I was there for two years. After that, I left because an opportunity came up, a different land. A friend passed it on to me and I had almost no money. I still went to rent. Uh, I almost went bankrupt. Imagine renting without money. . . . And then came the increases in electricity, in everything. On top of that, the rent went through the roof. So, well, we struggled. One day I heard that there was going to be a strike in Quintero. That's when I met Lautaro, Manso, Diego, Maru, and I don't know who else. I don't remember well. And we were there that day, that night, all night long! Until the next day at two o'clock I was there.*
>
> *(producer of Los Hornos, 2019)*

Within the framework of this strike, the Small Producers' Movement of La Plata grew exponentially, with its strength lying mainly in productive peri-urban territories. Since 2016, producers in the area massively joined the Union of Land Workers or the Movement of Excluded Workers—Rural Branch (currently reconfigured as FRPA). Today, FRPA is one of the most representative organizations in the horticultural sector in Argentina. It brings together more than 20,000 families belonging to family, peasant, and Indigenous agriculture, of which a large majority is dedicated to vegetable production in the green belts of the main urban centers. In the greater La Plata area, it brings together more than 4,000 family producers (Shoaie Baker & García, 2021).

Within the FRPA, there is a section dedicated to agroecology whose objective is to support the transition to agroecological production. Shoaie Baker and García (2020) point out limiting factors such as the risk and uncertainty involved for any producer when faced with the decision to change activity, taking into account the cultural legacy and a productive structure based on conventional production. In addition, these authors highlight limitations in terms of dissemination and access to information; inadequate technical advice from agronomists or insufficient training of farmers as a necessary technical barrier to the practical adoption of new knowledge; obstacles or impediments to marketing and access to markets in the face of a still incipient demand for agroecological products; among others. This is why the organization develops its territorial work mainly in the areas of cooperativism, agroecological transition, and land and housing. One of the great challenges the members of the agroecology unit face is how to work around these obstacles and incorporate new producers in this transition. Indeed, even in some cases where producers were essentially engaging in agroecological production, many did not define it as such:

Q: *And before you started testing, had you heard of agroecology?*

A: No.

Q: *Or before the movement, nothing?*

A: *No, not before.*

Q: *And how was it when you were told to produce without chemicals? Did it not generate doubts, for example?*

A: *Sure, doubts, yes. But, it wouldn't be a bad thing to try it, I was saying. Right. That part, it can be a little difficult, right? Because back in Bolivia, where I lived, no chemical, of any kind, was ever used. And now. . . . Well, now, yes, because you can see that the bugs are not from there. They arrived with the people, who knows. Now there are spider mites, there are thrips. Not before, they didn't exist. Nothing was ever used. They used goat guano, the soil was moved with a plow, with a couple of oxen. Then we sowed, watered and the children took the food from there with their hands and that was it, natural, everything.*

(Abasto producer, 2021)

Once a producer decides to engage in agroecological practices, the FRPA provides support to aid in the transition. It built and manages a plot of land where there is a plant nursery, a bio-inputs factory, and a storage shed where bags of seasonal vegetables are collected from producers and sold directly. The main interest behind this process is to assist agroecological producers in accessing urban markets, avoiding intermediaries. This same producer says that:

> *I joined agroecology because I liked it and we began to train with the technicians who came from INTA and other colleagues who were already there, the preparations, how to put the vegetables and I said: I'm going to try it. And that's where we started. I spent almost two years doing the workshops with Wildo* (FRPA referent and agroecology promoter). *After that I started to send the bags because at first they wouldn't give them to me. Of course. And now I am always participating.*
>
> *(Producer from Abasto, 2021)*

These passages allow us to observe the feedback between the organizational processes and the drive for agroecological transition. The organization provides education and resources to producers, aiding and accompanying them in the agroecological transition. The FRPA's work broadens producer's possibilities to access preferred markets, which incentivizes others to join the organization. According to Baldini (2020), "as a result of these advances, we are facing the challenge of moving towards a scaling-up process leading to the massification of agroecology as a productive and territorial development model" (op cit., pp. 28).

Pueblo a Pueblo, an example of synergy between fair trade and agroecology

In 2018, FRPA established a new marketing tool called "Pueblo a Pueblo" (PaP) to support local producers with the sale of vegetables and, over time, it incorporated a bag of "pesadas" (potatoes, onions, and squash) that comes from the south of the Province of Buenos Aires and a bag of seasonal fruits that come from different provinces. According to one of the members of the cooperative, the initiative grew out of the problem of logistics for small family farms:

> *We had a big problem of how to market our production. Among the proposals we came up with the idea of holding a fair in the neighborhoods. All this worked well, not 100%, but it helped us a little. Intermediaries are very complicated, they take the production without working it and they set the prices* (Producer Los Hornos, 2021).
>
> *Pueblo a pueblo was born with the perspective and the horizon of being able to consolidate a cooperative way of working, where family agriculture producers of the fruit and vegetable sector of La Plata can have a direct marketing line without intermediaries. . . . Once we put together the produce bags, we share lists of available products for the week in our communication channels so that consumers can order what they want and we establish a delivery date, at home or at a drop-off point.*
>
> *(member of PaP, 2021)*

Moreover, this same member states that, although the pandemic hit the farming sector very hard, it also opened up opportunities for new types of commercialization:

> *When all the stores were closed and people could not leave their homes, we were able to establish a routing circuit and logistics to deliver to homes. That was positive because sales exploded. We opened new distribution nodes in other districts. It helped the sector a lot because we guarantee a fixed salary in a dignified way. Seventy percent of everything that is sold goes directly to the producer.*
>
> *(PaP member, 2021)*

A large part of the increase in produce sales is due to the ability to maintain low sales prices in an inflationary context, as Sotiru (2022) shows comparing different indexes of price increases. The results show that all the indexes surveyed increased above the price of a bag of produce through a local distribution network for the same period, which was able to maintain prices once the pandemic was over.

Part of the success in maintaining the price was the strategy of opening its own markets. FRPA through PaP has opened markets in the cities of La Plata, Buenos Aires City, Rosario, and Córdoba, among others. By doing this, they have been able to incorporate other products that are not produced in-house. In other words, not only do they market their products directly but they have also become solidarity intermediaries.

> *Our objective is to get healthy, quality food directly from the producer to the consumer at fair prices, taking into account that the work must be dignified. From the community organization, we started to project things like this where we can inaugurate our own market. In this market there are not only producers from the federation, we have honey from Samborondón, Yerba from cooperatives in Misiones, and coffee that we buy from the MST in Brazil. This helps a sector that is very hard hit and allows lower food prices in a context where everyone speculates with them, especially because of the dollarization of inputs and the lack of access to land. And that is the biggest problem, because it depends on what the landowner wants to produce and it limits the margins of action.*
>
> *(PaP member, 2021)*

This limitation mentioned by the member, to the type of product and forms of production, is given not only by the landlord's definitions but also by the rental prices. The indiscriminate increase in prices requires producers to need money at the end of each month to be able to pay rent and utilities. This undermines the agroecological transition because, as this farmer says, it takes more time:

> *Agroecology takes time. It always takes a little longer than conventional. It only has fertilizer. The conventional one has everything, to cure the vegetables quickly. We have to wait. This plot of mine that has vegetables was just about to flower and my neighbor has already finished harvesting. We don't work anymore, maybe a little, but we have to wait a lot and plan so as not to run out of vegetables and have money to pay for things.*
>
> *(Producer from Los Hornos, 2019)*

In this sense, the strategy of FRPA to facilitate producers' planning and guarantee a certain degree of predictability was to open its own markets and, from there, to coordinate with other actors in the productive sector of the social and popular economy. These strategies make it possible to guarantee that all agroecological production has a decent price and is included in a direct marketing channel. Otherwise, as the following producer says, part of the value of the product is lost:

> *In the conventional sector, the intermediary is not interested in whether it is an agroecological product or not, he is going to sell it. There is no certification that*

says that, if he produces agroecological, he can raise the price, for example. So he sells it as common, when in the agroecological sector the construction of prices also includes our labor force, but not in the conventional sector.

(Abasto producer, 2021)

The creation of a direct marketing tool by the FRPA made it possible to generate greater autonomy for producers. Cataldi and Flores (2019) point out that this greater autonomy has a concrete expression, since agroecological production is less costly economically than conventional production and sales through these channels improve their profits. Baldini et al. (2019) explain that marketing is a key point for producers who are tenants, given that they face high fixed costs, so sustained sales contribute to their stability and ability to plan. In addition, if the level of sales is increased, this can allow and encourage the organization to invite other producers, who produce conventionally, to make an agroecological transition (Sotiru, 2022).

Although total production costs are reduced with agroecological production, the labor invested, the relative costs of production, and the difficulties of transportation increase due to the low volume produced and make the product more expensive. This makes agroecological production affordable primarily to sectors with more disposable income. This element is central when thinking about the "fair price", since, as mentioned earlier, its preparation focuses on the decent remuneration of the producers' work. However, it does not go into the accessibility of these prices for consumers in urban areas.

Difficulty of access to agro-ecological products in urban areas

According to some authors, these market mechanisms that were designed to strengthen collective and cooperative organizations also contribute to the scaling-up of agroecology (Mier y Terán et al., 2018). Part of this process which is due to the growing demand for healthy food, without chemicals and whose production takes into account the conservation of natural resources. encourages agricultural producers to adapt their systems (Easdale, 2015). Along the same lines, Mier et al. (2019) propose that one of the ways to scale agroecology is through external allies, which, in this case, would be the inhabitants of urban areas who support these forms of production as consumers.

However, the lack of knowledge about rural production generates uncertainty in urban areas and doubts about agroecological forms of production. One of the challenges for agroecological producers is to build forms of certification, validating their forms of production, without the need to apply for formal organic certification, which increases production prices and is inaccessible to many small producers. Participatory guarantee systems have emerged as a strategy which addresses the need to certify and communicate to urban consumers that the products they are buying are agroecologically produced (Cuéllar Padilla, 2009). With regard to this, the FRPA has adopted a participatory certification system that includes INTA, the

National University of La Plata, and consumer organizations. This has made it possible to generate confidence among consumers:

> *Several years ago* (a technician) *told me that they were trying to start a SPG* (participatory certification system). *Because he said that it is a tool to legitimize production. Like he was telling me that many times people have to trust that the production is agroecological and the SPG is like a badge that legitimizes, that at some point it has the endorsement of the University.*
>
> *(Abasto producer, 2019)*

According to Marasas (2012), there is a change in ethics and values from the creation of a sustainable link between the people who produce food and those who consume it. These new sociabilities are not based on the trust that a brand, a state entity, or an organic seal can give (Socolovsky, 2016), they are based on the trust of the encounter (Podolak, 2021). Nevertheless, and in terms of thinking about how to scale up production and widen commercialization possibilities, the SPG serves as a mechanism to build trust and allows various consumers to choose to consume agroecological products. At the same time, agroecological producers recognize that it is necessary to rethink the product exchange system since the form, time, place, and dialogue are important elements which serve to generate trust and transform the traditional exchange systems that constitute one of the main barriers to the agroecological transition (Polesello, 2022).

It was previously mentioned that during the pandemic, there was a large increase in the sales of agroecological fruits and vegetables due to an increase in the demand for healthy food and greater availability of time to receive and cook them. However, it should be noted that this situation was not generalized. According to Sudriá et al. (2020), in the broader Argentine population during the pandemic the consumption of fruits and vegetables fell below two servings per day on average. Although only 6% of the population consume the five servings of fruits and vegetables that the WHO recommends, 50% believe they eat the appropriate amount (Secretary of Government of Health, 2019). The same report states that there are economic barriers to access, especially in the lower quintiles, Therefore, these sale increases that were observed in some marketing channels of agroecological fruits and vegetables were not associated with a higher consumption of these foods in the average population. In line with Sudriá et al. (2020), the pandemic has modified food consumption patterns, deepening a structural inequality that exists in access to fruits and vegetables; where sectors with greater purchasing power were able to increase the consumption of fresh food and eat homemade food, while sectors with little purchasing power reduce their consumption of these foods.

Those with greater purchasing power can thus access the growing agroecological market, while people with fewer opportunities consume cheap, nutritionally deficient foods (Aguirre, 2004). While working-class populations seek quantity rather than quality in their consumption baskets, middle-income and high-income sectors diversify their diets with fruits, vegetables, white meats, and dairy products, especially cheese (Aguirre, 2010). This pattern is observed in the National Surveys of Risk Factors (Sudriá et al., 2020), which shows that in Argentina, lower-income populations mainly consume a low variety of foods, predominantly carbohydrates, oils, fats, and sugars, that is, calorically dense foods, but of low nutritional value. In contrast, the higher-income sector allocates a higher percentage of its income to the consumption of fresh and healthy products (vegetables, fruits, and legumes). More recent studies (Zapata & Rovirosa, 2021; Ballesteros et al., 2022) confirm that this nutritional gap has only increased in recent decades, in spite of the growth of agroecological production.

Aware of this situation, since the pandemic, the FRPA has opened a solidarity axis in its purchases, to assist with donations to those most affected. According to a member of PaP: *"We also set out to get our food to other soup kitchens and community centers. As a result, we were able to donate $960,000, which represented more than 50,000 kilos of merchandise"* (PaP member, 2021).

While these initiatives are important, it has not been possible to develop an efficient and sustained mechanism to supply agroecological fruits and vegetables to low-income sectors of the cities; even many of the people in these sectors are grouped in spaces that have a daily link with the FRPA.

Final thoughts

This chapter addresses the role of collectivist family producers' organization in supporting the growth of agroecological production, at the same time as they work toward improving living conditions and strengthening the rural roots of small-scale producers. Through their emphasis on fair trade and improving conditions for rural workers, the "Federación Rural para la Producción y el Arraigo" has promoted transformations in food systems that support a transition to agroecology and a more sustainable food future.

The FRPA, like other producers' organizations, faces difficulties in terms of cost, scaling up, reaching urban markets, and competing with conventional food systems. Yet through a variety of strategies, the organization has made improvements and managed to increase their membership, and the scale of agroecological production in the region. Through the creation of direct marketing channels, such as the "Pueblo a Pueblo" project, the FRPA has eliminated intermediaries and allowed producers to obtain fair prices for their products. However, in many cases this tool does not reach a large enough market, and producers are forced to sell their goods in the conventional market at reduced prices. Therefore, this experience is considered very valuable, but when it comes to replicating it, it is important to think about scalability, based on the association with other producers or organizations, in order to reduce the relative costs of production, logistics, and marketing.

Along with this increase in the scale of production, it is necessary to increase demand in major cities. In general, the reduced demand for agroecological deliveries (to homes or distribution nodes in cities) after the pandemic can be explained by many factors, including the return to daily life, the lack of time to buy fresh food and cook it, and the economic crisis, among others. Yet, at the same time, a central issue which is necessary to address is the difficulties that working-class sectors face in accessing these foods. Indeed, the higher cost associated with the dignified wages for producers as well as elevated costs associated with the time intensiveness and logistical challenges faced by small producers makes consuming agroecological products difficult for many urban consumers. The challenge, then, is how to avoid reproducing inequalities whereby urban elites are able to afford healthy and agroecological foods, of which working classes are excluded. Undoubtedly, this is an extremely difficult challenge, which can hardly be addressed by collective small farmer's organizations alone. Although the FRPA has started initiatives aimed at making their products available to low-income urban populations, there is a need for public policies that could encourage this type of production by building demand, for example, through subsidies or large-scale purchases of agroecological products by the public sector. Finally, it is considered that this discussion requires a perspective of the right to healthy food in order to observe the inequalities in access to this type of food and to be able to design the public policies and community networks necessary to democratize it, while improving the living conditions of producers and strengthening their roots in rural areas.

Bibliography

Aguirre, P. 2004. *Ricos Flacos y Gordos Pobres – La Alimentación En Crisis*. Buenos Aires, Argentina: Capital intelectual.

Aguirre, P. 2010. *Estrategias de consumo: qué comen los argentinos que comen*. CIEPP-Miño y Dávila (eds). Buenos Aires.

Aguirre, P. 2011. Consecuencias del ajuste en la alimentación. Voces en el Fénix, Ed. *Plan Fénix*, 7, 52–59.

Alejandre, María Agustina. 2016. *Las Ferias del Productor al Consumidor incluídas en la economía social: un análisis de las fases de producción y comercialización de los productos hortícolas*. Tesis de Grado.

Ambort, M. E. 2017. *Procesos asociativos en la agricultura familiar: un análisis de las condiciones que dieron lugar al surgimiento y consolidación de organizaciones en el cinturón hortícola platense, 2005–2015* (Bachelor's Thesis, Universidad Nacional de La Plata. Facultad de Humanidades y Ciencias de la Educación).

Baldini, C. 2020. *Territorio en movimiento: las transformaciones territoriales del Cinturón Hortícola Platense en los últimos 30 años* (Disertación doctoral, La Plata, Universidad Nacional de La Plata).

Baldini, C., Marasas, M. E., y Drozd, A. A. 2019. Entre la expansión urbana y la producción de alimentos: el conflicto rural/urbano en relación al patrón espacial de usos del suelo en el partido de La Plata, Buenos Aires. *Revista de la Facultad de Agronomía*, 118.

Ballesteros, M. S., Zapata, M. E., Freidin, B., Tamburini, C., & Rovirosa, A. (2022). Desigualdades sociales en el consumo de verduras y frutas según características de los hogares argentinos. *Salud colectiva*, 18, e3835.

Benencia, R. 2012. Los inmigrantes bolivianos en el mercado de trabajo de la horticultura en fresco en la Argentina. *El impacto de las migraciones en Argentina*, 2, 153.

Carballo, C. 2013. *El retroceso de la frontera agraria frente a la expansión de la frontera urbana* (Doctoral Dissertation, Facultad de Ciencias Económicas, Universidad de Buenos Aires).

Cataldi, V., y Flores, C. 2019. *Análisis comparativo entre sistemas convencionales y en transición agroecológica desde el punto de vista de la economía convencional y de la economía del medio ambiente en el Cinturón Hortícola de La Plata. Buenos Aires, Argentina.* Ponencia presentada en el Primer Congreso Argentino de Agroecología, Mendoza.

Cordara, C., Duarte, J. I., Lanfranchi, G., Hutton, T. G., Rodriguez, S., & Ferlicca, F. 2017. *¿Cómo crecen las ciudades argentinas? Estudio de la expansión urbana de los 33 grandes aglomerados.* Centro de Implementación de Políticas Públicas para la Equidad y el Crecimiento (CIPPEC).

Cuéllar Padilla, M. D. C. 2009. *Hacia un sistema participativo de garantía para la producción ecológica en Andalucía.* Universidad de Córdoba, Servicio de Publicaciones. Córdoba, España.

Easdale, M. H. 2015. *Una aproximación a la vulnerabilidad y robustez socio-ecológica de los sistemas ganaderos trashumantes* (Doctoral Dissertation, Escuela para Graduados Ing. Agr. Alberto Soriano, Facultad de Agronomía, Universidad de Buenos Aires).

FAO, IFAD, UNICEF, WFP and WHO. 2020. *The State of Food Security and Nutrition in the World 2020. Transforming food systems for affordable healthy diets.* Rome, FAO. https://doi.org/10.4060/ca9692en

Feito, M. C. 2014. *Agricultura familiar con enfoque agroecológico en zonas periurbanas. Análisis de una experiencia de intervención para el desarrollo rural en Luján.* Buenos Aires, Argentina.

García, M. 2012. *Análisis de las transformaciones de la estructura agraria hortícola platense en los últimos 20 años* (Tesis Doctoral. Cap. VIII. La Plata: UNLP).

García, M. 2014. Fuerza de trabajo en la horticultura de La Plata (Buenos Aires, Argentina): Razones y consecuencias de su competitividad. *Trabajo y sociedad*, 22, 67–85.

Gazzano, I., Achkar, M., Apezteguía, E., Ariza, J., Gómez Perazzoli, A., y Pivel, J. 2021. Ambiente y crisis en Uruguay. La agroecología como construcción contrahegemónica. *Revista de Ciencias Sociales*, 34(48), 13–40.

Giobellina, B., Mari, N., & Barchuk, A. 2017. *El cinturón verde de Córdoba: hacia un plan integral para la preservación, recuperación y defensa del área periurbana de producción de alimentos.* Manfredi: Ediciones INTA.

Gliessman, S. R. 2013. Agroecología: plantando las raíces de la resistencia. *Agroecología*, 8(2), 19–26.

Guber, R. (2019). *La etnografía: método, campo y reflexividad.* Siglo XXI editores.

Hasegawa, T., Havlík, P., Frank, S., Palazzo, A., & Valin, H. 2019. Tackling food consumption inequality to fight hunger without pressuring the environment. *Nature Sustainability*, 2(9), 826–833.

Lazarte, J., Tóffoli, M. M., Ambort, M. E., García, M., & Roca Pamich, B. 2020. *La organización de la patria precarizada: Apuntes para pensar la economía popular a partir de la experiencia del Movimiento de Trabajadores Excluidos.* Memoria Académica, Editorial FaHCE, UnLP. Disponible en: www.memoria.fahce.unlp.edu.ar/libros/pm.5753/pm.5753.pdf

López-García, D. 2012. Canales cortos de comercialización, un elemento dinamizador. *Soberanía alimentaria, biodiversidad y culturas*, 8, 20–24.

Manzanal, M., & González, F. 2010. Soberanía alimentaria y agricultura familiar. *Oportunidades y desafíos del caso argentino en Realidad Económica*, 255, 12–42.

Marasas, M. (Comp.). 2012. *El camino de la transición agroecológica.* Buenos Aires, Argentina: Ediciones INTA.

Martínez, A., Velarde, I., y Fasulo, S. 2020. "Consumo de hortalizas en transición agroecológica en circuitos cortos de comercialización de ciudad de La Plata, Argentina: Elecciones alimentarias en construcción." *Revista Americana de Empreendedorismo e inovação*, 2(1), 32–35. Raei (Paranaguá).

Mier, M., Giménez-Cacho, T., Giraldo, O. F., Aldasoro, M., Morales, H., Ferguson, B. G., & Campos, C. 2019. Escalamiento de la agroecología: impulsores clave y casos emblemáticos.

Mier y Terán, M., Giraldo, O. F., Aldasoro, M., Morales, H., Ferguson, B. G., Rosset, P., Khadse, A., & Campos, C. 2018. Bringing agroecology to scale: Key drivers and emblematic cases. *Agroecology and Sustainable Food Systems*, 42(6), 637–665. https://doi.org/10.1080/21683565.2018.1443313

Mitidieri, M. 2015. *Programa Nacional Hortalizas, Flores y Aromáticas. Plan de Gestión Integrador PNHFA 1106081 Contribución al desarrollo territorial de las producciones intensivas*. Buenos Aires, Argentina.

Monkes, J., & Easdale, M. H. 2023. Agroecología periurbana en la Argentina del siglo XXI: de los márgenes a la estatalidad. *Mundo Agrario*, 24(57).

Pérez Martín, J. 2022. *Impacto de la operación logística y comercial en la formación de precios en el abastecimiento frutihortícola del Área Metropolitana de Buenos Aires*. Buenos Aires, Argentina: Ponencia en el Segundo Congreso Nacional de Periurbanos para el Consenso.

Podolak, E. 2021. *Aprendizajes desde el Sistema Participativo de Garantías FAUBA para la construcción del paradigma agroecológico: un análisis de los vínculos y tramas sociales*. Buenos Aires: Tesis de Grado, Universidad de Buenos Aires, Facultad de Agronomía.

Polesello, M. A. 2022. *El rol de las cooperativas de trabajo en la expansión del comercio justo y el consumo saludable: Estudio de caso de la Cooperativa "Nuestra América Ltda."* [Tesis de Grado, Facultad de Agronomía de la Universidad de Buenos Aires, Buenos Aires].

Secretary of Government of Health. 2019. 4° *Encuesta Nacional de Factores de Riesgo: resultados definitivos* (1a ed.). Ciudad Autónoma de Buenos Aires: Instituto Nacional de Estadística y Censos – INDEC; Libro digital, PDF. Dispobible en www.indec.gob.ar/ftp/cuadros/publicaciones/enfr_2018_resultados_definitivos.pdf

Shoaie Baker, S., & García, M. 2020. Jóvenes, agentes para la transición hacia una producción agroecológica en el sector hortícola platense. *Revista Americana de Empreendedorismo e Inovação*, 2(1), 406–417.

Shoaie Baker, S., & García, M. 2021. « Argentina». *Eutopía. Revista De Desarrollo Económico Territorial*, n.° 19 (junio), 97–118. Disponible en: https://doi.org/10.17141/eutopia.19.2021.4966.

Simonatto, S. 2000. Cambio tecnológico en el Sector Hortícola de La Plata. Período 1985–1995. En *Espacio tecnológico, población y reproducción social en el sector hortícola de La Plata* (R. Ringuelet, coords.), pp. 23–30. Editorial FaHCE, UnLP. Disponible en: https://sedici.unlp.edu.ar/handle/10915/92993

Socolovsky, A. 2016. *Valoración de la certificación según el perfil del consumidor de productos orgánicos y agroecológicos*. Tesis de Grado, Facultad de Agronomía de la Universidad de Buenos Aires, Buenos Aires.

Sotiru, M. N. (2022). Bolsones Agroecológicos: ¿posible estrategia territorial para combatir la tendencia alcista del precio de las hortalizas? *Eutopía, Revista de Desarrollo Económico Territorial*, 21, 124–142.

Souza Casadinho, J. 2013. La agroecología: bases científicas, historia local y estrategias productivas en la construcción de un espacio de desarrollo integral, ético y humano. En *La Agroecología en Contexto: cruce de miradas entre Argentina y Francia* (V. Hernández, F. Goulet, D. Magad, & N. Girard, coords), pp. 13–29. Buenos Aires: INTA.

Sudriá, M., Emilce, M., Andreatta, D., Marta, M., Defagó, D., & Daniela, M. 2020. Los efectos de la cuarentena por coronavirus (COVID-19) en los hábitos alimentarios en Argentina. *Diaeta*, 38(171), 10–19.

UN. 2018. *Revision of world urbanization prospects*. New York, NY: United Nations.

Zapata, M. E., & Rovirosa, A. 2021. *La alimentación en la Argentina. Una mirada desde distintas aproximaciones. CAPA II. Consumo aparente de alimentos y nutrientes a nivel hogar*. Ciudad Autónoma de Buenos Aires, Argentina: Centro de Estudios sobre Nutrición Infantil – CESNI. Recuperado de Centro de Estudios sobre Nutrición Infantil – CESNI Website. https://cesni-biblioteca.org/la-alimentacion-en-la-argentina-capa2/

12

ACTOR CONSTELLATIONS AND CONTESTED GOVERNANCE IN THE MEXICO CITY PUBLIC MARKETS' NETWORK

León Felipe Téllez Contreras

Introduction

The diversity of actors converging around and shaping urban food systems has been at the core of academic and policy enquiry. Alongside processes, mechanisms, and structures, different notions of people, individuals, groups, and populations have been a primary concern for food systems scholars. These actors come together to create the socio-infrastructural networks that underpin the production, processing, distribution, and consumption of food in cities, and their classification is often based on their role and position within the food system (Smith, 1998; Wiskerke, 2015). As noted by Ingram (2019, p. 50), urban food systems are highly complex coupling systems that encompass "a set of dynamic actors and activities with a wide range of power and vested interests operating under fragmented governance."

Following conceptualizations of "people as infrastructure" (Simone, 2004, 2021; Wilson & Jonas, 2021), I approach these sets of actors as dynamic and adaptive actor constellations that underpin the reproduction of socio-material configurations. In this case, Mexico City's 329 public markets, a public food-and-other-basic-staples distribution network.[1] Actor constellations become essential factors influencing the capacity of food systems to perform different functions, from keeping a population fed to improving people's health, delivering food security, or advancing sustainability agendas. As this chapter discusses, such dynamic conglomerates propel the operational and material stability and transformation of urban food systems over different periods of time. This approach thus furthers Hayden's (2023, p. 91) description of Mexico City's food system as an infrastructure: "a series of channels connecting the countryside to the city through a combination of intermediaries, objects, and places that serve as nodes."

DOI: 10.4324/9781003471929-17

Mexico City's 329 public markets are part of these nodes, operating all year round as an economic, socio-political, and territorial network, therefore, as a central component of the city's infrastructure for food and other basic staples distribution. Like other networks in urban food systems (Kasper et al., 2017; Murray & Caraher, 2019; Felici & Mazzocchi, 2022; Fuertes & Gomez-Escoda, 2022; Guibrunet et al., 2023), the public markets' network consists of different constellations of actors that constantly contest and negotiate the institutional, regulatory, and material landscapes in which they operate. In this way, they play a decisive role in the shaping and reshaping of food and other products distribution.

Drawing on ethnographic and documentary research primarily conducted between 2016 and 2022, this chapter examines the evolution of actor constellations in the Mexico City public markets' network. For its qualitative approach, this study shares with other actor analysis strategies in food system studies an interest in mapping out economic, social, and political actors and their role and influence in the governance of specific components of the urban food system (Ingram, 2019; Murray & Caraher, 2019; Diehl, 2020; Rocker et al., 2022). A historical approach is also adopted to unpack the evolution of actor constellations in the public markets' network vis-à-vis key events that have transformed Mexico City's urban, economic, and political dynamics as well as the functions, forms, and meanings of the retail sector. The first section examines the socio-territorial formation and expansion of the public markets' network as a component of Mexico City's food system. The second section analyzes the network's actor constellations, their key transformations, and multiplication. The conclusion addresses the significance of this study for an understanding of the relationship between changing governance structures and the provision and preservation of socio-material configurations for food and other basic staples distribution—in both the Mexican and wider Latin American contexts.

The network

The creation and expansion of Mexico City's public markets as a modern food distribution network condenses the tensions between different formal and informal urbanization processes (Duhau & Giglia, 2008; Connolly, 2017). After all, the public markets' network is the product of both state and grassroots strategies for commercial infrastructure provision. The network's expansion connects the vendors' informal (popular) practices to provide themselves with workspaces and the state's formal strategies to plan, design, and build public commercial infrastructure. This also includes the state's long-standing tradition of regularizing informal practices and spaces through lengthy legal and administrative processes.

Since its beginnings in the 1950s, the public markets' network has been a highly contested component of Mexico City's food system. For decades, state and non-state agents have been constantly negotiating its form, function, and meaning for the city and its residents. The initial construction of the markets, for example, involved both the provision of capacious infrastructures and the implementation of urban technologies for the disciplining and displacement of the poor (López Rosado, 1988; Monroy, 2005; Meneses, 2011; Castillo, 2017). Thus, as noted by Vitiello and Brinkley (2014) and Fuertes and Gomez-Escoda (2022), the materiality of markets' networks speaks of the complex relationship between urban food systems and the construction of cities. In the case of Mexico City, this relationship has been characterized by a permanent contestation determined by the scale of the process that gave birth to the markets' network, its multitude of stakeholders, and its gradual expansion after 1966.

Provision

In the 1950s and 1970s, Mexico City was growing rapidly. Its urban area and population increased dramatically as a result of the country's industrialization and urban development plans. This was the time of the "Mexican miracle," when unabated economic growth contributed to consolidating Mexico City's existing urban communities and its metropolitan area (Ward, 2013). Public markets' construction is part of this process, in which, as Ziccardi (1991) points out, infrastructure provision became the means to materialize post-revolutionary aspirations of social progress and economic development.

With the federal government's financial support and under Mayor Ernesto P. Uruchurtu's command, the city implemented an extensive plan to modernize the public markets between 1952 and 1966. Publicly funded, this plan set the foundations of a network of state-owned, self-contained commercial facilities that were expected to play a key role in the distribution of basic staples at affordable prices across the city. Only the large investments in markets' construction and refurbishment in the 1950s give an indication of the plan's significance: 20 million pesos for eight markets in 1954; 40 million pesos for 10 markets in 1955; and 55 million pesos for 14 markets in 1957 (Monroy, 2005; Zenteno, 2016). Supplied with stalls, toilets, loading areas, subsidized energy and water services, and, in some cases, with nurseries, theatres, meeting rooms, and management offices, these markets were conceived as spearheads of a new era. Similarly, the active involvement of national and city authorities in the construction process, including presidents Miguel Alemán (1946–1952), Adolfo Ruiz Cortines (1952–1958), and Adolfo López Mateos (1958–1964), speaks of the plan's importance in broader modernization agendas.

The scale of the program and its impact cannot be underestimated given the speed at which it transformed the city's distribution network. In only 14 years, the number of Mexico City's public markets increased to almost 200. This amounts to 60% of today's network. Based on the markets' inauguration dates, Figure 12.1 helps describe this political-infrastructural process. The 1957, 1963, and 1964 peaks, for instance, reveal how intensive the process became during Uruchurtu's tenure. If measured in presidential terms, the periods 1952–1958 and 1958–1964

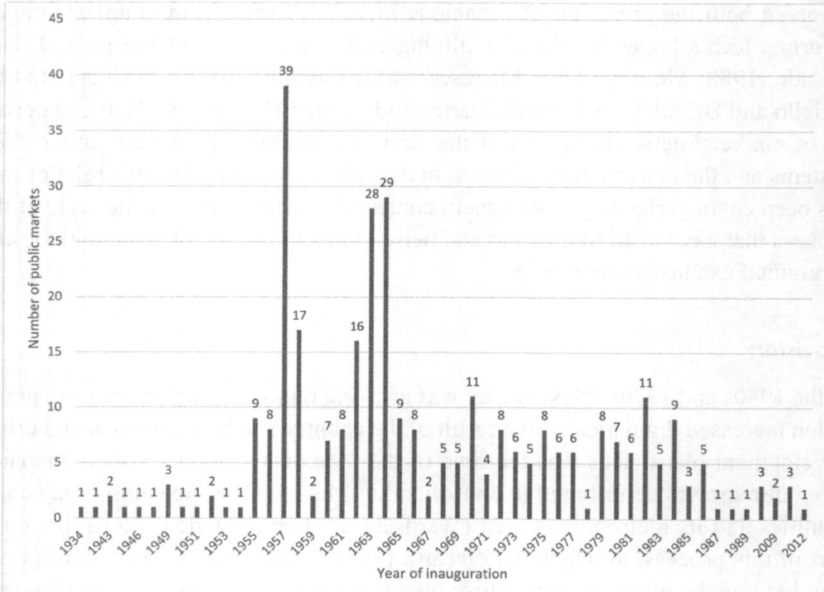

FIGURE 12.1 Public markets' provision (1934–2012)

Source: Author based on GDF (2015), Jiménez and González (2015), CES-CDMX (2017), Laboratorio para la Ciudad (2017), and Jiménez (2019).

delivered 77 and 90 facilities, respectively, indicating that markets' provision was considered, for some time, a political priority that facilitated the relocation of 56,090 traders and street vendors (Meneses, 2012, p. 20). Because of the speed and scale of the process, this period has been considered the public markets' "golden era" (Jiménez & González, 2015, p. 265).

Following the urbanization patterns at the time, the provision of the newly built or refurbished markets concentrated in six districts: Cuauhtémoc, Venustiano Carranza, Gustavo A. Madero, Álvaro Obregón, Benito Juárez, and Miguel Hidalgo (Map 12.1). Nonetheless, the impact of deploying this new commercial infrastructure was felt not only through the reorganization and transformation of the traders' practices but also through the reconfiguration of the urban fabric and consumption practices in hundreds of neighborhoods. The redefinition of local centralities is, therefore, one of the most impactful territorial effects of this process.

Expansion

Between 1967 and 2012, the construction and refurbishment of public markets took place at a different pace, significantly decreasing the number of markets inaugurated each year. Nonetheless, the network continued to grow, although without

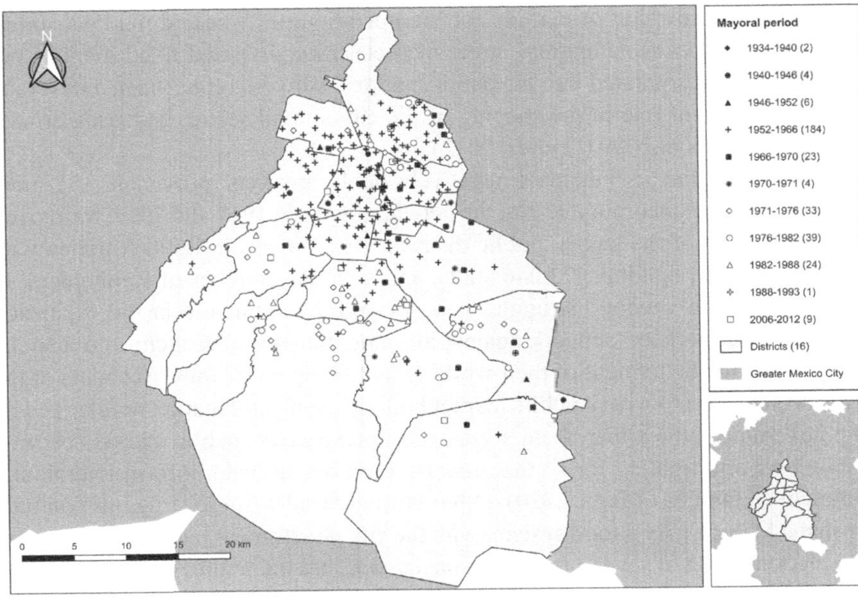

MAP 12.1 Expansion of Mexico City public markets' network (1932–2012)

Source: Author based on GDF (2015), Jiménez and González (2015), CES-CDMX (2017), Laboratorio para la Ciudad (2017), and Jiménez (2019)

the frenzy of the previous years. For example, between 1967 and 1986, during five mayoral tenures (see Figure 12.1 and Map 12.1), the markets' provision grew steadily with the inauguration of 72 public facilities. As the Map 12.1 shows, the provision of public markets after the "golden era" partially benefited Mexico City's peripheral districts. Public investment for new markets remained concentrated in the central districts notwithstanding that the urbanization process began to manifest more intensively in the periphery. From 1987, the pattern completely changed with public markets' provision decreasing dramatically one more time and even stopping between 1990 and 2005.

Behind these tendencies, we find economic and political factors. These include the increasing concerns about the financial burden the public markets represented for the city, and the limited political benefits trader communities represented for clientelist and corporatist structures (Cross, 1998; Meneses, 2011). The decision to prioritize the investment in the city's subway system since the late 1960s also played its part (Davis, 1991, 1994), as well as the implementation of neoliberal policies since the late 1970s, which facilitated the consolidation of corporate interests in the retail sector with the proliferation of supermarkets in the city (Gasca, 2017). In terms of state participation, these changes involved the prioritization of mobile and low-cost food distribution networks over the construction of public markets. The provision of permits for the operation of "wheeled markets" (*mercados sobre ruedas*), temporary street markets (*tianguis*), and fixed markets not yet officially incorporated into the public markets' network (*concentraciones*) took a more prominent role in the shaping of the city's retail sector, gathering around 100,000 vendors in 2009 (Gómez, 2012).

While these factors impacted negatively public markets' provision, 132 more markets were yet incorporated into the network between 1967 and 2012. Moreover, today, it is one of the largest public distribution networks in Latin America with 329 commercial facilities, 72,246 stalls, and a similar number of stallholders. In this process, the vendors' struggles have played a central role in the expansion of the public markets' network against all odds, transforming them into a social demand for the betterment of their working and living conditions. Accounts of the traders' struggles to have a public market built or a self-built market regularized by the government show that, from a grassroots perspective, public markets became facilities worth fighting for so that traders could obtain legal, infrastructural, and political certainties (Téllez, 2020). Often lasting decades, these struggles continue to shape Mexico City's food system, with the city government recently announcing the incorporation of seven more *concentraciones* into the public markets' network (Jefatura de Gobierno, 2022), which also reveals the multifaceted nature of and the political overlaps and interdependencies in infrastructure production (Téllez, 2025). These are, ultimately, instances in which contemporary informal urbanization practices meet and mesh with the mid-twentieth-century aspirations of a planned distribution network to improve Mexico City's food system.

Actor constellations

The history of infrastructures shows that every new socio-material configuration engenders its own governing bodies. Given the history of Mexico City, the constellations of actors directly and indirectly involved in marketplace governance have created a dynamic and complex social ecology with discursive, institutional, and regulatory continuities across centuries (Velázquez, 1997; Gruzinski, 2012; Iturriaga, 2012). Some of these consistent themes (re)emerging around marketplace governance are food supply and accessibility, health and safety and trading regulation, taxation, stall and market tenure, traders' organization, urban (dis)order, and infrastructure obsolescence and modernization. At different moments in time, different actor constellations have sought to deal with these issues; however, since the 1950s, the scale and nature of how marketplaces are governed were profoundly transformed in light of the size and complexity of the public markets' network.

The extensive provision of public markets in Mexico City has then involved the repurposing, adaptation, reinvention, and creation of regulatory, institutional, and political bodies, traditions, and imaginaries to facilitate the governance of this expansive network. Since the 1950s, these processes have primarily involved the (re)design of the public markets' norms, the (re)distribution of powers among markets' stakeholders, and the progressive incorporation of new actors into marketplace governance. Dominated by politically active communities, marketplace governance in Mexico City reveals itself as a highly contested arena whose impacts reach both the urban food system and broader urban political agendas.

Foundations

The actor constellations in the emerging public markets' network were primarily (re)organized with a legal instrument: the 1951 Markets Bylaw (Gobierno de la República, 1951). Published a year before the markets' "golden era" began, this short document defined the network's key actors, spaces, and processes, established the main institutional framework, and distributed powers and responsibilities among stakeholders. Its still-valid 101 articles set the legal foundations under which the public markets have been contentiously governed and their everyday operation regulated for decades. From a socio-political perspective, the 1951 Markets Bylaw establishes the key terms of the relationship between authorities, market traders, and other categories of vendors, the conditions to perform commercial activities in the markets, and the limits to the spatial practices associated with these activities.

A detailed analysis of the Markets Bylaw provides an initial understanding of the key actors in Mexico City's marketplace governance and the political architecture underlying the relationship between the state and the traders. At the top of the pyramid in a highly centralized system, the Department of the Federal District (*Departamento del Distrito Federal*)—and more specifically its Department of Markets, a branch of the city's Treasury (*Departamento de Mercados de la Tesorería del Distrito Federal*)—was responsible for the provision and operation of the public markets. Among this Department's activities, the Bylaw lists the following: license permanent and temporary vendors and allocate them stalls inside and outside the markets, apply sanctions, tax the traders' activities, manage the markets' everyday functioning (including additional services such as nurseries or health clinics), and assess the need for new markets. To ensure the observance of the rules, the Department of Markets would be assisted by the fiscal, city, and traffic police, and the Federal District's Office of Licences (*Oficina de Licencias*), the Department of Health (*Salubridad y Asistencia*), and the Bank for Small Businesses (*Banco del Pequeño Comercio*).

Regarding the traders, Chapter VI of the Bylaw outlined the new social and political structure through which traders' organization and representation would take place. Traders were expected to organize in associations, federations, and confederations democratically formed in assemblies and legally registered by a notary. As basic social and political units, associations would then be recognized by the Department of Markets and become the primary channel for traders to advance their interests and engage with state agents. Together with the Department of Markets, they were expected to contribute to the observance of the Markets Bylaw. The names and number of trader associations currently operating in the public markets' network are not publicly known, as the "special book" of registered associations kept by the authorities cannot be found and no new public records have been created (infoCDMX, 2019; see Table 12.1 for a sample). In the late 1980s, Rello and Sodi (1989, p. 252, in Giglia, 2018, p. 32) estimated the existence of around 500 associations and 50 federations. A considerable number that emerged in a political context in which trader associations were affiliated to the National Confederation of Popular Organisations (*Confederación Nacional de Organizaciones Populares*, CNOP) for clientelist purposes (Cross, 1998). This created a highly centralized structure for marketplace governance. Controlled by central government officials, trader representatives, and members of the Revolutionary Institutional Party (*Partido Revolucionario Institucional*, PRI), this structure was in place and only began to change when the calls for political reform intensified in the city.

Transitions

The administrative, political, and economic transitions that Mexico City experienced in the last quarter of the twentieth century transformed the actor constellations and the markets' governance. Through decentralization and deconcentration processes (Botero & Carvajal, 2011), the administrative reforms that took place between 1970 and the late 1990s played a key role in bringing new actors into the network. The reform of the Organic Law of the Department of the Federal District (*Ley Orgánica del Departamento del Distrito Federal*) in 1970 transferred some administrative responsibilities over the public markets to the 16 district authorities (then called *delegaciones*). Article 37 of the Law provided district officials with new powers to participate in marketplace governance (Gobierno de la República, 1970). Similarly, the 1987 reform led to the creation and incorporation of the Assembly of Representatives of the Federal District (*Asamblea de Representantes del Distrito Federal*) as a new political actor in the public markets' network. Article 73-VI-3a-A stated that its role would involve the enactment of edicts, ordinances, and regulations concerning food supply, distribution, and markets (Gobierno de la República, 1987).

Additional reforms in the 1990s and early 2000s led to multiple nominal changes and the expansion or limitation of competencies of these governing bodies, but they essentially kept the four-sided governance structure that directly manages the public markets' network. Today, public markets' governance revolves around a) numerous trader organizations (see Table 12.1 for a sample); b) Mexico City's Secretary of Economic Development (*Secretaría de Desarrollo Económico*) and its Department of Supply, Trade, and Distribution (*Dirección General de Abasto, Comercio y Distribución*); c) 16 district governments (*alcaldías*, known as *delegaciones* before 2017) and their Offices for Markets (e.g., *Jefatura de Unidad Departamental de Mercados y Concentraciones*); and d) the Congress of Mexico City and its Commission for Rural Development, Supply, and Food Distribution (*Comisión de Desarrollo Rural, Abasto y Distribución de Alimentos*). This formal structure oversees (i) the everyday functioning of the public markets, (ii) the provision and

TABLE 12.1 Mexico City's trader organizations (a sample)

Organization	*Key member*	*Source/Year*
Organización de Mercados Públicos y Concentraciones del Distrito Federal	Femando García	Newspaper, 2013
Coordinadora Nacional para la Defensa de la Economía Social	Joaquín Vela	Newspaper, 2014
Unión de los Comerciantes Establecidos de La Merced	–	Academic, 2015
Mesa Directiva Mercado Nave Mayor	–	Academic, 2015
Locatarios Unidos de La Merced en el Distrito Federal A.C.	–	Academic, 2015
Asociación de Locatarios del Mercado de Dulces Ampudia A.C.	–	Academic, 2015
Mesa Directiva Mercado de Comidas	–	Academic, 2015
Comité de Representates de Locatarios Afectados del Mercado Nave Mayor, Banquetón y Corredor Comercial Merced	–	Academic, 2015
Mesa Directiva Mercado Flores	–	Academic, 2015
Mesa Directiva Banquetón	–	Academic, 2015
Administración del Mercado de Flores	–	Academic, 2015
Unión de Comerciantes en Pequeño del Mercado Nave Mayor	–	Academic, 2015
Coordinadora Democrática de Mercados Públicos A.C.	–	Academic, 2015
Unión de Locatarios del Mercado 105 Merced Flores A.C.	–	Academic, 2015
Coordinadora Nacional Democrática de Mujeres A.C.	Rosa María García	Academic, 2015
Federación de Mercados y Concentraciones Populares de Anáhuac A.C.	Humberto García	Academic, 2015
Movimiento Nacional del Contribuyente Social 17 de Marzo A.C.	Alberto Vargas	Academic, 2017
Asociación de Locatarios del Mercado Jamaica		Newspaper, 2017
Frente de Comerciantes del Servicio Público de Mercados	Edgar Alvarez	Newspaper, 2018
Fundación Pro Mercados A.C.	Femando García	Newspaper, 2018
Organización Mercados Públicos Unidos	–	Newspaper, 2018
Asociación Nueva Generación Mercado Hidalgo	Alicia Férez	Newspaper, 2020

Source: Author based on PUEC (2015a, 2015b), newspaper articles from La Jornada, Excélsior, El Universal, Reforma, and Milenio (2006–2020).

preservation of their infrastructure, (iii) the design of policies and regulations for the markets, and (iv) the allocation of financial resources for these policies.

Alongside these administrative changes, the 1997 political transition and the consolidation of a multi-party political system in the 2000s and 2010s undermined the role of the PRI and the CNOP in the public markets' network. The hegemonic position of the Democratic Revolutionary Party (*Partido de la Revolución Democrática*, PRD) (1997–2018) and the National Regeneration Movement (*Movimiento Regeneración Nacional*, MORENA) (2018–present), as well as the fluctuating electoral victories of other parties at the district government level and within the legislative bodies (Tejera & Rodríguez, 2015; IECDMX, 2023), have contributed to making public markets' governance a highly dynamic political arena. In this context, the provision and preservation of public markets have become increasingly mediated and fragmented by diverse partisan interests, government agendas, changing electoral alliances, and the fast-moving electoral competition at the district level. Such diversity of political actors, who constantly take and leave government positions linked to marketplace governance, has reshaped the logics of clientelism and pushed market trader organizations to strategize and plan their interactions with multiple political affiliations (Téllez, 2020).

The main economic transition reconfiguring the public markets' actor constellations involves the implementation of neoliberal policies in the 1980s. As in other countries of the Global South, Mexico City's food system was deeply transformed by what has been called retailer dominance through supermarkets (Popkin & Reardon, 2018; Murray & Caraher, 2019). Although retail corporations already controlled a third of food sales nationally in 1975 and supermarkets outnumbered public markets in the early 1980s (308 to 282) (Schatan, 1982, p. 67), the implementation of the North American Free Trade Agreement (NAFTA) in 1994 provided the critical platform for this tendency to consolidate in the following decades. Thus, there were 332 supermarkets in 2013 and 462, plus 3,535 convenience stores, in 2018 (SEDECO, 2013; Seale & Associates, 2018; Giglia, 2018). The rapid expansion of private retail infrastructure has been a key factor in the public markets' marginalization from Mexico City's food system. According to official reports, the markets' participation in the distribution of food and other basic staples has decreased from 80% in the 1950s to 16% in 2018 (interview with Central Government Official, 2018; Gómez, 2013).

These transitions and the ways in which they transformed the public markets' actor constellations already suggest a progressive multiplication of those involved in marketplace governance. Such an increase in the number of actors comes in hand with the increase in the instances of contestation within the distribution component of Mexico City's food system. The traders' opposition to supermarkets, the competition between city and district authorities, the alliances between trader organizations and political parties, and the unequal distribution of financial resources for the markets are only some examples of the tensions between these key actors.

Multiplication

In highly dynamic arenas such as marketplace governance in Mexico City, administrative, regulatory, economic, and political landscapes are expected to be more complex. Over seven decades, the operation of the public markets' network has been historically influenced by a wide range of peripheral actors. These actors intervene in public markets' affairs more sporadically or in indirect ways, in the whole network or parts of it, as if orbiting around these commercial facilities and their main four stakeholders. Because of this, the relevance of these actors and their interventions is highly contextual, as frictions between them and key stakeholders last until the issue at hand is resolved.

Drawing on ethnographic and documentary research, Figure 12.2 groups some of these peripheral actors based on their involvement in specific public markets' governance issues. For instance, the Environmental and Territorial Prosecutor (*Procuraduría Ambiental y del Ordenamiento Territorial*), the Department of Housing and Urban Development (*Secretaría de Desarrollo Urbano y Vivienda)*, and the Supreme Court were involved in the enactment and abrogation of the Norm 29 in 2011 and 2013, which sought to limit the opening of supermarkets in the markets' vicinities. Similarly, the Federal Electricity Commission and the

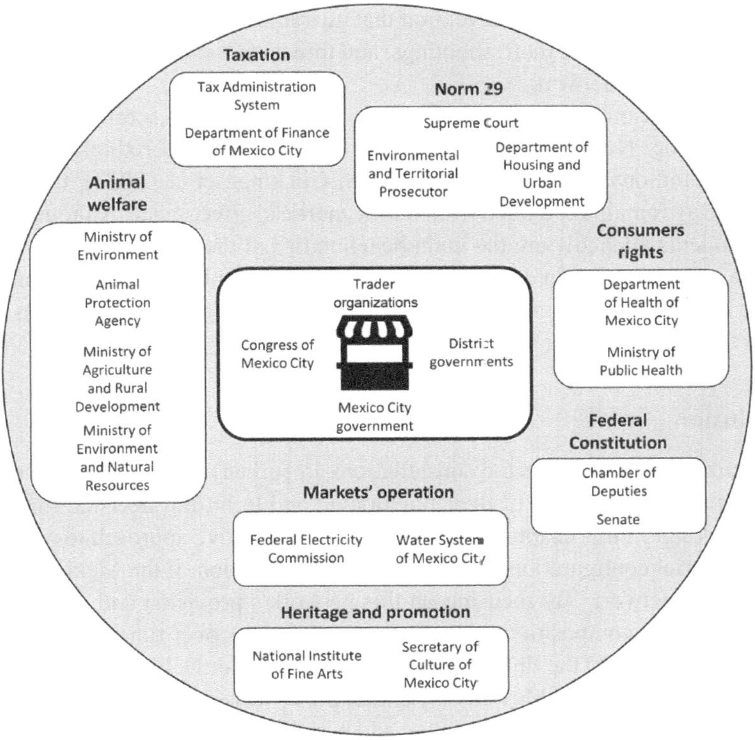

FIGURE 12.2 Core and peripheral governing bodies of the public markets' network

Source: Author based on interviews, field notes, official records, and newspaper articles.

Water System of Mexico City frequently negotiate with district authorities and trader organizations the debts the markets incur for the use of water and energy services. More localized, animal welfare governmental and non-governmental agencies occasionally engage in conflictive encounters with five public markets specialized in animal trade.

Since each public market also operates as an autonomous node in the network, the peripheral actors involved in their everyday lives can multiply at a local level. Defined by the markets' territorial nature, actor constellations can include street vendors, waste pickers, hawkers, seasonal fairground operators and vendors, indigenous and peasant communities, religious groups, homeless people, and taxi driver organizations, among many others, which also orbit and interact with key stakeholders. Tensions, conflicts, and instances of cooperation also emerge between these actors in formal and informal ways, as the markets' gravitational pull creates new socio-material connections between the food system and the city's diverse inhabitants. As noted by Hayden (2023), criminal organizations need to be counted among these actors, as their presence is increasingly impacting some parts of the public markets' network. In recent years, market traders have continuously demanded state intervention that guarantees their safety and the markets' operation, as extorsion, theft, shootings, and threats of kidnapping and murder have spread across the network.

The public can also be counted among these peripheral actors, but mostly as a missing one. Notwithstanding the calls for inclusion and rethinking food systems as commons (Vivero-Pol et al., 2018; Glickman et al., 2022), the public in Mexico City remains excluded from public markets' governance. Although Mexico City residents allegedly are the main beneficiaries of the public markets' network, they barely participate in decision-making and policymaking processes concerning public markets' provision, maintenance, and functioning. These processes remain under the control of four main stakeholders.

Conclusion

Recognizing the role of actor constellations in (urban) food systems is essential for a better understanding of their functioning and to inform decision-making and policymaking. In this chapter, I have adopted a qualitative approach to map out the socio-material configurations underlying the reproduction of the Mexico City public markets' network. By focusing on this network's provision and expansion first and then on the composition of its actor constellations over time, the chapter provides insights into 1) the links between the network and the history of planned and informal urbanization in Mexico City and 2) the contested, changing, and expansive nature of the connections between core and peripheral public markets' stakeholders. Overall, the chapter demonstrates the adaptive and resilient nature of both actors, spaces, and their relations as part of Mexico City's food system. After all, the public markets' network continues to operate 70 years after its foundation notwithstanding the chronic underfunding, economic decline, material deterioration, and political neglect that have afflicted them, particularly over the past three decades.

The history of these hundreds of public markets, thousands of market traders, diverse government bodies and regulations, and changing economic and political landscapes sheds light on the role of popular (retail) economies in the making of urban food systems. Notwithstanding the marginalization of public markets and its constellation of actors in urban (food) politics, their expansive tendencies are primarily led by trader communities in their struggles to preserve the network for decades to come. In advocating for the markets' preservation and improvement vis-à-vis different governing bodies, traders often challenge the logics of retailer dominance through supermarkets. In this sense, the defense of the public markets' network signals opportunities to rethink otherwise the urban infrastructure for food distribution in both Mexico and other Latin American countries. This is particularly salient given the shared colonial past and hegemonic modernization patterns across the region, which have had a critical role in the making of urban food systems. Similarly, the governance of Mexico City's public markets offers a glimpse into the evolving logics and multifaceted encounters between food system actors, food distribution infrastructures, and the city. The formal–informal foundations of these logics and encounters are particularly relevant for an understanding of actually existing urban food systems in Latin American countries.

Note

1 The city government officially recognizes 329 public markets, but the promise to regularize and incorporate seven *concentraciones* (fixed markets not yet officially incorporated into the public markets' network) into the network can increase the number to 336 in a few years (Jefatura de Gobierno, 2022).

References

Botero, M. H., & Carvajal, D. (2011). *El proceso de descentralización intraterritorial en el Distrito Federal mexicano: La ambigüedad generada por la tensión entre descentralización y centralización en la gestión de los territorios*. Universidad del Rosario. Retrieved December 3, 2023, from http://repository.urosario.edu.co/handle/10336/3356

Castillo, H. (2017). *La Merced: El comercio mayorista de alimentos en el Centro Histórico de la Ciudad de México (1900–1960)*. UNAM.

CES-CDMX. (2017). *Estudio de caracterización de la oferta de los mercados públicos en la Ciudad de México*. Consejo Económico y Social de la Ciudad de México.

Connolly, P. (2017). Latin American informal urbanism: Contexts, concepts and contributions with specific reference to Mexico. In F. Hernández & A. Becerra (Eds.), *Marginal urbanisms: Informal and formal development in cities of Latin America* (pp. 22–47). Cambridge Scholars Publishing.

Cross, J. C. (1998). Co-optation, competition, and resistance: State and street vendors in Mexico City. *Latin American Perspectives*, *25*(2), 41–61. https://doi.org/10.1177/0094582x9802500203

Davis, D. E. (1991). Urban transport, dependent development and change: Lessons from a case study of Mexico City's subway. *Canadian Journal of Development Studies/Revue Canadienne D'Études du Développement*, *12*(2), 329–355.

Davis, D. E. (1994). *Urban Leviathan: Mexico city in the twentieth century*. Temple University Press.
Diehl, J. A. (2020). Growing for Sydney: Exploring the urban food system through farmers' social networks. *Sustainability*, *12*(8), 3346. https://doi.org/10.3390/su12083346
Duhau, E., & Giglia, A. (2008). *Las reglas del desorden: Habitar la metrópoli*. Siglo XXI Editores.
Felici, F. B., & Mazzocchi, G. (2022). Territory matters: A methodology for understanding the role of territorial factors in transforming local food systems. *Land*, *11*(7), 1046. https://doi.org/10.3390/land11071046
Fuertes, P., & Gomez-Escoda, E. M. (2022). Supplying Barcelona: The role of public market halls in the construction of the urban food system. *Journal of Urban History*, *48*(5), 1121–1139. https://doi.org/10.1177/0096144220971821
Gasca, J. (2017). Centros comerciales de la Ciudad de México: El ascenso de los negocios inmobiliarios orientados al consumo. *Revista EURE. Revista de Estudios Urbano Regionales*, *43*(130), 73–96. http://dx.doi.org/10.4067/s0250-71612017000300073
GDF. (2015). Aviso por el que se da a conocer el Listado de los Mercados Públicos de la Ciudad de México. *Gaceta Oficial del Distrito Federal*, *18*(71), 7–34.
Giglia, A. (2018). *Comercio, consumo y cultura en los mercados públicos de la Ciudad de México*. UAM.
Glickman, A. R., Clark, J. K., & Freedman, D. A. (2022). Participatory modeling of the food system: The case of community-based systems dynamics. In C. Peters & D. Thilmany (Eds.), *Food systems modeling* (pp. 257–283). Academic Press. Retrieved November 14, 2023, from https://doi.org/10.1016/B978-0-12-822112-9.00003-5
Gobierno de la República. (1951). Reglamento de mercados para el Distrito Federal. *Diario Oficial de la Federación*, *CLXXXVI*(26).
Gobierno de la República. (1970). Ley Orgánica del Departamento del Distrito Federal. *Diario Oficial de la Federación*, *CIII*(47), 19–41.
Gobierno de la República. (1987). Decreto por el que se reforman los artículos 73 fracción VI, 79 fracción V, 89 fracciones 11 y XVII, 110 primer párrafo, 111 primer párrafo y 127; y se deroga la fracción VI del artículo 74 de la Constitución Política de los Estados Unidos Mexicanos. *Diario Oficial de la Federación*, *DCVII*(6), 5–9.
Gómez, L. (2013). Baja participación de mercados públicos en abasto de alimentos. *La Jornada*, March 4, p. 37.
Gómez, N. (2012). *Liderazgos y organizaciones en el comercio en vía pública de la Ciudad de México: el caso de la delegación Iztapalapa, 1998–2008*. El Colegio de México.
Gruzinski, S. (2012). *La Ciudad de México: Una historia*. Fondo de Cultura Económica.
Guibrunet, L., Rubio, M., & Flores Abreu, I. N. (2023). Reclaiming traditional food systems in alternative food networks: Insights from Mexico City peri-urban agriculture. *Local Environment*, *28*(9), 1153–1172. https://doi.org/10.1080/13549839.2023.2194618
Hayden, T. B. (2023). Insecure infrastructures: The affects and effects of violence in Mexico's food system. *American Anthropologist*, *125*(1), 89–99. https://doi.org/10.1111/aman.13807
IECDMX. (2023). *Historial de elecciones*. Instituto Electoral de la Ciudad de México. Retrieved December 4, 2023, from https://www.iecm.mx/elecciones/historial-de-elecciones
infoCDMX. (2019). *Inconformidad a la respuesta: Recurso de revisión RR.IP.4189/2019*. Instituto de Transparencia, Acceso a la Información Pública, Protección de Datos Personales y Rendición de Cuentas de la Ciudad de México. Retrieved December 3, 2023, from https://www.infocdmx.org.mx/LTAIPRC-2016-OT/Art133/Fr01/2019/A133Fr01B_2019_Relacion-de-las-resoluciones-RR.IP.4189-2019.pdf
Ingram, J. (2019). Food system models. In M. Lawrence & S. Friel (Eds.), *Healthy and sustainable food systems*. Routledge.

Iturriaga, J. E. (2012). *La categoría de Centro Histórico y su rescate: Ciudad de México*. Cámara de Diputados (Patrimonio Cultural y Divertimentos).

Jefatura de Gobierno. (2022). *Publica SEDECO normas para la regulación y funcionamiento de los mercados públicos de la Ciudad de México*. Gobierno de la Ciudad de México. Retrieved January 11, 2023, from https://jefaturadegobierno.cdmx.gob.mx/comunicacion/nota/publica-sedeco-normas-para-la-regulacion-y-funcionamiento-de-los-mercados-publicos-de-la-ciudad-de-mexico

Jiménez, A. D. (Ed.). (2019). *Mercados de la Ciudad de México*. Comité de Asuntos Editoriales del PRI Distrito Federal.

Jiménez, A. D., & González, C. (Eds.). (2015). *DF Festivo: Mercados de la Ciudad de México*. Comité de Asuntos Editoriales del PRI Distrito Federal.

Kasper, C., Brandt, J., Lindschulte, K., & Giseke, U. (2017). The urban food system approach: Thinking in spatialized systems. *Agroecology and Sustainable Food Systems*, *41*(8), 1009–1025. https://doi.org/10.1080/21683565.2017.1334737

Laboratorio para la Ciudad. (2017). *Mercados, Laboratorio de Datos*. Retrieved June 3, 2019, from http://labcd.mx

López Rosado, D. (1988). *El abasto de productos alimenticios en la Ciudad de México*. Fondo de Cultura Económica.

Luis, V. P. J., Tomaso, F., & De Schutter Olivier, M. U. (Eds.). (2018). *Routledge handbook of food as a commons*. Routledge. https://doi.org/10.4324/9781315161495

Meneses, R. (2011). *Legalidades públicas: El derecho, el ambulantaje y las calles en el Centro de la Ciudad de México (1930–2010)*. UNAM, CIDE.

Meneses, R. (2012). *La negociación jurídica del derecho a la ciudad: Los ambulantes y el Centro Histórico de la Ciudad de México* (Vol. 2, pp. 9–34). Seminario Permanente Centro Histórico de la Ciudad de México.

Monroy, F. P. (2005). *La selva de acero: Crónica de la Ciudad de México bajo la primera administración de Ernesto P. Uruchurtu (1952–1958)*. UNAM.

Murray, S., & Caraher, M. (2019). Food retail and distribution: A focus on supermarkets. In M. Lawrence & S. Friel (Eds.), *Healthy and sustainable food systems*. Routledge.

Popkin, B. M., & Reardon, T. (2018). Obesity and the food system transformation in Latin America. *Obesity Reviews*, *19*(8), 1028–1064. https://doi.org/10.1111/obr.12694

PUEC. (2015a). *Los mercados de La Merced: Un diagnóstico integral para su revitalización económica y desarrollo social*. UNAM. Retrieved December 17, 2019, from https://www.puec.unam.mx/pdf/libros_digitales/mercados_la_merced_un_diagnostico_integral_revitalizacion_economica_desarrollo_social.pdf

PUEC. (2015b). *Trayectorias de vida de las mujeres comerciantes de La Merced, Centro Histórico de la Ciudad de México*. UNAM, Autoridad del Centro Histórico.

Rello, F., & Sodi, D. (1989). *Abasto y distribución de alimentos en las grandes metrópolis*. Editorial Nueva Imagen, México.

Rocker, S., Kropczynski, J., & Hinrichs, C. (2022). Using social network analysis to understand and enhance local and regional food systems. In C. Peters & D. Thilmany (Eds.), *Food systems modeling* (pp. 231–256). Academic Press. Retrieved November 14, 2023, from https://doi.org/10.1016/B978-0-12-822112-9.00015-1

Schatan, J. (1982). *El abastecimiento de alimentos en la Ciudad de México (versión preliminar)*. INT-0301. PROCADES-CEPAL.

Seale & Associates. (2018). *Reporte de la industria de autoservicios*. Seale & Associates. Retrieved September 7, 2019, from http://mnamexico.com/wp-content/uploads/2018/07/Supermercados-Final-1.pdf

SEDECO (2013) *Política de protección y fomento para los mercados públicos de la Ciudad de México (2013–2018)*. Gobierno de la Ciudad de México.

Simone, A. (2004). People as infrastructure: Intersecting fragments in Johannesburg. *Public Culture*, *16*(3), 407–429. https://doi.org/10.1215/08992363-16-3-407

Simone, A. (2021). Ritornello: "People as infrastructure." *Urban Geography*, *42*(9), 1341–1348. https://doi.org/10.1080/02723638.2021.1894397

Smith, D. W. (1998). Urban food systems and the poor in developing countries. *Transactions of the Institute of British Geographers*, *23*(2), 207–219. https://doi.org/10.1111/j.0020-2754.1998.00207.x

Tejera, H., & Rodríguez, E. (2015). Las paradojas de la democracia: Partido dominante, gobierno y redes políticas en la Ciudad de México. *Estudios Sociológicos*, *33*(98), 375–408. https://doi.org/10.24201/es.2015v33n0.6

Téllez, L. F. (2020). *Popular infrastructural politics: Trader organisation and public markets in Mexico City* [PhD Thesis, The University of Leeds]. Retrieved April 5, 2021, from https://etheses.whiterose.ac.uk/28209/

Téllez, L.F. (2025). Infrastructural politics: A conceptual mapping and critical review, *Urban Studies*, *62*(1), 31–51. https://doi.org/10.1177/00420980241246206

Velázquez, M. (1997). *Evolución de los mercados en la Ciudad de México hasta 1850*. Consejo de la Crónica de la Ciudad de México.

Vitiello, D., & Brinkley, C. (2014). The hidden history of food system planning. *Journal of Planning History*, *13*(2), 91–112. https://doi.org/10.1177/1538513213507541

Ward, P. M. (2013). Mexico City. In M. Pacione (Ed.), *Problems and planning in Third World cities* (pp. 28–64). Routledge (Routledge Revivals).

Wilson, D., & Jonas, A. (2021). The people as infrastructure concept: Appraisal and new directions. *Urban Geography*, *42*(9), 1333–1340. https://doi.org/10.1080/02723638.2021.1931752

Wiskerke, J. S. C. (2015). Urban food systems. In H. de Zeeuw & P. Drechsel (Eds.), *Cities and agriculture: Developing resilient urban food systems*. Routledge.

Zenteno, C. (2016). *La valorización sociocultural y el proceso de transformación del centro de la Ciudad de México en tiempos de Ernesto P. Uruchurtu, 1952–1960* [Masters Dissertation, Instituto de Investigaciones Dr. José María Luis Mora].

Ziccardi, A. (1991). *Las obras públicas de la Ciudad de México, 1976–1982: Política urbana e industria de la construcción*. UNAM.

13

LOCAL URBAN FOOD POLICIES IN LATIN AMERICA

The Milan pact as translocal articulation network

Diego Martín

Introduction

As stated in the introduction to this book, more than half of the world's population currently resides in urban areas (Battersby et al., 2024). This figure is higher in Latin America, which is one of the most urbanized regions on the planet, with approximately 80% of its population living in cities (Mayer & Nguyen Long, 2020). In this context of increasing urbanization, the urban food issue acquires a centrality that puts local governments in front of the need to generate public responses to address issues related to food security, sustainability, justice, and sovereignty (FAO, 2019; Sonnino, 2016; Wiskerke, 2015; Yacamán, 2017; Karanja & Njenga, 2011; Moragues, 2014). As will be seen in this chapter, these responses have a dual purpose: First, the construction of food policies that can respond to this challenge at the local level and, second, the construction of an international agenda that supports and generates tools to frame and reinforce local territorial actions (Martín & de la Fuente, 2022).

In the construction of this international agenda, city networks appear as a key tool for local governments, as they facilitate cooperation amongst and between themselves, providing a variety of services to their members, ranging from political advocacy to knowledge management and transfer, in addition to supporting the implementation of innovative policies (Fernández de Losada & Zapata Garesché, 2022). Within the existing complex ecosystem of international city networks (Fernández de Losada & Abdullah, 2019), this paper focuses on the study of how one of them, the Milan Pact on Urban Food Policies (MUFPP), which is the first international protocol to promote sustainable urban food policies, influences the implementation of urban food strategies in three Latin American cities: Quito (Ecuador), Rosario (Argentina), and São Paulo (Brazil).

DOI: 10.4324/9781003471929-18

Although MUFPP is not the only network working on urban food, the Pact is the only network of cities created to specifically address this issue. In this sense, and in view of the proliferation of a growing debate regarding the functionality of networks as a tool that provides concrete solutions to local governments (Fernández & Abdullah, 2019), this chapter analyzes the constitution and contributions generated by the Milan Pact network in relation to the governance of urban food systems in specific sites. Bearing in mind the question of how urban food systems develop forms of governance that promote food security and sustainability—to which this book seeks to respond—this chapter attempts to determine whether there are, in the international articulations that local governments build, operational and reference frameworks for the implementation of governance schemes in the construction of sustainable urban food systems. By sustainable urban food system, we refer to a system "in which food is nutritious and accessible to all and in which the management of natural resources preserves ecosystem functions to support the satisfaction of current and future human needs FAO (2014, p. 12)." Specifically, then, this chapter asks what is the influence and capacity of the Milan Pact on Urban Food Policies (MUFPP) to generate frameworks for action at the local level and analyzes its implementation in Quito (Ecuador), Rosario (Argentina), and São Paulo (Brazil).

Methodologically, this chapter adopts a qualitative and empirical explanatory approach (Anduiza et al., 2009, p. 12), using a three-stage comparative method: information gathering, case selection, and intensive synchronic comparison. The information gathered included narratives, debates, and relevant policy documents. For the three selected cities, a comparative analysis is conducted that explores common patterns and particularities in the development of urban food strategies. Central to the study are key informant interviews, conducted between 2018 and 2023, which included city politicians and officials, MUFPP representatives, experts, and NGO representatives. These interviews, together with face-to-face visits to the selected cities, provided detailed information and territorial perspectives essential for the analysis. Finally, a comparative analysis is conducted using categories based on work by Sonnino (2016) and Baker and de Zeeuw (2015), of MUFPP documents and statements, covering the period 2015–2022, in which the impact of the COVID-19 pandemic is also considered.

Theoretical framework

This research addresses the international action of local governments and their networks, particularly the process of building the international urban food agenda and its territorial implementation in three Latin American cities. Without entering into the debate regarding the formal recognition of cities and their networks as actors in international relations, we seek to analyze the usefulness of tools developed by local governments around the generation of governance schemes that facilitate the implementation of various policies at the local level (Durmuş, 2021), in this case food policies.

In order to analyze the construction of agendas at the international level, the work of Javier Sánchez Cano (2016) entitled "*Non-central governments and their networks: analysis of their role as actors in global governance*" is taken as a theoretical reference. The author argues that one of the characteristics of the international order promoted by the United Nations in the post-Cold War period is the institutionalization of a global governance system structured around a system of international conferences and summits. In this order, the aim is to ensure the effectiveness of the agendas proposed, which is why local governments are progressively gaining some space in the international system (although it is a matter of fact and not of law), as agents to ensure the fulfillment of these agendas (Sánchez Cano, 2016). In this scenario, the construction of international networks and alliances is one of the main modalities that local governments develop in order to influence the international system, as well as to generate tools that facilitate the implementation of policies at the local level. Along the same lines, Durmus argues that "local governments are part and parcel of the patchwork of international law and governance" (2021, p. 11).

There is a considerable academic production around the ecosystem of international city networks, taking into account that their emergence dates back at least to the early twentieth century (Acuto, 2016; Le Saux, 2015; Acuto & Rayner, 2016; Curtis, 2014, 2018; Leffel, 2020; Acuto & Leffel, 2021). As mentioned earlier, one of the central debates currently taking place is related to the great proliferation of networks (Acuto & Leffel, 2021), their functionality (Fernández de Losada & Zapata Garesché, 2022), and the tension between traditional networks of a supposedly more rigid and bureaucratic character and new, more agile, and fluid networks (Malé, 2019, de la Fuente et al., 2019; Fernández de Losada & Zapata Garesché, 2022). At this point, the Milan Pact appears as one of the new forms of international articulation found by local governments, without a large bureaucratic structure, led in fact by the city of Milan, but with a presence on all continents through the creation of spaces for regional representation, as will be further discussed later. As Steyaert et al. (2023) argue, the issue of urban food policies and their networks and governance spaces has not been extensively studied, with the corpus comprised of just a dozen studies, including Blay-Palmer (2016), Coulson and Sonnino (2019), Jones and Hills (2021), Levkoe (2014), Martín and de la Fuente (2022), Mooney et al. (2014), Moragues-Faus (2014, 2021), Moragues-Faus and Sonnino (2019), Santo and Moragues-Faus (2019), and Sibbing et al. (2021).

In this sense, the scientific production of urban food governance networks and spaces can be classified into three groups (Steyaert et al., 2023). The first group focuses on the study of initiatives at the local level and examines how they relate to other levels of governance through Trans-Local Cities Food Networks (Coulson & Sonnino, 2019; Levkoe, 2014). The second, which focuses on the inner workings of the networks, includes the work of Moragues-Faus and Sonnino (2019); Moragues-Faus (2021); and Steyaert et al. (2023). The third, which includes the present chapter, starts from translocal articulations to study the impact they have on local (Jones & Hills, 2021; Santo & Moragues-Faus, 2019; Sibbing et al., 2021) and/or global food governance (Blay-Palmer, 2016; Martín & de la Fuente, 2022; Moragues-Faus, 2017; Santo & Moragues-Faus, 2019).

In conceptual terms, in order to understand the functioning of the network of cities of the Milan Pact, the concepts of internal and external functions proposed by Sánchez Cano (2016) are extremely useful. By external functions of a network it is understood that: "the network ensures representation and works for institutional recognition and policy advocacy" (2016, p. 68); and by internal functions, that it "promotes technical cooperation and *policy learning* among its members, facilitates their adaptation to their international political and regulatory environment, and thus organizes the responsible participation of local authorities, with their own competences, in global governance systems" (2016, p. 68). On the other hand, to analyze the emergence of urban food strategies, Roberta Sonnino (2016) finds the emergence of a new local approach to responding to the challenge of ensuring food security in a sustainable way, which presents valuable elements from both a practical and symbolic point of view, which would allow overcoming limitations inherent to traditional postulates on food security.

Results

As stated in the introduction to this chapter, the Milan Pact on Urban Food Policy (MUFPP) is the first international protocol dedicated to promoting sustainable urban food policies. Its origin dates back to October 15, 2015, during Expo Milano, where 123 mayors and representatives of local authorities from around the world signed it under the slogan "Feeding the Planet, Energy for Life," in collaboration with the United Nations Food and Agriculture Organization. From its inception, the compact set ambitious goals, highlighting the need to develop sustainable and resilient urban food systems that ensure healthy and accessible food for all. It also called for waste reduction, biodiversity preservation, and climate change adaptation. To achieve these objectives, the promotion of coordination between departments and sectors at the municipal and territorial levels was proposed, incorporating urban food policy considerations in various social, economic, and environmental areas.

The central challenge here is to mainstream food policies across different areas of government, recognizing the interconnectedness between food policy and other aspects of sustainable development, from poverty reduction to the promotion of decent work (MUFPP, 2015; Sonnino, 2016; Morley & Morgan, 2021). The Pact proposes that cities use a Strategic Framework for Action . . . "as a starting point for organizing their own urban food system" (MUFPP, 2015). This Framework for Action is built from the systematization of different policies that some of the signatory cities have been carrying out, and whose objective is to provide a series of policy options and recommendations, working methods, and decision-making processes to achieve sustainable urban food systems, for those local governments that want to apply it. These options are grouped into six thematic axes, for which a series of concrete actions—"strategic options"—is offered that cities can adopt. The thematic axes consist of preparing an enabling context for effective action (governance); promoting sustainable diets and adequate nutrition; ensuring social and economic equity; promoting food production; improving food supply and distribution; and reducing food waste.

Progressively, new cities have joined this network; currently, there are 270 cities in six different geographic regions, representing more than 450 million inhabitants. It should be noted that not only cities are part of the Pact, but there is also the active participation of international organizations such as FAO, non-governmental organizations such as RUAF, and coordination with other city networks such as UCLG, ICLEI, or C40, to mention a few. In terms of its internal functions (Grasa & Sánchez Cano, 2013), the Pact encourages cooperation between cities, facilitating the exchange of good practices through awards and financial allocations. This approach has led to a greater focus on governance in shared experiences. Among its external functions (Grasa & Sánchez Cano, 2013), the Pact seeks to influence mainly the specialized agencies of the United Nations, highlighting the contribution of cities to the 2030 Agenda, COP21, and Habitat III, to promote the participation of cities in the design of sustainable food systems. The creation of the Pact represents an impulse from local authorities in the face of the systemic crisis affecting the global food system (Morley & Morgan, 2021). It stands out as a bottom-up effort to build an urban food agenda and energize food strategies in cities that had not yet implemented them comprehensively, where it is the local actors themselves who propose an alternative to the traditional visions described earlier (the extremes between the macro and micro visions analyzed by Sonnino (2016).

In this context, it is relevant to incorporate the perspective of Rita Grandinetti, who served as a member of the jury at the Milan Pact Awards 2022, highlighting "the level of comprehensiveness with which the policy is approached and the effective structuring of all management mechanisms" (virtual communication, September 28, 2023) (*Ibid.*). This technical specificity of the network allows for a higher level of appropriation of the proposed agenda by local governments. On this point, Cecile Michel, an official of the MUFPP Secretariat & knowledge-sharing programs, within the Food Policy Department of the Municipality of Milan, maintains that it is an initiative "developed and managed by a city, Milan, that is, it is the only network of and for cities in relation to the food issue. It is important that the management of the network is not in the hands of national governments or international organizations" (telephone communication, C. Michel, October 5, 2023).

This distinctive feature of the city-managed network also brings with it a series of difficulties, the main one being budgetary, even more so when there is no fee required for membership.

In terms of geographic composition, the preponderance of European cities in the Pact is noteworthy although not unexpected, considering that this is where the initiative originated. However, there has been a progressive growth of cities from other parts of the world, with the creation of six regional operating spaces, including Africa; Asia Pacific; Eurasia and Southwest Asia; Europe; North and Central America; and South America. Grandinetti recognizes as a distinctive feature the true globality of the network, especially with regard to the profile of the municipalities that comprise it. She notes that the network "exhibits a territorial globality, encompassing a remarkable regional diversity, as well as a significant variability in terms of size and characteristics of the participating municipalities. This ranges from European municipalities with a population of 3,000 inhabitants to large Latin American cities" (personal communication, R. Grandinetti, September 28, 2023).

Moreover, this is important because it reflects a diversity in the actors participating and their commitment to the fulfillment of "very specific, very structured axes" (*Ibid*).

As a result of the regionalization processes, there has been a significant increase in South American cities joining the Pact, as will be discussed later. Indeed, the network's emergent regionalization makes it possible to address with greater specificity the food-related challenges presented, in this case, by the governments of South America. In this regard, Marina Borgatello, Head of the Program for Innovation and Improvement of Food Quality in Rosario, Argentina, argues that:

> *What is remarkable about the Compact lies in its capacity for regionalization, i.e. its global character combined with the flexibility to adapt to specific local contexts. The possibility of operating at the regional level adds a significant strategic component, thus enhancing its effectiveness and relevance in different geographical and socioeconomic environments.*
>
> *(virtual communication, M. Borgatello, August 29, 2023)*

On the other hand, Alexandra Rodríguez, Head of the Participatory Urban Agriculture Program of Quito (AGRUPAR) maintains that this regionalization has some shortcomings, among which is that Latin America has not "managed to build a regional voice as in the cases of Africa and Asia" (virtual communication, A. Rodríguez, October 13, 2023). The specific regional challenges and experiences of Latin American members will be discussed further in what follows.

The Milan pact and urban food Strategies in Quito, Rosario, and Sao Paulo

Rosario, Argentina

Rosario, a city located in the south of the province of Santa Fe, Argentina, stands as a pioneering reference in addressing the urban food issue. With about 40% of the provincial population concentrated in this urban area (INDEC, 2022), Rosario has cultivated a rich tradition in food production programs, especially through the Urban Agriculture Program (Lattuca et al., 2014), which has been in place for more than two decades.

Although the city already had food policies and programs in place before joining the Milan Pact, the signing of the MUFPP in 2020 brought with it a key organizing tool. Marina Borgatello, who was in charge of implementing the Program for Innovation and Improvement of Food Quality, reflects on this change, noting that although Rosario was already working on policies related to the Pact, it provided the organization and clarity the city needed (personal communication, M. Borgatello, August 29, 2023).

The main challenge that motivated the current administration to try to implement comprehensive food strategies in Rosario was the alarming prevalence of malnutrition, especially among the infant–juvenile population. In 2019, 40.5% of young people aged 2–19 years in Rosario suffered from malnutrition (La Capital, 2019). The COVID-19 pandemic not only exacerbated the demand for food aid but also evidenced the vulnerability of public procurement systems. Against this backdrop, the government response materialized through the Rosario Food Bank (BAR), which managed to benefit 300,000 people (personal communication, M. Borgatello, August 29, 2023). Another of the city's major food problems is related to food waste: to date, 20 tons of fruits and vegetables end up in landfill each month. The Recupebar Program at the Producers' Market is the only recovery initiative, managing to recover an average of seven tons per month (personal communication, M. Borgatello, August 29, 2023).

As mentioned at the beginning of this section, the Urban and Periurban Agriculture Program is the main policy that the city of Rosario has sustained for more than 20 years. Now called the Sustainable Food Production Program, it seeks not only to maintain a productive periurban area with a sustainable and agroecological approach but also to address the loss of food autonomy. In this sense, one of the great difficulties facing the city today is related to the progressive decrease in the area dedicated to horticulture, which has generated dependence on other regions and affected agroecological production (see Barksy, this volume). However, the city today continues to sustain 800 hectares dedicated to agroecological production of vegetables, for which it has received distinguished recognition from the MUFPP.

One of the main aspects highlighted by Roberto Barbieri, responsible for MUFPP monitoring at the General Directorate of International Relations of Rosario, is the regionalization that has been promoted in collaboration with Belo Horizonte in South America, combining the localization of the Pact through methodological tools perfected in the Barcelona 2030 Commitment. In this sense, since Rosario's adhesion and its designation as representative of the MUFPP Steering Committee in the representation of South America, the number of signatory cities in the region has increased by 60%. Regarding the localization of policies, Barbieri highlights the importance of the Milan Pact "by putting a clear focus on local food strategies, ordering the agendas and urban development of cities. The network operates under a governance scheme with the participation of various actors, including academic institutions and civil society" (Virtual communication with Roberto Barbieri, August 17, 2023).

While recognizing the importance of the Milan Pact network, Barbieri suggests the need for stronger leadership to amplify the voice of the more than two hundred cities participating in international forums and make a more significant impact on the global food security and climate change agenda.

In summary, the case of Rosario highlights the need to integrate existing food policies into a comprehensive strategy, a framework provided by the MUFPP. Membership in MUFPP has not only had a transformative impact but also served as a catalyst for the creation of new projects, such as Innovation in Food Quality and the Alliance for Innovation and Sustainability of the Local Food System (intended as a sort of Food Council). It has also guided existing programs, such as Sustainable Food Production, through the application of indicators proposed by MUFPP. While the city faces many food challenges, the officials interviewed concur that joining the Pact has provided it with a useful tool to try to generate a comprehensive approach to the food issue and at the same time exercise regional leadership on the issue in South America.

Quito, Ecuador

The Metropolitan District of Quito, the capital of Ecuador, stands out in the Latin American region for its commitment to urban and peri-urban food policies (FAO, 2014). The city, with a population of 1,928,000, gained international recognition as the host of the UN Habitat Summit in 2016, generating awareness of the importance of urban food issues globally. Quito joined the Milan Pact in 2016, lacking, until then, an urban food strategy, as did Rosario and São Paulo. However, since the 2000s, the city has promoted various initiatives, such as a strong urban agriculture policy (AGRUPAR) and support for small producers, which culminated in the presentation of its Strategy and the Agrifood Pact in 2018. Accession to the Milan Pact was motivated by the need for coherence and comprehensiveness in already existing programs. The formulation of the urban food strategy involved diverse actors, from universities to government representatives and civil society sectors. It was coordinated by the Quito Economic Development Agency (CONQUITO), with the collaboration of advisors from the Social Responsibility and Shared Value Area (personal communication, A. Rodríguez, June 24, 2018).

The urban food agenda in Quito is linked to the proliferation of urban gardens since the 1980s, a spontaneous strategy linked to internal migration (FAO, 2014). Since 2000, the city went from tolerating these gardens to promoting them through the AGRUPAR program, supported by the United Nations. Joining MUFPP in 2016 increased the visibility of the food issue, integrating it into strategies and programs, and culminated in the presentation of the Agrifood Strategy in 2018, which presented a broadened agenda, focused on ensuring food security and promoting sustainable practices in the city (personal communication, A. Rodríguez, June 24, 2018). These and other citywide efforts were hindered during the COVID-19 pandemic, when the closure of farmer's markets, gardens, and agroecological fairs limited many citywide efforts, but there has been resurgent support in recent years.

Despite these challenges, membership in MUFPP allowed for the comprehensive inclusion of the food issue in Quito's agenda, manifesting itself in initiatives such as the Agrifood Strategy and Pact, as well as in the city's development and climate action plans. Quito's synchronization of local and international efforts, especially with FAO, has strengthened the city's relevance in networks such as C40, ICLEI, and UCCI, evidencing the convergence of global and local objectives (personal communication, A. Rodríguez, July 3, 2019).

Sao Paulo, Brazil

São Paulo, the most populous city in the Americas, faces the challenge of implementing public food policies at the municipal level, with 22.6 million inhabitants in the metropolitan area and 11.5 million in the city proper (IBGE, 2023). As expressed in the 1st FNS Plan (CAISAN, 2016), the city presents great inequalities, in a country where more than 50% of the population faces some level of food insecurity (Rede PENSSAN, 2022). Severe food insecurity by color or race corresponds to 29.8% among Black and Brown populations, while among the White population the proportion is 14.4%, the infant mortality rate among Indigenous peoples is still 2.5 times higher than that of the rest of the population; the rate of indigenous children under five years of age with chronic malnutrition is 26% and acute malnutrition is 15%.

In this context, the city of São Paulo joined MUFPP in 2015. Similar to the cases of the cities of Quito and Rosario, one of the main contributions made by this network of cities in São Paolo is to provide a framework within which to organize municipal food policies. As mentioned in the previous cases, the city of São Paulo has an urban and peri-urban agriculture program that, although it began in the 1970s, presents a discontinuous trajectory and was only institutionalized in 2004 through Law No. 13,727 (Porto de Oliveira, 2017, p. 90).

Unlike Argentina and Ecuador, Brazil has a more robust legislative and institutional system for addressing food and nutritional security, mainly as a result of Constitutional Amendment No. 64 of 2010 to the 1988 Political Constitution, which incorporates the recognition of the right to food, established in Article 6 as a social right. In relation to this framework and national policies, in 2013 São Paulo established the municipal components of the National FSN System, through Law No. 15,920. The same provides for the obligation of the municipality regarding the development of actions and policies that tend to ensure FNS and the Human Right to Adequate Food (DHAA).

In this regard, MUFPP membership coincides with the regulation of the functioning of the SAN Municipal Council (COMUSAN) and the creation of the SAN Interministerial Chamber (CAISAN). COMUSAN has a composition in which two-thirds of its representatives belong to civil society, and one-third is made up of representatives of the public sector. Another of the main confluences generated between the signing of the Pact and the municipal FNS policies is evidenced in the development of the 1st Municipal Food and Nutrition Security Plan (2016–2020). In this context, there has been a growing participation of civil society and social and educational organizations in the installation and legitimization of the food strategy approach in the city of São Paulo (Porto de Oliveira, 2017).

Regarding the main influence exerted by the signing of the Covenant on municipal food policies, the implementation of waste reduction policies and food banks that "proved to have a fundamental value in the pandemic" (Personal communication, Palm, August 12, 2022) is highlighted. In fact, the MUFPP in 2019 awarded the city for its Policy "Municipal Programme on Food Waste and Loss Combat Campaign on food waste combat in public supply equipment". This program is part of Municipal Decree No. 58,862 of July 19, 2019. Initiated in October 2017, it seeks to raise awareness among merchants of public food supply logistics in São Paulo to avoid waste and donate food fit for consumption to the Municipal Food Bank. The project, which at the time was in a pilot phase in seven supply points, is currently "being implemented in 23 free fairs, avoiding 60 tons of waste" (Viviane dos Santos Fontana, personal communication, August 18, 2022) and aims to expand to all 32 public markets and 150 street markets. The evaluation shows 85% reuse of donated food, contributing to SDGs 8 and 12, and aims to achieve SDG 2. Since October 2017, the Program has impacted food and socioeconomic security, distributing food to 120 thousand people. Despite logistical challenges and labor dynamics, the initiative has generated environmental benefits by reducing solid waste and complying with the Federal Solid Waste Law. The direct connection of entities at the point of waste generation is a strategy to scale up action in a faster and more sustainable manner. In addition, the program addresses the labor dynamics of merchants through the participation of beneficiaries in the separation of suitable food, contributing to the training and job reinsertion of economically vulnerable people.

As in Quito and Rosario, the COVID-19 pandemic had a strong impact in São Paulo. The closure of spaces, such as markets and fairs, altered the dynamics of food sales, affecting the availability and access to fresh produce. In response to these challenges, the city implemented specific policies, focusing mainly on working with food banks and emphasizing waste reduction, a policy for which it had received an award from MUFPP.

In summary, the Milan Pact's effects in the city of São Paolo have supported the development of legal and institutional frameworks for addressing food security and sustainability by the state, and given greater support for existing frameworks. In particular, it is important to highlight the influence that the signing of the Pact has had on the development of the 1st Municipal Plan for Food and Nutritional Security (2016–2020), on the strengthening of governance schemes with increasing participation of civil society (Personal communication with Lia Palm, August 17, 2022), as well as on the generation of a municipal policy to reduce food waste.

Conclusion

The adherence to the Milan Pact by the cities of Quito, Rosario, and Sao Paulo has been an influential factor in the design of sustainable urban food systems and supporting food and nutritional security, beyond the different degrees of progress in its implementation in each of the reference cities. When asked what was the main influence of the Pact in the cases studied, the responses of the officials interviewed were practically the same: The MUFPP represents a tool that made it possible to organize and frame urban food policies, from a comprehensive and cross-cutting perspective across all areas of government and with multi-stakeholder participation. In Quito and São Paulo, adherence to the Milan Pact has enabled the preparation and implementation of Urban Food Strategies and the creation of the respective Food Councils, which are urban governance schemes with significant participation of civil society. In the case of Rosario, this initiative has remained at the project level, with the so-called Program for Innovation and Improvement of Food Quality, although it has not been implemented in practice.

In all three cases, the adhesion to MUFPP has generated a boost to the programs that were already being developed, while at the same time creating a reference framework that integrates and gives a holistic sense of the different food policies. As mentioned earlier, Rosario and Sao Paulo have been awarded for their Sustainable Food Production and Waste Reduction and Combating Programs, respectively. In the case of Quito, the city was selected to participate in the adaptation of indicators proposed in the Pact, together with Nairobi and Antananarivo. At this point, it can be seen how the implementation of concrete measures, aligned with MUFPP guidelines, can act as an effective tool to address specific challenges of Latin American cities.

On the other hand, it is important to highlight that, based on the data and characteristics of food and nutritional security presented throughout this chapter, the cities studied have countless challenges to address. In this sense, the creation of regional instances of the MUFPP network should make it possible to build a South American voice, which will bring the specific needs and demands of the region to the international level. As stated by several of the officials interviewed, it is necessary to build a greater political volume beyond the technical, in order to address the problems that are structured at the global level and are manifested, among others, in the cities studied in this section. Future lines of research should address the relationship between the technical support of a network such as the Milan Pact and the budgetary restrictions, social complexities, and political capacities of governments in the Latin American region.

Taking up the question on the consideration of the Milan Pact as an actor that contributes to developing forms of governance that support food security and sustainability in urban food systems in Latin America, the analysis of the cases has shown that the MUFPP has been a sort of structuring and energizing axis for the implementation of food strategies in those cities that, with different trajectories and specific programs, had not carried out an integral and transversal approach to it.

Bibliography

Acuto, M. (2016). City diplomacy. In C. Costantinou, P. Sharp & P. Kerr (Eds.), *The Sage handbook of diplomacy*. Sage.

Acuto, M., & Leffel, B. (2021). Understanding the global ecosystem of city networks. *Urban Studies*, *58*(9), 1758–1774.

Acuto, M., & Rayner, S. (2016). City networks: Breaking gridlocks or forging (new) lock-ins? *International Affairs*, *92*, 1147–1166. https://doi.org/10.1111/1468-2346.12700

Anduiza, E., Crespo, I., & Méndez, M. (2009). *Metodología de la Ciencia Política* (1ª ed.). Centro de Investigaciones Sociológicas.

Baker, L., & de Zeeuw, H. (2015). Urban food policies and programmes: An overview. En *Cities and agriculture: Developing resilient urban food systems* (pp. 26–55). RUAF Foundation.

Battersby, J., Hatab, A. A., Ambikapathi, R., Chicoma, J. L., Shulang, F., Kimani-Murage, E., & Resnick, D. (2024). Strengthening urban and periurban food systems to achieve food security and nutrition, in the context of urbanization and rural transformation, HLPE Report No. 19.

Blay-Palmer, A. (Ed.). (2016). *Imagining sustainable food systems: Theory and practice*. Springer.

Brazilian Institute of Geography and Statistics (IBGE). (2023). *2023 population census*. IBGE. https://www.ibge.gov.br

Borelli, S., Conigliaro, M., & Di Cagno, F. (2023). *Urban forests: A global perspective*. https://doi.org/10.4060/cc8216en

Câmara Intersecretarial de Segurança Alimentar e Nutricional (CAISAN). (2016). *1º Plano Municipal de Segurança Alimentar e Nutricional 2016/2020*. São Paulo

Coulson, H., & Sonnino, R. (2019). Re-scaling the politics of food: Place-based urban food governance in the UK. *Geoforum*, *98*, 170–179. https://doi.org/10.1016/j.geoforum.2018.11.010

Curtis, S. (2014). *The power of cities in international relations*. Routledge.

Curtis, S. (2018). Global cities and the ends of globalism. *New Global Studies*, *12*(1), 75–90.

de la Fuente, F. R., Martín, J., Agüero, B., García, A., Rodríguez, M., & Martín, D. (2019). *Alianzas locales para los retos globales*. Cuadernos para la Internacionalización de las Ciudades (N.º 9). Jefatura de Gobierno de la Ciudad de México, Intendencia de Montevideo, Alcaldía de Madrid, y Unión de Ciudades Capitales Iberoamericanas.

Dubbeling, M. (2013). *Cityfood: Linking cities on urban agriculture and urban food systems*. ICLEI – RUAF Foundation. http://www.iclei.org/index.php?id=1348

Durmuş, E. (2021). Cities and international law: Legally invisible or rising soft-power actors? *Monografías*, *81*, 45–53. CIDOB.

FAO. (2014). *Urban and peri-urban agriculture in Latin America and the Caribbean*. https://www.fao.org/ag/agp/greenercities/en/GGCLAC/downloads.html (consultado el 28 de diciembre de 2021).

FAO. (2019). *Marco de la FAO para la Agenda Alimentaria Urbana*. https://doi.org/10.4060/ca3151es

Fernández de Losada, A., & Abdullah, H. (Coords.). (2019). *Repensando el ecosistema de redes internacionales de ciudades*. Retos y oportunidades. CIDOB.

Fernández de Losada, A., & Zapata Garesché, E. (2022). Hacia una "red ideal" de ciudades. *CIDOB*. https://www.cidob.org/es/publicaciones/serie_de_publicacion/notes_internacionals_cidob/274/hacia_una_red_ideal_de_ciudades

Ganesan. (2023). *Reducción de las desigualdades en favor de la seguridad alimentaria y la nutrición*. GANESAN del CSA.

Grasa, R., & Sánchez Cano, J. (2013). Global and networking action of local governments: The case of development aid. In *CIDOB d'Afers Internacionals* (pp. 83–105). https://www.jstor.org/stable/23611649

HLPE. (2014). Food losses and waste in the context of sustainable food systems. *A report by the High Level Panel of Experts on Food Security and Nutrition of the Committee on World Food Security, Rome*. www.fao.org/cfs/cfs-hlpe

Instituto Brasileiro de Geografia e Estatistica (IBGE). (2023). *Censo 2022. Cidades e Estados do Brasil*. https://censo2022.ibge.gov.br/panorama/?utm_source=ibge&utm_medium=home&utm_campaign=portal (consultado el 30 de octubre de 2023).

Instituto Nacional de Estadística y Censos (INDEC). (2022). *Censo Nacional de Población, Hogares y Viviendas 2022*. INDEC. https://www.indec.gob.ar

Jones, M., & Hills, S. (2021). Scaling up action on urban sustainable food systems in the United Kingdom: Agenda setting, networking, and influence. *Sustainability*, *13*(4), 2156.

Karanja, N., & Njenga, M. (2011). Alimentar las ciudades. En *VVAA, La situación del Mundo* (pp. 45–53). Fuhem Ecosocial/Icaria.

La Capital. (2019, diciembre 16). En Rosario, el 40% de los niños y jóvenes de 5 y 19 años tiene sobrepeso. *La Capital*. https://www.lacapital.com.ar/la-ciudad/en-rosario-el-40-ciento-los-ninos-y-jovenes-5-y-19-anos-tiene-sobrepeso-n2534409.html

Lattuca, A. L., Terrile, R. H., & Sadagorsky, C. (2014). El programa de agricultura urbana de la Municipalidad de Rosario en Argentina. *Hábitat y Sociedad*, (7).

Le Saux, A. (2015). *Un siglo de internacionalización de los gobiernos locales*. Revista Mexicana de Política Exterior, Nº 104. Ciudad de México, mayo-agosto 2015. pp. 19–32

Leffel, B. (2020). *Urban political ecology of global urban climate change mitigation*. University of California, Irvine.

Levkoe, C. Z. (2014). The food movement in Canada: A social movement network perspective. *Journal of Peasant Studies*, *41*(3), 385–403.

Malé, J. P. (2019). *La emergencia de frentes y alianzas de ciudades: ¿Hacia nuevas formas de incidencia de los gobiernos locales?* Observatorio de Cooperación Descentralizada. Colección Monografías.

Martín, D., & de la Fuente, R. (2022). Global and local agendas: The Milan urban food policy pact and innovative sustainable food policies in Euro-Latin American cities. *Land*, *11*(2), 202. https://doi.org/10.3390/land11020202

Mayer, L., & Nguyen Long, L. (2020). Can city-to-city cooperation facilitate sustainable development governance in the global South? Lessons gleaned from seven north-south partnerships in Latin America. *International Journal of Urban Sustainable Development*, *13*. https://doi.org/10.1080/19463138.2020.1855433

Mooney, P. H., Tanaka, K., & Ciciurkaite, G., (2014). Food policy council movement in North America: A convergence of alternative local agrifood interests? In *Alternative agrifood movements: Patterns of convergence and divergence* (Vol. 21, pp. 229–255). Emerald Group Publishing Limited.

Moragues, A. (2014). Cambiar la política alimentaria empezando desde abajo. *Revista Soberanía Alimentaria, Biodiversidad y Culturas*, 16–20.

Moragues-Faus, A. (2020). Towards a critical governance framework: Unveiling the political and justice dimensions of urban food partnerships. *The Geographical Journal*, *186*(1), 73–86.

Moragues-Faus, A. (2021). The emergence of city food networks: Rescaling the impact of urban food policies. *Food Policy*, *103*, 102107.

Moragues-Faus, A., & Morgan, K. (2015). Reframing the foodscape: The emergent world of urban food policy. *Environment and Planning A*, *47*(7), 1558–1573.

Moragues-Faus, A., & Sonnino, R. (2019). Re-assembling sustainable food cities: An exploration of translocal governance and its multiple agencies. *Urban Studies*, *56*(4), 778–794.

Morgan, K. (2015). Nourishing the city: The rise of the urban food question in the Global North. *Urban Studies*, *52*(8), 1379–1394.

Morgan, K., & Sonnino, R. (2010). The urban foodscape: World cities and the new food equation. *Cambridge Journal of Regions, Economy and Society*, *3*(2), 209–224.

Morley, A., & Morgan, K. (2021). Municipal foodscapes: Urban food policy and the new municipalism. https://doi.org/10.1016/j.foodpol.2021.102069

MUFPP. (2015). Milan Urban Food Policy Pact. https://www.milanurbanfoodpolicypact.org accesed on December 28, 2021.

Patrouilleau, M., Anastasio, M., Le Coq, J., & Sotomayor, O. (2023). *Escenarios agroalimentarios para América Latina y el Caribe: estudio prospectivo al año 2040*. Editorial Teseo.

Porto de Oliveira, L. C. (2017). *Redes, ideias e ação pública na agricultura urbana: São Paulo, Montreal e Toronto* (Doctoral thesis, Fundação Getulio Vargas, Escola de Administração de Empresas de São Paulo)

Pothukuchi, K., & Kaufman, J. L. (1999). Placing the food system on the urban agenda: The role of municipal institutions in food systems planning. En *Agriculture and human values* (nº 16, pp. 213–224). Kluwer Academic Publishers.

Rede PENSSAN. (2022). *II VIGISAN: Encuesta Nacional sobre Inseguridad Alimentaria en el Contexto de la Pandemia de COVID-19 en Brasil*. Recuperado de https://olheparaafome.com.br/wp-content/uploads/2022/09/OLHESumExecutivoESPANHOL-Diagramacao-v2-R01-02-09-20224211.pdf

Russell, R. (2010). El Estado Nación y los actores gubernamentales no centrales: una relación complementaria. En L. Maira (Ed.), *La Política Internacional Subnacional en América Latina*. Libros del Zorzal.

Sánchez Cano, J. (2016). *Los Gobiernos no centrales y sus redes: análisis de su rol como actores en la gobernanza global*. Universitat Atutònoma de Barcelona. https://ddd.uab.cat/record/165306

Santo, R., & Moragues-Faus, A. (2019). Towards a trans-local food governance: Exploring the transformative capacity of food policy assemblages in the US and UK. *Geoforum*, *98*, 75–87.

Sibbing, L., Candel, J., & Termeer, K. (2021). A comparative assessment of local municipal food policy integration in the Netherlands. *International Planning Studies*, *26*(1), 56–69.

Sonnino, R. (2016). The new geography of food security: Exploring the potential of urban food strategies. *The Geographical Journal*, *182*, 190–200. https://doi.org/10.1111/geoj.12129

Sonnino, R., Marsden, T., & Moragues-Faus, A. (2016). Relationalities and convergences in food security narratives: towards a place-based approach. *Transactions of the Institute of British Geographers*, *41*(4), 477–489.

Steyaert, A., Dessein, J., & Provė, C. (2023). Exploring approaches to equal and effective participation of governance actors in trans-local city food networks. *Geoforum*, *145*. https://doi.org/10.1016/j.geoforum.2023.103831

United Nations Department of Economic and Social Affairs, Population Division. (2022). *World population prospects 2022: Summary of results*. UN DESA/POP/2022/TR/NO. 3.

United Nations Environmental Program. (2019). *Collaborative framework for food systems transformation: A multi-stakeholder pathway for sustainable food systems*. https://www.oneplanetnetwork.org/knowledge-centre/resources/collaborative-framework-food-systems-transformation-multi-stakeholder (consultado el 28 de diciembre de 2021).

Vía Campesina. (2001). Declaración Final del Foro Mundial Sobre Soberanía Alimentaria. *La Habana*. http://www.movimientos.org/cloc/show_text.php3?key=1178 (consultado el 28 de diciembre de 2021).

Wiskerke, J. (2015). Urban food systems. En *Cities and agriculture: Developing resilient urban food systems* (pp. 1–25). RUAF Foundation.

World Food Summit. (1996). *Rome declaration on World Food Security and Plan of Action of the World Food Summit, Rome*. https://www.fao.org/3/w3613e/w3613e00.htm (consultado el 28 de diciembre de 2021).

Yacamán, C. (2017). El Paradigma del Proyecto Agrourbano: La Agricultura Defendida Desde la Ciudad. *Urbano*. http://www.redalyc.org/articulo.oa?id=19853617002 (consultado el 4 de mayo de 2018).

Final reflections

FOOD AND THE PRODUCTION OF URBAN SPACE: REFLECTIONS FROM EXPERIENCES IN LATIN AMERICAN CITIES

María Mercedes Di Virgilio

Introduction

Despite the fact that the emergence and transformation of cities have historically been linked to the forms of food production and consumption, the power of food and gastronomy in the configuration of our urban spaces has remained largely invisible for centuries (Steel, 2009, 2023). In fact, studies that focus on the relationship between food, gastronomy, and the production of urban space are relatively recent. Even more so, those that seek to investigate these links from a systemic perspective capable of taking into account the complexity of rural–urban continuum or agro-food systems (FAO, 2023; Di Virgilio et al., 2024). In Latin America, studies on the complex interrelationships between food and the configuration of urban spaces have been virtually absent from the urban studies agenda.

Within this framework, this concluding chapter seeks to dialogue and integrate the evidence built from the set of studies in this volume that addresses the links between food and urban space in Latin America from different approaches, fields, and issues. As we will discuss later, as Latin American cities have evolved, they have done so in close relation to the forms of food production, distribution, and consumption. However, the impact of these processes on urban structure and dynamics has remained largely hidden, despite their importance for understanding contemporary social and economic transformations.

This chapter is organized into four sections that articulate the discussions addressed in the chapters of this volume. The first section examines the hyper-commercialization of food and cities. This phenomenon has led to a concentration of power in the hands of a few multinationals, affecting food diversity and the autonomy of local producers. The second section focuses on the role of food as a driver of urban transformations. Here we analyze how food practices, from

DOI: 10.4324/9781003471929-20

production to consumption, have influenced the reconfiguration of neighborhoods and cities, contributing to processes such as gentrification. The gourmetization of food products and the rise of gastronomic tourism are examples of how food can transform urban landscapes, attracting consumers with high purchasing power and displacing the original communities. The third section addresses food production and circulation in the current context, highlighting how global supply chains and industrial agricultural practices have impacted food security and environmental sustainability. This analysis is complemented by the fourth section, which focuses on social movement activism. These movements have emerged in response to excessive commodification, promoting sustainable agricultural practices and fair trade, and advocating for more equitable access to nutritious food.

By integrating evidence from diverse studies and approaches, the chapter seeks to offer a comprehensive and multidimensional view of how food shapes not only our cities but also our daily lives and social relations in Latin America. This approach invites a reconsideration of the role of food in urban planning and in the quest for more equitable and sustainable cities. At a time when cities face increasing challenges related to sustainability and social equity, this analysis is presented as a call to integrate the food issue into urban policies, recognizing its transformative potential in building a more just and resilient future.

When food and the city became commodities

If there is one thing that has characterized the evolution of post-Fordist capitalism, it is the hypercommodification of certain common goods. We call commons a broad set of resources or goods, of different natures, that are socially shared and whose forms of disposition, production, and consumption affect society as a whole. Among these resources or goods, land, housing, and food are key elements.

As Sassen (2015, p. 19) points out, the process of hypercommodification of the commons is rooted in "diverse and often ancient histories and genealogies." However, it has intensified from the last half of the twentieth century to the present day through complex processes. On the one hand, the global outsourcing of manufacturing, services, and office work and the relocation and extraction of industrial crops to areas of low costs and weak regulations. These trends are articulated with the development of a network of global cities necessary to convey advanced economic functions. Finally, they rely on the rise of finance as a driving force in the creation of new market niches in traditionally non-financial sectors—among them real estate and food production and consumption. In this context, the consumption of goods and services depends on the purchasing power and solvency of social groups (Pírez, 2016) and is subject to hypermarket logics that organize their forms of production, circulation, and consumption, becoming a powerful factor of inequality. In fact, for example, as food becomes a commodity, those social groups with greater resources have more access to quality food, while those with fewer resources are forced to consume highly processed and poorly nutritious food. At the same time, access to the city, in general, and to housing, in particular, becomes more unequal. Even as building space increases and cities continue to consume land, the supply of affordable housing fails to meet household requirements (for Latin America, see Di Virgilio, 2021; Benza & Kessler, 2020; Bouillon, 2012). The concomitance of these factors generates that the social groups with greater resources benefit not only from an adequate place to develop their daily life but also from good food, relegating the poorest households to precarious housing conditions and food.

As highlighted in the FAO report (2023), world hunger, as measured by the prevalence of undernourishment, currently affects some 735 million people, 43.2 million of whom are in Latin America. These figures are reached in a context in which, for the first time in history, the world is mostly urban—this proportion currently reaches 56% of the world's population and in Latin America more than 80% of its population. In this context, the assembly of the processes of hyper-mercantilization and their consequences are being felt with extreme brutality. As the world urbanizes, both food demand and supply are undergoing rapid changes along the rural–urban continuum. Indeed, one of the main effects of the hypercommodification of food is the industrialization of agriculture. Intensive agricultural practices, the use of agrochemicals, and the genetic modification of crops are some of the consequences of this market-oriented approach.

In addition, the hyper-commercialization of food has led to the concentration of power in the hands of a few multinational companies that control a large part of the food chain. This has resulted in the homogenization of the food supply, limiting the diversity of food available and affecting the autonomy of farmers and consumers. This trend is expressed, in part, in the expansion of supermarkets. As Pérez Martín (in this volume) shows, in Latin America, liberalization and the growth of foreign investments—especially since the 1990s—have driven this process, affecting both small retailers and consumers. On the one hand, the expansion of supermarkets has transformed the food retail trade, displacing small traders and increasing market concentration. In Chile, as the author shows, supermarket expansion has been more consistent and earlier, driven by local companies. In Argentina, Brazil, and Mexico, on the other hand, expansion has been characterized by the entry of multinationals and the adoption of format diversification strategies. These countries present a fragmented panorama in terms of consumption, with differences in purchasing patterns among different income levels. As can be seen, the expansion of supermarkets has had a significant impact on food environments, affecting the quality and diversity of the food supply. Promotions and discounts are key elements in supermarket operations, influencing purchasing and consumption patterns. In addition, expansion has led to increased competition and displacement of small traditional stores.

Likewise, the processes of concentration and centralization of capital in the food retail sector shape the production of urban space, especially in medium-sized cities. For example, the expansion of the[1] *grocery stores* has been fundamental for the growth of large shopping malls in Brazil, redefining the logics of food production and consumption. In this context, the retail sector, especially supermarkets, in the early 2020s, experienced a growing monopolization, with the food *retail* market concentrated in the hands of supermarkets. This concentration was driven by strategic acquisitions, such as the purchase of Makro and Grupo Big by Carrefour. These processes have a critical spatial dimension, impacting urban structure and socioeconomic dynamics. The expansion of *grocery* expansion has displaced traditional commerce, affecting local markets and small stores, and has driven an urban restructuring that favors socio-spatial fragmentation (Samalley, this volume).

In this context, food purchases are no longer exclusive to urban households but are also increasing in rural households far from urban centers. Likewise, in some regions, consumption of highly processed foods is increasing in peri-urban and rural areas, while consumption of vegetables, fruits, fats, and oils is becoming more homogeneous along this continuum. These significant changes are influencing the food security and nutrition of individuals and social groups according to their location and position along this continuum (FAO, 2023).

In this process, some traditional foods—such as tortillas—are stripped of their social context and transformed into a mass consumption product. As Lind and Barham (2004) show, the transformation of the tortilla into a mass product is associated with the emergence of new transnational corporate actors such as, for example, Maseca-Gruma, the world's leading producer of corn flour and tortillas. These corporations have not only transformed the meaning and material composition of the tortilla to commercialize it in a global market. In order to build a global image of the tortilla, they had to strip it of the meanings associated with strictly Mexican cuisine. In this transformation process, wraps, for example, emerged, which, together with fast food restaurants, are the modern descendants of the tortilla and the neighborhood tortilla shop. In the process, not only the form of commercialization changes but also the presentation and preparation. Increasingly, the wrap does not arrive as such on the supermarket shelf but is presented as frozen burritos, enchiladas, or a variety of other products that are oven-ready and can be served and eaten in five minutes.

In this context, cities, as the centers that concentrate potential consumers, become the main markets for the distribution of hyper-merchandised food. Large supermarket chains and fast food restaurants dominate the urban landscape, offering standardized and accessible products, but often at the expense of small local producers and traditional businesses.

Food and urban transformations

In this assembly of hyper-commodification processes, bars, restaurants, and specialized food stores have contributed to changing the physiognomy of cities. Gourmet cuisine, wine bars, breweries, and vintage cafés, to mention a few examples, play a central role in gentrification processes at a global level. Although gentrification has been analyzed mainly in its residential aspect and related to housing injustices, there is growing evidence of its effects on the urban foodscapes. Through gourmetization, food has become a pillar among the factors that structure gentrification (González, 2018). Gourmetization refers to the association of everyday gastronomic products with premium quality and aesthetics, leading to their consumption at high prices. Thus, the process involves traditionally consumed foods that become specialties and part of elitist and exclusive marketing circuits and practices. The paths of these foods are not linear, observing that in some cases, they derive from greater knowledge and dissemination of their attributes, improvement techniques in their production or elaboration (as in the case of coffee), promotion of consumption through cooking programs, fashionable gastronomic trends, social networks, among other incentives that lead to the gourmetization not only of the product itself but also of its consumption and associated practices.

Thus, the process, associated with an exaggerated aestheticization of products, endows food with a symbolic value that includes exclusivity, exoticism, and luxury and whose consumption can satisfy an unattainable desire (Johnston & Baumann, 2015). The process of gourmetization converges with gentrification to the extent that the consumption of gourmet products is only possible at a high price, and the offer is oriented to a particular public, with specific codes of distinction.

In this frame, food and gastronomy have become a significant pull factor in promoting tourism in urban contexts (Nelson, 2016). Local food consumption at a destination can influence tourists' decisions and consumer behavior (Okumus et al., 2013). For instance, for international tourists coming to South Korea, cognitive and affective images of food places influence their preferences for food destinations in India (Seo et al., 2017). Similarly, international tourists are likely to look for food tourism experiences that reflect their recreational habits at home, as in the case of Slow Food members seeking similar cooking and food-related activities while on holiday (Lee et al., 2015; Amore & Roy, 2020). Local and international gastronomic tourism contributes to the acceleration and intensification of gentrification processes by attracting consumers with economic resources and expertise in consolidating tastes and trends. To attract "foodies"—gastronomic tourists with high purchasing power—stores and spaces for food consumption and sale adapt and change their offer. As González (2018, p. 3) shows, in many Spanish cities, certain areas and neighborhoods become a kind of foodie theme park: "These are usually central neighborhoods that used to agglutinate lower/middle classes and immigrants and that due to their centrality, low land prices and architectural heritage attract visitors and new businesses." In the last decades, food and gastronomic tourism have been significantly related to transforming urban environments.[2]

Vázquez-Medina and Hernández Cordero (in this book) show how food gentrification affects urban food systems in Mexico. Based on the analysis of three cities, Mexico City, Cholula, and Mazatlán, the authors make it clear that food gentrification processes can leverage different drivers, assuming different modalities. In Mexico City, the Santa María La Ribera neighborhood has undergone a significant change in its culinary offerings, becoming a gastronomic cluster that attracts new residents with high cultural and purchasing capital. The arrival of new residents has prompted the opening of restaurants and cafés that appeal to culinary cosmopolitanism, coexisting with traditional establishments that resist change. Cholula, with its population composition diversified by the presence of universities, presents a hybrid food regime that combines the cosmopolitan with the regional. Touristification and gentrification have promoted the specialization of the gastronomic offer, with the municipality of San Pedro focusing on the more traditional offer and San Andrés on the modern and cosmopolitan. Finally, Mazatlán, in Sinaloa, with the arrival of US and Canadian retirees, has changed the food supply, introducing organic markets that favor short distribution chains. Although these initiatives boost local production, they also limit access to agroecological products for the local population due to their high cost. Thus, food gentrification in Mexico reflects a complex phenomenon that varies according to the local context, affecting the accessibility and diversity of urban food systems.

While tourist conglomerates or urban landowners appropriate the value caused by new consumption and production trends, the producers and residents of the neighborhoods where gourmet products are consumed at high prices are dispossessed or displaced. This leads to direct or indirect transformations in the social composition of the agents that fail to jump on the bandwagon of change, as well as in the arrival of other actors attracted by the new commercial and financial opportunities linked to a diversity of cultural, economic, productive, and financial practices in the places of consumption.

Despite this, the processes of food gentrification and gourmetization are not the only ones that promote transformations at the city level. As Jirón et al. show (in this book), the ways in which public spaces are practiced and their forms of appropriation are powerful drivers of urban transformations. In fact, subway stations in Santiago de Chile have gone from being transit points to becoming key spaces for the informal food trade. This phenomenon was driven by the implementation of the Transantiago transport system in 2007. In this context, metro stations, originally designed to facilitate the rapid flow of passengers, became centers of informal commerce in general, and of food in particular, especially in areas where there is a lack of services and stores. In this context, subway stations are integrated into the so-called care infrastructures, responding to the daily food needs of users and supporting the informal economy.

Migratory flows also have an impact on destination cities. This impact is multifaceted. On the one hand, infrastructure, the capacity of cities to provide social and basic services, to facilitate access to housing and also their capacity to produce and distribute accessible and quality food is strongly strained in a context in which large metropolitan areas play a fundamental role as regional nodes in migration networks and corridors (Vera & Adler, 2020). On the other hand, migrations affect other aspects of urban life, such as culture. Migrants introduce new ingredients and recipes, diversifying the food options available and enriching the local culinary culture. They also participate in the sale of food in informal and formal markets, strengthening food distribution networks in cities.

Hayden, Eguiguren & Alfaro (in this book) explore the relationship between migration and the development of urban food systems in Latin America. In this framework, they note how migrants, both internal and international, influence food production, distribution, and consumption in cities such as Quito (Ecuador) and Buenos Aires (Argentina). In these cities, the migrant collective leaves its mark on the food production and supply systems in both cities. On the one hand, Quito has been a destination for internal migrants, especially Indigenous people and peasants, who play a crucial role in the provision of food in urban markets. In recent decades, it has also received migrants from Colombia, Peru, Cuba, Haiti, and Venezuela. Interurban migrants, especially Venezuelans, find the sale of street food one of the few affordable alternatives available. The presence of these migrants has also introduced new foods and commercial practices in the city. In Buenos Aires, long-standing and more contemporary processes overlap. Italian migration in the nineteenth century left a lasting imprint on local gastronomy, while contemporary migrations from China, Bolivia, and Peru have reshaped the urban food system. Chinese supermarkets and Bolivian greengrocers are examples of how migrants have established important niches in the food trade, influencing both supply and market structure. Likewise, Peruvian restaurants have been articulated in broader circuits of food gentrification. In this way, urban food systems often provide early insertion points for migrants into local economies, allowing them to contribute new flavors, ingredients, and culinary practices. The contribution of migrant collectives thus transforms food landscapes—reshaping food supply and urban food systems—through the incorporation of new products and new culinary practices.

Likewise, app-based food delivery also constitutes a vector through which platform capitalism is reshaping socio-spatial practices and urban environments. As Zunino and Ferrer Sánchez (in this book) show, food delivery through digital platforms has grown significantly in Latin America, driven by the precariousness and informality of labor markets, the low cost of service, and the promise of self-regulating time. Companies such as PedidosYa and Rappi have dominated the market in countries such as Argentina, Colombia, and Mexico. However, this growth is supported by the precarious working conditions of delivery drivers, who face long hours and risks of accidents, theft, and harassment. These platforms affect the digital food environment, promoting unhealthy eating habits by prioritizing ultra-processed foods. Despite this, food delivery via bicycles is presented as a sustainable mobility. However, it implies vulnerabilities for delivery drivers due to frequent accidents and theft. Also, this food delivery infrastructure is characterized by the hyper-mobility of workers and the immobility of consumers, which generates an unequal relationship between the two.

Those foodscapes are related to specific places, subjects, and meanings (Johnston & Baumann, 2015). These new foodscapes can also be observed in different urban and rural areas. In all cases, they are based on and shape different social injustice issues related to food access, food production, the relationship between exchange prices, the impacts of new ways of consumption and production in rural and urban areas, the effects of new urban or rural activities, etc.

The production and distribution of food in the scenario of transformations

Although research has made considerable progress in analyzing the new food landscapes shaping cities, the transformations these processes generate beyond the consumption spheres have yet to be overlooked. Some authors delve into the links between urban changes and local food systems, examining the role of urban planning and policy in creating (or not) sustainable foodscapes.

Indeed, food systems in Latin America have undergone major transformations due to urbanization, agribusiness, and the globalization of food transactions. These changes have generated significant challenges, such as price volatility, the proliferation of ultra-processed products, the marginalization of small producers, and precarious labor conditions in supply chains. Pasquier Merino & Buratti (in this volume) show short marketing circuits as a tangible strategy for food sustainability in contemporary cities. These circuits, which have increased in the last two decades, promote geographic proximity and low intermediation, generating social and environmental value. However, they face logistical challenges, especially in the transportation of goods, a crucial aspect of their development. In Mexico City, urban mobility represents a significant challenge for the distribution of fresh produce due to traffic congestion and lack of adequate infrastructure. Producers must adapt to these conditions, using innovative strategies such as the use of bicycles, motorcycles, and modified vehicles to optimize distribution. Collaboration among producers to share resources and reduce transportation costs is a common practice, although the lack of specialized systems and reliance on conventional means of transport limit their effectiveness. In fact, many of these short marketing circuits rely on volunteer or low-paid labor, reflecting their alternative nature and dependence on the social economy. The lack of professionalization in the management of these circuits and their operation outside tax and health regulations are additional challenges. Despite their potential to promote sustainability and strengthen food security, short marketing circuits face significant barriers to their consolidation and expansion. Local government involvement in the promotion of fairs and farmers' markets has opened up opportunities. However, there is still a need for greater integration of agroecological producers into conventional distribution systems.

Although literature (Monkes, this volume; Barsky, this volume) stresses the need to sustain periurban production belts as key stabons in these short (production and) marketing chains, periurban agriculture faces challenges due to urban sprawl and a hegemonic agrifood model. For example, the horticultural belt of La Plata (Argentina) is crucial for supplying the Buenos Aires metropolitan area. However, it faces problems such as real estate speculation, rising rents, and the relocation of producers to less favorable areas (Monkes, this volume). Uncontrolled urban sprawl affects peri-urban productive belts, reducing their capacity to supply cities with fresh, local produce. Also, as urban development puts pressure on peri-urban land, land prices increase and make access to land more difficult for farmers, especially those with lower incomes. Uncontrolled urbanization also causes land fragmentation and puts pressure on the management of natural resources, including water and soil. In addition, pollution and intensive resource use can negatively affect not only agricultural productivity but also the quality of the peri-urban environment and the resilience of local ecosystems. Uncontrolled urban sprawl thus represents a significant challenge to the sustainability of peri-urban productive belts, requiring planned and coordinated interventions to mitigate its negative impacts (Barsky, this volume). Within this framework, Barsky highlights some initiatives in the management of peri-urban agriculture in different Latin American countries. In Cuba, he recovers the experience of the Urban and Periurban Agriculture Movement, which fed into the Comprehensive Program for Urban and Suburban Agriculture. Brazil has developed pioneering legislation on urban law and urban agriculture programs. In Colombia, food supply plans have been implemented in Bogota and Medellin. Finally, it should be noted that in Argentina, peri-urban agriculture has gained visibility on the national public agenda through policies to support family farming. However, urban sprawl and the operational difficulties of the State have severely limited the effectiveness of such initiatives. Thus, the preservation of peri-urban agriculture in Latin America requires the adaptation of territorial management instruments to the complex socioeconomic and environmental dynamics of peri-urban spaces. These include territorial governance arrangements for preservation to protect horticultural green belts and strengthen food security in cities.

From a complex and interdisciplinary perspective, the bibliography aims to investigate the relations between processes in eminently urban environments—gentrification and gourmetization—with others that occur beyond the cities and neighborhoods (Barsky, in this book; Di Virgilio et al., 2024). The phenomena, which we could call food gentrification or gourmetization, concomitantly impact consumption processes—usually occurring in urban environments—and production processes associated with rural or peri-urban environments. Likewise, these phenomena are articulated with processes such as the "gentrification" of food delivery, understood as a gear in supply chains. In this framework, the work of food delivery mediated by platforms defines a new consumption pattern. In fact, in Latin American cities, food delivery through apps has grown massively, showing the capacity of these infrastructures to mediate and sustain new food consumption patterns (Zunino and Ferrer Sánchez, this volume).

Based on this conception, some researchers seek to expand the frontiers of knowledge by highlighting the links in the food chain between gentrified neighborhoods and food-producing areas. In this chain, which is technically and economically related, from the production of primary materials to the consumer, revaluation, and devaluation processes that unequally affect the actors involved are generated.

Street vending is undoubtedly one more cog in this chain of production, provision, circulation, and consumption of food in the urban–urban continuum, representing an important source of income and employment for large sectors of the urban population. Despite this, street food vending has historically been seen as an "urban problem" due to its association with precariousness, disorder, lack of hygiene, and criminality. This has led to an ambivalent relationship between city governments and street vendors, alternating between tolerance and criminalization (Hayden & Farah, this volume). In Mexico City, for example, it is estimated that there are more than 442,000 food vendors operating in public spaces. In that framework, the governance of street vending takes place through a complex interaction between municipal and delegacional governments, as well as a variety of local actors. Legal frameworks for governing street vending in Latin America have been ambiguous, and Mexico has been no exception.

In Mexico City, public markets also constitute a key piece in the provision of social infrastructure for the distribution of food and other basic products in the city. The city's public markets, with their 329 facilities, represent one of the most extensive experiments in the provision of commercial infrastructure in Latin America during the twentieth century. These markets are central to the city's retail sector and urban policy, and their preservation is led primarily by market traders, who emphasize their importance as valuable urban infrastructures. These commercial infrastructures operate as an economic, socio-political, and territorial network and are a central component of the city's food distribution infrastructure. Over time, these constellations have undergone key transformations due to economic, regulatory, institutional, and political changes. The expansion of the network of public markets reflects tensions between formal and informal urbanization processes, and their history is marked by constant negotiation between state and non-state actors over their form, function, and meaning. Indeed, administrative and political reforms since the 1970s have introduced new actors into the network, transforming the governance of markets. Moreover, the implementation of neoliberal policies and the growth of supermarket chains have marginalized public markets, reducing their share of food distribution from 80% in the 1950s to 16% in 2018 (Tellez, this volume).

Urban planning and efforts to govern public space in Mexico City have not recognized the importance of either markets or street vendors for urban life and food security. On the one hand, public markets configure a resilient and adaptive infrastructure that persists over time and plays a key role in food distribution. On the other, food vendors play a crucial role in providing affordable food to urban populations on the move. However, recent policies have followed negative portrayals of street food vendors. Despite this, vendors have learned to contest these logics in multiple ways, differentiating their work from other criminalized activities.

The interactions between ecological, social, economic, and administrative layers that make up the foodscape must be inquired consciously. The relationship between urban planning and food production and consumption needs to be studied more regarding food access. Likewise, local food systems demand increased attention insofar as they have explicit implications for everyday life and the socio-spatial politics of inequality (McEntee & Agyeman, 2010).

For the right to food in fairer and more resilient urban environments

Finally, understanding the everyday geography of food also assumes an understanding of emerging local food social movements and practices faced to ensure food access. Indeed, in response to the challenges posed by the provision of and access to affordable, quality food, movements have developed around the world that seek to reverse the processes of hypermarketization. These movements promote sustainable agricultural practices, fair trade, support for small-scale producers, and equitable access to nutritious food.

In fact, farm-to-table movements encourage the use of local ingredients, which reduces the distance between production and consumption, reduces the carbon footprint, and limits the consumption of ultra-processed foods. In addition, the creation of community rooftop gardens and orchards and other initiatives to promote urban biodiversity contribute to greener and more livable cities. Sustainable practices such as beekeeping and urban gardening, as well as the strengthening of local market networks, increase the resilience of food systems in Latin America and the Caribbean. When a city improves its capacity to produce food, it becomes less susceptible to supply chain disruptions. Likewise, programs to reduce food waste and residues, together with support for nearby rural economies, have a positive impact on the environment and general welfare, ensuring greater access to affordable and nutritious food and guaranteeing food security (IDB, 2024).

These initiatives not only ensure access to affordable and healthy food but also contribute to improving the living conditions of family producers and strengthening their rural roots. In some cases, such as the horticultural belt of La Plata (Argentina), agroecology has advanced toward associativism, facilitating access to technical information, alternative marketing, and the strengthening of community networks. The Federación Rural para la Producción y el Arraigo is an outstanding example of an organization of family producers promoting agroecology. FRPA brings together more than 20,000 families engaged in family, peasant, and indigenous agriculture, with a focus on agroecological transition. This organization has developed initiatives such as "Pueblo a Pueblo" (PaP), a direct marketing project that eliminates intermediaries and allows producers to obtain fair prices. PaP began in Buenos Aires in 2018 and has expanded its reach to other cities, offering agroecological products at affordable prices and guaranteeing a decent income for producers. FRPA has created marketing channels that value agroecological production, allowing producers to access direct markets and improve their earnings. However, challenges are faced such as the scalability of these initiatives and the need to increase demand in the cities. Despite this, access to agroecological products in urban settings remains limited, especially for low-income sectors. FRPA has attempted to address this inequality through donations to canteens and community centers but has not yet developed a sustainable mechanism to ensure access to these products for all (Monkes, this volume).

In some contexts, international pacts or agreements appear to be useful channels for the promotion of sustainable food policies at the city level. For example, the Milan Pact on Urban Food Policies has influenced the food strategies of Quito, Rosario, and São Paulo. This pact, signed in 2015, is the first international protocol designed to promote sustainable urban food policies. In the context of increasing urbanization, especially in Latin America, where 80% of the population lives in cities, the pact seeks to support local governments in creating sustainable food systems. In Quito, accession to the compact in 2016 spurred the creation of an urban food strategy that integrates sustainable practices such as urban agriculture, coordinated by the Economic Development Agency of Quito (Ecuador). The COVID-19 pandemic not only presented significant challenges, such as the disruption of markets and fairs, but also reinforced the importance of food security on the local agenda. Rosario (Argentina), recognized for its tradition of food production programs, signed the compact in 2020. This provided a structure to address critical issues such as malnutrition and food waste. The city has developed initiatives such as the Sustainable Food Production Program, although it faces challenges such as the decrease in land dedicated to horticulture. The pact has thus enabled Rosario to organize its food policies and strengthen its regional leadership. São Paulo (Brazil), the most populous city in Latin America, joined the pact in 2015. The city has implemented policies to reduce food waste and strengthen its food security system, supported by a national legislative framework that recognizes the right to food. The pandemic highlighted the importance of these policies, especially in food bank management and waste reduction. In Latin American cities, the Milan Pact seems to have played a fundamental role in structuring and energizing food policies, fostering inclusive and multi-stakeholder governance. However, budgetary restrictions and state capacities in the cities of the region affect the implementation of these initiatives (Martín, this volume).

Conclusion

The chapter sought to recover the contributions of a set of texts in the investigation of the relationship between food, gastronomy, and the configuration of urban spaces in Latin America, a link that has remained largely hidden until recent times. In this context, he proposes the hypercommercialization of food and cities as the backdrop against which these links are inscribed. Thus, hypermercantilization is presented as a key process where food and cities become commodities, exacerbating social inequalities. This phenomenon has led to intensive agricultural industrialization, where a few multinationals control a large part of the food chain, reducing food diversity and limiting the autonomy of producers and consumers. The expansion of supermarkets has transformed retail trade, displacing small traders and centralizing the market, negatively affecting local economies and the diversity of food options available to consumers.

In this context, food has played a crucial role in urban gentrification processes. The gourmetization of food products, where everyday foods are revalued as luxury items, has transformed neighborhoods and cities, attracting consumers with high purchasing power and contributing to the exclusion of the original residents. This phenomenon, together with the rise of gastronomic tourism, has accelerated gentrification, creating urban environments that are more homogeneous and less accessible to local populations, leading to a significant transformation in the social and economic composition of cities.

Nevertheless, in response to these onslaughts of global capitalism, social movements have emerged that promote sustainable agricultural practices and fair trade. These movements seek to counteract hyper-commercialization by promoting equitable access to nutritious food and supporting small-scale producers. Initiatives such as agroecology and short marketing circuits are presented as viable strategies to improve food security and strengthen the resilience of urban food systems. These practices seek not only to ensure access to healthy food but also to improve the living conditions of producers and foster stronger rural roots, promoting a fairer and more sustainable economy.

Thus, even as urbanization and globalization have profoundly transformed food systems, they have also opened up opportunities to develop sustainable food policies. International agreements such as the Milan Pact on Urban Food Policies have played a crucial role in structuring food policies in Latin American cities, promoting more inclusive and sustainable governance.

Notes

1 Combination of wholesale and retail, characterized by large stores and low-price policies aimed at low-income consumers.
2 Food also plays a key role in promoting tourism initiatives in rural areas, relating to the search for freshness, taste, and authenticity, support for local producers, and environmental concerns (Sidali et al., 2015).

Bibliography

Amore, A., & Roy, H. (2020). Blending foodscapes and urban touristscapes: International tourism and city marketing in Indian cities. *International Journal of Tourism Cities*, *6*(3), 639–655.

Banco Interamericano de Desarrollo. (2024). *Seguridad alimentaria en América Latina y el Caribe*. BID. https://www.iadb.org/es/noticias/seguridad-alimentaria-en-america-latina-y-el-caribe

Benza, G., & Kessler, G. (2020). *La ¿nueva? estructura social de América Latina: Cambios y persistencias después de la ola de gobiernos progresistas*. Siglo XXI editores.

Bouillon, C. P. (2012). *Un espacio para el desarrollo. Los mercados de vivienda en América Latina y el Caribe*. Banco Interamericano de Desarrollo, Washington, DC.

Di Virgilio, M. M. (2021). Desigualdades, hábitat y vivienda en América Latina. In *Nueva Sociedad*, 293, Mayo–Junio 2021, ISSN: 0251–3552.

Di Virgilio, M. M., Frisch, M. A., González, S., Grenoville, S., Hernández, M. C., Nussbaumer, B. B., & Vega Barbero, J. M. (2024). *Gourmetización y gentrificación: un recorrido por los paisajes alimentarios en disputa, desde la ciudad hasta el campo.*

FAO. (2023). *El estado de la seguridad alimentaria y la nutrición en el mundo 2023. Urbanización, transformación de los sistemas agroalimentarios y dietas saludables a lo largo del continuo rural-urbano.* FAO. https://doi.org/10.4060/cc3017es

González, S. (2018). La gourmetización de las ciudades y los mercados de abasto. Reflexiones críticas sobre el origen del proceso, su evolución e impactos sociales. *Boletín Ecos*, *43*(Junio–Agosto 2018), 1–8.

IDB. (2024). Gastronomy as a catalyst for urban development. *Sustainable Cities Blog.* https://blogs.iadb.org/ciudades-sostenibles/en/gastronomy-as-a-catalyst-for-urban-development/

Johnston, J., & Baumann, S. (2015). *Foodies: Democracy and distinction in the gourmet foodscape* (2nd ed.). Routledge.

Lee, K. H., Packer, J., & Scott, N. (2015). Travel lifestyle preferences and destination activity choices of slow food members and non-members. *Tourism Management*, *46*, 1–10.

Lind, D., & Barham, E. (2004). The social life of the tortilla: Food, cultural politics, and contested commodification. *Agriculture and Human Values*, *21*, 47–60.

McEntee, J., & Agyeman, J. (2010). Towards the development of a GIS method for identifying rural food deserts: Geographic access in Vermont, USA. *Applied Geography*, *30*(1), 165–176.

Nelson, V. (2016). Food and image on the official visitor site of Houston, Texas. *Journal of Destination Marketing & Management*, *5*(2), 133–140.

Okumus, F., Kock, G., Scantlebury, M. M., & Okumus, B. (2013). Using local cuisines when promoting small Caribbean Island destinations. *Journal of Travel & Tourism Marketing*, *30*(4), 410–429.

Pírez, P. (2016). Las heterogéneas formas de producción y consumo de la urbanización latinoamericana. Quid 16. *Revista del Área de Estudios Urbanos*, *6*, 131–167.

Sassen, S. (2015). *Expulsiones: brutalidad y complejidad en la economía global* (Vol. 3090). Katz editores.

Seo, S., Yun, N., & Kim, O. Y. (2017). Destination food image and intention to eat destination foods: A view fromKorea. *Current Issues in Tourism*, *20*(2), 135–156.

Sidali, K. L., Kastenholz, E., & Bianchi, R. (2015). Food tourism, niche markets and products in rural tourism: Combining the intimacy model and the experience economy as a rural development strategy. *Journal of Sustainable Tourism*, *23*(8–9), 1179–1197.

Steel, G. (2009). Chapter 8: Dishing up the city: Tourism and street vendors in Cuzco. In *Cultural tourism in Latin America* (pp. 161–176). Brill.

Steel, C. (2023). Sitopia: How food shapes civilisation. *Metode Science Studies Journal*, (13), 77–83.

Vera, F., & Adler, V. (2020). *Inmigrando: Fortalecer ciudades destino.* Banco Interamericano de Desarrollo.

INDEX

For Product Safety Concerns and Information please contact our
EU representative GPSR@taylorandfrancis.com Taylor & Francis
Verlag GmbH, Kaufingerstraße 24, 80331 München, Germany